40 QUESTIONS ABOUT
The Text and Canon of the New Testament

Charles L. Quarles
L. Scott Kellum

Benjamin L. Merkle, Series Editor

KREGEL
ACADEMIC

40 Questions About the Text and Canon of the New Testament
© 2023 Charles L. Quarles and L. Scott Kellum

Published by Kregel Academic, an imprint of Kregel Publications, 2450 Oak Industrial Dr. NE, Grand Rapids, MI 49505-6020.

This book is a title in the 40 Questions Series edited by Benjamin L. Merkle.

The Greek font GraecaU and the Hebrew font New JerusalemU are from www.linguistsoftware.com/lgku.htm, +1-425-775-1130.

ISBN 978-0-8254-4275-9

Printed in the United States of America

23 24 25 26 27 / 5 4 3 2 1

To Julie and Cathy,
our precious wives—two ladies who deserve the
highest praise for their support and sacrifice
for the sake of our ministries.

Contents

Part 2: The Canon of the New Testament

Acknowledgments

Several people have made helpful contributions to this book and we are deeply grateful for their assistance. Seth Ellington, Eric Emmons, Jarrett Fletcher, Brad Grizenko, Will Lawson, Mark Lockyear, and Mark Silverthorn (students in the graduate Introduction to New Testament Textual Criticism class at Southeastern Baptist Theological Seminary in the Spring of 2021) read and offered feedback on the initial draft of the first twenty chapters. Research assistants Seth Ellington, Hayden Fleming, Yeongwhi Jo, and James Willison carefully proofread Part 1, and Charlie Gilbert proofed Part 2.

Two scholars were kind enough to read and provide thorough comments on individual chapters related to their areas of expertise. Comments from Maurice Robinson improved the content addressing Question 14 and hopefully ensured that the Byzantine priority approach was given fairer treatment than one sometimes encounters in an introductory work. Feedback from James Snapp, Jr. significantly strengthened the treatment of Question 18 and prevented the author from repeating some of the common errors regarding the ending of Mark that mar the work of several generations of textual critics. Elijah Hixson and Alex Carr read the entire first half of the book and suggested important revisions that have improved the accuracy and clarity of Part 1. These four scholars were especially kind and generous with their time despite their own busy schedules and important responsibilities. Obviously, any remaining errors are solely the responsibility of the authors.

We are also grateful to the administration, trustees, and support staff at Southeastern Baptist Theological Seminary. The seminary provided a half-sabbatical to each author that was deeply appreciated. Faith Haberer was diligent in helping us produce the Scripture index and provided other assistance. We would also like to thank the staff at the Southeastern Library for acquiring numerous important and sometimes rare volumes for us.

Abbreviations

1 Apol.	Justin Martyr, *Apologia*
1 Clem.	*1 Clement*
2 Clem.	*2 Clement*
AB	Anchor Bible Commentary
ABD	*Anchor Bible Dictionary.* Edited by David Noel Freedman. 6 vols. New York: Doubleday, 1992
ABRL	Anchor Bible Reference Library
Adumbr.	Clement of Alexandria, *Adumbrationes in epistulas canonicas*
Adv. Haer.	Irenaeus, *Adversus Haeresis*
Adv. Jud.	Tertullian, *Adversus Judaeos*
ANF	*Ante-Nicene Fathers*
Apol.	*Apologia/Apologeticus*
Att.	Cicero, *Epistulae ad Atticum*
Autol.	Theophilus, *Ad Autolycum*
Barn.	*Barnabas*
BASP	*Bulletin of the American Society of Papyrologists*
BBR	*Bulletin for Biblical Research*
BDAG	Danker, Frederick W., Walter Bauer, William F. Arndt, and F. Wilbur Gingrich. *Greek-English Lexicon of the New Testament and Other Early Christian Literature.* 3rd ed. Chicago: University of Chicago Press, 2000 (Danker-Bauer-Arndt-Gingrich)
BECNT	Baker Exegetical Commentary on the New Testament
BGBH	Beiträge zur Geschichte der biblischen Hermeneutik
Bib	*Biblica*
BibInt	Biblical Interpretation Series
BJRL	*Bulletin of the John Rylands University Library of Manchester*
BMC	Bodmer Miscellaneous Codex
C. Ap.	Josephus, *Contra Apion*
CBGM	The Coherence-based Genealogical Method
CBQ	*Catholic Biblical Quarterly*
Cels	Origen, *Contra Celsum*
CNTTS	The Center for New Testament Textual Studies
Comm. Jo.	Origen, *Commentarii in evangelium Joannis*

Comm. Matt.	Origen, *Commentarium in evangelium Matthaei*
Comm. Zach.	Didymus, *Commentarii in Zachariam*
ConBNT	Coniectanea Neotestamentica or Coniectanea Biblica: New Testament Series
Conf.	Augustine, *Confessionum*
Contempl.	Philo, *De vita contemplativa*
CSB	Christian Standard Bible
CSEL	Corpus Scriptorum Ecclesiasticorum Latinorum
CSHB	Corpus Scriptorum Historiae Byzantinae
CSNTM	Center for the Study of New Testament Manuscripts
Cult. fem.	Tertullian, *De cultu feminarum*
Dial.	Justin Martyr, *Dialogus cum Tryphone*
Did.	*Didache*
Diogn.	*Diognetus*
ECC	Eerdmans Critical Commentary
ECM	Editio Critica Maior
EGGNT	Exegetical Guide to the Greek New Testament
Eleem.	Cyprian, *De opere et eleemosynis*
Ep. Barn.	Epistle of Barnabas
Ep. Can.	Peter of Alexandria, *The Canonical Epistle*
Ep. Fest.	Athanasius, *Epistulae festales*
Epid.	Irenaeus, *Epideixis tou apostolikou kērygmatos*
Epigr.	Cicero, *Epigrammata*
Epist.	Jerome, *Epistula*
ESV	English Standard Version
ExpTim	*Expository Times*
Fam.	Cicero, *Epistulae ad familiares*
FC	Fathers of the Church
Frag.	*Fragment*
GE	General Epistles
GTJ	*Grace Theological Journal*
Haer.	Hippolytus, *Refutatio omnium haeresium*
Herm. Mand.	Shepherd of Hermas, Mandte(s)
Hist. eccl.	Eusebius, *Historia ecclesiastica*
Hom. Jos.	Origen, *Origenis Homiliae in librum Josua*
HTR	*Harvard Theological Review*
HTS	*Harvard Theological Studies*
IEJ	*Israel Exploration Journal*
Ign. Smyrn.	Ignatius, *To the Smyrnaeans*
INTF	Institut für Neutestamentliche Textforschung
JBL	*Journal of Biblical Literature*
Jejun.	Tertullian, *De jejunio*
JETS	*Journal of the Evangelical Theological Society*

JR	*The Journal of Religion*
JSNT	*Journal for the Study of the New Testament*
JTS	*Journal of Theological Studies*
LCL	Loeb Classical Library
LDAB	Louvain Database of Ancient Books
LNTS	The Library of New Testament Studies
LXX	Septuagint
Marc.	Tertullian, *Adversus Marcionem*
Mart. Pet.	*Martyrdom of Peter*
MF	Muratorian Fragment
Mon.	Tertullian, *De monogamia*
Mort.	Lactantius, *De mortibus persecutorum*
MS	Manuscript
MSS	Manuscripts
NA[28]	*Novum Testamentum Graece,* Nestle-Aland, 28th ed.
NAC	New American Commentary
NCBC	New Cambridge Bible Commentary
NHMS	Nag Hammadi and Manichaean Studies
NIBC	New International Biblical Commentary
NICNT	New International Commentary on the New Testament
NIGTC	New International Greek Testament Commentary
NIV	New International Version
NovT	*Novum Testamentum*
NPNF	Nicene and Post-Nicene Fathers
NT	New Testament
NTL	New Testament Library
NTS	*New Testament Studies*
NTTS	New Testament Tools and Studies
NTTSD	New Testament Tools, Studies, and Documents
OECS	Oxford Early Christian Studies
OT	Old Testament
PA	*Pericope Adulterae*
Paed.	Clement of Alexandria, *Paedogogus*
Pan.	Epiphanius, *Panarion*
PG	Patrologia Graeca [= Patrologiae Cursus Completus: Series Graeca]. Edited by Jacques-Paul Migne. 162 vols. Paris, 1857–1886
P.Köln	Kölner Papyri
PL	Patrologia Latina [= Patrologiae Cursus Completus: Series Latina]. Edited by Jacques-Paul Migne. 217 vols. Paris, 1844–1864
P.Mich.inv.	Michigan Medical Papyri
Pol. Phil.	*Polycarp, To the Philippians*

P.Oxy.	Oxyrhynchus papyri
Praescr.	Tertullian, *De praescriptione haereticorum*
Princ.	Origen, *De principiis*
PRSt	*Persepectives in Religious Studies*
Pud.	Tertullian, *De pudicitia*
Quint. fratr.	Cicero, *Epistulae ad Quintum fratrem*
Quis div.	Clement of Alexandria, *Quis dives salvetur*
Retract.	Augustine, *Retractionum*
RP	Maurice Robinson and William Pierpont. *The New Testament in the Original Greek: Byzantine Textform 2005.* Southborough, MA: Chilton, 2005
RSV	Revised Standard Version
SBLGNT	The Greek New Testament: SBL Edition
SD	Studies and Documents
Sel. Ps.	Origen, *Selecta in Psalmos*
SJT	*Scottish Journal of Theology*
Strom.	Clement of Alexandria, *Stromateis*
Symp.	Methodius of Olympus, *Symposium*
TC	*TC: A Journal of Biblical Textual Criticism*
TCSt	Text-Critical Studies
TENTS	Texts and Editions for New Testament Study
THGNT	Tyndale House Greek New Testament
TR	Textus Receptus
Treg	Tregelles
TS	Texts and Studies
TynBul	*Tyndale Bulletin*
TZ	*Theologische Zeitschrift*
UBS	*The Greek New Testament*, United Bible Societies, 5th ed.
VC	*Vigiliae Christianae*
Vir. ill.	Jerome, *De viris illustribus*
Vit. Const.	Eusebius, *Vita Constantini*
WBC	Word Biblical Commentary
WH	Westcott-Hort
WUNT	Wissenschaftliche Untersuchungen zum Neuen Testament

Introduction

The forty questions answered in this volume could easily be reduced to one fundamental question that is preliminary and foundational for all New Testament research: What is the New Testament? Most readers will probably assume that the answer to that question is both simple and obvious. The New Testament is the text of the twenty-seven books that form the latter portion of the Christian Scriptures. In fact, the question is a bit more complex than is commonly assumed. The question "What is the New Testament?" encapsulates two distinct but related questions: What books compose the New Testament, and what is the original text of those books?

First, let's briefly consider the matter of the original text of the New Testament. Careful readers of modern English translations of the New Testament should be aware that the ancient manuscripts of the Greek New Testament sometimes differ from each other. This is one of the reasons for the occasional differences in wording between modern translations. Additionally, readers will find notes in the margin of their Bibles explaining that some ancient manuscripts say one thing but other manuscripts say something else. When the ancient manuscripts differ, scholars must seek to determine which wording is original. Sometimes the differences in wording in the ancient manuscripts do not significantly affect their meaning. On other occasions, the differences are very significant. In either case, the differences cannot be ignored. Modern editors of the Greek New Testament must choose a reading to print as the New Testament text and modern translations must choose a reading to translate as the New Testament text. These decisions affect the words that Bible readers meditate on, memorize, use in their witness, and serve as the basis for the sermons that their pastors preach on the Lord's Day. In other words, these decisions really matter.

Why do some Bibles contain the Trinitarian statement in 1 John 5:7 but most modern translations do not? Why do some Bible versions place Mark 16:9–20 and John 7:53–8:11 in brackets and note that some early manuscripts do not contain these verses? Did the resurrected Jesus command his disciples to "Go into all the world and preach the gospel to all creation"? Did he promise that they would pick up snakes and drink poison without suffering harm? Did he pronounce forgiveness on the adulteress and insist that only one who was sinless was qualified to participate in her stoning? Given the differences in the ancient manuscripts, how confident can we be that the Scriptures that we read preserve what God originally inspired? We will consider questions like this in the first half of this book.

Second, let's briefly consider the question regarding the specific books that should be included in the New Testament. Most readers probably take it for granted that the contents of the New Testament are the twenty-seven books including our Four Gospels (Matthew, Mark, Luke, and John), Acts, fourteen letters of Paul (Hebrews was considered by many to have been written by Paul), the General Epistles (James, 1 & 2 Peter, Jude, and 1, 2, & 3 John), and the Book of Revelation. However, the early church, the Protestant Reformers, and some modern scholars debated the contents of the New Testament. For example, the well-known Jesus Seminar gave the title *The Five Gospels* to its "search for the authentic words of Jesus."[1] "Five Gospels? I thought there were only four!" you might reply. Not according to this group of scholars. They not only include the Gospel of Thomas in the Gospel collection but prefer its account of Jesus's teaching to that preserved in our traditional Gospel corpus. Some scholars have suggested that a text called Secret Mark and excerpts from the Gospel according to Peter are earlier than and superior to our traditional Gospels.

Although some would like to add books to our New Testament, other influential figures would like to subtract books from our New Testament. They have dismissed or questioned the inclusion of some of our New Testament books in the Christian Scriptures. These figures not only include heretics like Marcion but even one of the most respected Protestant reformers, Martin Luther. Luther dismissed claims that James was written by the half-brother of Jesus. He described the Epistle of James as "an epistle of straw"[2] and argued that the book "mangles the Scripture and thereby opposes Paul and all Scripture."[3] This negative assessment impacted his presentation of the books of the New Testament in the first edition of his German Translation. Luther's Table of Contents assigns numbers to only twenty-three of our twenty-seven New Testament books. Luther left four books, Hebrews, James, Jude, and Revelation, unnumbered and relegated these books to the very end of the list. He also distinguished these four books from the numbered books of the New Testament by indenting this portion of the Table of Contents. The resulting impression on the reader is that these books appear to be more of an appendix to the New Testament than part of the New Testament itself. Luther's Preface to James in the 1530 edition of his New Testament made his intention clear: "Therefore, I will not have him [James] in my Bible to be numbered among

---

1. Robert W. Funk, Roy W. Hoover, and the Jesus Seminar, *The Five Gospels: The Search for the Authentic Words of Jesus: New Translation and Commentary* (New York: Macmillan, 1993).
2. E. Theodore Bachmann, ed., *Word and Sacrament I*, vol. 35 of *Luther's Works* (Philadelphia: Fortress, 1955), 362.
3. Bachman, *Word and Sacrament I*, 397.

the true chief books."[4] So, should our New Testament contain the Epistle of James (not to mention Hebrews, Jude, and Revelation) or not? And what about letters that claim to be written by Paul but whose Pauline authorship is rejected by many scholars today? What about the books that were a topic of debate in the early church?

Obviously, these are very important questions. We will attempt to address these crucial questions in the following pages. Our book is divided into two major parts. Part 1, titled "The Text of the New Testament," was written by Quarles. He divides his twenty questions into four major sections. "The Transmission of the New Testament Text" focuses on the journey of the New Testament text from the original autographs to today. "The New Testament Manuscripts" considers the differences between the ancient manuscripts and introduce some of the most important manuscripts. "Textual Criticism" examines the definition, history, and various theories and methods of the science devoted to recovering the original text of the New Testament. Finally, "The Practice of Textual Criticism" gives an overview of some of the tools and recent advances in the discipline and walks through two practical examples of how scholars using critical-thinking skills to restore the original reading.

Part 2, titled "The Canon of the New Testament," was written by Kellum. He divides his twenty questions into three major sections: "Definitions and Theories of Canon," "The Physical Evidence of Canon," and "The Literary and Theological Dimensions of Canon." The first section answers questions about the different theories and definitions current in scholarship. This initial step sets the parameters for how we examine the evidence. It also gives us the ability to adjudicate various views that we encounter in our reading on the Canon. In other words, if you have ever asked, "Where is this scholar coming from?", this section should help you. The second division, "The Physical Evidence of the Canon," explores the little-discussed firsthand evidence regarding the canon in the ancient New Testament manuscripts. Instead of these only providing evidence for the words of the New Testament, they also serve as the vehicle of the canon. Finally, we will address the issues related to interpreting the church fathers and the contemporary relevance of our findings. The ultimate goal is to answer the question: So what now?

After addressing each question, we provide a summary that digests the most important elements of the discussion. We also provide reflective questions designed to guide readers in reviewing and thinking through the implications of the discussion. These features should assist individual readers and facilitate meaningful dialogue for those who study the book as a group.

---

4.   For the original German, see the second paragraph of the second page of Luther's preface to James and Jude. It may be accessed here: https://bibles-online.net/flippingbook/1530/382.

The Text of the New Testament

The Transmission of the
New Testament Text

Has the Text of the New Testament Been Preserved?

The Christian church has historically recognized that the New Testament is divinely inspired and provides the standard for the church's faith and practice. This inspiration and authority, of course, are why this question about the state of the New Testament text really matters. Our concern in this book is not the text of Homer's *Iliad* or Josephus's *Antiquities of the Jews*, as important as these texts are. Our concern is divine revelation. The New Testament is no ordinary collection of interesting ancient writings. It is God's Word, and Christians rely on its teachings to inform them of the way of salvation. Millions of people are staking their eternal destiny on the message of the New Testament. Ensuring that we have the correct text of this book is of the highest importance. So, has this text been faithfully preserved or is it irretrievably corrupted?

Clarification of the Question

The "text" of the New Testament refers to what was originally written and published by the authors of the twenty-seven books of the New Testament.[1] The authors wrote these books in Koine Greek, the *lingua franca* of the Mediterranean world in their day. Thus, our question is not about whether there are differences in the wording of modern English translations of the New Testament. Those differences may well be due to different theories of translation rather than to the underlying Greek text which is being translated. But our question focuses on the wording of the original Greek text of the individual books of the New Testament.

In decades past we might have briefly mentioned the "original text" of the New Testament and moved on because most scholars assumed that everyone

---

1. The New Testament canon will be the focus of the second half of this book so no lengthy treatment will be offered here.

agreed that the "original text" referred simply to the text of the autographs of the individual books of the New Testament. That is, the "original text" was contained in the manuscripts penned by the apostles and their associates. However, the situation has recently become significantly more complicated since scholars now debate precisely what the original text is. This question will be treated in greater detail in Question 7. To be specific, by original text we mean the published text of each of the New Testament books, the form in which the authors intended them to be distributed and read publicly.

Our question then is whether the wording of these final polished editions of the New Testament books distributed to a wider reading audience has been preserved to the present day. The answer is unequivocally "Yes." However, the answer does require some qualification. This preservation may be of a different sort than many readers expect.

What Preservation Does Not Mean

To avoid giving false impressions through the affirmation of the preservation of the New Testament text, several important qualifications must be clearly stated:

1. The manuscripts on which the original text was first penned (the "autographs") no longer exist. As we will see in Question 2, these autographs disappeared in the first few centuries of Christian history.
2. No single ancient manuscript of the Greek New Testament in existence today appears to perfectly preserve the original text. Although a few scholars have called for a "single text model" as a method for restoring the New Testament text, they acknowledge that even the best options for this model (e.g., Sinaiticus or Vaticanus) contain errors that must be corrected based on the readings of other manuscripts.[2]
3. Although we have thousands of manuscripts of the Greek New Testament, no two manuscripts are exactly alike. No two manuscripts have identical texts.

These statements will alarm some readers. Even though they may have never heard anyone explicitly teach that every copy or at least some copy of the New Testament text perfectly preserves the text of the original, they may assume that to be the case. This assumption is natural for those from cultures and times that have access to technology like printing presses or computer printers that enable mass production of completely identical copies of a work. This technology, however, is a fairly recent development—the movable-type printing press was invented only about five centuries ago.

---

2. See Stanley Porter and Andrew Pitts, *Fundamentals of New Testament Textual Criticism* (Grand Rapids: Eerdmans, 2015), 59–60; 95–96.

Prior to the first printed Bible (a Latin Bible printed by Johannes Gutenberg between 1452 and 1456), every Bible was copied by scribes by hand. Some of these scribes were amateurs and others were professionals. Some scribes spoke Greek as their mother tongue, others as a second language, and a few of the scribes seem to have known very little Greek at all. Some were highly trained and experienced scribes, and others were complete novices. But all scribes were fallible human beings. As the old saying goes: "To err is human." Despite their best efforts, the scribes all made mistakes. They were copyists, not copy machines. None of them perfectly reproduced the exact text of the manuscripts that they copied.[3]

Even our oldest and best manuscripts of the Greek New Testament contain mistakes. The earliest complete manuscript of the New Testament known to exist today is Codex Sinaiticus. This manuscript dates to the mid-fourth century and is generally considered to be one of the two most reliable manuscripts. However, it still contains clear errors that must be corrected to restore the original reading. These include singular readings, that is, readings that are unparalleled in any of the other roughly 5,800 Greek manuscripts. They also include readings that make no sense at all, accidental omissions, insertions of new material, and other similar errors. Some of these errors were spotted by proofreaders at the scriptorium and corrected before the release of the volume. Later generations of scribes also made corrections up through the twelfth century. In fact, Codex Sinaiticus has been corrected more fully than any other manuscript. David Parker has estimated that the manuscript contains nearly 23,000 corrections, an average of almost thirty per page, though most of these merely correct spelling, darken fading letters, and make other such minor changes.[4] The discoverer of Sinaiticus, Constantine Tischendorf, preferred this manuscript to all others and described it as *omnium antiquissimus* ("the most ancient of all"). However, the large number of careless errors led Kurt Aland to dismiss Tischendorf's glowing appraisal of Sinaiticus as "highly overrated."[5]

Codex Vaticanus, which is generally regarded as the most reliable manuscript of the New Testament, also contains singular readings and clear errors. Furthermore, the manuscript has been damaged and is now sadly missing the last half of Hebrews (9:14–13:2) as well as the entirety of 1 and 2 Timothy, Titus, and Revelation.

---

3. For some of the factors that led to an increased number of scribal errors, see Question 3.
4. D. C. Parker, *Codex Sinaiticus: The Story of the World's Oldest Bible* (Peabody, MA: Hendrickson, 2010), 3, 89. Note, though, that the OT text has been more heavily corrected than the NT. See also Klaus Wachtel, "The Corrected New Testament Text of Codex Sinaiticus," in *Codex Sinaiticus: New Perspectives on the Ancient Biblical Manuscript*, eds. Scot McKendrick, David Parker, Amy Myshrall, and Cillian O'Hogan (Peabody, MA: Hendrickson, 2015), 97–106.
5. Kurt Aland and Barbara Aland, *The Text of the New Testament: An Introduction to the Critical Editions and to the Theory and Practice of Modern Textual Criticism*, trans. Erroll F. Rhodes, 2nd ed. (Grand Rapids: Eerdmans, 1989), 107.

The thousands of manuscripts of the Greek New Testament still in existence have many differences between them. Sometimes these differences are minor and relate only to the spelling of a word, its specific form, or word order and have no impact on the meaning of the text. In some cases, however, the differences are significant and affect the meaning of the text. In rare cases they even affect the theology of a particular passage.

Nevertheless, claims that the text of the New Testament is terribly corrupt and that modern Bible readers can have no confidence that what they read reflects the actual thought of the authors of the New Testament are grossly exaggerated. An example of this exaggeration is a 2015 *Newsweek* article by Kurt Eichenwald titled "The Bible: So Misunderstood It's a Sin."[6] Eichenwald compared the transmission of the text of the New Testament to "playing telephone with the word of God." In the telephone game (sometimes called "Gossip"), a group of people sit in a circle or row. The leader whispers a message into the ear of the person next to him, who then whispers it into the ear of the person sitting next to her, and so on. The person at the very end then shares the reported message out loud with the entire group. Almost without fail, after being passed on by a dozen or more people, the message is drastically, usually hilariously, different from the original message. Eichenwald drew this conclusion from the telephone-game analogy:

> No television preacher has ever read the Bible. Neither has any evangelical politician. Neither has the pope. Neither have I. And neither have you. At best, we've all read a bad translation—a translation of translations of translations of hand-copied copies or copies of copies of copies, and on and on, hundreds of times.[7]

This description is a terrible distortion of the actual transmission of the text of the New Testament. It is so packed with fallacies that space does not permit us to address them all here.[8] Although the telephone game is a favorite analogy for those who want to undermine confidence in the Christian Scriptures, it is a very poor one. First, the analogy overlooks the difference between oral and written transmission. In the telephone game, the entire message, sometimes a lengthy one, is whispered once and only once to the next person in line. That person has to attempt to transmit the entire message from memory no matter how poorly they heard or understood. In the transmission of a written text, however, a scribe typically used a clearly legible text as his exemplar and copied line by line, word for word, or in some cases, even letter by letter. This placed

---

6. Kurt Eichenwald, "The Bible: So Misunderstood It's a Sin," *Newsweek,* January 2, 2015.
7. Eichenwald, "The Bible."
8. Some other fallacies will be addressed in other chapters, such as the claim that multiple hundreds of copies stand between the original text of the NT and manuscripts in existence today.

a much smaller burden on the memory of the scribe than the telephone game places on its players. Furthermore, if the scribe feared that he forgot or confused something from the exemplar, he could easily consult it again.

Second, during the telephone game, participants often attempt to distract the recipients of the message so that they cannot hear it clearly or so that they will remember it poorly. Scribes were generally able to give much greater concentration to their work and were able to labor with fewer distractions. Third, in the telephone game the message is often intentionally and completely distorted by one or two humorous participants in order to give the participants a few laughs when the message is reported. That is all part of the game. But the scribes who copied the New Testament did not view their work as a game and their goal was not to amuse. Most were either amateur Christian scribes who wanted to copy the New Testament faithfully or professional scribes who wanted to produce quality work. One of the four "basic assumptions" that guides the work of the Institute for New Testament Textual Research, the recognized world leader in the study of the text of the New Testament, is this principle: "A scribe wants to copy the *Vorlage* [the manuscript that serves as his source] with fidelity."[9] This assumption is by no means a presumption; it is factually based. Gerd Mink explains that it is "supported by the fact that in the late, richly documented phase we can determine a close relative for nearly each witness."[10]

Eichenwald is not the only writer to give the impression that currently available manuscripts of the New Testament contain a text with numerous layers upon layers of scribal errors so that the original text is irretrievably lost. Bart Ehrman's *Misquoting Jesus* left many readers with the same impression. In fact, Eichenwald's article parrots elements of Ehrman's book and probably expresses his (mis)understanding of Ehrman's arguments. Eichenwald seems to echo this thought of Ehrman:

> Moreover, the vast majority of Christians for the entire history of the church have not had access to the originals, making their inspiration something of a moot point. Not only do we not have the originals, we don't have the first copies of the originals. We don't even have copies of the copies of the originals, or copies of the copies of the copies of the originals. What we have are copies made later—much later. In most instances, they are copies made many centuries later. And these copies all differ from one another, in many thousands

---

9. Gerd Mink, "Contamination, Coherence, and Coincidence in Textual Transmission: The Coherence-based Genealogical Method (CBGM) as a Complement and Corrective to Existing Approaches," in *The Textual History of the Greek New Testament: Changing Views in Contemporary Research*, ed. Klaus Wachtel and Michael W. Holmes, TCSs 8 (Atlanta: SBL, 2011), 151.

10. Mink, "Contamination, Coherence, and Coincidence in Textual Transmission," 151.

of places. As we will see later in this book, these copies differ from one another in so many places that we don't even know how many differences there are. Possibly it is easiest to put it in comparative terms: there are more differences among our manuscripts than there are words in the New Testament.[11]

What Eichenwald overlooked was Ehrman's blunt admission that a very large proportion of these differences are completely inconsequential. In his summary of *Misquoting Jesus*, Ehrman insisted: "The vast majority of these changes are insignificant, immaterial, and of no importance for the meaning of the passages in which they are found."[12] Responding to the objection that his book gives the impression that the problems with the New Testament text are greater than they truly are, Ehrman protested:

> In fact, in the book I regularly point out the facts that the very scholars who raise the objection want to emphasize—for example, that most of the textual variants in the manuscript tradition of the New Testament are of no real importance: they don't change the meaning of the text or have any bearing on its interpretation. The majority of changes have to do simply with spelling mistakes. But why would I want to devote most of the book to discussing textual differences that don't matter for anything? They don't matter for anything![13]

In summary, the preservation of the text of the New Testament does not mean that the actual autographs of the New Testament have been miraculously preserved for two thousand years. Nor does it mean that the scribes who copied the New Testament were prevented from making mistakes as they reproduced the text. The miracle of divine inspiration was limited to the authors of Scripture. The New Testament does not promise that this same inspiration would extend to everyone who copied Scripture any more than it promises inspiration to everyone who reads and interprets Scripture.

What Preservation Does Mean

What then does "preservation" mean in relationship to the text of the New Testament? It means that God in his gracious providence has sufficiently preserved the text of the New Testament that it can be restored from the available evidence. An amazing amount of evidence is available to assist in the task of

---

11. Bart D. Ehrman, *Misquoting Jesus: The Story Behind Who Changed the Bible and Why* (New York: HarperCollins, 2005), 10.
12. Ehrman, *Misquoting Jesus*, 260.
13. Ehrman, *Misquoting Jesus*, 260.

restoring the text of the New Testament. As we will see in Question 8, we have approximately 5,800 manuscripts of the Greek New Testament or portions of it. Some of these manuscripts are remarkably early. In addition, we have quotations of the New Testament in the writings of the early church fathers and thousands and thousands of ancient manuscripts of the New Testament in languages other than Greek including at least 10,000 Old Latin and Vulgate manuscripts. The original text of the New Testament is certainly to be found among these many ancient witnesses.[14] But that text must be reconstructed after considering the evidence of these many different sources.

A given manuscript will consist largely of correct readings—though, sometimes it will contain errors. When it has errors, the correct reading must be drawn from another manuscript(s). The process for weighing variant readings to determine which is most likely the original will be described in Question 14. The text of the New Testament that results from this approach will be a collage of different readings from different manuscripts.

Think of reestablishing the text this way: If a person took several one-thousand-piece jigsaw puzzles, mixed their pieces together, and then placed one thousand of the mixed pieces into the puzzle boxes, would it be possible to assemble one of the puzzles? Of course! It would be a ton of work and would take much more time than if all the pieces were in the proper box. But someone who was up to the challenge could complete the task. One would likely find that quite a few of the pieces were in the proper box. One would also quickly identify others that clearly did not belong. That piece of a ship's anchor probably did not belong in the fir-covered mountains, for example. One would then look for pieces that matched from each of the other boxes, one by one, until the puzzle was complete.

Although the analogy is admittedly imperfect, the reconstruction of the text of the New Testament is somewhat like this. Many of the correct readings can

---

14. Only very rarely do the editors of the most widely used critical edition for scholarly research (i.e., NA[28]) feel that it is necessary to resort to a conjectural emendation. Conjectural emendation involves hypothesizing a presumably original reading that is not supported by any Greek manuscripts (though it may be supported by other ancient witnesses). Two conjectural emendations appear in the NA[28] and the UBS[5]: the addition of a single letter (ς) to πρώτη in Acts 16:12 and the insertion of the negative οὐχ in 2 Peter 3:10. Otherwise, the editors are convinced that the original reading appears in at least one of our ancient Greek witnesses.

Jan Krans defines a conjectural emendation as "a reading that is not found as such in any known manuscript." See "Conjectural Emendation and the Text of the NT," in *The Text of the New Testament in Contemporary Research: Essays on the Status Quaestionis*, NTTSD, 2nd ed., eds. Bart D. Ehrman and Michael W. Holmes (Leiden: Brill, 2012), 614. The context suggests that by "any known manuscript" Krans means Greek manuscripts specifically. See note 4 on page 613. Parker's definition narrows the application of the term to include only readings not found in any extant witness including the ancient versions. See his *An Introduction to the New Testament Manuscripts and Their Texts* (New York: Cambridge, 2008), 308–9. By this definition, the NA[28] and the UBS[5] do not contain any conjectural emendations since the Acts 16:12 reading is supported by Latin and Old Church Slavonic manuscripts and the 2 Peter 3:10 reading by Sahidic Coptic manuscripts.

be found in a single manuscript. Most textual scholars are convinced that the earliest complete or nearly complete manuscripts of the Greek New Testament (Sinaiticus and Vaticanus) very closely resemble the original text. But frankly, just about any New Testament manuscript has a text that generally resembles the original. Although it is true that no two extensive manuscripts have identical texts, it is also true that any two manuscripts that are compared have more similarities than differences. These basic similarities are what enables a scholar to recognize the text as a *New Testament* text. Yet an examination of the puzzle pieces (alternative readings) in some of the other puzzle boxes (Greek manuscripts) will often discover that those pieces are a better fit than those in the first puzzle box (the base manuscript). A text reconstructed from different ancient witnesses is called an "eclectic" text. The adjective "eclectic" comes from the Greek verb ἐκλέγομαι ("to select" or "to pick out something") and refers to a text composed of readings selected from various sources.

Admittedly, the task of choosing between alternative readings is not best performed by the average Joe. To do the task well and to produce reliable results, one must have a special set of skills. In addition to being able to read Greek well, the scholar should be able to read a variety of ancient Greek scripts (majuscule and minuscule), be able to work in some of the other ancient languages into which the New Testament text was translated in the early centuries (e.g., Latin, Coptic, or Syriac), have a knowledge of the mistakes most common to ancient scribes, be familiar with the works of the church fathers that quote the New Testament, and have some knowledge of the history of the quest to restore the New Testament.

The fact that readers of the English Bible must trust scholars to decide what the original text was and then translate it accurately frustrates some. Ehrman expressed this frustration felt by many when he wrote:

> How do these millions of people know what is in the New Testament? They "know" because scholars with unknown names, identities, backgrounds, qualifications, predilections, theologies, and personal opinions have *told* them what is in the New Testament. But what if the translators have translated the wrong text?[15]

Ehrman seems to imply that the average Bible reader cannot trust the message of the Bible and must rely on anonymous scholars to determine what the original text of the New Testament was.[16] The fact is that we depend daily, we

---

15. Ehrman, *Misquoting Jesus*, 208–9.
16. For a description of the growing distrust of experts and its causes, see Thomas M. Nichols, *The Death of Expertise: The Campaign against Established Knowledge and Why It Matters* (Oxford: Oxford University Press, 2017).

even stake our lives, on the work of experts that we do not know—the architects that designed the buildings we work in, the engineers who developed the automobiles we drive and the elevators that we ride, the pilots who fly airplanes, and the doctors who pioneered new surgical techniques. The list is practically endless. It should not shock the Bible reader that experts worked to restore the text of the New Testament and experts labored to translate it. If that concern prevents someone from reading and trusting the New Testament, if we determine that the only reliable knowledge is that which we personally possess, then consistency demands that we design our own buildings, perform our own surgeries, and engineer, build, and repair our own vehicles. In many areas of life, we either trust the experts or we must invest the time and energy to become the expert ourselves. Few of us can become true experts in all the subjects that impact our lives.

Admittedly, the experts sometimes disagree. But this does not mean that the entire text of the New Testament is in question. There is little room for disagreement about the vast majority of the New Testament text. Scholars in past generations divided manuscripts into several different text types based on their similar readings. The most important of these were the Alexandrian text type and the Byzantine text type. While most scholars affirmed the superiority of the Alexandrian text, others affirmed the superiority of the Byzantine text. That debate will be the focus of Questions 12 and 14. Although manuscripts in each of these groups are recognized by the similarities to one another and their differences from manuscripts in the other groups, the fact remains that the texts in these two major groups are identical an estimated 80 percent of the time![17]

To offer another example, Kurt and Barbara Aland compared six different editions of the Greek New Testament with the Nestle-Aland text. They discovered that in 4,999 of the New Testament's 7,947 verses, all seven editions either completely agreed or differed by a single word. They concluded: "Thus in nearly two-thirds of the New Testament text the seven editions of the Greek New Testament which we have reviewed are in complete accord, with no differences other than in orthographical details (e.g., the spelling of names, etc.)."[18]

B. F. Westcott and F. J. A. Hort argued that more than 87.5 percent of the words of the New Testament are certain.[19] The vast majority of the remaining issues relate to "changes of order and other comparative trivialities" such as

---

17. Aland and Aland, *The Text of the New Testament*, 28. This is similar to Hort's estimate: "The proportion of words virtually accepted on all hands as raised above doubt is very great, not less, on a rough computation, than seven eighths of the whole" (B. F. Westcott and F. J. A. Hort, *Introduction to the New Testament in the Original Greek with Notes on Selected Readings* [1882; repr., Peabody, MA: Hendrickson, 1988], 2).
18. Aland and Aland, *The Text of the New Testament*, 29.
19. Westcott and Hort, *Introduction*, 2. Although Hort wrote this *Introduction*, he clearly considered it to be a joint work. Thus, I cite the *Introduction* as the work of both scholars. See Peter Gurry, "Why I Cite Westcott and Hort's *Introduction* as a Joint Work," *Evangelical Textual Criticism Blog*, December 14, 2022, http://evangelicaltextualcriticism.blogspot.com.

"differences of orthography."[20] They estimated that "the amount of what can in any sense be called substantial variation is but a small fraction of the whole residuary variation, and can hardly form more than a thousandth part of the entire text."[21] In other words, in Westcott and Hort's opinion, only 0.1 percent of the text of the New Testament both remains in question and affects the meaning of the text. That is remarkable preservation for a book that is nearly two thousand years old. Kurt and Barbara Aland wrote: "Textual critics themselves, and New Testament specialists even more so, not to mention laypersons, tend to be fascinated by differences and to forget how many of them may be due to chance or to normal scribal tendencies, and how rarely significant variants occur—yielding to the common danger of failing to see the forest for the trees."[22]

Summary

Although the original manuscripts of the New Testament no longer exist, the original text contained in those manuscripts has been remarkably preserved. The claim of preservation does not mean that any single manuscript perfectly preserves the original or that any two manuscripts have identical texts. It means that the original text may be reconstructed from the readings present in the thousands of different manuscripts known today. No serious question remains about the original text of the vast majority of the words of the New Testament. Most of the remaining questions do not significantly impact the meaning of the text.

REFLECTION QUESTIONS

1. What were some of the false ideas that you had about the preservation of the New Testament before reading this chapter?

2. What factors prompted these false ideas?

3. Why are none of the copies of the New Testament perfect?

4. What would you say to a person who rejects Christianity by arguing "We don't really know what the New Testament actually says"?

5. Why is it reasonable to trust experts to reconstruct the original text from the available manuscript evidence?

---

20. Westcott and Hort, *Introduction*, 2.
21. Westcott and Hort, *Introduction*, 2.
22. Aland and Aland, *The Text of the New Testament*, 28.

What Happened to the Original Manuscripts of the New Testament?

The previous chapter stated that the original manuscripts (autographs) of the New Testament no longer exist. This chapter will discuss the fate of the original manuscripts more completely. Is there any possibility that an autograph could still be found? How long were the autographs available for Christians to consult when they discovered differences in their copies? What likely happened to these manuscripts? And why would God choose not to preserve them? We will now explore these questions.

Could We Still Find the Autographs?

No recognized textual scholar believes that the autographs still exist. Over the last several hundred years, scholars have examined a couple of manuscripts that were purported to be autographs. In both cases, these claims were found to be false.

In his commentary on the gospel of Mark, the Jesuit scholar Cornelius à Lapide claimed that an autograph of Mark's gospel was still preserved in Venice:

> The original of the Gospel of S. Mark is religiously preserved at Venice, but the letters are so corroded and worn away by age that they cannot be deciphered. When I was inquiring about the matter at Rome, several reliable persons, who had carefully investigated the subject, wrote to me to this effect, that the following is the tradition among the Venetians. They say that this Gospel was written by S. Mark at Aquileia, and left by him there, and that it was brought from thence to Venice.[1]

---

1. Cornelius à Lapide, *The Great Commentary of Cornelius à Lapide*, trans. Thomas Mossman (London: John Hodges, 1891), 362–63.

As it turns out though, the fragment in Venice is actually in Latin and is a very early copy of the Vulgate. Bernard de Montfaucon, known as the father of paleography, demonstrated that the manuscript was probably copied in the sixth century, and this was acknowledged by later Catholic commentators.[2]

Some have also claimed that fragments of a Latin manuscript of the gospel of Mark containing 12:21–16:20, preserved at the Prague Metropolitan Chapter, were from the autograph. However, this claim was disproven by Josef Dobrovsky who showed that the fragment was copied in the sixth or seventh century and is dependent on the Vulgate. It contains the eight missing leaves of the Old Latin manuscript in Venice.[3] Fragments of Luke and John located elsewhere were originally part of this manuscript which is called Codex Foro-Juliensis.[4]

Neither of these false claims seems to have been an attempt to deceive. They were likely a result of a simple misunderstanding. Some scholars of previous generations were convinced that Mark wrote his gospel in Latin rather than Greek since it was originally intended for use by the church in Rome. Furthermore, since the manuscript was once believed to be the earliest copy of Jerome's version of the Gospels, statements about the antiquity of the manuscript were probably confused, resulting in the belief that the manuscript was original.

Spectacular claims have been made about some recent manuscripts. Only a few years ago, several scholars reported the existence of a fragment of Mark believed to have been produced in the first century. It was later confirmed that this manuscript actually dated to the late second or early third century.[5] In 1972, José O'Callaghan claimed that seven fragments from Cave 7 at Qumran contained portions of Mark, Acts, Romans, 1 Timothy, James, and 2 Peter and that all but one of these fragments dated to AD 70 or earlier.[6] This claim was almost universally rejected by textual scholars. However, even in these cases,

---

2. Bernard de Montfaucon, *Diarium Italicum* (Paris, 1702). See, for example, the "Introduction to Mark" in George Leo Haydock, *Catholic Family Bible and Commentary* (New York: Edward Dunigan and Bro., 1859).

3. Josef Dobrovsky, *Fragmentum pragense Euangelii S. Marci: vulgo autographi* (Prague, 1778; Prague: Ceskoslovenske Akademic Ved, 1953).

4. F. H. A. Scrivener, *A Plain Introduction to the Criticism of the New Testament*, 4th ed., ed. Edward Miller (1894; repr. Eugene, OR: Wipf and Stock, 1997), 265.

5. The manuscript is P. Oxy. 5345. See D. Colomo and D. Obbink, "5345. Mark I 7–9, 16–18," in *The Oxyrhynchus Papyri LXXXIII* (London: The Egypt Exploration Society, 2018). Although not as early as initially reported, the manuscript remains the earliest known fragment of Mark. For a discussion of the early claims, see Elijah Hixson, "'First-Century Mark,' Published at Last?" May 23, 2018, at http://evangelicaltextualcriticism.blogspot.com/2018/05/first-century-mark-published-at-last.html.

6. José O'Callaghan, "New Testament Papyri in Qumran Cave 7," *JBL* 91, Suppl 2 (1972): 1–14; Carsten P. Theide, *The Earliest Gospel Manuscript? The Qumran Fragment 7Q5 and Its Significance for New Testament Studies* (London: Paternoster, 1992).

no textual scholar suggested that these manuscripts were actual autographs. If claims regarding the discovery of the autographs or even incredibly early manuscripts are made, readers would be wise to be skeptical unless peer-reviewed scholarly publications support the claim, and the manuscripts are made available for examination by the scholarly community.

How Long Did the Autographs Last?

Most scholars probably agree with Westcott and Hort's view: "The originals [of the New Testament documents] must have been early lost, for they are mentioned by no ecclesiastical writers, although there were many motives for appealing to them, had they been forthcoming, in the second or third centuries."[7] Westcott and Hort acknowledge that some scholars believed one or two references to the autographs existed, but they claim that the scholars misinterpreted the references.

Several early Christian documents may refer to the autographs.[8] The earliest of these is Tertullian's *On Prescription Against Heretics* 36.1–2. Tertullian, who is known as the "father of Latin Christianity," was an early Christian apologist from the city of Carthage in Northern Africa. He probably wrote *On Prescription Against Heretics* around AD 200. Two pieces of evidence support this date: (1) Tertullian does not yet appear to have embraced Montanism; and (2) several of Tertullian's other works refer to this earlier work and one of these can be dated to AD 207.[9]

In this section of his *Prescription*, Tertullian argued that the orthodox faith, unlike heretical views, is based on the teachings of the apostles. He then urged any reader who might doubt this to consult the writings of the apostles:

> Run over the apostolic churches, in which the very thrones
> of the apostles are still pre-eminent in their places, in which
> their own authentic writings are read, uttering the voice and
> representing the face of each of them severally.[10]

The question is precisely what Tertullian meant by "their own authentic writings." Tertullian's Latin phrase is *ipsae authenticae litterae eorum*. Peter

---

7. B. F. Westcott and F. J. A. Hort, *Introduction to the New Testament in the Original Greek with Notes on Selected Readings* (1882; repr., Peabody, MA: Hendrickson, 1988), 4.
8. Other scholars also strongly deny that any references to the autographs appear in ancient literature. For example, E. W. E. Reuss (*History of the Sacred Scriptures of the New Testament*, trans. E. L. Houghton, 2 vols. [Cambridge: Houghton, Mifflin and Company, 1884], 367 [§351]) insisted: "It is certain that no ancient writer makes mention of them."
9. *Against Marcion* 1, *Against Praxeas* 2, *The Flesh of Christ* 2, and *Against Hermogenes* 1. The reference in *Against Marcion* is particularly important since this is the only work for which Tertullian states the date of composition—the fifteenth year of the emperor Severus (AD 207).
10. *ANF* 3, 260.

Holmes, the translator for the standard but dated English translation, noted that the adjective *authenticus* could here mean that the writings are (1) the autographs (that is the actual original manuscripts of the New Testament documents), (2) copies of the documents in the original language (i.e., Greek rather than Latin), or (3) copies that are free from the corruptions of the heretics. Holmes preferred the second definition.[11] Although this is possible, both the ordinary sense of the terms and the context suggest that Tertullian was referring to the autographs.

The Oxford Latin Dictionary which treats "classical Latin from its beginning to the end of the second century AD" glosses *authenticus* "(of documents) Original."[12] The related noun *authenticum* is defined as "an original document, autograph." The adjective modifies the noun *litterae* which means "a document" or "writings." The phrase would be an unusual expression for copies in a particular language.

The immediate context suggests that Tertullian is referring to the autographs. It is likely no accident that he suggests that those indulging their curiosity visit cities like Corinth, Philippi, Thessalonica, Ephesus, and Rome because the churches in these locations were among those that Paul addressed in his letters. If the apologist were merely referring to churches that had accurate copies, one would have expected him to mention the great intellectual centers of the ancient world where greater concern for and skill in accurate copying might be found. The fact that he instead lists the original recipients of Paul's letters suggests that the phrase *authenticae litterae* carries its normal sense.[13]

This interpretation also fits well with Tertullian's argument in the book as a whole. In chapter 17, Tertullian charged that the heretics perverted the Scriptures that were contrary to their false teaching "by means of additions and diminutions." Similar statements appear in chapters 18, 30, 32, 33, 34, 35, 37, 38, and 39. In light of this consistent theme, Tertullian's appeal to the wording of the autographs suits his argument especially well. At the very least, Tertullian must believe that very accurate copies of the autographs were preserved at these churches.

What is unclear is whether Tertullian just assumed this or had direct knowledge of the preservation of these autographs. Even if Tertullian is

---

11. *ANF* 3, 260n12.
12. *Oxford Latin Dictionary*, ed. P. G. W. Glare, 2nd ed. (New York: Oxford University Press, 2012), viii, 241.
13. For similar views, see Daniel B. Wallace, "Claim One: The Original New Testament Has Been Corrupted by Copyists So Badly That It Can't Be Recovered," in *Dethroning Jesus: Exposing Popular Culture's Quest to Unseat the Biblical Christ*, eds. Darrell L. Bock and Daniel B. Wallace (Nashville: Thomas Nelson, 2007), 45; Craig Evans, "How Long Were Late Antique Books in Use? Possible Implications for New Testament Textual Criticism," *BBR* 25 (2015): 30–32.

expressing a mistaken assumption, his testimony remains significant. Daniel Wallace expressed this well:

> Our point, however, is simply that by Tertullian's day carefully made copies of the originals were considered important for verifying what the New Testament authors wrote and may still have been available for consultation. Even taking the worst-case scenario, Tertullian's statement tells us that some early Christians were concerned about having accurate copies and that the earliest ones still in existence were not quietly put on the shelf.[14]

A clear reference to the autograph of a New Testament book appears in a sermon of Peter, the bishop of Alexandria in the late third and early fourth century. The *Chronicon Paschale* from the seventh century twice quotes Peter's reference in a discussion of the timing of Jesus's hearing before Pontius Pilate. The subject was a topic of debate since some manuscripts of John's gospel state that the time was the sixth hour (noon) and others state that it was the third hour (9 a.m.). Peter is quoted as writing that the correct reading is "the third hour" because this is the reading that "the accurate books contain, even the autograph of the Evangelist itself, which until the present time has been guarded by the grace of God in the most holy church of the Ephesians, and there is being venerated by the faithful."[15]

But could the autograph of John have possibly lasted this long? Most scholars are convinced that John's gospel was written in the 80s or 90s. By Peter's time, the autograph would be around two hundred years old. Such longevity is not implausible. The most detailed study on the topic suggests that manuscripts of literary texts in Egypt remained in use for an average of 150 years.[16] The climate in Ephesus was not nearly as favorable for the preservation of manuscripts as the climate in Egypt. Yet, Craig Evans points out that Pliny the Elder claimed to have seen autographs of the Gracchi letters that would have been about two hundred years old, and Galen claims to have possessed

---

14. Bock and Wallace, *Dethroning Jesus*, 46.

15. Ludwig Dindorf, *Chronicon Paschale*, Vol. 2, CSHB (Bonn: Weber, 1832), 11, 411. The English translation is mine. For confirmation that the sermon was from Peter of Alexandria, see page 4, lines 21–22.

16. G. W. Houston, "Papyrological Evidence for Book Collections and Libraries in the Roman Empire," in *Ancient Literacies: The Culture of Reading in Greece and Rome*, eds. W. A. Johnson and H. N. Parker (Oxford: Oxford University Press, 2009), 248–51. Timothy Mitchell suggests that Houston's findings "likely represent best-case scenarios" ("Myths about Autographs: What They Were and How Long They May Have Survived," in *Myths and Mistakes in New Testament Textual Criticism*, eds. Elijah Hixson and Peter Gurry [Downers Grove, IL: InterVarsity Press, 2019], 43).

volumes that were three hundred years old.[17] Even more importantly, manuscripts such as Codex Vaticanus and Codex Sinaiticus have survived for a millennium and a half. Since the fifteenth century, Vaticanus has been located in Rome and yet has remained in remarkably good condition. Thus, it is feasible that an autograph of John could last two centuries in Ephesus.

All other references to the autographs appear in sources that are much later, and most contain elements that prompt serious doubts about their reliability. For example, Theodorus Lector, a reader at the Hagia Sophia in Constantinople during the early sixth century, wrote a history of the Christian church that is preserved only in quotations in later works.[18] Theodorus claimed that an autograph of the gospel of Matthew had been placed on the chest of the apostle Barnabas at his burial and was later discovered in his tomb on the island of Cyprus.[19] This autograph was later deposited by Zeno in the church of St. Stephen on the Palatine Hill in Rome. Theodorus goes on to explain that the church in Cyprus appealed to this important find to claim that the church in Cyprus was autocephalous and not under the authority of the church in Antioch.[20] The survival of a manuscript in a tomb for more than four hundred years is incredible. The use of the manuscript to declare the church's autonomy could be a motive for exaggerated claims.

Philostorgius (*Church History* 7.14) claims that when the emperor Julian in the fourth century attempted to rebuild the temple to disprove Jesus's predictions, one of the workmen discovered a manuscript of the gospel of John on a pillar in a cavern filled with water beneath the city. The book "appeared to be newly made and untouched," was written in large letters, and "the writing contained the entire Gospel proclaimed by the tongue of the virgin disciple in speaking about God."[21] The survival of a manuscript in these damp conditions is highly unlikely, and the description of the manuscript's condition sounds fanciful. The discovery of the manuscript during the rebuilding of the temple is suspiciously similar to 2 Kings 22:8–13 and suggests that the account is a legend based on this OT text.

Some of the autographs of New Testament books could have survived for a few centuries. During that time, they may have continued to be consulted and in some cases even venerated by local believers. Unfortunately, we do

---

17. Evans, "How Long Were Late Antique Books In Use?," 28.
18. These include John Damascenus, Nilus, and Nicephorus Callisti.
19. Although Theodorus's statement is normally interpreted as referring to an original manuscript of Matthew, the Greek phrase ἰδιόγραφον τοῦ βαρνάβα is ambiguous. It could refer to an autograph that belonged to Barnabas (possessive genitive) or a manuscript written by Barnabas's own hand (subjective genitive).
20. See Migne, PG 86: 183 (§571).
21. Philostorgius, *Church History*, trans. Philip Amidon (Atlanta: SBL, 2007), 107–8. Philostorgius's account is repeated in Nicephorus Callisti, *Church History* 10.33. The Greek text and Latin translation can be found in Migne, PG 146:539–44.

not have sufficient data to be sure. Tertullian's statement may have merely expressed his assumptions, and Peter of Alexandria's statement may have been based on unconfirmed thirdhand information.[22]

What Likely Happened to the Autographs?

Reuss mentions possible causes for the disappearance of the autographs: (1) they became illegible; (2) they were intentionally destroyed by the persecutors of the church; and (3) the availability of more complete copies caused them to be abandoned.[23]

The twenty-seven books of the New Testament were first published individually. Soon, however, Paul's letters began to circulate as a collection. The four Gospels also circulated as a collection. These collections surpassed the individual books in usefulness. Since the New Testament documents were prized for their content, rather than the material on which they were written, Reuss suggests that the autographs were neglected and, in some cases, even lost.

The text of the books could have been damaged to the point that they could no longer be read due to mold, mildew, bookworms, water damage, or fire. The earliest Christians worshipped in homes or rented facilities and had no permanent church buildings or libraries in which to store texts. The Scriptures were stored in private homes, carried to the place of worship, or handed off to other believers for copying or reading. Even in the period in which churches had their own buildings, those responsible for the public reading of Scripture apparently took the church's copies of New Testament books home so that they could practice their readings. Since the earliest manuscripts were written in *scriptio continua* (i.e., one letter after another without spaces between paragraphs, sentences, or even words, and without punctuation), readers had to familiarize themselves with the assigned reading in advance. All this transport and use placed the manuscripts in greater risk of damage. Once the text was no longer legible, the manuscripts would likely be ritually buried or discarded since the manuscripts were valued entirely for their texts and not as historical artifacts.[24]

Autographs that survived up to the early fourth century might have been destroyed in the Great Persecution under emperor Diocletian. Diocletian's first edict against the Christians, issued in AD 303, ordered the confiscation and

---

22. Timothy Mitchell concluded: "It is unlikely that the New Testament autographs still existed and influenced the text by the time of our earliest copies" ("Myths about Autographs," 47). This is a reasonable conclusion given the fragility of ancient writing materials in many environments. This evidence must be weighed together with the claims of ancient Christians regarding the existence of the autographs in their time.
23. Reuss, *History of the Sacred Scriptures of the New Testament*, 368.
24. On the discarding and ritual burial of Christian Scriptures, see AnneMarie Luijendijk, "Sacred Scriptures as Trash: Biblical Papyri from Oxyrhynchus," *VC* 64 (2010): 217–54, esp. 231–40.

burning of all Christian books including especially the Christian Scriptures.[25] Christians who hid or otherwise refused to surrender copies of the Scriptures were executed. Although Diocletian's edict was the first empire-wide destruction of the Scriptures, some of the local persecutions in the two previous centuries may have involved the destruction of the Scriptures also.

We simply do not know what happened to the autographs. Since the individual autographs of the New Testament books were scattered around the world, it is unlikely that they all met the same fate. Some were likely ruined in one way, and others were destroyed in another.

Why Didn't God Preserve the Autographs?

Theologians have attempted to explain why God did not choose to preserve the actual autographs. Perhaps the most common explanation is that God knew that the autographs would be worshipped as an idol, so he prevented this by permitting their destruction. There is no doubt that, if the autographs had survived, they would be worshipped by some today. The same people who kneel before the index finger of St. Thomas (according to tradition, the one he inserted in the crucifixion wounds of the resurrected Jesus) at the Basilica of the Holy Cross in Rome would assuredly bow before the autograph of the Epistle to the Romans. If Peter of Alexandria was correct that the autograph of the gospel of John was venerated by the Ephesians in his day, the autographs were on their way to becoming something of an idol before they disappeared. Still, there remains doubt that this is the reason God permitted their destruction. Peter Gurry observed that God permits many other idols to exist. It would certainly be odd for God to ordain the loss of the autographs but permit us to keep our idols that are much more dispensable such as money, power, popularity, and sex.[26]

A better explanation is offered by Frederick Henry Ambrose Scrivener, the textual scholar of the nineteenth century. God operates by the principle of "parsimony in the employment of miracles."[27] By this Scrivener meant that God does not waste miracles when his ordinary governance of the universe is enough. He uses miracles only as necessary to fulfill his purposes.

The preservation of the autographs would require multiple perpetual miracles. God would have to place something like an impenetrable force field around each of the autographs to protect it from the attacks of the persecutors,

---

25. Eusebius, *Church History*, 8.2.4. See the interesting, detailed account of the confiscation of Christian books in Cirta from *Gesta apud Zenophilum* cited in Harry Gamble, *Books and Readers in the Early Church: A History of Early Christian Texts* (New Haven, CT: Yale University Press, 1995), 145–46.

26. Peter Gurry, "Why Didn't God Preserve the Biblical Autographs?" *Evangelical Textual Criticism,* Nov 30, 2018, https://evangelicaltextualcriticism.blogspot.com/2018/11/why-didnt-god-preserve-biblical.html.

27. Scrivener, *A Plain Introduction to the Criticism of the New Testament*, 1:2.

the violence of war, the assault of the elements, the heat of the flame, and the appetites of vermin. But that would not be enough. Ink, papyrus, and parchment are all susceptible to the ravages of time, even within such a force field. Ink fades, parchment rots, and papyrus fragments. Everything on this earth is corruptible; it ages and decays. The only material object not subject to decay is Jesus's resurrection body (1 Cor. 15:35–58). Nothing else is rescued from this corruption until the return of Christ, the general resurrection, and the restoration of all creation (Rom. 8:18–25). The preservation of the autographs would require that the same incorruptibility that characterizes Jesus's resurrection body be imparted to the twenty-seven autographs of the New Testament books.[28] God simply does not choose to perform such miracles when the ordinary course of copying by faithful scribes sufficiently preserves the text of the New Testament and when the careful work of textual scholars is sufficient to restore it.

David Alan Black honestly answers this question by stating: "No one can say why this is so—except that a sovereign God designed it that way."[29] When we ask, "Why didn't God preserve the autographs," we may as well ask, "Why didn't God inscribe the text of the New Testament indelibly on the heavens so that everyone can read it?"[30] Or "Why didn't God write the New Testament in an eternal and universal language so that no translation is ever necessary?"[31] It seems we all like to second-guess God. Ultimately, rather than posing questions that cannot be definitively answered, we should roll up our sleeves to be about the difficult tasks of restoring the New Testament and translating it into all the languages of the world.

Summary

The autographs of the New Testament no longer exist. They apparently were destroyed one by one during the first few centuries of church history by various means such as aging and anti-Christian persecution. Although God did not choose to preserve the autographs miraculously, we can confidently assume that he regards the preservation accomplished through the copying by faithful scribes and the restoration of the text of the New Testament by scholarly activity to be sufficient.

---

28. We should actually imagine significantly more autographs since both letters and books were produced in multiple copies approved by the author.
29. David Alan Black, *New Testament Textual Criticism: A Concise Guide* (Grand Rapids: Baker, 1994), 12.
30. See Scrivener, *A Plain Introduction to the Criticism of the New Testament,* 1:2.
31. This objection to inspiration was suggested by Bart D. Ehrman, *Misquoting Jesus: The Story Behind Who Changed the Bible and Why* (New York: HarperCollins, 2005), 11: "If he wanted his people to have his words, surely he would have given them to them (and possibly even given them the words in a language they could understand, rather than Greek and Hebrew)."

REFLECTION QUESTIONS

1. How would you react if a journalist suddenly published an article with the headline: "Original Manuscript of Mark's Gospel Discovered That Refutes Historic Christianity"?

2. What importance did early Christians like Tertullian and Peter of Alexandria ascribe to the original manuscripts?

3. Can you imagine other reasons why God would not choose to preserve the autographs?

4. What explanation makes the most sense to you?

5. What are the dangers in trying to guess why God has acted differently than what we would prefer?

How Did Errors Enter into the Manuscripts?

The old adage, "Nobody's perfect," applies to the ancient scribes who copied the New Testament for future generations. The scribes were imperfect people who made mistakes. Samuel Tregelles wrote: "It is *impossible* (unless human infirmity were overruled by a miracle) for a writing to be copied again and again without the introduction of some errors of transcription."[1] He added: "God did not see fit to multiply the copies of his Scripture for the use of mankind by miracle; and just as He left it to the hands of men to copy His Word in the same manner as other books, so was it left exposed to the same changes, from want of skill in copyists, from carelessness or misapprehension, as affect all other ancient writings."[2] Imperfect copyists produced imperfect copies.

What Were the Conditions Under Which Scribes Did Their Work?

Although the mere humanity of the scribes is enough to explain why they made mistakes in their work as copyists, other factors exacerbated their tendencies toward error. Helpful information about the ancient procedure for hand-copying a book comes from diverse sources such as artwork depicting scribes at work, descriptions of scribal activity in ancient literature, and the evidence of the manuscripts themselves. Modern readers likely envision ancient scribes sitting at a desk with their exemplar (the manuscript that served as the basis for his copy) and their blank parchment or papyrus side by side on the desktop at a comfortable height. They would be surprised to discover that scribes probably

---

1. Samuel P. Tregelles, *An Account of the Printed Text of the Greek New Testament: with Remarks on Its Revision upon Critical Principles* (London: Samuel Bagster, 1854; repr., Cambridge: Cambridge University Press, 2013), 37 (italics original).
2. Tregelles, *An Account of the Printed Text of the Greek New Testament*, 37.

did not normally use writing desks or tables until the Middle Ages.[3] Before then, ancient scribes usually sat on a stool, bench, or even cross-legged on the floor and held their blank writing material in their lap.[4]

Modern writers have suffered writer's cramps after sitting too long at a desk at a comfortable height. We can imagine the discomfort of hand-copying a book for hours in the more awkward ancient position. Metzger and Ehrman mention a traditional formula that appears at the end of many ancient manuscripts and complains of the fatigue and pain produced by the scribe's labors: "Writing bows one's back, thrusts the ribs into one's stomach, and fosters a general debility of the body."[5] This pain and fatigue could prevent a scribe from producing his best work.

The environment in which the scribe did his work often made it even more difficult. They did not work in climate-controlled offices with fluorescent lighting! Scribes in Egypt tried to write while swatting insects in sweltering heat. On the other hand, scribes laboring much farther north might labor in chilling cold. The scribe who produced an Armenian manuscript of the four Gospels wrote an interesting colophon (a note placed at the end of a book). His note complained that he performed his work while a blizzard blasted the region with such cold that his ink had frozen, and his fingers had grown so numb that he could no longer feel his pen and repeatedly dropped it.[6] These conditions made concentration more difficult and impacted the accuracy of a scribe's work.

A. C. Myshrall has helpfully gathered, transcribed, and translated the marginal notes written by Neilos, the scribe who copied lectionary 299.[7] The scribe's comments provide helpful insights into the challenges of the ancient scribe who desired to copy the New Testament faithfully. Neilos wrote prayers for God to aid him in his work as a copyist such as "Christ, guide my works," "Unclean hands: spare, Lord, spare this most holy writing," and "Spare, Lord, spare the one who is completely slow." The scribe admits his (and others') tendency to make mistakes as they copy: "The one who writes tends toward errors." He warns of the dangers of making such errors: "Woe also to those

3. Bruce Metzger, "When Did Scribes Begin to Use Writing Desks?" in *Historical and Literary Studies, Pagan, Jewish, and Christian* (Grand Rapids: Eerdmans, 1968), 123–37.
4. In the Louvre in Paris, a limestone statuette depicts a stripped-down Egyptian scribe sitting on the floor writing on pages stacked in his lap.
5. Bruce Metzger and Bart Ehrman, *The Text of the New Testament: Its Transmission, Corruption, and Restoration*, 4th ed. (Oxford: Oxford University Press, 2005), 29.
6. Bruce Metzger, *Manuscripts of the Greek Bible: An Introduction to Palaeography* (New York: Oxford University Press, 1981), 20.
7. Lectionary 299 is the Gospel lectionary text of the twelfth century that was written over the erased New Testament text of Codex Zacynthius. All of the following quotations of Neilos's notes are from A. C. Myshrall, "An Introduction to Lectionary 299," in *Codex Zacynthius: Catena, Palimpsest, Lectionary, Text and Studies* (Third Series) 21, eds. H. A. G. Houghton and D. C. Parker (Piscataway, NJ: Gorgias, 2020), 197–99.

writing errors." Another note complains of a scribe who miscopied the text (or dictates it incorrectly) due to his failing eyesight: "The error of Theodore the squinter." The scribe speaks of forcing himself to write quickly in order to stay focused on his work: "In haste, for laziness leads to a lack of attention." The notes describe the weariness that comes from lengthy sessions of copying: "I am very tired with a heavy head, and what I write I do not know." Elsewhere the scribe admits that he is "very drowsy and foolish." Myshrall noted that many of the references to the scribe's weariness are on pages with errors, poor handwriting, and lengthy erasures in which the scribe had to recopy text due to significant mistakes.[8] Neilos's humble confessions are a window into the struggles of the scribe.

What Kinds of Errors Did Scribes Most Frequently Make?

Spelling

The uniformity of spelling of Greek words in modern editions may give readers the false impression that the ancient manuscripts agree in spelling. Most modern editions simply adopt the standardizing Greek spellings of the Middle Ages and later.[9] In fact, the manuscripts of the Greek New Testament sometimes exhibit a wide range of different spellings for the same word. The proper spelling of Greek words changed over time and likely was different in various regions of the world even in the same period.[10] Codex Vaticanus provides an example of different spellings in different periods. When the ink of the fourth-century Codex Vaticanus began to fade, a corrector (probably in the tenth or eleventh century) traced over every letter. He disliked the frequent use of the moveable nu (the Greek letter ν) and chose not to darken the ν in many of these cases.

Another example of different spellings in the same period is seen through a comparison of Codex Sinaiticus and Codex Vaticanus. Despite their other remarkable similarities and the fact that they were copied within only a few decades of each other, they frequently use different spellings. Westcott and Hort noted that Codex Sinaiticus "shows a remarkable inclination to change ∈ι to ι, and [Codex Vaticanus] to change ι to ∈ι, alike in places where either form is

---

8. Myshrall, "An Introduction to Lectionary 299," 200.

9. Modern editions that have attempted to restore the original spellings include Westcott and Hort's Greek New Testament and the recent edition produced at Tyndale House. See B. F. Westcott and F. J. A. Hort, *Introduction to the New Testament in the Original Greek with Notes on Selected Readings* (1882; repr., Peabody, MA: Hendrickson, 1988), 393–404; THGNT, 508–12.

10. Hort observed, "A large proportion of the peculiar spellings of the New Testament are simply spellings of common life. In most cases either identical or analogous spellings occur frequently in inscriptions written in different countries, by no means always of the more illiterate sort" (Westcott and Hort, *Introduction*, 304).

possible and in places where the form actually employed in the MS is completely discredited by the want of any other sufficient evidence or analogy."[11] Based on careful tabulations of various spellings in ancient manuscripts, Westcott and Hort came to the conclusion that various authors of the New Testament documents originally spelled words differently from one another and that sometimes even the same author spelled words differently in a single New Testament book.[12] Even scribes who were attempting to copy the text exactly could accidentally let the spelling with which they were most familiar slip from their pen. Ehrman acknowledges that these different spellings make up the majority of differences between the manuscripts of the New Testament.[13]

These differences in spelling should not completely surprise us since our own English spelling was not standardized until the publication of the influential dictionaries by Samuel Johnson (1755) and Noah Webster (1806) and the first edition of the American Spelling Book (1783).[14] Even today spelling differences not only exist between American English and British English, but dictionaries of American English sometimes allow for alternative spellings (e.g., adapter/adaptor; doughnut/donut; glamour/glamor).[15]

Errors Related to Sight

Reading and accurately copying texts was difficult when the scribe labored in the dark indoors with only the flickering flame of an oil lamp to illuminate the pages. Scribes who were farsighted or whose cataracts thickened as they aged had no corrective lenses (until the fourteenth century) or surgeries (eighteenth century) to assist them. Poor eyesight and a dimly lit workspace were a bad combination for producing accurate copies. Not surprisingly, scribes often confused one Greek letter for another letter that was similar in appearance. Examples of easily confused letters are: (1) The letters C, Є, Θ, O; 2) Γ, Τ, Π; and 3) Δ, λ. One of the best-known instances of suspected letter confusion is 1 Timothy 3:16. The earliest manuscripts identify Jesus as "the one who" (OC), but many later manuscripts refer to him as "God" (using the abbreviation ΘC).[16] The earliest manuscripts and

---

11. Westcott and Hort, *Introduction*, 306.
12. Westcott and Hort, *Introduction*, 304, 308.
13. Bart D. Ehrman, *Misquoting Jesus: The Story behind Who Changed the Bible and Why* (New York: HarperCollins, 2005), 260.
14. An amusing example of diverse spellings by the same author appears in the journal of the explorer William Clark. Clark spelled the name of the Sioux tribe twenty-seven different ways! See Donald Jackson, "Some Books Carried by Lewis and Clark," *Bulletin of the Missouri Historical Society* 16 (1959): 11–13.
15. On orthographical differences in the manuscripts, see Westcott and Hort, *Introduction*, 141–72.
16. This form, known as a *nomen sacrum*, was very common in the early manuscripts. On this interesting feature, see Larry Hurtado, *The Earliest Christian Artifacts: Manuscripts and Christian Origins* (Grand Rapids: Eerdmans, 2006).

church fathers support the reading "the one who." But the clear reference to the incarnation in the verse prompted a Christian scribe to read the Ο mistakenly as a Θ. Similarly, the scribe who produced Δ (037) confused a Ο for a Θ in Matthew 5:4 so that he accidentally wrote ΠΕΝΟΟΥΝΤΕC (which is not a word) instead of ΠΕΝΘΟΥΝΤΕC ("those who are mourning").

Sometimes scribes accidentally skipped a few letters of a word as they copied. An example is the scribe behind Θ (038) who should have written ἀδελφῷ (to a brother) in Matthew 5:22 but instead wrote ἀλφῷ (to a leper).[17] The scribe of K (017) accidentally left the first letter off of σκότος in Matthew 8:12 so that unbelieving Israelites were cast into the outer wrath instead of the outer darkness. The scribe behind L (019) accidentally skipped the ην in γαλήνη in Matthew 8:26 so that the sea became a great weasel instead of a great calm![18]

Errors Related to Sound

In the early centuries during which the New Testament was copied, certain vowels and diphthongs (combinations of vowels) began to be pronounced alike. Since the scribe dictated the remembered text to himself as he wrote, he sometimes accidentally substituted another vowel or diphthong for one with a similar sound. This is similar to some errors that modern writers make. I sometimes accidentally substitute homophones for one another as I write or type so that "their" becomes "there" or "hear" becomes "here."

An error related to sound is the probable cause of the variant in Matthew 18:15. Some manuscripts say, "if your brother sins." Others say, "if your brother sins against you." Which is it? Is this a passage about church discipline or is it about resolving personal conflict? The variant probably arose because the last two syllables of the verb (ἁμαρτ**ήσῃ**) sound similar to the prepositional phrase (εἰς σέ). The prepositional phrase is probably original. The scribe dictated to himself the verb as he copied it and when he glanced back at the exemplar and saw the prepositional phrase, he imagined that he had already copied it due to the almost identical sound.

Errors Related to Memory

An early scribe would read a phrase or line from his exemplar, attempt to remember that phrase or line as he turned away from the exemplar, and then dictate the portion of text to himself as he wrote it on his blank sheet, scroll, or book. The process was interrupted by the need to dip his pen frequently into an ink well. Quintilian complained of how the constant need to supply

---

17. See E. A. Sophocles, J. H. Thayer, and H. Drisler, *Greek Lexicon of the Roman and Byzantine Periods (from B.C. 146 to A.D. 1100)* (New York: C. Scribner's Sons, 1900), 121.
18. See John Lowndes, *A Modern Greek and English Lexikon* (London: Black, Young, and Young, 1837), 162.

the pen with ink "interrupts the stream of thought."[19] Judging from the variation in the darkness of letters on a page from darker to lighter then suddenly
darker again, scribes had to reink their pens anywhere from once or twice
per line to every four to six characters.[20] Scholars have demonstrated that the
reinking of the pen often broke the scribe's concentration and led to unintentional errors.[21]

Sometimes the scribe remembered the words in the line perfectly but confused the order of those words. An example is Mark 15:29 in which scoffers
describe Jesus as the one who destroys the temple and rebuilds it in three
days. Some manuscripts have the order οἰκοδομῶν ἐν τρισὶν ἡμέραις, but
others have ἐν τρισὶν ἡμέραις οἰκοδομῶν.[22] The temporal phrase obviously
modifies the participle in either order, so the different orders do not significantly affect the meaning.

Word order matters much more in a language like English in which the
order of words determines the function of a word in a sentence. Since the
grammatical function of Greek nouns in a sentence is indicated by their case
endings, these differences in word order often have little, if any, impact on the
meaning of the text. In fact, scholars are not entirely certain what the significance of word order is in the Greek New Testament.[23]

Not only did scribes confuse the order of words, sometimes they confused
the order of letters in a single word (transposition). For example, although the
scribe who produced (032) intended to write μάγων (in the phrase "by the
magi") in Matthew 2:16, he accidentally switched the positions of the μ and
γ and wrote γαμων instead. Thus, rather than writing about how Herod was
tricked by the magi, he wrote that Herod was tricked by the wedding celebra-
tions! This is a clear example of a nonsense reading.

Memory plays a much smaller role in transcribing written material today.
For example, when modern "touch typists" type a quotation from a book,
they are able to type as they read without looking away from the exemplar.
Thus, they have no need to retain even the smallest portion of the text in their
memory as they reproduce it.

---

19. Quintilian, *Institutio Oratoria* 10.3.31.
20. The scribe of P.Oxy. 657 reinked once or twice per line. See P. M. Head and M. Warren,
    "Re-inking the Pen: Evidence from P.Oxy. 657 (P13) Concerning Unintentional Scribal
    Errors," *NTS* 43 (1997): 466–73, esp. 469. The classical example of reinking every four to
    six letters is Codex Laudianus 35, a Latin manuscript.
21. Head and Warren give four examples in P.Oxy. 657 in which reinking coincides with sin-
    gular readings, i.e., readings that appear in only this particular manuscript ("Re-inking the
    Pen," 469–73).
22. Several manuscripts adopt one of these two basic word orders but drop the preposition
    (which does not affect the meaning since the dative phrase is obviously a dative of time).
23. See Chrys Caragounis, *The Development of Greek and the New Testament* (Tübingen: Mohr
    Siebeck, 2004), 405–33; Heinrich von Siebenthal, *Ancient Greek Grammar for the Study of
    the New Testament* (New York: Peter Lang, 2019), 178–80, esp. 178n3.

Ancient Christian scribes also could confuse the wording of texts they were copying with that of parallel texts that were more familiar to them. These changes are especially common in the Synoptic Gospels but occur in Paul's letters as well. Modern English readers share this tendency also. Many of us have heard someone who was reading aloud a modern translation accidentally revert to the wording of an older translation, especially when reading particularly memorable passages. The memory of the translation studied in years past overrides what the eyes see on the printed page. Similarly, the long-term memory of the scribe sometimes overrode his short-term memory when copying line by line.

Summary

We should not find it surprising that scribes made mistakes as they copied the New Testament. They were fallible human beings working with primitive tools and often in difficult conditions. They sometimes accidentally changed the spelling of a word in their exemplars to a spelling with which they were more familiar. They sometimes change spellings intentionally, thinking that they were correcting mistakes in the exemplar. They also made mistakes due to the similar appearance of letters or sounds of vowels and diphthongs. And their memories sometimes failed them as they turned from their exemplars to their blank manuscripts. Usually, these errors are easily spotted, and the original reading can be confidently determined. Often these kinds of errors do not significantly impact the meaning of the text.

REFLECTION QUESTIONS

1. Have you sometimes made mistakes when writing that are similar to the scribal errors discussed in this chapter?

2. When you catch a spelling error in a document, can you normally determine what word the author intended to write?

3. When a writer accidentally substitutes a homophone for another word in a sentence, can you normally determine what word the author intended to write?

4. When a poet deviates from normal English word order so that he can achieve the rhyme or meter that he intends, is the meaning still clear (e.g., "forest primeval")?

5. What do these parallels to ancient scribal errors suggest about our ability to restore the original text of the New Testament?

How Reliable Are the Manuscripts We Possess?

In Question 2, we saw that the original manuscripts of the New Testament no longer exist. All of the surviving manuscripts have differences between them and clearly contain mistakes. This leads to the question: "How reliable are the manuscripts that we possess?" Are the manuscripts early enough, sufficiently accurate, and adequately numerous to provide the information needed to reconstruct the original text?

Early Manuscripts Are Available

When it comes to the usefulness of a manuscript for restoring the Greek New Testament, age matters. Greater antiquity is not a guarantee of greater accuracy, but most scholars have recognized a general correlation between age and accuracy. Westcott and Hort wrote, "[The proposition] that a relatively late text is likely to be a relatively corrupt text is found true on the application of all available tests in an overwhelming proportion of the extant MSS in which ancient literature has been preserved."[1] Scribes made mistakes as they copied. In general, a manuscript that is fewer generations of copies removed from the original will be more accurate than one that is many generations of copies removed from the original. Ordinarily, an older manuscript preserves a text that is fewer generations of copies removed from the autograph, so older texts are generally preferred evidence for identifying the original reading. And the greater number of early manuscripts that are available, the better.

We have significantly more ancient manuscripts of the New Testament than of other ancient books. A search of the *Liste* for manuscripts that potentially date to AD 250 or earlier located sixty-seven papyrus manuscripts and

---

1. B. F. Westcott and F. J. A. Hort, *Introduction to the New Testament in the Original Greek with Notes on Selected Readings* (1882; repr., Peabody, MA: Hendrickson, 1988), 5–6. See also p. 31.

four majuscules.[2] Although most of these manuscripts consist now only of brief fragments, a few are extensive. For example, P[46] contains most of Paul's letters (see the discussion in Question 9). Our earliest complete manuscript of the Greek New Testament (Sinaiticus) and our earliest nearly complete manuscript (Vaticanus) both date to the fourth century.

Metzger noted, "We can appreciate how bountiful the attestation is for the New Testament if we compare the surviving textual materials of other ancient authors who wrote during the early centuries of Christianity."[3] The early evidence for the New Testament text compares very favorably to that of other ancient books. For example, two very important works for understanding New Testament backgrounds (like the differences between the major sects of Judaism in the first century) are the *Antiquities of the Jews* and *The Jewish War* by Flavius Josephus. However, the Leuven Database of Ancient Books which catalogs ancient manuscripts from the fourth century BC to AD 800 only lists one ancient Greek manuscript for either of these works, a third-century manuscript containing just two verses of Book 2, Chapter 20 of *The Jewish War*.

Database #	Language	Work	Portion of Text	Century
61315	Greek	*Wars of the Jews*	2.20.6–7	3rd
61316	Latin	*Antiquities of the Jews*	5.334–10.204	6th
66826	Latin	*Wars of the Jews*	Excerpts	6th–7th
67026	Latin	*Antiquities of the Jews*	9.10–12	8th–9th
67906	Latin	*Antiquities of the Jews*	Books 1–12	8th
69156	Latin	*Antiquities of the Jews*	4.8	8th–9th
69364	Latin	*Antiquities of the Jews*	Books 1 and 8	8th–9th
117847	Syriac	*Wars of the Jews*	Book 6	6th–7th

---

2. The qualifier "potentially" is important. The manuscripts were dated based on the script that was used and other features. Paleographical dating is merely a rough estimate and cannot pinpoint the date of copying with precise accuracy. The *Liste* is the official registry of manuscripts of the Greek New Testament. The registry is maintained by the Institute for New Testament Textual Research in Münster, Germany. The search in the online *Liste* conducted on June 6, 2019, resulted in sixty-eight hits from among the papyri but this was reduced by one since P[67] is now recognized as a portion of P[64]. Of the majuscules, 0212 was not included in my count since it preserves the *Diatesseron*.

3. Bruce Metzger and Bart Ehrman, *The Text of the New Testament: Its Transmission, Corruption, and Restoration*, 4th ed. (Oxford: Oxford University Press, 2005), 50. Tregelles made a similar argument: "[T]he providence of God has transmitted to us far more ample materials for the restoration of the text of the New Testament, than we have in the case of any other work of similar antiquity" (Samuel P. Tregelles, *An Account of the Printed Text of the Greek New Testament: with Remarks on Its Revision upon Critical Principles* [London: Samuel Bagster, 1854; repr., Cambridge: Cambridge University Press, 2013], 38).

Translations of Josephus's *Jewish Wars* today are dependent primarily on Codex Parisinus Graecus 1425 and Codex Ambrosianus both of which date to the tenth or eleventh century and Codex Laurentianus which dates to the eleventh or twelfth century.[4] Translations of Books 1–10 of his *Antiquities* are based primarily on six late manuscripts dating from the eleventh to the fifteenth century.[5] Translations of Books 11–20 are based on seven manuscripts dating from the ninth to the fifteenth century. The earliest manuscript to contain all twenty books of the *Antiquities* appears to be Codex Medicaeus from the fifteenth century.[6]

Although both Josephus's works and the New Testament were written in Greek in the first century, only one small Greek fragment is extant from before AD 800 compared to sixty-seven papyrus fragments and four majuscules of the New Testament that potentially date before AD 250! The earliest complete Greek manuscript of the *Antiquities* dates nearly a millennium and a half after the original but the earliest complete Greek manuscript of the New Testament dates less than three hundred years after the original. After conducting his own similar comparison, Metzger concluded: "In contrast with these figures, the textual critic of the New Testament is embarrassed by the wealth of material."[7]

These early manuscripts are very important. In some cases, later manuscripts are just as important. Vincent warned that one cannot assume that an earlier manuscript preserves a purer text since "it must first be settled how many copies there are between it and the autograph, and whether it followed an earlier or a later copy, and whether the copy which it followed correctly represented the autograph or not."[8] For example, minuscule 1739 was copied in the tenth century, but it appears to be a copy of a very reliable exemplar written at the end of the fourth century and preserves an earlier and more accurate text than some much earlier manuscripts. Still, most scholars affirm the principle espoused by Lachman, Griesbach, Tischendorf, Tregelles, Metzger, and Ehrman that a reading should not be viewed as original unless it is supported by ancient witnesses, preferably ancient manuscripts of the Greek New

---

4. H. St. J. Thackeray, *Josephus: The Jewish War, Books 1–2*, LCL 203 (London: Harvard University Press, 1927), xxvii–xxx. These translations include both the Loeb editions and the new Brill Josephus project. See Honora Chapman and Steve Mason, *Flavius Josephus: Translation and Commentary*, vol. 1b (Leiden: Brill, 2008), xiii.
5. H. St. J. Thackeray, *Josephus: Jewish Antiquities, Books I–III*, LCL 242 (London: Harvard University Press, 1930), xvii–xviii.
6. Ralph Marcus, *Josephus: Jewish Antiquities, Books 9–11*, LCL 326 (London: Harvard University Press, 1937), vii–viii.
7. Metzger and Ehrman, *The Text of the New Testament*, 51.
8. Marvin Vincent, *A History of the Textual Criticism of the New Testament* (London: Macmillan, 1899), 4.

Testament.[9] The existence of an abundance of early witnesses places us in a much better position to restore the original text.

Most textual scholars have little doubt that the original text of the New Testament can be found among the early manuscripts. Westcott and Hort wrote confidently: "The books of the New Testament as preserved in extant documents assuredly speak to us in every important respect in language identical with that in which they spoke to those for whom they were originally written."[10] They went so far as to speak of the "approximate non-existence of genuine readings unattested by any of the best Greek uncials."[11] They later referred to the "approximate sufficiency of existing documents for the recovery of the genuine text, notwithstanding the existence of some primitive corruptions."[12] In other words, in very few cases did he believe that the critic had to resort to conjectural emendation. Almost always, the original readings were to be found among the existing manuscripts.

All Manuscripts Share Remarkable Similarities

Although some discussions of the manuscript evidence emphasize the differences between the ancient manuscripts, we cannot overlook their remarkable similarities. We can quickly recognize that a manuscript contains a text of the New Testament, as opposed to some other book like Tacitus's *Annals*, because that manuscript shares the same general content as any other New Testament manuscript. We can likewise identify the New Testament book, the chapter, and the verses contained in a tiny fragment of a New Testament manuscript because the similarities extend down even to the level of individual phrases and words.

Of all the New Testament manuscripts, the one that is often more different than any other is Codex Bezae. Metzger wrote: "No known manuscript has so many and such remarkable variations from what is usually taken to be the normal New Testament text."[13] The most notable feature of Codex Bezae is its freedom in adding new material ranging from single words to entire incidents. The greatest differences between this manuscript and others appear in the Book of Acts. Metzger estimated that the manuscript's version of Acts is approximately ten percent longer than the normal text. Despite the

---

9. Tregelles, *Account of the Printed Text*, 113, 119–20; Tregelles also adopted this principle (pp. 174–76). For a carefully qualified statement on the probable corruption of later manuscripts, see Westcott and Hort, *Introduction*, 5–6, 31. See also Metzger and Ehrman, *The Text of the New Testament*, 302. In contrast, Vaganay refers to the appeal to the age of the witness to choose the correct reading as a "defective principle" even though age is "never to be completely overlooked." See Léon Vaganay, Christian-Bernard Amphoux, and Jenny Heimerdinger, *An Introduction to New Testament Textual Criticism*, 2nd ed. (Cambridge: Cambridge University Press, 1991), 62–63.
10. Westcott and Hort, *Introduction*, 284.
11. Westcott and Hort, *Introduction*, 276.
12. Westcott and Hort, *Introduction*, 272.
13. Metzger and Ehrman, *The Text of the New Testament*, 71.

dramatic differences, Bezae agrees with Vaticanus in 3514 out of 5142 variant units, that is, in 68.34 percent of the variant units (places in which different manuscripts have different readings).

Remember that this is a truly extreme example, a worst-case scenario.[14] Other manuscripts are much more similar. For example, a comparison of Codex Vaticanus with several other manuscripts for the Book of Acts shows that Sinaiticus agrees on 92.07 percent of the variant units, manuscript 049 agrees on 84.42 percent of the variant units, and the Majority Text (see Question 14) agrees on 87.47 percent of the variant units.[15] Traditionally, these manuscripts have all been regarded as belonging to distinct groups. Sinaiticus was viewed as belonging to the Alexandrian text type, 049 and the Majority Text represent the Byzantine text type, and Codex Bezae belongs to the Western text type.[16] But the manuscripts are far more similar than different. The very precise data produced by recent detailed studies show why Westcott and Hort were not far off base in their "rough computation" that virtually all critics agreed on more than seven-eighths of the words of the New Testament (87.5 percent). This agreement is, in part, the result of the broad similarities between the ancient manuscripts.

Differences Do Not Change the Gospel or the Essential Claims of Christianity

When a person reads some of the modern skeptics' critiques of the New Testament, one quickly gets the impression that the ancient manuscripts give wildly different accounts of the life of Jesus and the nature of the Christian faith. But this impression is a false one. Could Jesus really have been conceived by a union of Mary and a Roman soldier? Was he a wandering philosopher who performed no miracles? Was his unburied corpse eaten by wild dogs after his crucifixion? None of these claims by modern skeptics are taught in *any* New Testament manuscript—not a single one! No manuscript of the Greek New Testament denies the virginal conception of Jesus, his miracles, his sacrificial death, his bodily resurrection, or the promise of his return. No New Testament manuscript denies the holy Trinity and teaches that there are two or four or twenty-one persons in the Godhead.

We will later see that the lengthiest portions of text contained in some New Testament manuscripts but not in others are the story of the woman caught in

---

14. Of recent scholars, David Parker has most closely studied Codex Bezae. Despite his affection for the manuscript, he stated: "The longer I have studied it, the more I have become convinced that its many unique readings only very rarely deserve serious consideration if one is trying to establish the best available text." Parker, *Codex Bezae: An Early Christian Manuscript and Its Text* (New York: Cambridge University Press, 1992), 1.
15. These comparisons were generated using the "Comparison of Witnesses" tool in Phase 4 of the ECM of Acts (https://ntg.uni-muenster.de).
16. For an explanation of the traditional view of these text types, see Question 12.

adultery (John 7:53–8:11) and the ending of Mark (Mark 16:9–20). But if we affirm that the first account belongs in John, this does not mean that we, for example, treat sin dismissively or flippantly. Jesus forgave the woman for her adultery, but he also insisted that she repent of her adultery, that she "go and sin no more." But if we believe that the account was added to the gospel of John by early scribes and is not an original part of the gospel, this does not mean that we conclude that adultery is an unforgivable sin. First Corinthians 6:9–11 indisputably teaches that adulterers can be both forgiven and changed.

Similarly, Mark 16:9–20 clearly affirms Jesus's resurrection and his ascension. But even without that ending, the gospel clearly affirms the resurrection. When the women are puzzled by the empty tomb, they see a young man clothed in white inside the tomb who not only announces that Jesus is raised but also offers evidence of his resurrection. And Jesus's resurrection and ascension are obviously affirmed by many other passages in the New Testament. Without the longer ending, Mark's gospel admittedly offers no description of Jesus's post-resurrection appearances to his disciples. But these post-resurrection appearances are clearly described in other texts in which the original reading is not in question (Matt. 28:1–20; Luke 24:1–49; John 20:1–30; 21:1–25; Acts 1:1–11; 1 Cor. 15:3–8).

Most Scribes Attempted to Copy Their Exemplar Faithfully

Most scribes sought to copy a manuscript as accurately as possible. Some were more capable and thus more successful in this endeavor than others. Although a few were copying New Testament texts for personal use and adapted the text as necessary to make it understandable to a particular reader(s), most recognized that their job was to reproduce the text of the exemplar. This has long been recognized by textual scholars. Ehrman admitted:

> Later scribes who were producing our manuscripts, on the other hand, were principally interested in copying the texts before them. They, for the most part, did not see themselves as authors who were writing new books; they were scribes reproducing old books. The changes they made—at least the intentional ones—were no doubt seen as improvements of the text, possibly made because the scribes were convinced that the copyists before them had themselves mistakenly altered the words of the text. For the most part, their intention was to conserve the tradition, not to change it.[17]

---

17. Bart Ehrman, *Misquoting Jesus: The Story Behind Who Changed the Bible and Why* (New York: HarperCollins, 2005), 215. In context, "later scribes" refers to scribes who began their work after the NT authors had completed theirs and not to the scribes who copied the NT in the later history of its transmission.

These claims have been confirmed by comparisons of related manuscripts. For example, P[75] has what Gordon Fee described as a "remarkable homogeneity" with Codex Vaticanus, a homogeneity that includes both readings and stylistic features.[18] Fee's comparison of the two manuscripts prompted him to conclude that the two manuscripts were either related through a common ancestor or, less likely, that Vaticanus was a copy of a copy (possibly of a copy) of P[75]. Based on the high percentage of agreement between the two manuscripts, Fee argued that "both MSS are faithfully preserving textual phenomena that are anterior to them."[19] In other words, neither scribe intentionally created new readings. His design was to transmit the readings found in the exemplar. An earlier examination of P[75] by Colwell showed that the scribe who produced the text was "a disciplined scribe who writes with the intention of being careful and accurate."[20] Although Kurt Aland argued that some of the early papyri exhibit a "free text" in which early scribes felt the liberty to adapt the text, he denied that this freedom was typical of the early period.[21] He stated: "The fact that this was not the normative practice has been proved by P[75], which represents a strict text just as P[52] represents a normal text. It preserves the text of the original exemplar in a relatively faithful form (and is not alone in doing so)."[22]

Several dozens of our extant Greek manuscripts appear to be copies of a surviving exemplar. These have recently been carefully researched in order to determine what changes scribes tended to make.[23] For example, two manuscripts, Codex Sangermanensis (0319) of the ninth century and Codex Waldeccensis (0320) of the tenth century, appear to be copies of the fifth-century Codex Claromontanus (06). Alan Farnes discovered that both copies have an identical word count to the exemplar. The scribes did not add or omit a single word or make any adjustments to the word order.[24] The scribe who copied the Greek text of 0319 "was characterized by a strict attention to detail" and "near perfect accuracy when the *Vorlage* was clear."[25] Although the scribe who copied the Greek text of 0320 was more prone to make substitutions, his

18. Gordon Fee, "The Myth of Early Textual Recension in Alexandria," in *Studies in the Theory and Method of New Testament Textual Criticism*, SD 45, eds. Eldon J. Epp and Gordon D. Fee (Grand Rapids: Eerdmans, 1993), 258–61.
19. Fee, "The Myth of Early Textual Recension in Alexandria," 261.
20. Ernest C. Colwell, "Method in Evaluating Scribal Habits: A Study of P45, P66, P75," in *Studies in Methodology in Textual Criticism of the New Testament*, NTTS 9 (Leiden: Brill, 1969), 117.
21. Kurt Aland and Barbara Aland, *The Text of the New Testament: An Introduction to the Critical Editions and to the Theory and Practice of Modern Textual Criticism*, trans. Erroll F. Rhodes, 2nd ed. (Grand Rapids: Eerdmans, 1989), 59–60.
22. Aland and Aland, *The Text of the New Testament*, 63–64.
23. Alan Taylor Farnes, "Scribal Habits in Selected New Testament Manuscripts, Including Those with Surviving Exemplars" (PhD dissertation: University of Birmingham, 2017).
24. See especially Farnes, "Scribal Habits," 155–57, 159–60.
25. Farnes, "Scribal Habits," 161.

exemplar was also "carefully copied."[26] Normally, these scribes did not create variants but drew them from trusted sources that had different readings. The vast majority of differences between the source and the copy were simple matters of orthography in which the scribe updated the text to the spelling that was common in his time and location. Neither text had a single instance in which the scribe appeared to have altered the text intentionally to impose his personal theology on it. Farnes's research confirmed one of the guiding principles of the Coherence-Based Genealogical Method (CBGM) that scribes seek "to copy the *Vorlage* with fidelity."[27]

Summary

The manuscripts of the New Testament available today are numerous and early enough to enable scholars to establish the original readings of the New Testament. In fact, the manuscript evidence is vastly superior to any other ancient book. Although these manuscripts have their differences, they are remarkably similar. Solid evidence shows that the ancient scribes did their best to copy their exemplars faithfully. The differences between the manuscripts do not threaten the essential truths of the Christian faith.

REFLECTION QUESTIONS

1. What are four reasons to believe that the original text can be established from the available manuscripts?

2. Why would we expect early manuscripts to preserve a text closer to the original than a later text might? Are there any exceptions? If so, why?

3. Practically all scholars agree that a large percentage of the New Testament text has been established since all the major textual groups agree on these readings. What is that percentage?

4. What is one of the lengthiest variants in the New Testament? How does the addition or omission of that text affect the Christian faith?

5. How do we know that ancient scribes wanted to copy their exemplar faithfully?

---

26. Farnes, "Scribal Habits," 161.
27. Farnes, "Scribal Habits," 271; Gerd Mink, "Contamination, Coherence, and Coincidence in Textual Transmission: The Coherence-Based Genealogical Method (CBGM) as Complement and Corrective to Existing Approaches," in *The Textual History of the Greek New Testament: Changing Views and Contemporary Research*, eds. Klaus Wachtel and Michael W. Holmes, TCSt 8 (Atlanta: SBL, 2011), 151–52.

Did Scribes Attempt to Change the Theology of the Text?

Textual scholar Bart Ehrman has insisted that scribes who copied the New Testament made "theologically motivated alterations of the text."[1] He claims that "this happened whenever the scribes copying the texts were concerned to ensure that the texts said what they wanted them to say; sometimes this was because of theological disputes raging in the scribe's own day."[2] Statements like these have prompted some readers to wonder if the "theology of the New Testament" is really the theology of Jesus, the apostles, and their associates or the opinions of later scribes who had a theological axe to grind.

Early Accusations of Theological Tampering

Both early orthodox Christians and leaders of heretical groups accused one another of tampering with the text. We have already seen Tertullian's claim that the heretics of his day rejected entire books of the New Testament that did not suit their teachings and then perverted what remained by adding or subtracting material at their whim (*On the Prescription Against Heretics* XVII). Eusebius quotes an anonymous pamphlet written to refute the heresy of

---

1. This is the title of Chapter 6 of Bart Ehrman's *Misquoting Jesus: The Story Behind Who Changed the Bible and Why* (New York: HarperCollins, 2005), 151–176.
2. Ehrman, *Misquoting Jesus*, 151. This charge stands in tension with claims of Ehrman's scholarly work. In his book for scholars (Bart Ehrman, *The Orthodox Corruption of Scripture: The Effect of Early Christological Controversies on the Text of the New Testament* [New York: Oxford University Press, 1993], 276), he merely asserted that "scribes altered their sacred texts to make them 'say' what they were already known to 'mean.'" That statement does not imply that the scribes were intentionally changing the meaning of texts. One wonders why the claim escalated to the charge that scribes "were concerned to ensure that the texts said what they wanted them to say." In this work, Ehrman repeatedly admits that modern scholars cannot pretend to assess the motives of ancient scribes (e.g., pp. 28, 275).

Artemon that also charges that heretics "insert each one his own corrections" that the author insisted were actually "corruptions." The author claimed that they could not provide older manuscripts that contained these new readings.[3]

Despite these repeated claims, no trace of these efforts to revise the text of the New Testament to conform it to aberrant doctrines can be found in the manuscripts of the Greek New Testament that have survived. Evidently, these revised texts were recognized for what they were by Christian scribes and they were not copied extensively.

Lack of Evidence for Theological Tampering

Some of the leading scholars in the history of New Testament textual criticism repudiated the claim that scribes attempted to conform the New Testament text to support a personal theology that was foreign to the authors of the New Testament. Westcott and Hort wrote:

> It will not be out of place to add here a distinct expression of our belief that even among the numerous unquestionably spurious readings of the New Testament there are no signs of deliberate falsification for dogmatic purposes. The license of paraphrase occasionally assumes the appearance of willful corruption, where scribes allowed themselves to change language which they thought capable of dangerous misconstruction; or attempted to correct apparent errors which they doubtless assumed to be due to previous transcription; or embodied in explicit words a meaning which they supposed to be implied. But readings answering to this description cannot be judged rightly without taking into account the general characteristics of other readings exhibited by the same or allied documents. The comparison leaves little room for doubt that they merely belong to an extreme type of paraphrastic alteration, and are not essentially different from readings which betray an equally lax conception of transcription, and yet are transparently guiltless of any fraudulent intention. In a word, they bear witness to rashness, not to bad faith.[4]

He added: "Accusations of willful tampering with the text are accordingly not infrequent in Christian antiquity; but, with a single exception [Marcion],

---

3. Eusebius, *Church History* 5.28.
4. B. F. Westcott and F. J. A. Hort, *Introduction to the New Testament in the Original Greek with Notes on Selected Readings* (1882; repr., Peabody, MA: Hendrickson, 1988), 282–83. Spelling has been modernized in this and the following quote.

wherever they can be verified they prove to be groundless, being in fact hasty and unjust inferences from mere diversities in inherited text."[5]

To summarize, Westcott and Hort contested the claim that scribes attempted to change the theology of the text on several grounds. First, in those cases in which ancient writers claimed that their opponents had changed the text to support their theology, it turned out that the reading actually predated the theological debate. Second, the readings originated from scribes who felt responsible to clarify, not change, what they thought was the meaning of the text. Third, the assumed theological revision of the text is never thorough or systematic.

Gordon Fee has argued that Westcott and Hort were wrong to deny completely that "deliberate changes were made to the text for the sake of some theological axe to grind."[6] However, he agreed in general with them, writing, "The view that most corruption to the text was deliberate, theological, and malicious stands almost as the antithesis to what actually appears to have been the case" and insisted that corruption to the text "was seldom theologically motivated in the sense of trying to score a theological point."[7] Scholars today generally agree that some scribes did alter the text for theological reasons. The question is how frequently this happened and to what degree has it impacted our ability to restore the original New Testament. Many scholars see scribal attempts to deliberately change the theology of the New Testament as "relatively limited, either to certain MSS (e.g., P[72] or codex Bezae) or to some isolated passages."[8]

Alleged Examples of Theological Tampering

Fee's claims are essentially confirmed when we examine some of the supposed cases of the "orthodox corruption" of the New Testament. For example, Bart Ehrman has argued that the change from ὅς to θεός in 1 Timothy 3:16 was not an accident as was argued in Question 3,[9] but is instead "an anti-adoptionistic corruption that stresses the deity of Christ."[10] But Ehrman failed to present a compelling case for an intentional corruption of the text here. The

---

5. Westcott and Hort, *Introduction*, 283.
6. Gordon Fee, "The Majority Text and the Original Text of the NT," in *Studies in the Theory and Method of New Testament Textual Criticism*, SD 45, eds. Eldon J. Epp and Gordon D. Fee (Grand Rapids: Eerdmans, 1993), 194.
7. Fee, "The Majority Text and the Original Text of the NT," 194–95.
8. Tommy Wasserman, "Misquoting Manuscripts? The Orthodox Corruption of Scripture Revisited," in *The Making of Christianity: Conflicts, Contacts, and Constructions: Essays in Honor of Bengt Holmberg*, ConBNT, eds. Magnus Zetterholm and Samuel Byrskog (Winona Lake, IN: Eisenbrauns, 2012), 325–50.
9. Note that Ehrman's view was not the view of his mentor, Bruce Metzger. See Bruce Metzger and Bart Ehrman, *The Text of the New Testament: Its Transmission, Corruption, and Restoration*, 4th ed. (Oxford: Oxford University Press, 2005), 251.
10. Bart Ehrman, *The Orthodox Corruption of Scripture*, 77–78.

argument that the reading "God" was an intentional change is not new. Back in the sixth century, Liberatus Diaconus claimed that Emperor Anastasius expelled Macedonius from the patriarchate of Constantinople in AD 506 for daring to corrupt the Scriptures by changing the "who" to "God" in 1 Timothy 3:16.[11] This same account was later mentioned in the *Chronicon* of Victor.[12] Despite these accounts, Macedonius clearly did not introduce this reading into the manuscript tradition since figures from earlier church history like Pseudo-Dionysius (fifth century), Apollinaris (d. 390), Diodore (d. before 394), Gregory-Nyssa (d. 394), Chrysostom (d. 407), and Theodoret (d. 466) already found the reading in manuscripts available to them. In several cases, these manuscripts predate Macedonius's birth by nearly one hundred years![13]

Porter and Pitts have articulated a principle that is helpful in cases like the variant unit in 1 Timothy 3:16: "Variants should be explained as doctrinally motivated alterations only when more standard (and common) canons for accounting for textual variation fail."[14] Since the variant in 1 Timothy 3:16 can be explained as a common error of sight in which scribes confused one letter for a similar-looking letter, no need exists to hypothesize about theological motivations for the change. Even Ehrman admits that "it is impossible to establish an argument on scribal intentions."[15]

No surviving Greek New Testament manuscripts prior to the eighth or ninth century have "God" as their original reading in 1 Timothy 3:16. The earliest evidence for the θέος reading in a surviving manuscript of the Greek New Testament is the correction to codex Ephraemi Rescriptus (fifth century). However, this correction was by the second corrector whose work probably dates to the sixth century. Thus, the earliest surviving manuscripts that identify Jesus as God in 1 Timothy 3:16 date centuries after the great Christological controversies that led to the Council of Nicaea (AD 325) and Council of Chalcedon (AD 451). Even the earliest references to the reading in the church fathers date after the Council of Nicaea. Ehrman claimed that "proto-orthodox scribes of the second and third centuries occasionally

---

11. *Brevarium* 19 (PL 68:1033–1034).
12. Samuel P. Tregelles, *An Account of the Printed Text of the Greek New Testament: with Remarks on Its Revision upon Critical Principles* (London: Samuel Bagster, 1854; repr., Cambridge: Cambridge University Press, 2013), 229.
13. Anastasius (a Miaphysite) had attempted to remove Macedonius several times because Macedonius refused to release the emperor from the commitment he made at his coronation to submit to the Christology affirmed by the Council of Chalcedon. The emperor had initiated rumor campaigns against the patriarch and even hired an assassin to kill him. After the emperor sent Macedonius into exile, Pope Homisdas attempted to have Macedonius restored as Patriarch. Anastasius agreed to this in his treaty with Vitalian but never honored his promise.
14. Stanley Porter and Andrew Pitts, *Fundamentals of New Testament Textual Criticism* (Grand Rapids: Eerdmans, 2015), 120.
15. Ehrman, *The Orthodox Corruption of Scripture*, 275.

modified their texts of Scripture in order to make them coincide more closely with the Christological views embraced by the party that would seal its victory at Nicaea and Chalcedon."[16] But we have no firm evidence that the "God" reading emerged early enough to influence the debates at Nicaea or that this passage was a topic of discussion at Chalcedon.[17]

Furthermore, these manuscripts that contain the "God" reading do not have the changes one would expect elsewhere if the goal was to clarify or correct any text that might seem to speak of Jesus's mere humanity. For example, earlier in this same letter (1 Tim. 2:5), we read that "there is one God, and one mediator for God and human beings, the human Christ Jesus." The text contrasts the Father's deity with Jesus's humanity in a way that some opponents of orthodox Christianity might conveniently use to challenge Jesus's deity. However, not a single manuscript known to us makes any changes in the text to prevent this misunderstanding. This suggests that the change from "who" to "God" was accidental and not intentional, certainly not an effort to systematically revise the theology of the text. Ehrman suggests that "scribes were more likely to modify texts that could serve as proof texts for the opposition."[18] Yet he provides no evidence that 1 Timothy 3:16 was ever used as such a proof text either by the orthodox or those who rejected an orthodox Christology. Although 1 Timothy 2:5 would be a suitable proof text for arguing that the Father is divine and Jesus is merely human, no evidence of scribal alteration of this text has been found.

In a few cases, scribes do seem to have changed the text for theological purposes. However, the purpose of the changes was usually to clarify what the author meant, not to make the text say what the scribe wanted it to say.[19] Ehrman points out that the earliest witnesses describe Joseph and Mary in Luke 2:33 as "his [Jesus's] father and mother." However, later witnesses have "Joseph and his mother" instead. In this case (and in a similar example in 2:43) scribes altered the wording in order to avoid the impression that Joseph was Jesus's biological father. Luke had already stressed that Jesus was miraculously conceived in the womb of Mary without an act of copulation (1:34–35). In the genealogy of Jesus in Luke 3:23, Luke describes Jesus as the son of Joseph but clarifies the nature of their relationship by adding the parenthetical clause "as

---

16. Ehrman, *The Orthodox Corruption of Scripture*, 275.

17. Ehrman is aware of the problem that this potentially poses for his thesis and argues that we should not hesitate to date a particular variant reading centuries earlier than can be proven from the surviving witnesses (*The Orthodox Corruption of Scripture*, 28).

18. Ehrman, *The Orthodox Corruption of Scripture*, 277.

19. Jerome argued that scribes often copied what they understood the text to mean rather than the exact wording found in their exemplar: "They write not what they find, but what they understand, and as long as they try to correct the errors of others, they introduce their own" (Jerome, *Epistulae* LXXI–CXX, ed. I Hilberg, CSEL 55 [Leipzig: G. Freytag, 1912], 5; author's translation).

it was thought/supposed." The clarification reminds the reader that although Joseph was assumed to be Jesus's father in the ordinary sense, he was in fact Jesus's legal but not biological father. When Luke wrote 2:33 he assumed that readers would read at least several chapters at a time and interpret the statement about Jesus's father in light of the preceding and following contexts.

When smaller sections of the gospel of Luke began to be read publicly in church services, the possibility of misunderstanding statements like Luke 2:33 naturally increased. When the manuscripts that contained the reading "Joseph and his mother" were copied, the New Testament was read in church services according to a lectionary calendar. The calendar assigned particular readings for particular days. On February 2, Luke 2:22–40 was read as part of the liturgy celebrating the presentation of Christ in the temple.[20] Since the reading did not contain the reference to the virginal conception in 1:34–35 or the clarification about the nature of Joseph's relationship to Jesus in 3:23, scribes adapted the wording of the text to avoid giving the mistaken impression that Joseph was Jesus's biological father. It is important to note that this adaptation did not change the texts to make them say "what they wanted them to say." They were seeking to clarify the meaning of the text intended by the author when the text was read in a setting that was not anticipated by the author.

Even Ehrman admits that the scribes "did not effect the changes that one might expect with any kind of rigor or consistency."[21] He pointed out that texts that one would have expected a scribe to change in order to conform the text consistently to his theology "apparently escaped the pens of the early scribes unscathed."[22] This inconsistency undermines claims that scribal changes were motivated by a desire to alter the theology of the text.[23]

Summary

Although several early Christian writers claimed that opponents revised the New Testament text to support their false teachings, the manuscripts of the New Testament that have survived give little indication of any effort to

---

20. See F. H. A. Scrivener, *A Plain Introduction to the Criticism of the New Testament*, 4th ed., ed. Edward Miller (1894; repr. Eugene, OR: Wipf and Stock, 1997), 1:88.

21. Ehrman, *The Orthodox Corruption of Scripture*, 277.

22. Ehrman, *The Orthodox Corruption of Scripture*, 277.

23. For a refutation of claims of doctrinal revision in manuscripts, see Tregelles, *An Account of the Printed Text of the Greek New Testament*, 222–25. Klaus Wachtel has argued that many variants that seem to imply theological tendencies are actually either adaptations to a more popular mode of expression or towards mainstream thinking, or an example of the scilicet phenomenon which attempts to express the meaning of the text in a clearer manner. See Wachtel, "Towards a Redefinition of External Criteria: The Role of Coherence in Assessing the Origin of Variants," in *Textual Variation: Theological and Social Tendencies?*, TS 3rd Series 6, eds. Hugh Houghton and David Parker (Piscataway, NJ: Gorgias Press, 2007), 109, 112.

adapt the text of the New Testament to make it say what the scribe wanted it to say. Although some variants exhibit the scribe's effort to clarify the theology of the text, they do not nefariously seek to impose a different theology on the text. Dirk Jongkind sums up the debate nicely:

> Another way of answering the reliability question is to look for signs of deliberate tampering with the text. People have claimed to have found these, but they have also had to admit that these are few and far between and do not occur on the scale and frequency that one might expect if there were an attempt to systematically change the text.[24]

REFLECTION QUESTIONS

1. Compare Ehrman's statement describing "orthodox corruption" in his scholarly book with the description in his popular-level book. Is the difference significant? Why?

2. Does the absence of examples of deliberate theological modification of the New Testament text in the manuscripts available today necessarily mean that the accusations made by Tertullian and others were false?

3. Do you think it is more likely that the change in 1 Timothy 3:16 was deliberate or accidental?

4. Do you think that the change in Luke 2:23 alters the meaning of the text intended by the author or clarifies that meaning?

5. What is the biggest problem with the claim that scribes attempted to make the text say what they wanted it to say?

---

24. Dirk Jongkind, *An Introduction to the Greek New Testament Produced at Tyndale House, Cambridge* (Wheaton, IL: Crossway, 2019), 22.

The New Testament Manuscripts

SECTION 8

The New Testament
Manuscripts

How Many Variants Are in the Ancient Manuscripts?

If a person reads an English translation of the New Testament, he will likely assume that there are very few differences between the manuscripts. Even those translations that mention these differences typically do so only in the instances in which they matter most. A Greek student might have the same impression if he uses a "reader's edition" of the Greek text. These editions were produced primarily to provide a reliable Greek text for rapid reading rather than a tool for scholarly text-critical work.[1] The editors chose not to clutter the edition with a detailed text-critical apparatus. For example, the Reader's Edition of the United Bible Societies' fifth edition (UBS[5]) does not list any variants for Matthew 1:11–5:21. The Tyndale House Greek New Testament identifies sixteen variant units for the same section of text. However, the Nestle-Aland, twenty-eighth edition (NA[28]) identifies eighty-seven variant units for this same portion. But even the NA[28] is a handbook edition that does not attempt to identify all variant units or variants. Editions with a more detailed text-critical apparatus will identify many more variants.[2] Although a beginning student might glance at some editions of the Greek New Testament and assume that the New Testament has very few variants, detailed editions will quickly shake that false assumption. So how many variants are there?

---

1. The editors of the THGNT write: "Other New Testament editions have a much fuller apparatus, but we believe that this edition's chief significance, like that of Westcott and Hort, lies not in its apparatus but in the text itself" (THGNT, 507).
2. For Matthew, this includes Tischendorf, Legg, and the CNTTS apparatus. The *Editio Critica Maior* is presently available only for Acts, the Catholic Epistles, Mark, and selected Gospel pericopes.

Important Definitions

Before proceeding, a few preliminary definitions are necessary. When manuscripts are compared and it is discovered that one manuscript says one thing and another manuscript something different, these differences in the wording of the manuscripts are called "textual variants." The places in the text where variants appear are called "variant units." For example, important early witnesses end Mark 1:1 after the word "Christ." Many other manuscripts have the words "son of God" after Christ. The two different readings are textual variants. The ending of Mark 1:1 (which we might call 1:1c) is the variant unit, the place in the text at which the two options appear.

In order to give a helpful estimate of the number of variants in the New Testament, a more precise definition of "variant" than the preliminary definition given above is necessary. The number naturally depends on factors such as whether one counts differences in spelling, use of or differences in abbreviation, readings supported by only one manuscript, nonsense readings, and obvious scribal errors.[3] It also depends on whether one only counts different readings in the manuscripts of the Greek New Testament available today or also counts different readings contained in the ancient versions or in quotations by the early church fathers. Our discussion will not count spelling differences, differences in abbreviation, or different readings in ancient witnesses other than Greek manuscripts of the New Testament. Our count will include readings found in only one manuscript, nonsense readings, and clear scribal errors, but we will later separate these from the variants that are serious candidates for the original reading.

Efforts to Count the Variants

Until recently, the number of variants suggested by scholars amounted to little more than a "wild guess."[4] However, in the last few years, two scholars have produced careful scientific studies seeking to determine the number of variants. Based on a research sample of about 3 percent of the Greek New Testament, Gurry estimated the number of variants at approximately 500,000.[5] His study was based on detailed studies of the text of John 18 by Bruce Morrill, Philemon by Matthew Solomon, and Jude by Tommy Wasserman, in addition to studies on the collation of selected passages by the

---

3. On the definition of "textual variant" and for the distinction with "textual readings," see Eldon J. Epp, "Toward the Clarification of the Term 'Textual Variant,'" in *Studies in the Theory and Method of New Testament Textual Criticism*, SD 45, eds. Eldon J. Epp and Gordon D. Fee (Grand Rapids: Eerdmans, 1993), 47–61.

4. This is the expression that Eldon Epp ("Why Does New Testament Textual Criticism Matter: Refined Definitions and Fresh Directions," *ExpTim* 125 [2014]: 419) used to characterize his own estimate.

5. Peter J. Gurry, "The Number of Variants in the Greek New Testament: A Proposed Estimate," *NTS* 62 (2016): 97–121, esp. 113.

Institute for New Testament Textual Research in Germany. Gurry further estimated that each of the scribes, who produced manuscripts of the portions of the New Testament that he examined, contributed one new variant for every 150 (Philemon and Jude) to 430 (John 18) words.

A detailed study by Gregory Lanier soon followed Gurry's using a significantly different approach.[6] Lanier attempted to count the total number of textual variants that appear in the most important sixteen manuscripts of Acts and the Catholic/General Epistles. His more focused study eliminated the textual clutter that resulted from including the thousands of late and relatively less valuable manuscripts. He also excluded a group of texts that were especially erratic and very unlikely to represent the original text.[7] Lanier found that approximately 15 percent of this section of the New Testament was free from any variants in any manuscripts. All sixteen of the manuscripts in his focused study agreed with each other in 69 percent of the variant units, leading Lanier to conclude that the Greek New Testament enjoys "a relatively stable core textual tradition."[8] He also found that in 91 percent of the variant units among the sixteen witnesses, there were only two variants per unit.[9] An attempt to extrapolate an approximation of the number of variants for the entire New Testament concluded that these sixteen witnesses contained between 75,696 and 96,396 variants.

Putting Things into Perspective

Some readers will view the existence of half a million variants as troubling. The shock produced by the large number of variants is significantly reduced by three considerations. First, the large number of variants is due to the large number of manuscripts available to us. Three centuries ago, Richard Bentley noted that as more and more manuscripts of an ancient author's work become available, "the various readings always increase in proportion."[10] The studies by Gurry and Lanier essentially confirmed this. Gurry observed that "the data confirm that the large number of variants is a reflection of the frequency with which scribes copied more than a reflection of their failure to do so faithfully."[11] Lanier showed that when one limits the pool of variant

---

6. Gregory Lanier, "Quantifying New Testament Textual Variants: Key Witnesses in Acts and the Catholic Letters," *NTS* 64 (2018): 551–72.
7. I am referring to the D-tradition, the "Western text." Lanier, "Quantifying New Testament Textual Variants," 554.
8. Lanier, "Quantifying New Testament Textual Variants," 563.
9. Lanier, "Quantifying New Testament Textual Variants," 567.
10. Richard Bentley, "Remarks upon a Late Discourse of Free Thinking, in a Letter to F. H., D.D. by Phileleutherus Lipsiensis." Quoted in Samuel P. Tregelles, *An Account of the Printed Text of the Greek New Testament: with Remarks on Its Revision upon Critical Principles* (London: Samuel Bagster, 1854; repr., Cambridge: Cambridge University Press, 2013), 51.
11. Gurry, "The Number of Variants in the Greek New Testament," 117. He pointed out that, contrary to Bentley, the increase is not proportional but "logarithmic" since the majority

readings to the most important manuscripts, the number of variants is significantly reduced.

Although Ehrman shocked readers with the claim that "there are more differences among our manuscripts than there are words in the New Testament,"[12] this is only true when one includes the large number of late manuscripts that contribute little to our understanding of the New Testament text anyway. The text of the NA[28] has 138,151 words. Yet Lanier's estimation of the number of variants in the New Testament that appear in the sixteen most important manuscripts is significantly lower (roughly 76,000–96,000). Furthermore, Ehrman's use of the statistic is baffling since, in his scholarly work, he admitted that "it is pointless . . . to calculate the numbers of words of the New Testament affected by such variations."[13]

Second, the really important variants are (1) viable, that is they must be worthy of consideration for preserving the original text, and (2) significant, they actually impact the meaning of the text. The vast majority of variants fail to satisfy these criteria. Many variants have no claim to being the original reading since they are singular readings, that is, variants that appear in a single manuscript. Given the vast number of manuscripts of the Greek New Testament currently available, it is highly improbable that the original reading would be preserved in only one copy.[14] About half (50.3 percent) of the variants counted in Gurry's total are singular readings. Even readings that only appear in two witnesses ("sub-singular readings") are very seldom considered to be original unless one of these manuscripts is very early and deemed to be especially reliable.[15] Kurt and Barbara Aland expressed this principle, followed by many textual critics, in one of their twelve basic rules for establishing the original text: "The principle that the original reading may be found in any single manuscript or version when it stands alone or nearly alone is

---

of manuscripts are Byzantine and are characterized by greater uniformity. Paolo Trovalto, *Everything You Always Wanted to Know about Lachmann's Method: A Non-Standard Handbook of Genealogical Textual Criticism in the Age of Post-Structuralism, Cladistics, and Copy-Text*, Storie e linguaggi (Padova: Libreriauniversitaria.it, 2014), 62.

12. Bart D. Ehrman, *Misquoting Jesus: The Story Behind Who Changed the Bible and Why* (New York: HarperCollins, 2005), 10.

13. Bart D. Ehrman, *The Orthodox Corruption of Scripture: The Effect of Early Christological Controversies on the Text of the New Testament* (New York: Oxford University Press, 1993), 276.

14. Colwell and Tune argued that singular readings are highly unlikely to be the original readings given the vast number of manuscripts that preserve the NT text. See Ernest C. Colwell and Ernest W. Tune, "Method in Classifying and Evaluating Variant Readings," in *Studies in Methodology in Textual Criticism of the New Testament*, NTTS 9 (Leiden: Brill, 1969), 104.

15. Hort defined subsingular readings as those which, in addition to support in one early manuscript, otherwise have "only secondary support, namely, that of inferior Greek MSS, of Versions, or of Fathers, or of combinations of documentary authorities of these kinds" (*Introduction to the New Testament in the Original Greek with Notes on Selected Readings* [1882; repr., Peabody, MA: Hendrickson, 1988], 230).

only a theoretical possibility."[16] They added that if a critic accepts singular readings or subsingular readings, he "will hardly succeed in establishing the original text of the New Testament."[17]

Gurry also identified about a third (30.8 percent) of the variants as "non-sense" variants.[18] These variants simply do not fit the literary or grammatical context and can be excluded on these grounds from consideration in the search for the original reading. It is important to note that these two categories (singular and nonsense) often overlap.[19] A search of the critical apparatus produced by the Center for New Testament Textual Studies located approximately 5,275 nonsense readings in the New Testament in a select group of manuscripts. An example is a reading unique to minuscule 2. Rather than writing χοίρων in Matthew 8:30, the scribe accidentally wrote ξυρων so that a herd of razors (rather than pigs) was feeding. This was clearly a simple mistake by an absent-minded scribe since (1) no other manuscript preserves this reading, (2) it makes no sense, and (3) the scribe correctly wrote "pigs" in 8:31 and 32.

A Couple of Examples

We can easily illustrate both why the number of variants is so high and why the high number of variants should not shake confidence in the New Testament. To keep things simple, let's just consider the two shortest verses in the Greek New Testament. In terms of word count, the shortest verse is 1 Thessalonians 5:16 which consists of only two words: πάντοτε χαίρετε ("Rejoice always"). However, one manuscript has παντοτετε and another παντε instead of πάντοτε ("always"). Other manuscripts have χαιρεται and χερετε instead of χαίρετε ("Rejoice"). One manuscript adds the phrase εν τω κω ("in the Lord" using a special abbreviation for "Lord" [κυρίῳ] called a *nomen sacrum*). The temporal adverb can be considered one variant unit; the verb can be considered a second; and the prepositional phrase can be considered a third. The first variant unit has three variants from which one must choose. The second variant unit has three variants. The third variant unit has two variants (the presence or absence of the prepositional phrase).

---

16. Kurt Aland and Barbara Aland, *The Text of the New Testament: An Introduction to the Critical Editions and to the Theory and Practice of Modern Textual Criticism*, trans. Erroll F. Rhodes, 2nd ed. (Grand Rapids: Eerdmans, 1989), 281.

17. Aland and Aland, *The Text of the New Testament*, 281.

18. Gurry, "The Number of Variants in the Greek New Testament," 108–9.

19. In John 18, 86.3 percent of nonsense variants are also singular. The percentages for Philemon and Jude are 64.2 percent and 84.7 percent, respectively. One cannot simply add the 30.8 percent to the 50.3 percent and conclude that 81.1 percent of variants are singular or nonsense readings.

The correct reading is clearly πάντοτε χαίρετε.[20] But this two-word verse has no less than eight variants.[21]

The variants παντοτετε and παντε are probably the result of a simple scribal error and both are "nonsense" readings since neither is even an actual word! The variant χαιρεται does not fit the grammatical context which is a lengthy series of second person plural imperatives (1 Thess. 5:14–22). Χαιρεται, by contrast, is third person singular indicative. Additionally, the middle/passive form makes no sense in context.[22] The form χερετε is not a known verb.[23] The prepositional phrase is a singular reading, apparently drawn from parallels in Philippians 3:1 and 4:4. Of the eight known variants, none creates any doubt about the reading of the original text.

In terms of letter count, the shortest verse in the Greek New Testament is Luke 20:30, which contains only twelve letters: καὶ ὁ δεύτερος ("and the second").[24] However, one manuscript omits the καί from this reading. A considerable number of manuscripts dating to as early as the fifth century have καὶ ἔλαβεν ὁ δεύτερος τὴν γυναῖκα, καὶ οὗτος ἀπέθανεν ἄτεκνος ("and the second brother took the woman, and this one died childless").[25] Some manuscripts have this longer reading but omit ὁ δεύτερος. Others place ἄτεκνος before the verb ἀπέθανεν instead of after it. This variation appears both with and without ὁ δεύτερος. Still another manuscript has καὶ ἔλαβεν ἄτεκνος. Thus, this brief verse contains no fewer than seven variants. None of these variants are nonsense readings or the result of obvious scribal error. In other words, several of these variants could be considered viable options for the original text. On the other hand, none of these variants significantly impact the meaning of the text. The shorter reading of Luke 20:30 clearly implies the content of the longer reading(s). The longer readings only make explicit what is already implicit in the shorter reading. Regardless of which major variant a textual critic selects, the meaning of the text basically remains the same.

---

20. The NA[28], SBLGNT, THGNT, and RP not only agree, but also consider the text so well-established that none of the variants are listed in these editions.
21. Notice that three of these variants actually make up the correct reading. Some scholars define a variant as deviations from the correct reading, so they would count five variants in this verse.
22. Future and aorist passive forms of the verb are used in the NT, but the verb is always active in the present tense. Note, however, that Codex D uses a middle/passive form of the present participle in Acts 3:8.
23. Westcott and Hort state that substitutions of ε and αι for each other are a "frequent permutation" and add that the substitution of ε for αι "is merely the shortening of an individual sound" (*Introduction*, 309, 150–51). Consequently, this difference does not necessarily affect the sense.
24. This is the reading in the NA[28], SBLGNT, and THGNT.
25. This is the reading in RP.

Summary

There are probably around 500,000 variants in all the manuscripts of the Greek New Testament. The large number of variants is a direct result of the frequency with which the New Testament was copied and the large number of New Testament manuscripts that have survived to the present day. Many of these variants appear in late manuscripts that do not contribute much to the endeavor of restoring the original Greek New Testament. In the sixteen most important manuscripts available to us less than 100,000 variants appear. About two-thirds of these variants are readings that only appear in a single manuscript or that make no sense at all and are not worthy of serious consideration in the search for the original text. Many of the remaining variants do not significantly change the meaning of the text.

REFLECTION QUESTIONS

1. Were you alarmed to discover that the Greek New Testament has approximately half a million variants? If so, why?

2. How does the definition of the term "variant" affect attempts to count the number of variants?

3. Why are singular and sub-singular readings not likely to preserve the original text?

4. Why do some scholars exclude late manuscripts in the effort to count the number of variants?

5. Do you think that the majority of the variants are really important? Why or why not?

Do the Differences Between the Manuscripts Really Matter?

In Question 6, we saw that the vast majority of variants in the New Testament do not significantly affect the meaning. For example, although Luke 20:30 has seven variant readings, they all have the same basic meaning. But one must not confuse "the vast majority of variants" with "all variants." Sometimes the variant readings do have different meanings, and sometimes the differences are theologically important. Sometimes the differences between the manuscripts matter greatly, but the differences impact the meaning of a verse or paragraph, rather than the meaning of an entire book or the entire New Testament.

Variants May Affect the Meaning of the Text at the Micro Level

Students sometimes say that they need not bother examining the variants in the apparatus at the bottom of the page in their Greek Testament because "the differences do not really matter." When asked to clarify, they normally reply, "They don't really affect the meaning of the text." However, this all depends on what one means by "the text." If the reference is to the New Testament text as a whole, then the statement is accurate. However, if the reference is to a specific text of the New Testament, the statement is clearly incorrect. Variants do not affect the meaning of the New Testament text at the macro level. No single variant unit will change the theology of the New Testament as a whole. But variants do sometimes significantly affect the meaning of the text at the micro level, so much so that deciding the original reading is a prerequisite to any serious exegetical work. Greenlee was correct when he wrote:

> Textual criticism is the basic study for the accurate knowl-
> edge of any text. New Testament textual criticism, therefore,
> is the basic biblical study, a prerequisite to all other biblical
> and theological work. Interpretation, systematization, and

application of the teachings of the New Testament cannot be done until textual criticism has done at least some of its work. It is therefore deserving of the acquaintance and attention of every serious student of the Bible.[1]

To pretend that textual variants do not matter at all is intellectually dishonest. Furthermore, it stifles the advancement of text-critical research by discouraging people from devoting themselves to this important area of study.

By "micro level" we mean the level of the clause, sentence, and even paragraph. Many people study the New Testament at this level of detail. When a commentator explains a clause or an expositional preacher explains a verse, textual variants can significantly impact meaning.

After admitting that most of the variant readings in the New Testament are insignificant, Ehrman quickly added:

> It would be wrong, however, to say—as people sometimes do—that the changes in our text have no real bearing on what the texts mean or on the theological conclusions that one draws from them. We have seen, in fact, that just the opposite is the case. In some instances, the very meaning of the text is at stake, depending on how one resolves a textual problem.[2]

Ehrman is absolutely right. The different theological meanings between variants becomes obvious by taking a close look at two of his examples. He asks, "Is the doctrine of the Trinity explicitly taught in the New Testament? Is Jesus actually called the 'unique God' there?"[3]

The first of these questions is related to a well-known textual issue in 1 John 5:7–8. A few late manuscripts add to these verses a reference to three heavenly witnesses: "and there are three who testify in heaven, the Father, the Word, and the holy Spirit, and these three are one." Although this reference was included in the text of the King James Version, it is relegated to a footnote in modern translations. Why? No Greek manuscript dating earlier than the fourteenth century has the trinitarian reference in the text. A few earlier Greek manuscripts have the reference as a variant reading in the margin added by a later scribe. However, none of the marginal readings appear to predate the fourteenth century.[4] The variant appears to have emerged as a marginal reading in Latin manuscripts and was later accidentally incorporated into the

---

1. J. Harold Greenlee, *Introduction to New Testament Textual Criticism* (Grand Rapids: Baker Academic, 1995), 7.
2. Bart D. Ehrman, *Misquoting Jesus: The Story Behind Who Changed the Bible and Why* (New York: HarperCollins, 2005), 207–8.
3. Ehrman, *Misquoting Jesus*, 208.
4. See, for example, minuscule 221.

text of 1 John itself.[5] Although the reference is not a reasonable candidate for the reading of the original text, one certainly cannot dismiss the variant as doctrinally insignificant. If the reference to the three heavenly witnesses were original to the letter (and it is not), it would be the clearest expression of the doctrine of the Trinity in the entire New Testament.

But 1 John 5:7–8 is not the best text to illustrate the importance of textual variants since the variant there is significant but not viable. Other variants in the New Testament are both viable and theologically significant as well as hotly debated. Ehrman offers John 1:18 as his second example. Manuscripts of the gospel refer to Jesus as either "one and only God" (μονογενὴς θεός)[6] or "one and only Son" (μονογενὴς υἱός). Since the earliest manuscripts used *nomina sacra* (ΘC and ῩC), the two readings differ by only a single letter.[7] The change from one reading to the other could easily have been the result of an error of sight. Ehrman argued that orthodox scribes intentionally changed "Son" to "God": "It appears, though, that some scribes—probably located in Alexandria—were not content even with this exalted view of Christ, and so they made it even more exalted."[8] This explanation is unlikely. If the scribes intentionally made this perceived improvement, one would expect them to make the same change in other texts that originally referred to Jesus as the "one and only Son" (John 3:16, 18; and 1 John 4:9). But such a change does not appear in a single extant manuscript. Furthermore, the earliest Greek manuscripts support the description of Jesus as God, including P[66] and P[75] (early third century) and three of the four major majuscules. The earliest manuscript to have the "Son" reading is Alexandrinus (fifth century). Most likely scribes familiar with the more frequent expression "one and only Son" misread the unique expression "one and only God" and introduced an unintentional change into the text. But does the difference really matter? Yes! Although the description of Jesus as the "one and only Son" is compatible with an identification of Jesus as the one and only God, it is not equivalent to that identification. The description "one and only Son" could be misinterpreted as a reference to Jesus's mere adoption by God so that the reader concludes Jesus is less than fully God. The descriptor "one and only God" is not subject to such misinterpretation. Against the background of Jewish monotheism, "one and only God" is about as clear a reference to Jesus's true deity as one can possibly imagine. So Ehrman is right in this regard—some variants do matter and do affect the theology of a text.

---

5. See Bruce Metzger, *A Textual Commentary on the Greek New Testament*, 2nd ed. (Stuttgart: Deutsche Bibelgesellschaft, 1994), 647–49.
6. The adjective μονογενής is sometimes taken as substantival: "the one and only [Son], God . . .". The CSB seems to take this option: "The one and only Son, who is Himself God."
7. For a more detailed discussion of this variant unit, see Question 17.
8. Ehrman, *Misquoting Jesus*, 162.

Variants Do Not Affect the Meaning of the Text at the Macro Level

If textual variants can make a significant difference in the meaning of a specific text, how can some scholars make the claim that textual variants do not undermine the essential teachings of the Christian faith? For example, Dan Wallace has claimed:

> Our fundamental argument is that although the original New Testament has not been recovered in all its particulars, it has been recovered in all its essentials. That is, the core doctrinal statements of the New Testament are not in jeopardy because of any textual variations. That has been the view of the majority of textual critics for the past three hundred years, including Dr. Bruce Metzger.[9]

The examples above in no way contradict Wallace's claim. Neither variant unit is one in which one variant affirms the deity of Jesus and the other denies it. The reading that omits the reference to the three heavenly witnesses in 1 John 5:7–8 in no way disputes the doctrine of the Trinity. It simply fails to address it. The reading "one and only Son" in John 1:18 does not deny Jesus's deity. In fact, it asserts it, just not as clearly as the alternative reading does.

But one must not forget that the doctrines of the Trinity and Jesus's deity do not depend on these two texts. Jesus's deity is very clearly affirmed in other New Testament passages such as Colossians 2:9: "The entire fullness of God's nature dwells bodily in Christ." The doctrine of the Trinity is seldom neatly packaged in the New Testament. The doctrine is a conclusion drawn from an assembly of many different passages that (1) assert that God is one; (2) affirm the deity of the Father, the Son, and the Spirit; and (3) teach that the Father, Son, and Spirit are distinct persons. But single texts like Matthew 28:19–20 certainly imply the doctrine of the Trinity. Jesus commanded disciples to baptize new disciples in the name (sing.) of the Father, the Son, and the Holy Spirit. The fact that the three persons in the baptismal formula all share the same name implies that they are one God, Yahweh. And all the extant manuscripts affirm Jesus's deity in Colossians 2:9, and all the extant manuscripts affirm that Father, Son, and Spirit share a single name in Matthew 28:19–20. Any doctrinal ambiguity caused by variants in particular texts is cleared up by consulting other New Testament texts for which the original reading is well-established and clear. Even theologically significant variants do not change the theology of the New Testament as a whole.

---

9. Daniel B. Wallace, "Claim One: The Original New Testament Has Been Corrupted by Copyists So Badly That It Can't Be Recovered," in *Dethroning Jesus: Exposing Popular Culture's Quest to Unseat the Biblical Christ*, eds. Darrell L. Bock and Daniel B. Wallace (Nashville: Thomas Nelson, 2007), 72.

To go even further, they do not normally change the theology of the individual New Testament book or even a single chapter. Consider John 1:18 again as an example. Even if this single verse did not clearly affirm the deity of Jesus by describing him as "the only God" (ESV) or "the one and only Son, who is himself God" (CSB), the gospel of John clearly affirms Jesus's deity in numerous other texts. The Prologue itself describes Jesus as the Word who "is God" (John 1:1), who created all created things (1:3), who embodies God's glory and is filled with the grace and truth that are the fundamental characteristics of Yahweh (1:14; Exod. 34:6). Thus, even if the reading "God" in John 1:18 were the result of a scribal error, the variant would not change the theology of the Prologue.

Summary

Textual variants do matter. They sometimes affect the meaning of the text at the level of clauses, sentences, and in rare cases even paragraphs. Scholarly study of the Bible certainly requires some knowledge of the different readings in the ancient manuscripts and of the reasons for selecting one variant as the probable original reading. Anyone studying the Bible in detail, especially those who preach and teach it, should pay attention to variant readings, how they affect the meaning of a particular passage, and why a particular translation chose a specific variant.

On the other hand, one must not exaggerate their importance. No essential doctrine of the Christian faith depends on a textual variant that remains in question. We can concur with Jongkind's statement:

> Clearly, many of the differences affect how we read a particular sentence and how the text says what it says. But the actual content of a paragraph or a chapter—let alone that of a whole book—stands firm regardless. The message that is communicated comes across clearly even though there is interfering noise.[10]

---

10. Dirk Jongkind, *An Introduction to the Greek New Testament Produced at Tyndale House, Cambridge* (Wheaton, IL: Crossway, 2019), 21. The disagreement with my statement regarding the impact of variants is merely apparent. The rare cases in which variants affect the meaning of paragraphs would minimally include variants that encompass entire paragraphs such as John 7:53–8:11 and Mark 16:9–20. Jongkind later (p. 78) describes these "important variants" as those that "have a big impact" and adds that both "concern around 170 words."

REFLECTION QUESTIONS

1. Do differences in the readings of the ancient manuscripts ever affect the meaning of a text? If so, how?

2. Do differences in the readings of the ancient manuscripts ever affect the theology of a text? Do they affect the theology of a book as a whole or the New Testament as a whole?

3. How was the term "micro level" used in this discussion?

4. How was the term "macro level" used in this discussion?

5. Does the Christology of the gospel of John depend on the variant readings in John 1:18?

With All the Variants, Can We Still Speak of Inspiration and Inerrancy?

A person's view of the text of the New Testament will necessarily impact his view of the inspiration and authority of the New Testament. If a person holds that the message of the New Testament was only clear to the first few generations of Christians but then radically changed and was irretrievably lost, he will not likely affirm the inspiration of the New Testament. It is hard to imagine that God would go to the trouble of inspiring a book only to assign it to the dustbin of history a few decades later. If the New Testament carries any authority for a person with this view, the authority would be reduced to that of respected church tradition and not the authority of divine revelation. In light of what we have discovered about the differences between the ancient manuscripts, is it still reasonable to affirm the inspiration and inerrancy of the New Testament?

Inspiration and Inerrancy

The doctrine of inspiration affirms that the authors of Scripture wrote exactly what God intended to communicate through them. The doctrine of inerrancy further asserts that the Scriptures given by God had no factual errors. However, some Christians wrongly assume that when evangelical scholars speak of inspiration and inerrancy, they are referring to a particular modern English translation.

No translation can factually claim absolute and complete inerrancy, not even the very finest of the modern versions. Every translation is by necessity an interpretation. Since modern English lacks perfect word-for-word equivalencies with Koine Greek, a translator must attempt to interpret what the text means and then determine how to most clearly express that meaning in the receptor language. And translators are no more perfect than ancient scribes were. That is why there are sometimes significant differences between major translations today.

Scholarly definitions of "inerrancy" reserve the term for the original text of Scripture rather than copies that contain scribal changes or versions that express the translators' interpretation of the text.

The standard definition of inerrancy was produced by a group of conservative Christian scholars at a meeting in Chicago in 1978. The group produced a detailed statement on inspiration and inerrancy called "The Chicago Statement on Biblical Inerrancy" that consists of a preface, a one-page summary, and nineteen articles of affirmation and denial. Article X directly addresses issues related to textual criticism:

> We affirm that inspiration, strictly speaking, applies only to the autographic text of Scripture, which in the providence of God can be ascertained from available manuscripts with great accuracy. We further affirm that copies and translations of Scripture are the Word of God to the extent that they faithfully represent the original.
>
> We deny that any essential element of the Christian faith is affected by the absence of the autographs. We further deny that this absence renders the assertion of Biblical inerrancy invalid or irrelevant.

The word "only" in the first sentence plainly restricts inspiration (and inerrancy) to the original text of the New Testament, that is, the wording of the autographs. The statement affirms that God has providentially preserved the original readings among the many manuscripts available but implicitly denies that any modern editions of the Greek New Testament have perfectly restored the original text in every detail. The statement affirms the possibility ("can be") of restoring the original text with "great accuracy." But "great accuracy" is not absolute perfection. The statement adds that the authority and inspiration of copies and translations are derivative and relative, not absolute. The inspiration and authority of copies and translations are dependent on the degree to which they preserve the readings of the original. Changes made to the original text by scribes and translators do not have divine authority. Finally, the statement asserts that minimally the Scripture has been preserved and restored sufficiently that the Christian should have no doubt regarding "any essential element of the Christian faith."

Some will naturally object that affirming the inerrancy of a document that is no longer extant is meaningless. This objection seems to overlook the difference between a hypothetical document and a nonextant document. The autographs no longer exist, but they did once exist. They are the ultimate ancestors of all the extant New Testament manuscripts. The textual tradition exhibits general stability so that each copy contains a text that closely resembles that of the autographs. But the quality and purity of the Scriptures as originally given by God matters greatly. Thus, the assertion of the inerrancy of the text of the autographs is both valid and relevant.

Defining the Term "Autograph"

Scholars currently debate what "original text" or "autograph" means precisely. Recent research has concluded that some old assumptions about the identity of the "original text" are anachronistic. They wrongly assume that the authorship and publication of ancient books and letters followed the same procedure as the composition and publication of books in the twenty-first century. In fact, significant differences exist between the ancient and modern practices.[1]

Timothy Mitchell recently illustrated some of these differences by describing the authorship and publication of the works of Cicero, Pliny the Younger, and Galen.[2] These first two writers are especially helpful examples of ancient publication processes. Cicero often wrote a first draft, which was then carefully proofread by his slave Tiro[3] or by Cicero's brother Quintus.[4] Cicero and Tiro would often discuss in detail the changes that Tiro recommended and produce a more polished draft. Cicero then sent the more polished draft to his friend Atticus, who carefully proofread the draft and made editorial suggestions using his dreaded red pencil.[5] Cicero would then make the final decision about what changes were appropriate. Finally, Atticus supervised a team of copyists who produced multiple copies of Cicero's works.[6] Sometimes Cicero continued to make some changes in his own work even after the draft was in the hands of his copyists.[7] After the copyists completed their work, Cicero or Atticus corrected any copyist errors that they spotted.[8] These corrected copies were sent to the dedicatees and others, and Cicero kept a copy for his records. Cicero sometimes continued to make changes in his own retained copy and to request these same changes be made to other copies that had circulated.[9]

Pliny the Younger also composed and edited his work in various stages. He wrote his own initial draft and then used his notes to dictate the

---

1. For a helpful discussion of these differences, see Harry Gamble, *Books and Readers in the Early Church: A History of Early Christian Texts* (New Haven, CT: Yale University Press, 1995), 83–84.
2. Timothy Mitchell, "What Are the NT Autographs? An Examination of the Doctrine of Inspiration and Inerrancy in Light of Greco-Roman Publication," *JETS* 59 (2016): 287–308.
3. Cicero said that Tiro loved to be the "rule" (κανών) of Cicero's writings (*Fam.* 16.17).
4. *Quint. Fratr.* 3.6.
5. *Att.* 15.14; 16.11.
6. *Att.* 12.6a.
7. *Att.* 12.6a.
8. *Att.* 13.23.
9. *Att.* 12.6a; 13.21a; 16.5.

composition to a scribe. He then dismissed the scribe, so he could work in private and then called him back for more dictation.[10] He proofread his own work and then read it to several friends and entertained their feedback. He distributed it to a small group of colleagues who noted suggestions for improvement. If he was hesitant about any of the suggested revisions, he then discussed these with trusted advisors. Then he recited his composition before a large audience that made him even more aware of needed improvements.[11] After making these last changes, he retained one of the final copies and then distributed the rest.

Mitchell also discussed four papyrus autographs (P.Köln VI 245; P.Oxy. VII 1015; P.Mich.inv. 1436; P.Mich.inv 1440). The first two papyri have numerous revisions, suggesting that they are corrected first drafts that were intended to serve as the basis for a polished draft intended for distribution. The last two papyri are especially interesting, because P.Mich.inv. 1436 appears to be the first corrected draft of which P.Mich.inv. 1440 is the polished copy.

Since "the process by which a literary composition saw the light of day was a long, drawn-out procedure of correction, editing, polishing, and rewriting," Mitchell urges a precise identification of the "autograph" or original text as "the completed authorial work which was released by the author for circulation and copying, not earlier draft versions or layers of composition."[12] Mitchell's definition serves as a helpful clarification to the Chicago Statement. The goal of evangelical textual criticism is to seek to restore this completed authorial work released by the author for circulation and copying.

Summary

Many of the leading scholars in the field of textual criticism have been devout believers who dedicated their lives to the restoration of the New Testament text because of their love for the Holy Scriptures. They recognized that every word of the text is important because these words are the very words of God. The differences in the manuscripts available to us do not undermine an informed and properly nuanced doctrine of inspiration and inerrancy.

---

10. *Epigr.* 9.36.
11. *Epigr.* 7.17.
12. Mitchell, "What Are the NT Autographs?" 306.

REFLECTION QUESTIONS

1. Do well-informed biblical inerrantists intend to affirm the inerrancy of a specific translation of the Bible? Why or why not?

2. Do well-informed biblical inerrantists intend to affirm the inerrancy of the text of a specific edition or manuscript of the Greek New Testament? Why or why not?

3. How does the ancient publication process challenge your understanding of how NT books may have been composed and published?

4. In what sense can the inerrancy of manuscripts, editions, and translations of the Greek New Testament be described as "relative" and "derivative"?

5. What are the dangers in failing to recognize these distinctions?

What Are Some Important New Testament Manuscripts?

Westcott and Hort, two of the most important figures in the quest to restore the original Greek New Testament, famously stated: "The first step towards obtaining a sure foundation is a consistent application of the principle that KNOWLEDGE OF DOCUMENTS SHOULD PRECEDE FINAL JUDGMENT UPON READINGS."[1] They explained that, before a decision was made about which variant was the original reading, scholars should first consider features of the manuscripts that supported each reading such as their date and general reliability. This discussion will introduce the various classifications of New Testament manuscripts and give a brief description of some of the most important manuscripts for reconstructing the original text.

Kinds of Manuscripts

A "manuscript" is a text written by hand and, for our purposes, refers to texts produced by hand out of necessity because a printing press was not accessible. New Testament manuscripts are assigned to different categories based on factors such as (1) the material that they are written on; (2) the script used by the scribe; and (3) the way in which the text is presented. In some cases, classification depends on a combination of these factors.

Some types of Greek texts are identified and classified according to the material on which they are written. Papyri (sing. papyrus) are Greek manuscripts in which the text is written on something like a thick paper made from pressing together the split reeds of the papyrus plant that grew in the delta of the Nile River in Egypt. Generally, the papyri are the earliest surviving manuscripts of the Greek New Testament. The currently available papyri date from

---

1. B. F. Westcott and F. J. A. Hort, *Introduction to the New Testament in the Original Greek with Notes on Selected Readings* (1882; repr., Peabody, MA: Hendrickson, 1988), 31.

the second to the seventh (or very early eighth) century. Although papyrus is a hardy material when kept dry, it does not tolerate moisture well. Papyrus was used as a writing material all around the Mediterranean world, but surviving papyri have been found almost exclusively in dry areas such as Egypt (especially), Palestine, and Mesopotamia.[2] Papyrus manuscripts are identified using a Gothic or plain Roman upper-case P followed by a superscripted number indicating the order in which the manuscript was placed on the official registry of New Testament manuscripts (e.g., $\mathfrak{P}^{46}$ or P[46]).[3]

Ostraca are texts written on pieces of pottery. Amulets or talismans are small portions of text, often only a few words, written on an object and worn to ward off evil.[4] Some older editions of the Greek New Testament listed these texts as witnesses, and one scholar has recently argued that editors of the Greek New Testament should begin to utilize this kind of evidence again.[5]

The remaining categories of Greek texts are written on another material, parchment or vellum. Parchment refers to animal skins that were preserved and scraped thin to serve as a writing material. Vellum refers to the highest quality parchment. Though already used as a writing material for centuries, parchment began to replace papyrus as the writing material of choice for the most important books in the fourth century.

Parchment manuscripts are divided into two major categories based on the type of script used to write the text. Majuscules are written with a script that looks like capital block letters in which the letters generally fit between two imaginary horizontal lines. Majuscule manuscripts generally date from the fourth century to eighth century (though in some cases the script continued to be used even after this). Majuscule manuscripts are identified using several different systems. The older system developed by Johann Jakob Wettstein and later expanded by others used upper-case letters from the Greek, Latin, and Hebrew alphabets (e.g., Θ B א) to represent manuscripts. This system became confusing since some letters had to be used more than once to refer to

---

2. Eldon Epp, "The Papyrus Manuscripts of the New Testament," in *The Text of the New Testament in Contemporary Research: Essays on the Status Quaestionis*, NTTSD, 2nd ed., eds. Bart D. Ehrman and Michael W. Holmes (Leiden: Brill, 2012), 7. Exceptions include finds at Herculaneum in Italy, Dura-Europos in Syria, and Vindolanda in northern Britain (though these were not NT manuscripts). See Roger S. Bagnall, ed., *The Oxford Handbook of Papyrology* (New York: Oxford University Press, 2009), xvii–xviii.
3. Sometimes ancient manuscripts, including papyri, majuscules, and minuscules, are identified using the cataloging system of the library where they are held. For example, P[46] may be referred to as P. Chester Beatty II or Ann Arbor, Univ. of Michigan, Inv. 6238 since different portions of the codex are held by two different libraries.
4. The classification "amulet" or "talisman" is technically based on the object on which the text is written and the use of that object rather than the material on which it is written.
5. Brice C. Jones, *New Testament Texts on Greek Amulets from Late Antiquity*, LNTS 554 (New York: Bloomsbury T&T Clark, 2016). See Charles Quarles, review of *New Testament Texts on Greek Amulets from Late Antiquity*, by Brice C. Jones, *BBR* 27 (2017): 118–19.

different manuscripts. C. R. Gregory developed a better system that identifies majuscules with a number preceded by zero. For example, Codex Sinaiticus was formerly identified using the Hebrew *aleph* (‏א‎) but is now often identified as 01. In the past, the term "uncial" was used to refer to these manuscripts, but scholars now prefer to reserve the term "uncial" for Latin script.

Parchment or vellum manuscripts written with minuscule script are called minuscules. Minuscule script is characterized by connections between letters that permitted scribes to copy more quickly without the need to lift the pen to begin a new letter. Minuscule script also extends portions of letters above and below the two lines and uses smaller letters. Minuscule manuscripts often combine several letters into a single formation (ligatures) and use many different abbreviations for words or constructions that appear frequently in order to save space. Minuscule manuscripts date to the ninth century and later. Minuscule manuscripts are identified by a plain Arabic number (without the prefixed "P" or zero to distinguish them from papyri and majuscules).

Lectionaries, the final category of manuscripts of the Greek New Testament, are classified according to the presentation of the New Testament text. "Lectionaries" divide and order readings from the New Testament based on ancient religious calendars that assigned specific readings for specific days. Papyri and majuscules are described as "continuous text" manuscripts since they present the New Testament text verse-by-verse. "Lectionaries" are classified as "non-continuous text" manuscripts since they divide the text up into brief readings and change the order of these readings. The Book of Revelation is not included in the lectionaries. However, some lectionaries also contain readings from sources other than the Bible.[6] Lectionaries are identified with an italic lowercase letter "*l*" (sometimes just an uppercase "L") followed by an Arabic number (e.g., *l* 991).

Important Papyri Collections

Early editions of the Greek New Testament depended largely on minuscules and a few majuscules. Tischendorf was the first to use a papyrus in an edition of the Greek Testament. He collated the papyrus he called Q in 1862, which is now known as P^{11}. Only a few papyri were discovered prior to the twentieth century, and they were not seen as of great importance since they were so fragmentary (covering a combined total of only 176 verses) and also dated after the major majuscules. However, over a hundred papyri were discovered in the twentieth century, and some of these were significantly earlier

---

6. For a helpful introduction, see Carroll Osburn, "The Greek Lectionaries of the New Testament," in *The Text of the New Testament in Contemporary Research: Essays on the Status Quaestionis*, NTTSD, 2nd ed., eds. Bart D. Ehrman and Michael W. Holmes (Leiden: Brill, 2012), 93–113. See also F. H. A. Scrivener, *A Plain Introduction to the Criticism of the New Testament*, 4th ed., ed. Edward Miller (1894; repr. Eugene, OR: Wipf and Stock, 1997), 1:80–89, 327–76.

than any other known manuscripts. Interest in the papyri naturally increased. The official registry of New Testament manuscripts now lists 141 papyri.[7] Space will permit mention of only a few of the most important.

The dates given for these papyri are those given in the NA[28]. Although these dates reflect the opinions of respected paleographers who carefully examined these manuscripts, the dates are not universally accepted. A few scholars date some of these manuscripts considerably earlier, but other scholars date some of these considerably later.[8]

In the 1930s, a private collector named Chester Beatty purchased a group of papyri from a dealer in Egypt. Three of these are New Testament manuscripts that are both very early and unusually extensive. P[45] is a third-century manuscript that contains portions of thirty leaves of a codex that originally contained about 220 leaves covering all four Gospels and Acts. P[46] is a manuscript dated to approximately AD 200 and contains eighty-six of an original 104 leaves. Originally this codex contained all of Paul's letters (plus Hebrews which was widely believed to have been authored by Paul) except for possibly 1, 2 Timothy and Titus.[9] Second Thessalonians is now missing in its entirety, but the codex originally contained this letter also. Approximately a third of the manuscript is housed at the library of the University of Michigan. The Chester Beatty Papyri collection also includes P[47]. This manuscript contains approximately a third of a manuscript of Revelation (Rev. 9:10–17:2) and dates to the third century.

The Martin Bodmer collection includes P[66], a manuscript that contains most of the gospel of John and dates to the early third century. P[72] is perhaps the earliest known copy of the Epistles of Peter and Jude and dates to the third or fourth century. P[75] is a codex of Luke and John written in the third century (dated by its original editors to between AD 175 and 225). The manuscript often agrees with Codex Vaticanus in its readings. It serves to demonstrate that the excellent text of Vaticanus could be traced back more than a century earlier.

Finally, P[52] should be mentioned since it is believed to be the very oldest of the papyri. This fragment of the gospel of John contains 18:31–33 on one side and 18:37–38 on the other. The manuscript dates to the second century. A number of eminent paleographers have dated the papyrus to the first half

---

7. However, six of these are portions or duplicates of other papyri in the list and have now been struck from the registry.

8. For earlier dates, see Philip Comfort, *The Text of the Earliest New Testament Greek Manuscripts* (Wheaton, IL: Tyndale House, 2001). For later dates, see Brent Nongbri, "Grenfell and Hunt on the Dates of Early Christian Codices: Setting the Record Straight," *BASP* 48 (2011): 149–62. For high-resolution images of these manuscripts, see the website of The Center for the Study of New Testament Manuscripts (www.csntm.org).

9. For the view that P[46] contained these three letters also, see Jeremy Duff, "P46 and the Pastorals: A Misleading Consensus?" *NTS* 44 (1998): 578–90.

of the second century, potentially only a few decades after the autograph was written.[10]

Important Majuscules

Although approximately 324 majuscules are currently listed in the official registry, five are called the "major majuscules" because of their antiquity and importance. These five codices are Sinaiticus, Alexandrinus, Vaticanus, Ephraemi Rescriptus, and Bezae.

Codex Sinaiticus (‭א‬ or 01) is from the fourth century AD and was probably produced in either Caesarea or Egypt.[11] Not only is this codex the oldest complete manuscript of the Greek New Testament by half a millennium, but it is also the only complete manuscript of the Greek New Testament in majuscule script. Constantine Tischendorf was the first modern scholar to study the codex after spotting it at the monastery of St. Catherine on Mt. Sinai.[12] The manuscript clearly remained in use over the centuries, since corrections were made to the text periodically. David Parker counted 27,305 places where the text had been altered by later scribes and readers, though the majority of these are in the OT portion.[13] Parker suggested that the great number of corrections in this codex implies "that it has already a sufficiently high status in the first centuries after its creation to be treated with extraordinary care."[14] The codex also contains two books from the collection now called the Apostolic Fathers: the Epistle of Barnabas (which was previously known only through a poor Latin translation) and a large portion of the Shepherd of Hermas (which previously was known only by its title).

Codex Alexandrinus (A or 02) is a fifth-century manuscript.[15] The codex originally contained the entire Old and New Testaments, although it is now missing the leaves that contained Matthew 1:1–25:6; John 6:50–8:52 and 2 Corinthians 4:13–12:6. It also contains portions of the Old Testament Apocrypha and 1 and 2 Clement. An Arabic inscription on the back of the Table of Contents claims that the manuscript was copied by Thecla the Martyr who was executed in AD 286. However, this claim conflicts with evidence from the text itself since it contains features that require a date in the late

---

10. Bruce Metzger and Bart Ehrman, *The Text of the New Testament: Its Transmission, Corruption, and Restoration*, 4th ed. (Oxford: Oxford University Press, 2005), 56.
11. For high resolution images of Codex Sinaiticus, see https://codexsinaiticus.org/en.
12. For Tischendorf's account, see Stanley Porter, *Constantine Tischendorf: The Life and Work of a 19th Century Bible Hunter* (New York: Bloomsbury T&T Clark, 2015), 117–29. See also D. C. Parker, *Codex Sinaiticus: The Story of the World's Oldest Bible* (Peabody, MA: Hendrickson, 2010), 127–50.
13. Parker, *Codex Sinaiticus*, 79, 89.
14. Parker, *Codex Sinaiticus*, 89.
15. For high resolution images of Codex Alexandrinus, see https://www.bl.uk/collection-items/codex-alexandrinus.

fourth century or later. For example, the codex inserts a letter from Athanasius (d. 373) to Macellinus before the Psalms. Alexandrinus was the first of the codices to be widely studied by European scholars.[16] Although most of the New Testament largely agrees with other ancient codices like Sinaiticus and Vaticanus (Alexandrian group), in the Gospels, it often agrees with the majority of late manuscripts (Byzantine group).[17] Metzger claimed Alexandrinus preserves the best text of Revelation of any manuscript.[18]

Codex Vaticanus (B or 03) was written in the first half of the fourth century AD.[19] A section from Hebrews 9:14 on is missing so the manuscript no longer contains the ending of Hebrews or any of the text of 1–2 Timothy, Titus, Philemon, and Revelation. The end of Hebrews and Book of Revelation currently in the codex was added by a scribe in the fifteenth century.[20] Unlike Sinaiticus, Vaticanus has no ornamentation, suggesting that the text is slightly older.[21] Its greater antiquity is also implied by the absence of features such as the numbering system that Eusebius developed in the early fourth century to identify parallel accounts in the Gospels. Although Hebrews follows Thessalonians, the chapter numbers indicate that it followed Galatians in the exemplar.[22] The New Testament books are placed in the standard ancient order: Gospels (Matthew, Mark, Luke, John), Acts, General Epistles, Paul, and Revelation. Vaticanus is considered an excellent example of the Alexandrian group. Westcott and Hort regarded Vaticanus as the very best surviving manuscript, and most scholars today seem to share this opinion. Comparisons to the papyri have confirmed that it preserves a very early text.

Codex Ephraemi Rescriptus (C or 04) is a fifth-century manuscript that may have originally contained the entire Bible.[23] The volume now contains the OT Wisdom books and the New Testament (except for 2 Thessalonians and 2 John). However, based on differences in the script on the Old Testament

---

16. Joel C. Slayton, "Codex Alexandrinus," *ABD* 1:1069.

17. Scrivener, *A Plain Introduction to the Criticism of the New Testament*, 1:97–105.

18. Bruce Metzger, *Manuscripts of the Greek Bible: An Introduction to Palaeography* (New York: Oxford University Press, 1981), 86.

19. For high resolution images of Codex Vaticanus, see https://digi.vatlib.it/view/MSS_Vat.gr.1209.

20. D. C. Parker, "Codex Vaticanus," *ABD* 1:1074. This supplement is in minuscule script and is classified as minuscule 1957.

21. Those who examine photographs or the color facsimile will quickly notice the beautiful ornamentation, but this is the work of a later scribe. The colorful and highly ornamented first letter of each book placed to the left of the column also appears within the column in the original hand. Though the original letter was not reinked with the rest of the text, it is still visible. In manuscripts in which the ornamentation is original, the ornamented initial letter is absent from within the column of text.

22. Chapter numbers run consecutively through the Pauline corpus rather than starting over at the beginning of each new epistle.

23. For high-resolution images of Codex Ephraemi Rescriptus, see https://gallica.bnf.fr/ark:/12148/btv1b8470433r/f1.item.r=.langEN.zoom.

pages and New Testament pages, Parker has questioned whether the two actually belonged to a single manuscript originally.[24] In the twelfth century when majuscule script had been replaced by minuscule script, the parchment was erased, and its sheets were rewritten with a Greek translation of thirty-eight sermons by St. Ephraem (Syrian church father from the fourth century). A manuscript that was erased to serve as writing material for another work is called a palimpsest. The erased text was recovered by applying a chemical agent to the manuscript.[25] Tischendorf was able to transcribe the manuscript, but now many portions of the manuscript are illegible. The manuscript contains portions of all books except 2 Thessalonians and 2 John. The text is a mixture of readings from the Alexandrian and (predominantly) Byzantine groups.

Codex Bezae or Cantabrigiensis (D or 05) is dated by Parker to around AD 400,[26] though other scholars date it to the fifth or even sixth century.[27] The manuscript contains the text of most of the four Gospels and Acts and a small fragment of 3 John. The Greek text is written on the left page with a Latin translation on the facing page. The Latin translation does not exactly match the Greek text and sometimes appears to translate another Greek exemplar. Parker shows that the Greek text is characterized by harmonization, adaptation to the context, insertion of material from other sources, use of a colloquial style, and sometimes changing the Greek text to correspond to the Latin version.[28] The fundamental characteristic is "a freedom to transmit the text loosely."[29] The order of the Gospels is interesting: Matthew, John, then Luke, and Mark. This order (which is known as the "Western order") suggests that preference was given to the Apostles over the companions of the apostles.[30] Bezae is usually classified as belonging to the "Western group." However, the "Western group" refers to texts that share an important feature rather than

---

24. D. C. Parker, *An Introduction to the New Testament Manuscripts and Their Texts* (Cambridge: Cambridge University Press, 2008), 73.
25. Although more recent works claim that Tischendorf applied the chemical agents (e.g., Metzger and Ehrman, *The Text of the New Testament*, 69), Scrivener says that this was done "at the instance of Fleck in 1834" (*A Plain Introduction to the Criticism of the New Testament*, 1:121). However, Marvin Vincent (*A History of the Textual Criticism of the New Testament* [London: Macmillan, 1899], 16) indicates that the application of prussiate of potash was performed by Carl Hase in 1834–35.
26. David Parker, *Codex Bezae: An Early Christian Manuscript and Its Text* (Cambridge: Cambridge University Press, 1992), 277.
27. For high-resolution images of Codex Bezae, see https://cudl.lib.cam.ac.uk/view/ MS-NN-00002-00041/1.
28. For these and other characteristics, see Parker, *Codex Bezae*, 256–58.
29. Parker, *Codex Bezae*, 258.
30. Parker, *An Introduction to the New Testament Manuscripts and Their Texts*, 288. See also Parker, *Codex Bezae*, 109–10.

necessarily agreeing on variant readings.[31] The shared feature is a tendency to paraphrase.[32]

Important Minuscules

The official registry of Greek New Testament manuscripts currently lists approximately 2,967 minuscules. Space permits a discussion of only a couple of these. The discussion of these two manuscripts should be sufficient to demonstrate that although minuscules are later (sometimes significantly later) than the papyri and majuscules, they must not be neglected. They can be very helpful witnesses in the effort to restore the original text.

Minuscule 33 is widely recognized not only as one of the earliest minuscules but also one of the most important. Since the nineteenth century 33 has been called the "Queen of the cursives."[33] The manuscript contains the entire New Testament except for a few pages of Mark and Luke and the entire Book of Revelation, which were lost. The manuscript was produced in the ninth century, but its text often closely resembles the early majuscules Vaticanus and Sinaiticus in the Gospels and General Epistles (though it largely agrees with later manuscripts in Acts and Paul). Sadly, this manuscript is difficult to read due to water damage.[34]

Minuscule 1739 is a tenth-century manuscript that originally contained all of the New Testament except possibly Revelation, but now contains Acts, Paul's letters, and the General Epistles.[35] A colophon identifies the scribe who copied the manuscript as Ephraim. The manuscript has marginal notes drawn from the writings of several early Greek church fathers: Irenaeus, Clement, Origen, Eusebius, and Basil. The ancestor of 1739 was copied some time after Basil's death in 379. However, that ancestor must have been relatively early since a note on James 2:13 refers to a manuscript written by Eusebius of

---

31. Parker correctly noted: "Thus, the apparent confederacy of what was once described as the 'Western text' is a similarity not in detail, but in character. We have not a text, but a genre. That is why the representatives of this free genre are distinct from all other types, but puzzlingly unlike each other" (*Codex Bezae*, 284).
32. Metzger and Ehrman, *The Text of the New Testament*, 307–8.
33. "Cursive" was an alternative term for minuscule.
34. The ink from some pages has transferred to the facing page and must be read backwards superimposed over the other text. Although Samuel P. Tregelles was a skilled and accomplished collator, after collating 33, he complained: "I have had some experience in the collation of MSS.; but none has ever been so wearisome to the eyes, and exhaustive of every faculty of attention" (*An Account of the Printed Text of the Greek New Testament: with Remarks on Its Revision upon Critical Principles* [London: Samuel Bagster, 1854; repr., Cambridge: Cambridge University Press, 2013], 162).
35. Kirsopp Lake and Silva New, *Six Collations of New Testament Manuscripts*, HTS 17 (Cambridge, MA: Harvard University Press, 1932), 142.

Caesarea "with his own hand."[36] A note also indicates that the "very ancient codex" from which the exemplar of 1739 was copied contained Origen's text. This was confirmed by the early scribe's comparison of the codex to Origen's commentary. The scribe who compiled the exemplar drew his text of most of Romans (except for Romans 9 and 12:16–14:10 which he drew from the ancient codex directly) from quotations in Origen's commentary, though he continued to consult his ancient codex. These features suggest that the ancestor of 1739 may have been produced in Caesarea. Günther Zuntz pointed out that although the text of Romans in 1739 did indeed essentially preserve Origen's text, the rest of the text of Paul's letters in 1739 was from a manuscript as old as or even older than Origen's text.[37]

Zuntz demonstrated that 1739 preserved "rare, ancient readings."[38] In particular, Zuntz noted important agreements of 1739 with both P[46] and B, but especially P[46]. An example was 1739's omission of the phrase ἐν Ἐφέσῳ in Ephesians 1:1. Of the minuscules known to Zuntz, only 1739 supported the omission and stood in agreement with P[46], ℵ, B, Origen, Basil, and Marcion.[39]

These two manuscripts demonstrate that even manuscripts copied nearly a millennium after the New Testament era may be copies of a very early and reliable exemplar. Thus, the minuscules cannot be ignored simply due to their age. Early readings may also be found in some of the approximately 2,506 lectionaries that have survived.

Summary

Scholars have a rich store of ancient manuscripts to guide them in reconstructing the original text of the Greek New Testament. Additional study of some of these manuscripts is needed. New manuscript discoveries are still being made surprisingly often. A recent volume of the Oxyrhynchus papyri contains fragments from three different New Testament manuscripts all dated to the second to the fourth century.[40] But the evidence is already so abundant that these new discoveries do not require any radical changes to the New Testament text. Elijah Hixson wrote: "As exciting as they are, textually speaking, new manuscript discoveries tend to confirm or at most fine-tune our Greek New Testament editions. As an example, our Greek New Testament

---

36. A mutilated note on Galatians 5:15 also refers to a manuscript written in prison. Some scholars suggest that the manuscript was the one written by Pamphilus mentioned several times in the colophons in Sinaiticus.
37. Günther Zuntz, *The Text of the Epistles: A Disquisition up the Corpus Paulinum* (British Academy, 1953; repr., Eugene, OR: Wipf and Stock, 2007), 81.
38. Zuntz, *The Text of the Epistles*, 81.
39. Minuscule 6 (13th c.) and the correction in 424 also support the omission.
40. P. J. Parsons and N. Gonis, eds., *Graeco-Roman Memoirs 104*, vol. 83 of Oxyrhynchus Papyri (London: Egypt Exploration Society, 2018).

would be exactly the same with or without our current earliest New Testament manuscript, P[52]."[41]

REFLECTION QUESTIONS

1. Why are earlier manuscripts generally assumed to preserve the original text better than later manuscripts?

2. What are some important exceptions to this general principle?

3. Some scholars are arguing that some of the early papyri were assigned dates that were too early. Does it affect the text of the New Testament if we adjust the date of our potentially earliest fragment, P[52], ahead another 50–150 years?

4. What challenges do scholars face in working with very old manuscripts?

5. Which of the manuscripts discussed in this chapter is most interesting to you and why?

---

41. Elijah Hixson, "Despite Disappointing Some, New Mark Manuscript Is Earliest Yet," *Christianity Today* May 30, 2018: https://www.christianitytoday.com/ct/2018/may-web-only/mark-manuscript-earliest-not-first-century-fcm.html.

Textual Criticism

What Is New Testament Textual Criticism?

Although the term "textual criticism" often conjures very negative images in the minds of people who are unfamiliar with the discipline, it is actually a constructive and necessary branch of New Testament research. One scholar described textual criticism as his "sacred task, the struggle to regain the original form of the New Testament."[1] This discussion will define textual criticism, identify its primary goal, and explain its importance.

What Is Textual Criticism?

Common misconceptions about textual criticism make it necessary to define the term precisely. The terminology can be particularly confusing since some readers may not be familiar with the technical use of the word "criticism." The Merriam-Webster dictionary identifies the most common meaning of "criticism" as "the act of criticizing usually unfavorably." Thus, one might wrongly assume that textual criticism is the act of negatively criticizing the text of the New Testament. The terminology might cause a reader to imagine a skeptical scholar, his horns and tail barely concealed beneath his mortar board and academic robes, poring over the text of the New Testament hoping to catch the biblical authors in a mistake. He cackles wickedly at the discovery of any potential error, for he plans to add the problem to his arsenal of arguments that he uses to attack the veracity of the Christian faith. This is decidedly *not* what is meant by "textual criticism."

---

1. The quotation is from a letter from Constantin Tischendorf to his fiancé, cited in Bruce Metzger and Bart Ehrman, *The Text of the New Testament: Its Transmission, Corruption, and Restoration*, 4th ed. (Oxford: Oxford University Press, 2005), 172. Unfortunately, the authors provide no further documentation.

An alternative definition of "criticism" is "the scientific investigation of literary documents (such as the Bible) in regard to such matters as origin, text, composition, or history."[2] "Scientific investigation" is the intended sense of the term "criticism" in the discipline of textual criticism—though many scholars would argue that textual criticism is both a science and an art. The adjective "textual" shows that the focus of this particular scientific investigation is the text of the New Testament, that is, the precise wording of the New Testament documents. Thus, we may define New Testament textual criticism as "the scientific investigation of the original text of the New Testament." Marvin Vincent defined textual criticism as "that process by which it is sought to determine the original text of a document or of a collection of documents, and to exhibit it, freed from all errors, corruptions, and variations which it may have accumulated in the course of its transmission by successive copyings." Vincent adds that, by "original text," he means "what the author himself wrote."[3]

What Is the Primary Goal of Textual Criticism?

Scholars debate the specific purpose of the discipline of New Testament textual criticism. Most scholars in the history of the discipline have held that the purpose of the investigation is the recovery of the wording of the original text of the New Testament. For example, B. F. Westcott and F. J. A. Hort stated that the purpose of their edition of the Greek New Testament was "an attempt to present exactly the original words of the New Testament, so far as they can now be determined from surviving documents."[4] Bruce Metzger, who has been called the dean of New Testament textual criticism, defined textual criticism as the investigation that "seeks to ascertain from the divergent copies which form of the text should be regarded as most nearly conforming to the original."[5] Similarly, Kirsopp Lake wrote that "the object of all textual criticism is to recover so far as possible the actual words written by the writer."[6] F. H. A. Scrivener wrote that the purpose of the science of textual criticism of the Greek New Testament is "bringing back that text, so far as may be, to the condition in which it stood in the sacred autographs; at removing all spurious additions, if such be found in our present printed copies; at restoring whatsoever may have been lost or corrupted or accidentally changed in the lapse of

2. Merriam-Webster's Collegiate Dictionary, 11th ed., s.v. "criticism."
3. Marvin Vincent, A History of the Textual Criticism of the New Testament (London: Macmillan, 1899), 1–2.
4. B. F. Westcott and F. J. A. Hort, Introduction to the New Testament in the Original Greek with Notes on Selected Readings (New York: Harper and Brothers, 1882), 3.
5. Bruce M. Metzger and Bart D. Ehrman, The Text of the New Testament: Its Transmission, Corruption, and Restoration, 4th ed. (New York: Oxford University Press, 2005), xv.
6. Kirsopp Lake, The Text of the New Testament, Oxford Church Text Books, 6th ed. (London: Billing and Sons, 1959), 1.

eighteen hundred years."[7] Samuel Tregelles wrote: "The object of all Textual Criticism is to present an ancient work, as far as possible, in the very words and form in which it proceeded from the author's own hand."[8] Paul Maas, a textual critic working mainly in Classical literature, wrote: "The business of textual criticism is to produce a text as close as possible to the original (*constitutio textus*)."[9]

Although Vincent defined textual criticism as a quest for the original text of the New Testament, he later argued that the discipline of textual criticism was "slowly but surely moving" toward "the abandonment of the idea of the original autograph as an object of search."[10] This was due to the view that some New Testament authors themselves issued multiple editions of the same work and that the author viewed the later editions as improvements that were intended to replace the original edition. In 1966, Kenneth Clark referred to the effort to restore the original text as a "retreating mirage."[11]

The definition of textual criticism has recently been modified by scholars such as David Parker. Parker argued, "Textual criticism is the analysis of variant readings in order to determine in what sequence they arose."[12] Several factors prompted this shift in approach to the primary goal of the discipline. Perhaps most importantly, these scholars emphasize that all textual critics can do is establish the earliest recoverable text possible based on the currently available evidence. This text, from which all available later forms of the text were derived, is called the "Initial Text" (German: "Ausgangstext"). This is not necessarily identical to the "authorial text," that is, the text of the New Testament books directly produced by the New Testament authors. Parker stated: "No editor of the Greek New Testament would claim either the tools or the ability to produce an authorial text. . . . [W]hat is available is not an authorial text, but the product of a more complicated process in which the author's writings have been preserved but also to some degree changed, for better or for worse, by his readers."[13]

It is true that no editor of the Greek New Testament claims to have produced the authorial text with absolute perfection. However, many editors of the Greek New Testament have been convinced that they restored a very close

---

7. F. H. A. Scrivener, *A Plain Introduction to the Criticism of the New Testament*, 4th ed., ed. Edward Miller, 2 vols. (1894), 1:5.
8. Samuel P. Tregelles, *An Account of the Printed Text of the Greek New Testament: with Remarks on Its Revision upon Critical Principles* (London: Samuel Bagster, 1854; repr., Cambridge: Cambridge University Press, 2013), 174.
9. Paul Maas, *Textual Criticism*, trans. Barbara Flower (Oxford: Clarendon Press, 1958), 1.
10. Vincent, *A History of the Textual Criticism*, 176.
11. Kenneth Clark, "The Theological Relevance of Textual Criticism in Current Criticism of the Greek New Testament," *JBL* 85 (1966): 15.
12. D. C. Parker, *An Introduction to the New Testament Manuscripts and Their Texts* (Cambridge: Cambridge University Press, 2008), 159.
13. Parker, *An Introduction to the New Testament Manuscripts and Their Texts*, 184.

approximation of the "authorial text." Westcott and Hort clearly stated that their text was no more than "an approximation to the purest text that might be formed from existing materials," and they explained the steps that needed to be taken "for the perfecting of the results obtained so far."[14] They refused to retreat from the goal of restoring the original text since they "at the same time found it alike undesirable and impossible to take any intermediate text, rather than that of the autographs themselves, as the pattern to be reproduced with the utmost exactness which the evidence permits."[15]

Holger Strutwolf concluded that "as long as we have no evidence that suggests a radical break in the textual transmission between the author's text and the initial text of our tradition, the best hypothesis concerning the original text still remains the reconstructed archetype to which our manuscript tradition and the evidence of early translations and the citations point."[16] He added that "the reconstruction of the original text of the New Testament is of vital theological and historical interest: we want to know what Paul really wrote to the Romans and what was the original form of the gospel of Luke. The quest for the original text does not as such involve contradictions and logical impossibilities."[17]

Is Textual Criticism a Science, an Art, or Both?

Readers who are first learning about textual criticism will probably be puzzled to find that some scholars describe it as a science, others as an art, and others as a combination of the two. Most scholars fall into this last category. For example, in his famous lecture "The Application of Thought to Textual Criticism," A. E. Housman defined textual criticism as "the science of discovering error in text and the art of removing it."[18] E. J. Kenney similarly defined textual criticism as the "art and science of balancing historical probabilities."[19]

Textual criticism clearly utilizes aspects of science. The scientific method defines the purpose of an inquiry, constructs hypotheses, tests hypotheses, collects and analyzes data, and draws conclusions. All components of this method are utilized in reasoned eclecticism. Housman emphasized the scientific aspects of the discipline by insisting that textual criticism is "purely a matter of reason and of common sense."[20]

---

14. Westcott and Hort, *Introduction*, 284–85.
15. Westcott and Hort, *Introduction*, 289.
16. Holger Strutwolf, "Original Text and Textual History," in *The Textual History of the Greek New Testament: Changing Views in Contemporary Research*, eds. Klaus Wachtel and Michael W. Holmes (Leiden: Brill, 2012), 41.
17. Strutwolf, "Original Text and Textual History," 41. See Question 1 for an argument that the New Testament has been sufficiently preserved to enable scholars to restore the original text.
18. A. E. Housman, "The Application of Thought to Textual Criticism," Proceedings of the Classical Association 18 (1922): 68.
19. E. J. Kenney, *The Classical Text: Aspects of Editing in the Age of the Printed Book* (Berkeley and Los Angeles: University of California Press, 1974), 146.
20. Housman, "Application of Thought," 68.

Is textual criticism also an art? The answer depends on how one defines the term. If by "art" one means "the conscious use of skill and creative imagination in the production of aesthetic objects,"[21] then no. A textual critic should not imaginatively create the text that is most aesthetically pleasing. Textual criticism is not a purely subjective discipline in which beauty is in the eye of the beholder so that one critic can craft the text that he prefers and another can craft the text that she prefers. When scholars refer to textual criticism as an art, they are using the term in a very different sense to refer to the "skill acquired by experience, study, or observation."[22] Westcott and Hort were adamant that becoming a good textual critic required practice and experience:

> [I]t is from the past exercise of method that personal discernment receives the education which tends to extinguish its illusions and mature its power. All instinctive processes of criticism which deserve confidence are rooted in experience, and that an experience has undergone perpetual correction and recorrection.[23]

When scholars challenge the classification of textual criticism as a science and describe it as an art, they usually mean merely that textual criticism cannot be reduced to a mechanical process in which the same steps and methods apply to every variant unit. Günther Zuntz, the author of a groundbreaking study of the text of Paul's letters, stated this bluntly: "[Textual criticism] cannot be carried out mechanically. At every stage the critic has to use his brains. Were it different, we could put the critical slide-rule into the hands of any fool and leave it to him to settle the problems of the New Testament text."[24] Housman expressed the same view in a more entertaining way:

> A textual critic engaged upon his business is not at all like Newton investigating the motions of the planets: he is much more like a dog hunting for fleas. If a dog hunted for fleas on mathematical principles, basing his researches on statistics of area and population, he would never catch a flea except by accident. They require to be treated as individuals; and every problem which presents itself to the textual critic must be regarded as possibly unique.[25]

21. Merriam-Webster Dictionary, entry 4a.
22. Merriam-Webster Dictionary, entry 1.
23. Westcott and Hort, *Introduction*, 65–66.
24. Günther Zuntz, *The Text of the Epistles: A Disquisition upon the Corpus Paulinum* (London: Oxford University Press, 1953; repr. Eugene, OR: Wipf and Stock, 2007), 12.
25. Housman, "Application of Thought," 68–69.

Accurate analysis of the evidence requires sharp critical thinking skills, carefully nuanced and qualified criteria for evaluating readings, and the willingness to adapt the methodology or consider different categories of evidence in some scenarios. Housman correctly emphasized that textual criticism deals with a subject as complex as "the frailties and aberrations of the human mind, and of its insubordinate servants, the human fingers." Consequently, textual criticism

> is not susceptible of hard-and-fast rules. It would be much easier if it were; and that is why people try to pretend that it is, or at least behave as if they thought so. Of course you can have hard-and-fast rules if you like, but then you will have false rules, and they will lead you wrong; because their simplicity will render them inapplicable to problems which are not simple, but complicated by the play of personality.[26]

Summary

Textual criticism is the scientific investigation that seeks to establish the original text of the Greek New Testament. Some scholars no longer believe that reconstructing the original text should be the primary goal of the discipline. However, this was universally recognized as the goal of textual criticism by previous generations of textual critics as well as by those who apply textual criticism to classical literature. Textual criticism is based on reason and uses the scientific method. However, like an art, it requires skill and experience.

REFLECTION QUESTIONS

1. What does the term "criticism" mean when referring to textual criticism?

2. What other terms might be used to describe the discipline?

3. What is the primary goal of textual criticism?

4. Why have some scholars argued that the goal should change?

5. How is textual criticism a science? How is it an art?

---

26. Housman, "Application of Thought," 68.

What Is the History of Modern New Testament Textual Criticism?

In a sense, the textual criticism of the New Testament began when early scribes became aware of variants in manuscripts and had to choose between them when they produced their copies. Some of these early scribes were probably influenced by the librarians of the famous library in Alexandria and sought to preserve or restore the original readings in their copies.[1] Early Christian scholars like Origen adopted some of the critical signs developed by the Alexandrian librarians for their text-critical work. Several, including Origen, Pamphilus, Eusebius, Irenaeus, Basil, Isodore, Socrates, Augustine, and Jerome, show consciousness of some of the principles that guide modern textual criticism.[2] However, scholars normally trace the origins of modern textual criticism to the first printed editions of the Greek New Testament.[3] This discussion will trace some of the highlights in the history of modern textual criticism. The discussion will focus on scholars associated with the most important printed editions.

Early Editions

Although portions of the Greek New Testament had been printed as early as 1481,[4] the entire Greek New Testament was first printed in 1514 in Venice.

---

1. Amy Donaldson, "Explicit References to New Testament Variant Readings among Greek and Latin Church Fathers" (PhD diss., University of Notre Dame, 2009), 1:98–110.
2. Donaldson, "Explicit References to New Testament Variant Readings among Greek and Latin Church Fathers," 1:312.
3. Marvin Vincent, *A History of the Textual Criticism of the New Testament* (London: Macmillan, 1899), 45.
4. Evro Layton, *The Sixteenth Century Greek Book in Italy: Printers and Publishers for the Greek World* (Venice: Istituto Ellenico di Studi Bizantini e Postbizantini di Venezia, 1994), 355.

Cardinal Francisco Ximenes of Cisneros in Spain supervised the preparation of the edition. This Greek New Testament text was volume 5 of an entire Bible called the Complutensian Polyglot. For the New Testament, Greek and Latin were placed in parallel columns. Although the manuscripts used by Ximenes for the New Testament have not been positively identified,[5] they are generally regarded as inferior manuscripts.[6]

The edition by Desiderius Erasmus was printed shortly after the Complutensian text. However, Erasmus succeeded in publishing his text first in 1516, six years before the actual publication of the Polyglot, since Ximenes had patiently held his copies until they were approved by Pope Leo X. Erasmus rushed his preparation of the edition in hopes of cornering the market by releasing his Greek New Testament first. The rush resulted in an excessive number of errors. Although the Dedication of the edition boasted of its accuracy, Erasmus later admitted that the edition was "thrown together rather than edited."[7] Scrivener said that with respect to typographical errors, Erasmus's first edition was "the most faulty book I know."[8] Erasmus based his edition primarily on four minuscule texts. None of these were earlier than the tenth century.[9] He had only one manuscript of Revelation which lacked the final six verses of the book. Erasmus created the Greek text for those portions by translating from the Latin of the Vulgate into Greek. In the process, he created readings that do not appear in any Greek manuscript. Five editions of Erasmus's Greek New Testament appeared.

Robert Stephanus (Estienne) published four editions of the Greek New Testament based on the Complutensian and Erasmian editions and fifteen manuscripts available to him.[10] Although not all of the manuscripts have been identified, Codex Bezae (D 05) and Codex Regius (L 019) were clearly among them. These manuscripts date to the fifth and eighth centuries respectively. The third edition listed readings from the Complutensian Polyglot and the fifteen manuscripts in the margin. This was the first edition to collect and print variants in this fashion. Stephanus's 1551 edition was also the first to divide the New Testament into the verses that are still utilized in modern editions of the Bible.[11]

---

5. Bruce Metzger and Bart Ehrman, *The Text of the New Testament: Its Transmission, Corruption, and Restoration*, 4th ed. (Oxford: Oxford University Press, 2005), 140.
6. Kirsopp Lake, *The Text of the New Testament*, 6th ed., Oxford Church Text Books (London: Billing and Sons, 1959), 63; Alexander Souter, *The Text and Canon of the New Testament* (New York: Charles Scribner's Sons, 1917), 94–95.
7. "[P]raecipitatum fuit verius quam editum," quoted in F. H. A. Scrivener, *A Plain Introduction to the Criticism of the New Testament*, 4th ed., ed. Edward Miller (1894; repr. Eugene, OR: Wipf and Stock, 1997), 2:183.
8. Scrivener, *A Plain Introduction to the Criticism of the New Testament*, 2:185.
9. Vincent, *A History of the Textual Criticism*, 52.
10. Lake, *The Text of the New Testament*, 63.
11. Scrivener, *A Plain Introduction to the Criticism of the New Testament*, 2:192.

The reformer Theodore Beza published ten editions between 1565 and 1611.[12] Beza possessed at least two ancient codices, Codex Bezae (D for the Gospels) and Codex Claromontanus (D for Paul's letters), which date from the fifth and sixth centuries respectively. Unfortunately, he made little use of them for his editions.

Bonaventure and Abraham Elzevir published seven editions between 1624 and 1678. These were largely based on the earlier editions by Beza and Erasmus as well as the Complutensian Polyglot and the Vulgate. The 1633 edition became the standard text throughout Europe. The Preface to the edition contained the statement "Textum ergo habes nunc ab omnibus receptum" ("the text that you have [that is] now received by all") became the basis for the description of this edition as the Textus Receptus.[13]

Several sought to build upon the foundation of the Textus Receptus by comparing additional manuscripts and other ancient sources. Scholars such as Brian Walton and John Fell collated new manuscripts and added their readings to the margins of the editions of the Greek New Testament that they published. The greatest contribution was that of John Mill.[14] In 1707, he published an edition of the Greek New Testament that was the product of more than thirty years of research. Although the printed text was based on prior editions, his edition contained a new feature—a critical apparatus with a list of all the variants that he had identified. Scrivener lauded Mill's contribution to the discipline of textual criticism by stating that his contributions to textual criticism "surpass in extent and value those rendered by any other, except perhaps one or two men of our own time" and quipping: "He found the edifice of wood, and left it marble."[15]

In 1711, Gerhard von Maestricht published an edition of the Greek New Testament that contained a lengthy discussion of forty-three canons for evaluating variants. According to Vincent, "this appears to have been the first attempt to lay down canons for various readings."[16]

The Rise of Critical Editions

John Albert Bengel (1662–1742) has been described as the father of modern textual criticism.[17] As scholars became overwhelmed by the mass

12. Lake, *The Text of the New Testament*, 63.
13. See the scathing criticism of this claim in Vincent, *A History of the Textual Criticism*, 61. See also Question 13.
14. See the detailed discussion in Scrivener, *A Plain Introduction to the Criticism of the New Testament*, 2:196–200.
15. Scrivener, *A Plain Introduction to the Criticism of the New Testament*, 2:201–2; cf. Lake, *The Text of the New Testament*, 64.
16. Vincent, *A History of the Textual Criticism*, 69. See also C. R. Gregory, "*Prolegomena*," in *Novum Testamentum Graece*, ed. Constantine Tischendorf, 8th ed., 3 vols. (Leipzig: Hinrichs, 1869–94), 3:229; Scrivener, *A Plain Introduction to the Criticism of the New Testament*, 2:204.
17. Lake, *The Text of the New Testament*, 65.

of manuscript evidence, Bengel suggested simplifying matters by dividing manuscripts into major families. His Asiatic and African classifications were roughly equivalent to the Byzantine and Alexandrian text types, respectively, of later generations of scholars. Although Bengel is known as a pioneer in departing from the Textus Receptus, he required that, except in Revelation, no reading would appear in his main text that had not previously appeared in the editions of his predecessors. However, he expressed his judgments on variants at the foot of each page using a grading system. Bengel assigned the letter α to readings definitely better than those in the text, β to those more probable, γ to those equal, δ to those somewhat inferior, and ε to those much inferior.[18]

John James Griesbach (1745–1812) collated a large number of manuscripts and further developed the theory of manuscript families proposed by Bengel. Griesbach classified manuscripts in three groups: (1) Alexandrian (or Origenian) represented by the uncials A B C L, Origen's quotations, and Coptic versions; (2) Western represented by the Latin fathers and versions and D; and (3) Byzantine represented by the vast majority of manuscripts. Griesbach argued that, unless internal evidence precluded this assessment (and it often did, in his view), the reading supported by two families is more likely original than that supported by only one.[19] Griesbach also described and carefully qualified fifteen canons of textual criticism, most of which remain helpful guides to textual critics today.[20] These include:

1. The reading must have support from ancient witnesses.
2. The shorter reading is generally to be preferred.
3. The more difficult reading is generally to be preferred.
4. The reading that initially seems to be incorrect but upon more careful study is recognized as suitable to the context is to be preferred.

Westcott and Hort identified Griesbach as "the name which we venerate above that of every other textual critic of the New Testament," even though he could not affirm all of this earlier scholar's conclusions.[21]

Karl Lachmann (1793–1851) produced a Greek text in 1842–50 that was the first since the time of Erasmus to be based entirely on ancient manuscripts rather than previous printed editions. Lachmann also attempted to use a scientific method for evaluating variants. He is often recognized as the first textual critic to make a decisive break from the Textus Receptus by

---

18. Scrivener, *A Plain Introduction to the Criticism of the New Testament*, 2:210–13.
19. Lake, *The Text of the New Testament*, 65; Scrivener, *A Plain Introduction to the Criticism of the New Testament*, 2:216, 222–26.
20. Metzger and Ehrman, *The Text of the New Testament*, 166.
21. B. F. Westcott and F. J. A. Hort, *Introduction to the New Testament in the Original Greek with Notes on Selected Readings* (1882; repr., Peabody, MA: Hendrickson, 1988), 185. See his criticisms of Griesbach on 183–85.

daring to print his reconstructed text as the main text of the edition rather than merely identifying it in the accompanying apparatus. Lachmann made his decisions based solely on manuscript evidence (external or documentary evidence) without attempting to remove common scribal errors, nonsense readings, or readings inconsistent with an author's normal style. Lachmann sought to simplify the process of criticism by dismissing the evidence of the late manuscripts. Lachmann generally accepted the reading supported by the majority of early manuscripts.[22] Since so few early manuscripts were available to Lachmann, he often made decisions based on only two or three manuscripts.[23]

Samuel Tregelles (1813–1875) and Lobegott Friedrich Constantin von Tischendorf (1815–1874) basically followed a critical approach similar to the one developed by Lachmann.[24] However, both developed more extensive critical apparatuses for their editions of the Greek text that were fairly exhaustive for their time. Tischendorf's apparatus contained a complex system of abbreviations and symbols that made it difficult to use. Tregelles's apparatus was far easier to read and understand.[25]

Tischendorf's contribution to textual criticism can hardly be overestimated. He published more manuscripts and produced more critical editions of the Greek New Testament than any other scholar even to the present time.[26] He had devoted himself to the task of reconstructing "if possible, the exact text, as it came from the pen of the sacred writers" in 1839 at the age of 24.[27] Tischendorf's principles for establishing the text of the New Testament were influenced by Griesbach's.[28]

---

22. See the criticism of Lachmann in Lake, *The Text of the New Testament*, 66; Westcott and Hort, *Introduction*, 13.
23. Scrivener, *A Plain Introduction to the Criticism of the New Testament*, 2:233. Lachmann's preferred witnesses for the Gospels were A, B, and C. However, he had only indirect knowledge of B which was not entirely accurate. Tregelles gives an extensive treatment of Lachmann's work, primarily due to the broad similarities of his own approach to Lachmann's (Samuel P. Tregelles, *An Account of the Printed Text of the Greek New Testament: with Remarks on Its Revision upon Critical Principles* [London: Samuel Bagster, 1854; repr., Cambridge: Cambridge University Press, 2013], 97–115).
24. Tregelles saw Lachmann as the primary influence on Tischendorf (*An Account of the Printed Text of the Greek New Testament*, 117–18). Tregelles, however, insisted that his own similarities to Lachmann were due, not to dependence on Lachmann, but to the mutual influence of Richard Bentley (pp. 115–16).
25. Lake, *The Text of the New Testament*, 66.
26. Metzger and Ehrman, *The Text of the New Testament*, 172.
27. Constantine Tischendorf, *When Were Our Gospels Written? An Argument by Constantine Tischendorf with a Narrative of the Discovery of the Sinaitic Manuscript*, trans. J. B. Heard (London: Religious Tract Society, 1866), 12. For a recent biography, see Stanley E. Porter, *Constantine Tischendorf: The Life and Work of a 19th Century Bible Hunter* (London: Bloomsbury, 2015).
28. Tregelles, *An Account of the Printed Text of the Greek New Testament*, 119–26.

Tregelles, a contemporary of Tischendorf, published far less. However, his work tends to be characterized by greater accuracy than that of the more prolific textual critic.[29] Like Lachmann and Tischendorf, Tregelles believed that the ancient manuscripts were the key to restoring the original Greek New Testament. He explains his principles for restoring the New Testament at length in his book *An Account of the Printed Text of the New Testament* published in 1854. Although these principles are very similar to Lachmann's, Tregelles developed his approach before he was aware of Lachmann's work and primarily under the influence of Richard Bentley and Griesbach.

Tregelles identified two principles that are "of the utmost importance" in restoring the New Testament.[30] First, the critic had to distinguish "good and useful witnesses" from others that were of little help in reconstructing the original text due to their corruption.[31] Second, the critic must accept the "fixed and settled principle" that the only proof that a reading was truly ancient was its discovery in an ancient document.[32]

Tregelles devoted himself to the textual criticism of the New Testament because of his reverence for the New Testament documents as inspired Scripture.[33]

Westcott and Hort

In 1881, Brooke Foss Westcott (1825–1901) and Fenton John Anthony Hort (1828–1892) published a critical edition of the Greek New Testament that has been described as "the foundation of nearly all modern criticism" and "truly epoch-making."[34] Although some modern critics suggest that the attempt to reconstruct the original New Testament text is not the primary goal of textual criticism, Westcott and Hort boldly stated in the first sentence of their Introduction: "This edition is an attempt to present exactly the original words of the New Testament, so far as they can now be determined from surviving documents."[35] This task was facilitated by the fact that the vast majority of the New Testament lacks any substantial variation and "stands in no need of a textual critic's labours."[36]

Westcott and Hort acknowledged that reliance on internal evidence is "the most rudimentary form of criticism."[37] In the evaluation of internal evi-

---

29. Vincent, *A History of the Textual Criticism*, 132.
30. Tregelles, *An Account of the Printed Text of the Greek New Testament*, 175.
31. Tregelles, *An Account of the Printed Text of the Greek New Testament*, 175.
32. Tregelles, *An Account of the Printed Text of the Greek New Testament*, 175.
33. This is the final paragraph of the Preface to *An Account of the Printed Text of the Greek New Testament* signed by Tregelles on April 25, 1854 in Plymouth.
34. Lake, *The Text of the New Testament*, 67; Metzger and Ehrman, *The Text of the New Testament*, 174, 183.
35. Westcott and Hort, *Introduction*, 1.
36. Westcott and Hort, *Introduction*, 2–3.
37. Westcott and Hort, *Introduction*, 19.

dence of readings, judgments are based on the merits of the reading alone without reference to the quality, age, number, geographical distribution, or classification of the witness(es) in which the reading appears. Internal evidence consists of two kinds: intrinsic probability and transcriptional probability. Intrinsic probability relates to what the author was most likely to have written based on knowledge of his style, literary context, and theology. Transcriptional probability relates to the changes the scribes were most likely to make. Unfortunately, intrinsic probability and transcriptional probability often conflict. Since scribes were more likely to attempt to improve the text than to insert inferior readings, the reading that they were most likely to supply was also the one that they, at least, thought best fit the context and the author's theology.

Therefore, critics need to consider "internal evidence of documents," that is, determine the relative credibility of the documents that preserve the various readings. Westcott and Hort placed the following maxim in all caps for emphasis: "KNOWLEDGE OF DOCUMENTS SHOULD PRECEDE FINAL JUDGMENT UPON READINGS."[38] Judgments of the relative credibility of manuscripts should be based primarily on the percentage of readings that the manuscript contains which can be established confidently based on internal evidence of readings alone. It must be assumed that the manuscripts that have the highest percentages of demonstrably correct readings are more reliable than other manuscripts as a whole. This knowledge about the general reliability of specific manuscripts can then help with assessing variants for which no choice could be made by comparing the readings alone. Thus, Westcott and Hort advocated a three-step process:

1. Evaluate variants based on the intrinsic and transcriptional evidence.
2. Use the decisions from step 1 to determine the general reliability of specific manuscripts.
3. Use the decisions from step 2 to evaluate variants for which a firm decision could not be reached in step 1.[39]

Westcott and Hort argued that assessments of the general reliability of specific manuscripts are complicated by the facts that (1) good manuscripts do contain occasional errors, (2) scribes may have used a good exemplar for one portion of the New Testament and a poorer one for another, and (3) scribes may have even referred to multiple texts at the same time.[40] Furthermore, the

---

38. Westcott and Hort, *Introduction*, 31.
39. Westcott and Hort, *Introduction*, 30–34. Westcott and Hort admitted that the processes "depend ultimately on judgements upon Internal Evidence of Readings" (p. 34).
40. Westcott and Hort, *Introduction*, 35–39.

initial steps described earlier become less helpful as the number of manuscripts increases.

These factors required a "second great step" that "consists in ceasing to treat Documents independently of each other, and examining them connectedly as parts of a single whole in virtue of their historical relationships."[41] Thus, the team emphasized a second principle: "ALL TRUSTWORTHY RESTORATION OF CORRUPTED TEXTS IS FOUNDED ON THE STUDY OF THEIR HISTORY, that is, of the relations of descent or affinity which connect the several documents."[42] They proposed a "genealogical method" that attempted to construct a family tree of manuscripts. This genealogical method is discussed in greater detail in Question 20.

Westcott and Hort divided witnesses into four major groups: the Syrian text (which consisted of Codex A, late majuscules, and the vast majority of minuscules), the Western text (which was represented by Codex D and the Old Latin manuscripts), the Alexandrian text (represented by C, L, 33, and the Coptic versions), and the neutral text (represented especially by Codex B and to a lesser extent by א). Based on readings in which the Syrian witnesses conflated readings from Alexandrian and Western texts, they concluded that the Syrian text is a mixed text that was dependent on and thus later than the other two groups. This was supported by internal evidence, both transcriptional and intrinsic. It was confirmed by evidence in the writings of the Ante-Nicene church fathers.[43] Westcott and Hort viewed the Syrian text as a "recension," which they defined as "a work of attempted criticism, performed deliberately by editors and not merely by scribes."[44]

These same categories of evidence also suggested that the Western readings were secondary. Westcott and Hort noted that the Western text is characterized chiefly by a tendency to paraphrase, to supplement the text with additions from tradition and extrabiblical sources, and to assimilate the text to parallel passages.[45]

The Alexandrian text lacked these tendencies.[46] Although the label "Alexandrian" had been used by Westcott and Hort's predecessors due to the similarity of the text with quotations of the New Testament in Origen, Cyril, other Alexandrian fathers, and the Coptic versions, Westcott and Hort objected that the label was not entirely accurate since "Alexandrian" wrongly implied that texts with these readings originated from this single locale. In fact, "in various and perhaps many other places the primitive text in varying degrees of purity survived the early Western inundation which appears to

---

41. Westcott and Hort, *Introduction*, 39.
42. Westcott and Hort, *Introduction*, 40.
43. Westcott and Hort, *Introduction*, 93–108.
44. Westcott and Hort, *Introduction*, 133.
45. Westcott and Hort, *Introduction*, 122–26.
46. Westcott and Hort, *Introduction*, 131–32.

submerge it."[47] The Alexandrian text does, however, contain differences from the original text. The scribes responsible for this text especially tended to improve the grammar and style, though they relatively rarely introduced paraphrases and harmonizations.

The neutral text is the text most similar to the autographs of the New Testament. Codex Vaticanus (B) is the purest extant text and, when its readings were supported by Sinaiticus (ℵ), the critic should accept the reading as the "true" reading unless there is strong evidence to the contrary.[48]

Editions after Westcott and Hort

Soon after the Westcott and Hort edition appeared, Bernard Weiss (1827–1918) published a three-volume edition of the Greek New Testament (1894–1900). Weiss's textual decisions were based primarily on intrinsic probability. Westcott and Hort had repeatedly dismissed such a procedure as far too subjective.[49] Despite using a very different method from Westcott and Hort, Weiss also determined that Codex Vaticanus was the purest extant manuscript. The text produced by Weiss is very similar to that of Westcott and Hort, due largely to their mutual preference for Vaticanus. Weiss's use of internal evidence to demonstrate the supremacy of Vaticanus lent strong support to the conclusions reached by Westcott and Hort's textual research.

Eberhard Nestle (1851–1913) published a pocket edition of the Greek New Testament in 1898 that would become immensely popular. The purpose of the edition was to collate three of the most important current critical editions of the Greek New Testament and thus express the consensus of text-critical scholarship at the end of the nineteenth century. The first two editions compared the texts of Tischendorf, Westcott and Hort, and Richard Francis Weymouth and printed the text supported by two of the three. Beginning with the third edition, Weiss's edition replaced Weymouth's. In addition to supplying information from these three editions, Nestle's text cited an increasing number of early witnesses with each new edition and did so with greater accuracy than had previously been achieved since Tischendorf.

Alexander Souter (1873–1949) produced an edition of the Greek New Testament in 1910.[50] His text was a reproduction of the Greek text behind the Revised Version of 1881 which was constructed by Edwin Palmer. The text is very similar to the Textus Receptus. Souter's main contribution was a critical apparatus that contained nearly exhaustive treatment of evidence from the early church fathers.

---

47. Westcott and Hort, *Introduction*, 129.
48. Westcott and Hort, *Introduction*, 225.
49. Westcott and Hort, *Introduction*, 31, 286.
50. Alexander Souter, ed., *Novum Testamentum Graece* (Oxford: Clarendon, 1910).

Hermann Freiherr von Soden (1852–1914) published a Greek New Testament with an apparatus in 1913.[51] Von Soden had invested years in the study of Greek minuscules and the history of the Greek text. The publication of the text was preceded by the publication of an introduction more than two thousand pages in length with a large amount of small type. Unfortunately, von Soden's complicated system for referring to manuscripts and his somewhat eccentric approach ensured that his edition would not be as widely used as the texts by Westcott and Hort or Souter. Von Soden classed witnesses as belonging to three different recensions. He adopted the reading affirmed by two of the three recensions unless that reading harmonized with a parallel or was supported by Tatian. The edition was criticized for giving too much weight to Koine (Byzantine) readings, mingling text types, allowing Marcion and Tatian to play too great a role in the corruption of the text, and having an excessive number of mistakes in the critical apparatus. Still, Metzger and Ehrman shower praise on the edition:

> Despite these and other justifiable criticisms that have been leveled against von Soden, his edition remains a monument of broad research and immense industry that, with the extensive prolegomena dealing with the history of the transmission of the text, must be taken into account by every serious textual critic.[52]

The most important editions of the Greek New Testament in the twentieth and twenty-first centuries are undoubtedly the Nestle-Aland editions, the United Bible Societies's editions, and the multivolume Editio Critica Maior. These editions are discussed in Question 16.

Summary

In a sense, New Testament textual criticism is a very ancient practice. Early scribes were forced to select a specific reading for their copies when they encountered different readings in different manuscripts. However, most scholars trace the origins of New Testament textual criticism from the first printed editions of the Greek New Testament. Although many scholars have contributed to our knowledge of the New Testament text by searching for, transcribing and collating ancient manuscripts, by gathering manuscript data into textual apparatuses, and by theorizing the best approaches to the discipline of textual criticism, three scholars have had an especially significant impact on modern approaches to the task of restoring the original text. John

---

51. Hermann Freiherr von Soden, *Die Schriften des Neuen Testaments*, 4 vols. (Göttingen: Vandenhoeck und Ruprecht, 1913). The text of the New Testament is in volume 4.
52. Metzger and Ehrman, *The Text of the New Testament*, 189.

Albert Bengel is considered the "father of modern textual criticism" since he divided manuscripts into textual groups and classified many readings as superior to the Textus Receptus. Westcott and Hort have probably exerted a greater influence on current text-critical methods than anyone. The standard critical editions of the Greek New Testament are remarkably similar to the Greek New Testament edited by these two scholars. As we will see in the discussion of new developments in the field, modern technology now permits scholars to implement the "genealogical method" envisioned (but not fully applied) by Westcott and Hort.

REFLECTION QUESTIONS

1. Who produced the first printed edition of the Greek New Testament?

2. Who produced the first published edition of the Greek New Testament?

3. What was the first edition of the Greek New Testament to include a critical apparatus?

4. Who is known as the "father of modern textual criticism" and why?

5. What were the major contributions of Westcott and Hort to text-critical approaches?

What Are the Major Groups of Manuscripts?

The massive amount of manuscript evidence available to textual critics can be overwhelming. Thus, for nearly three centuries, textual critics have attempted to reduce the evidence to something more manageable. One convenient way to simplify the methodology is to compare the readings and tendencies of larger groups of manuscripts rather than every single manuscript. Scholars have referred to these larger textual groups as "text types." What are these text types? How have they served in making text-critical decisions? And why do some scholars see most of these categories as defunct?

A Brief History of Textual Groups

In 1725, Johann Albrecht Bengel published an essay that served as a forerunner to his edition of the Greek New Testament that would be published nearly a decade and a half later (1739). Bengel argued that the best way to manage the large number of witnesses to the New Testament text was to divide them into "companies, families, tribes, nations." He divided witnesses into two major groups: the Asiatic (later manuscripts associated with Constantinople) and the African (a small number of early manuscripts believed to be of higher quality). He then subdivided the African group into two subgroups based on their similarities to Codex Alexandrinus (the earliest major majuscule available at that time) and the Old Latin version.[1]

In 1765, Johann Salomo Semler also argued for categorizing textual witnesses into major groups (which he called "recensions").[2] He originally

---

1. Marvin Vincent, *A History of the Textual Criticism of the New Testament* (London: Macmillan, 1899), 87–89.
2. Samuel P. Tregelles, *An Account of the Printed Text of the Greek New Testament: with Remarks on Its Revision upon Critical Principles* (London: Samuel Bagster, 1854; repr.,

proposed two major groups (Oriental and Western) but two years later suggested three: Alexandrian (associated with Egypt); Oriental (used at Antioch and Constantinople); and Western. A similar view was adopted by J. J. Griesbach who published multiple editions of the Greek New Testament from 1785 to 1806. Griesbach divided witnesses into three groups: Western, Alexandrian, and Constantinopolitan. He argued that restoring the Greek New Testament depended on studying these three groups. When two of the three groups agreed on a reading, that reading was likely original.[3]

Scholars such as Karl Lachmann, Samuel Prideaux Tregelles, Constantin von Tischendorf, B. F. Westcott and F. J. A. Hort, Herman von Soden, and B. H. Streeter continued the practice of dividing witnesses into major groups associated with particular regions.[4] Up to the end of the twentieth century, scholars affirmed the existence of these groups (which came to be called "text types") though occasionally a scholar called for refinements or proposed the existence of another text type.

The Major Text Types

In the recent history of New Testament textual criticism, most scholars affirmed the existence of three major text types: the Western text, Alexandrian text, and Byzantine text. These major groups of witnesses were identified by (1) observing similarities with other witnesses in the group and (2) noting differences from witnesses in the other groups.

The so-called Western text is a group of witnesses characterized by the license taken by the copyist.[5] The scribes who produced this group of witnesses felt the freedom to paraphrase the New Testament text rather than restrict themselves to transmitting the text unchanged. Apparently, making the text clear and understandable to the reader was more important to these scribes than preserving the original text. These witnesses changed words, entire clauses, and even whole sentences. They sometimes conformed the wording of one New Testament book to that of another New Testament book (harmonization). They often added new material drawn from other sources. They sometimes omitted material from their exemplar.

Important witnesses in this group include P[38], P[48], Codex Bezae, the Old Latin manuscripts, and quotations by Marcion, Justin Martyr, Heracleon,

Cambridge: Cambridge University Press, 2013), 84; Vincent, *A History of the Textual Criticism of the New Testament*, 92.

3. F. H. A. Scrivener, *A Plain Introduction to the Criticism of the New Testament*, 4th ed., ed. Edward Miller (1894; repr. Eugene, OR: Wipf and Stock, 1997), 2:224–25.

4. See Eldon Jay Epp, "Textual Clusters: Their Past and Future," in *The Text of the New Testament in Contemporary Research: Essays on the Status Quaestionis*, 2nd ed., NTTSD, eds. Bart D. Ehrman and Michael W. Holmes (Leiden: Brill, 2012), 520–41.

5. Bruce Metzger and Bart Ehrman, *The Text of the New Testament: Its Transmission, Corruption, and Restoration*, 4th ed. (Oxford: Oxford University Press, 2005), 307–8.

Irenaeus, and Tertullian. The Western text refers specifically to the text of the Gospels, Acts, and Paul's letters. A Western text of the General Epistles and Revelation does not appear to have circulated. Scholars generally argue that the Western text emerged early in the history of transmission, no later than the second century.[6]

In some ways, the term "Western text" is a misnomer. As noted earlier, this group refers to witnesses that share the same character, a tendency to handle the text loosely, rather than to specific shared readings. Thus, the witnesses lack the similarities found in the other text types. Furthermore, this type of text was not restricted to the West (North Africa, Italy, Gaul) but appears also in Egypt (as the papyri show) and the East.[7]

The Alexandrian text is generally regarded as the most reliable text type. Scholars at the library of Alexandria worked to restore and preserve the text of ancient works and even developed a rudimentary system of text-critical symbols. The practices of the scholars of the library clearly influenced local Christian scholars. Origen, for example, used the text-critical symbols developed by the librarians in compiling his Hexapla.[8] Not surprisingly, witnesses associated with Alexandria are of very high quality and show that the Christian scholars of Alexandria were dedicated to preserving an ancient and accurate form of the New Testament text. Important witnesses belonging to the Alexandrian text type include P^{66}, P^{75}, Codex Sinaiticus, Codex Vaticanus, copies of the Coptic New Testament, Origen, Athanasius, and Didymus the Blind. The name "Alexandrian text" is somewhat problematic since the papyri, almost all of which were found in Egypt, have texts of several different kinds. Some also argue that this group of closely related witnesses is too small to legitimize classifying them as belonging to a "text type."

The Byzantine text refers to the text that appears in the vast majority of minuscule manuscripts. This type of text became dominant in the ninth century. However, this textform clearly existed earlier. Westcott and Hort showed that the text of church fathers associated with Antioch like Chrysostom in the fourth century as well as Diodorus (fourth century) and Theodore of Mopsuestia (fifth century) was "beyond all question identical" with the later text of the minuscules and that this text must have predated the second half of the fourth century.[9] Westcott and Hort even noted this meant that this form of text was "either contemporary with or older than our oldest extant MSS," referring to the major majuscules (since the earlier papyri had not yet been discovered).[10] However, they argued that Byzantine readings emerged later

---

6. See Metzger and Ehrman, *The Text of the New Testament*, 276–77.
7. This criticism was made by Semler in 1764. See Epp, "Textual Clusters," 554–55.
8. Amy Donaldson, "Explicit References to New Testament Variant Readings among Greek and Latin Church Fathers" (PhD diss., University of Notre Dame, 2009), 1:98–110.
9. Westcott and Hort, *Introduction*, xiii, 91–92.
10. Westcott and Hort, *Introduction*, 92.

than those of the other two text types since the Byzantine text (1) conflated variant readings; (2) was not supported by quotations of the New Testament in Christian writers prior to the fourth century; and (3) was not supported by internal evidence (see Question 14). This view dominated twentieth-century textual scholarship.[11]

However, several recent scholars have expressed renewed appreciation for later manuscripts. Gerd Mink observed: "Nearly all manuscripts from the first millennium are lost. What we have from the early phases of transmission is not likely to be representative of the text in those times; therefore, we have to rely on later sources to trace older variants."[12] This recognition that later manuscripts may preserve much older texts has prompted scholars to consider the possibility that the Byzantine (Majority) text may be a richer deposit of original readings than most twentieth-century scholars assumed. Guideline 5 of the CBGM states: "The priority of a majority reading is indicated if it is linguistically more difficult or contextually less suitable and thus atypical of the majority text."[13] Of the thirty-three changes made from the UBS[4] to the UBS[5], twelve abandoned a Byzantine reading but nineteen adopted a Byzantine reading.

The earliest manuscript preserving a Byzantine text is Codex Alexandrinus (in the Gospels). The most important Byzantine majuscules are K L P.[14] Maurice Robinson has noted, "For most of the New Testament the Byzantine Textform is supported by nearly the whole of the manuscript tradition; in almost every case the Byzantine reading reflects the concurrence of at least 70% and usually more than 80% of the extant manuscripts."[15]

Some older works also refer to a Caesarean text type. However, most current scholars seriously doubt that the manuscripts in this group have enough similarity to be classified in the same text type. Metzger and Ehrman noted that "the Caesarean text appears to be the most mixed and least homogeneous of any of the groups that can be classified as distinct text types."[16] These factors prompted Epp to view this text type as "non-existent."[17] The term refers to texts that blend readings from the Alexandrian and Byzantine text types.

---

11. For important exceptions, see Question 14.
12. Gerd Mink, "Contamination, Coherence, and Coincidence," in *The Textual History of the Greek New Testament: Changing Views in Contemporary Research*, eds. Klaus Wachtel and Michael W. Holmes, TCSs 8 (Atlanta: SBL, 2011), 146.
13. Georg Gäbel, Annette Hüffmeier, Gerd Mink, Holger Strutwolf, Klaus Wachtel, "The CBGM Applied to Variants from Acts—Methodological Background," *TC* (2015): 3.
14. UBS[5], 11*.
15. Maurice Robinson and William Pierpont, *The New Testament in the Original Greek: Byzantine Textform 2005* (Southborough, MA: Chilton, 2005), xiv.
16. Metzger and Ehrman, *The Text of the New Testament*, 312.
17. Epp, "Textual Clusters," 556.

The Legitimacy of Text Types

Several scholars including Holger Strutwolf, Klaus Wachtel, and David Parker have recently called for an abandonment of the theory of text types based on several weaknesses of the approach. Parker objected to the concept of text types based on these observations:

1. The term "text type" means very different things simultaneously since it may refer to texts merely sharing a characteristic (Western), thousands of texts from a lengthy period with many common readings (Byzantine), or a mere handful of forms of texts from a brief period (Alexandrian).
2. The categories use geographical labels but it is now known that the various texts circulated and were copied in various regions.
3. The categories were probably developed based on the study of Gospel texts specifically and may not apply to other sections of the New Testament.[18]

Epp argued that these classifications of texts remain helpful. He noted that scholars since 1764 have realized that the text types did not exclusively belong to one geographical region. Informed students of textual criticism recognize that the geographical labels are used only on "the basis of tradition and habit."[19] He argued that, although the Alexandrian text type had only a handful of witnesses, this was not surprising since so few manuscripts survived from the early period. The small number of witnesses in no way undermined the legitimacy of the type. Nevertheless, Epp admitted that the text type concept has only limited applicability in Paul's letters and the General Epistles, and the traditional types simply did not apply at all to Revelation. He also argued that the term "type" should be abandoned in favor of the term "cluster" since the word "type" normally refers to a group of items that are very similar, a description that is not true of the various clusters of New Testament texts which sometimes differ significantly.

Even scholars who wish to preserve the concept of textual clusters admit that previous classifications need to be reconsidered since they were based on relatively small numbers of test passages rather than the readings of a particular text at all variant units. Some previous studies classified manuscripts based on the analysis of a single book or even a single chapter and overlooked the possibility of "block mixture" in which a scribe used an exemplar from one cluster for a portion of a book and then shifted to another exemplar from

---

18. D. C. Parker, *An Introduction to the New Testament Manuscripts and Their Texts* (Cambridge: Cambridge University Press, 2008), 171.
19. Epp, "Textual Clusters," 557. Epp himself proposed new terms for the text types that were geographically neutral in 1989.

another cluster for another portion of the book. Accurate and precise classi-fication of manuscripts requires a full study of entire texts.[20] Fortunately, the Coherence-Based Genealogical Method (see Question 20) is committed to the accomplishment of this important task. Computer technology now gives scholars the ability to handle the massive amount of data related to the rela-tionships between texts, data that was previously unmanageable for textual scholars. Since Bengel's original motivation for division into text types was finding a way to manage the overwhelming number of witnesses, the text-type approach has become unnecessary. The Coherence-Based Genealogical Method enables scholars to see the percentage of agreement between the texts of the New Testament manuscripts of the first millennium of Christian his-tory and make better informed decisions about the relationships between these texts.

Summary

In 1725, Bengel proposed dividing manuscripts into major groups to pre-vent scholars from being overwhelmed by the massive amount of data from the numerous manuscripts being discovered. By the nineteenth and twentieth centuries, most scholars acknowledged the existence of at least three major text types: Alexandrian (generally preferred by scholars), Western (characterized by freedom in making changes to the text), and Byzantine (the vast majority of later manuscripts). In the late twentieth and early twenty-first centuries, scholars have called for either the abandonment or revision of this approach.

REFLECTION QUESTIONS

1. What are some of the ways that theories about text types changed throughout history?

2. Are the objections raised against the approach legitimate?

3. Should the approach be completely abandoned or merely revised?

4. What changes are needed to make the approach helpful?

5. How should scholars determine how to group manuscripts to aid them in making text-critical decisions?

---

20. Epp, "Textual Clusters," 548–49.

Why Not Just Follow the Greek Text Behind the King James Version?

The King James Version of the Bible remains one of the most widely read and cherished English translations of the Bible. Many Christians in the English-speaking world have found the elegant wording of the translation to be moving and memorable. For some, however, the King James Version is not merely a good Bible translation. Rather, it is the only reliable (and, for some, inspired) Bible translation. Any departure from the wording of the King James Version is a corruption of God's inspired words. This view, sometimes called King James Only-ism, is not defended currently by any competent New Testament scholars. The view is defended largely by pamphlets and websites written by well-meaning people who have little knowledge of biblical languages and lack skill in the study of ancient manuscripts. Unfortunately, when many people have questions about the Bible, they simply conduct an online search. Suddenly dozens of defenses of the inerrancy of the King James Version pop up, and the average reader has no way of knowing how many of the claims made in these defenses are factually incorrect.

Naturally, those who affirm this view and know that the New Testament was first written in Greek rather than English (and not all do) are compelled to argue that the Greek text used by the translators of the King James Version is the pure and unadulterated text of the autograph. For these, modern efforts to restore the original text of the Greek New Testament are wrongheaded. The efforts are sometimes even described as heretical and unchristian. The staunch adherents of the King James Version insist that the Greek text used by the King James translators, known as the Textus Receptus, is the perfectly preserved text of the original.

A Perfect Translation?

Those who insist that the Greek text behind the King James Version is the original text usually base this claim primarily on the assumption that the King James Version is the perfect translation of the inspired Word of God. However, a few simple facts reveal the fallacy of this view.

First, the King James Version contains some translation errors. In the original 1611 edition, Matthew 23:24 referred to the Pharisees as blind guides which "strain *at* a gnat," which evokes the images of a person with poor eyesight straining his eyes to view something tiny, when it should have said, "strain *out* a gnat," since the metaphor referred to the process of filtering wine to remove insects. The error is followed even in some modern editions. The 1611 King James Version also accidentally substituted the name Judas for Jesus in Matthew 26:36.[1]

Later editions introduced new errors. The second edition accidentally printed Exodus 14:10 twice. In 1631, Cambridge printers were fined £300 by Archbishop Laud for inadvertently omitting the "not" from the Seventh Commandment so that it read, "Thou shalt commit adultery."[2] The edition became known as the "Wicked Bible." In a 1702 edition now known as the "Scribes' Bible," a typesetter made Psalm 119:161 read, "Printers have persecuted me without a cause!" when it should have read "Princes have persecuted me without a cause."[3] A 1795 edition came to be called the "Murderer's Bible" by accidentally changing just one letter in Mark 7:27 so that, instead of "Let the children first be filled," it read, "Let the children first be killed." Obviously, it would be hazardous to affirm the inerrancy of any of these editions!

The original translators of the King James Version would likely be surprised to discover that modern readers affirm the inerrancy of their translation. The King James Only movement might never have arisen if publishers continued to publish the original Preface to the 1611 King James Bible entitled "The Translators to the Readers" and if readers carefully read and trusted the opinions of the translators. Several times in this Preface, the translators deny the perfection of their translation. For example, the Preface includes the translators' response to critics who argued that the text of Scripture should not be translated into English since no English translation can exactly and perfectly communicate the sense of the original. They replied that a man could be considered virtuous even though he had "made many slips in his life." A man could

---

1. One recent study identified 387 typographical errors in the first edition of the King James Version. See David Norton, *The King James Bible: A Short History from Tyndale to Today* (New York: Cambridge University Press, 2011), 127–33.
2. Norton has suggested that this error was the result of an act of intentional sabotage by Bonham Norton (see Norton, *The King James Bible*, 139).
3. Norton argues that the mistake was probably purposeful, an act of revenge by a typesetter who felt abused by a tyrannical printer (*The King James Bible*, 140). For these and other variants in editions of the King James Version, see Paul Wegner, *The Journey from Texts to Translations: The Origin and Development of the Bible* (Grand Rapids: Baker, 1999), 310.

be considered handsome even though he had warts on his hand or freckles and scars on his face. They concluded: "No cause therefore why the word translated should be denied to be the word, or forbidden to be current, notwithstanding that some imperfections and blemishes may be noted in the setting forth of it." Notice that they did not reply to the claim that the translation would be imperfect by insisting that their translation was, in fact, perfect. Instead, they acknowledged that careful readers would discover "imperfections and blemishes." But they argued that the translation was sufficiently accurate to be considered the word of God. They went on to acknowledge that no human translation of Scripture could be perfect: "For what ever was perfect under the Sun, where Apostles or Apostolic men [the authors of the New Testament], that is, men endued with an extraordinary measure of God's spirit, and privileged with the privilege of infallibility, had not their hand?"

In response to the claim that producing a new translation implied that previous translations were bad, they insisted:

> Truly (good Christian Reader) we never thought from the beginning, that we should need to make a new Translation, nor yet to make of a bad one a good one . . . but to make a good one better, or out of many good ones, one principal good one, not justly to be excepted against; that hath been our endeavor, that our mark.

The intention here is not to disparage the King James Version. I am quite fond of it. The kinds of criticisms leveled here would need to be made if inerrancy were claimed for any translation of the Bible (see Question 7). But I know of no other English Bible translation whose modern supporters claim inerrancy for it. Both the clear statements of the translators and the obviously mistaken readings of the King James Version show that this extraordinary claim cannot be substantiated.

Which Textus Receptus?

The translators of the King James Version used several different Greek texts to produce their New Testament translation. These included Robert Stephanus's 1550 edition, which was called the "royal edition," his 1551 edition, and Theodore Beza's 1598 edition, which made only minor changes to Stephanus's Greek text. These editions essentially reprinted the text from the 1527 and 1535 editions of the Greek text produced by Desiderius Erasmus. Defenders of the King James Version refer to these Greek texts as the Textus Receptus. The label is somewhat anachronistic. The moniker Textus Receptus ("received text") is actually derived from the Preface to a Greek New Testament published by Bonaventure and Abraham Elzevir in 1633. The clever publishers touted their edition with the statement: "*Textum ergo habes nunc ab omnibus receptum*" ("the text that you have [that is] now received by all"). The description was not entirely accurate. Many of the publishers introduced changes into this standard Greek text in an effort to improve it. Scrivener, for example, compared the 1550 edition of Stephanus and the 1633 Elzevir edition and found at least 287 differences between them even though both are referred to as the Textus Receptus.

Furthermore, the King James Version departs from all of these editions of the Greek text at some points. Maurice Robinson has pointed out that in a few places the King James Version seems to have drawn from the Latin Vulgate and adopts readings not found in any early printed Greek text, Greek manuscript, early version, or quotation from the early church fathers! An example is John 10:16 in which the translation "one fold" follows the Latin Vulgate (*unum ovile*) even though all Greek witnesses have "one flock" (μία ποίμνη rather than μία αὐλή).[4] Thus, when defenders of the King James Version insist that the Textus Receptus is the original text and assume that the Textus Receptus is the Greek text behind the King James Version, they are actually referring in a few places to a hypothetical Greek text that can only be reconstructed by translating from English back into Greek!

Problems with the Textus Receptus

Even the most stalwart of the defenders of the Textus Receptus in the twentieth century had to admit that the text had its problems. Edward F. Hills appears to be the only *bona fide* scholar of the last century to defend the Textus Receptus. Nevertheless, in his book *The King James Version Defended*, Hills admitted that the Textus Receptus contained readings that were "unquestionably erroneous."[5] For example, when Erasmus prepared his Greek text of Revelation, his single manuscript of the book was missing the last six verses. Rather than take the time to seek out another manuscript, he simply translated the Latin Vulgate back into Greek. He also applied this same method to other portions of Revelation where he suspected that his one Greek manuscript was inaccurate. In Revelation 17:4, he even invented a new Greek word that did not previously appear in Greek literature! Hills acknowledged: "Some of this manufactured Greek was removed by Erasmus himself in his later editions of the New Testament. Some of it, however, still remains in the Textus Receptus."[6] Hills dismissed these problems as "minor blemishes."[7] They nevertheless undermine the claim that the Textus Receptus preserves the pure text of the autograph of the Greek New Testament.

---

4. See Maurice Robinson, "Introduction to Scrivener's Textus Receptus 1894" https://scripture4all.org/help/isa2/DatabaseInfo/ScrTR/ScrTR.html.

5. Edward Hills, *The King James Version Defended: A Christian View of the New Testament Manuscripts* (Des Moines: Christian Research Press, 1956), 122–23.

6. Hills, *King James Version Defended*, 123.

7. Hills, *King James Version Defended*, 123.

The Comma Johanneum

First John 5:7–8 contains a prime example of a doubtful text that has made its way into the King James Version. The Textus Receptus inserts a clear Trinitarian statement known as the Comma Johanneum that reads: "there are three who are bearing witness in heaven, the Father, the Word, and the Spirit, and these three are one." When Erasmus produced the first published Greek New Testament in 1516 followed by his second edition in 1519, he did not include this Trinitarian statement in his Greek text.[8]

Archbishop of York Edward Lee and Stunica (the editor of a rival Greek text that was actually printed before Erasmus's first edition but was not published until afterward) harshly criticized this presumed omission. In a reply to Lee in May of 1520, Erasmus explained that he had not omitted anything. He had simply followed the Greek texts that were available to him, none of which contained the Trinitarian statement. Sometime over the next year (May 1520–1521), Erasmus received a transcription from a manuscript now called Codex Montfortianus (61) that contained the passage in question. Some scholars have suggested that the manuscript was made specifically to convince Erasmus to include the passage in his next edition.[9] Although Erasmus's writings give no indication that he suspected that this manuscript was essentially a forgery, he did note that the manuscript appeared to be of recent origin and that he suspected the reading had been revised from the Latin Vulgate.[10] Based on the reading of this late manuscript, Erasmus caved to pressure to include the Trinitarian statement in his 1522 (third) edition. The statement remained in future editions of the Textus Receptus and consequently made its way into the King James Version.[11]

The last scholar to suggest that this statement was original was Edward Hills, and he was probably the only scholar to do so in the twentieth century. Even he expressed his doubts and admitted, "the external evidence against the

---

8. For a high-resolution image of the relevant page of Erasmus's first edition, see http://images.csntm.org/PublishedWorks/Erasmus_1516/Erasmus1516_0257a.jpg.

9. J. Rendel Harris, *The Origin of the Leicester Codex of the New Testament* (London: C. J. Clay, 1887), 46–53.

10. Grantley McDonald, *Biblical Criticism in Early Modern Europe: Erasmus, the Johannine Comma and Trinitarian Debate* (Cambridge: Cambridge University Press, 2016), 27, 319. The story about Erasmus's text and the inclusion of the Trinitarian passage has become the stuff of legend. Some of the details reported in texts even to this day cannot be substantiated from the available evidence and are probably distortions. I have chosen to report here only what can be firmly established from Erasmus's correspondence with his opponents and his other writings. For important corrections to modern accounts, see H. J. de Jonge, "Erasmus and the Comma Johanneum," *Ephemerides Theologicae Lovainienses* 56 (1980): 381–89.

11. Interestingly, Martin Luther did not include the Johannine Comma in the German translations of the New Testament that were published during his lifetime. See Ezra Abbot, "I John v.7, and Luther's German Bible," in *The Authorship of the Fourth Gospel and Other Critical Essays* (Boston, G.H. Ellis, 1888), 458–63.

genuineness of the Johannine comma seems almost overwhelming."[12] Only eight manuscripts include the Trinitarian statement, and none of them date before the fourteenth century. After appealing to other evidence that might (weakly) support the genuineness of the statement, the most Hills could say was: "in spite of the very unfavorable state of the external evidence, the possibility still exists that the Johannine comma is a genuine portion of the New Testament text."[13]

Summary

The King James Version of the Bible was an excellent Bible translation for its time, and it is worthy of respect even today. However, claims that the translation is perfect or that the Greek text of the New Testament on which it was based is the purely preserved text of the autographs are clearly incorrect. The discussion of Question 7 showed that copies and translations are inspired and inerrant only to the extent that they accurately preserve the original text of the New Testament. Yet, the King James Version and its underlying Greek text undoubtedly deviate from the original text. Modern scholars now have the advantage of many recent manuscript finds that enable them to restore the original text far more accurately than was possible in the early seventeenth century when the King James Version was produced.

REFLECTION QUESTIONS

1. What concerns likely motivate claims that a translation is perfect and inerrant?

2. What were some of the errors in the early editions of the King James Version?

3. What are some of the different ways that the term "Textus Receptus" is used? Does the Textus Receptus of the King James Version exist in any single manuscript?

4. What is the Comma Johanneum and how did it end up in the King James Version? What evidence shows that this statement was not a part of the original Greek text of 1 John?

5. Has your view of the King James Version changed in any way after reading about its history? If so, how?

---

12. Hills, *The King James Version Defended*, 128.
13. Hills, *The King James Version Defended*, 132.

Why Not Just Follow the Reading Preserved in the Majority of Manuscripts?

Some scholars have argued that the original text of the New Testament is (at least generally) the text that has been preserved in the vast majority of surviving manuscripts. As seen earlier (Question 11), most manuscripts of the Greek New Testament have texts belonging to the Byzantine text type. Robinson and Pierpont state, "For most of the New Testament the Byzantine Textform is supported by nearly the whole of the manuscript tradition; in almost every case the Byzantine reading reflects the concurrence of at least 70% and usually more than 80% of the extant manuscripts."[1] In this approach, determining the original reading is normally a straightforward and simple process—follow the Byzantine text.

Method

Byzantine priorists are those who affirm the preference of the Byzantine text type to other types and see all other text types as stemming from an early Byzantine ancestor. The method employed by these scholars is different is several ways from a strict "Majority Text" approach. Although critics of the method of Byzantine priorists sometimes allege that they "count noses" and simply let the majority reading rule, the method is actually a bit more sophisticated than this. For example, Robinson and Pierpont sought to locate "primary Byzantine readings" from texts that were from the eleventh century and earlier. Even though nearly 80 percent of Byzantine manuscripts are from

---

1. Maurice Robinson and William Pierpont, *The New Testament in the Original Greek: Byzantine Textform 2005* (Southborough, MA: Chilton, 2005), xiv.

the twelfth century or later, these were viewed as generally "irrelevant" and served only to confirm readings based on the earlier evidence.[2]

Furthermore, although the method relies primarily on the consensus reading to establish the original text, it also evaluates the reading in light of what is known about common scribal mistakes before a final decision is made.[3] Robinson and Pierpont state: "At all times, pertinent transmissional, transcriptional, external, and internal factors are considered as component elements of weight."[4] Especially in cases in which the Byzantine witnesses are divided and no clear consensus emerges, the text must be established on "non-numerical grounds" by considering common scribal alterations, the reading that best fits the context and the style of the author, etc.[5] In such instances, the approach closely resembles the standard method.

Rationale

Byzantine priorists also argue that normal processes of transmission of a text will result in the original text ordinarily being the dominant text. Since scribes generally wanted to copy their exemplar faithfully and were reasonably competent, they produced texts that closely resembled the exemplar. Thus, "this 'normal' state of transmission assumes that the aggregate consentient testimony of the extant manuscript base is more likely to reflect its archetypal source (in this case the canonical autographs) than any single manuscript, small group of manuscripts, or isolated versional or patristic readings that failed to achieve widespread diversity or transmissional continuity."[6] In other words, because the process of transmitting the text was generally stable (scribes were faithful and accurate) and self-correcting (earlier scribal errors were often obvious to later copyists, and they sometimes had other copies available for comparison), the readings shared by the majority of manuscripts will likely preserve the original.[7]

---

2. Robinson and Pierpont, *The New Testament in the Original Greek: Byzantine Textform 2005*, xiv.
3. Robinson and Pierpont, *The New Testament in the Original Greek: Byzantine Textform 2005*, xiv.
4. Robinson and Pierpont, *The New Testament in the Original Greek: Byzantine Textform 2005*, x.
5. Robinson and Pierpont, *The New Testament in the Original Greek: Byzantine Textform 2005*, xiv.
6. Robinson and Pierpont, *The New Testament in the Original Greek: Byzantine Textform 2005*, v. Westcott and Hort affirmed the "theoretical presupposition" that "a majority of extant documents is more likely to represent a majority of ancestral documents at each stage of transmission" (*Introduction to the New Testament in the Original Greek with Notes on Selected Readings* [1882; repr., Peabody, MA: Hendrickson, 1988], 45). However, they argued that "the smallest tangible evidence of other kinds" outweighs this presumption and that the presumption "falls to the ground" when one considers the impossibility of determining how many copies were made of each individual ancestor or how many of the copies made were preserved to be copied in a future age.
7. My term "self-correcting" is an attempt to explain the view that "while a minority of scribes might adopt any difficult reading for at least a time, the chances are slim that the vast majority of scribes would adopt such a reading were a simpler one originally dominant

Byzantine priorists strongly affirm the inspiration of the New Testament. They generally argue that the God who inspired the New Testament also providentially preserved the New Testament. Robinson and Pierpont wrote: "A corollary to these doctrinal beliefs [biblical inspiration] is the confessional declaration that this revelation has been kept pure in all ages by the singular care and providence of God."[8] Even more emphatically, Pickering wrote: "God has preserved the text of the New Testament in a very pure form and it has been readily available to His followers in every age throughout 1900 years."[9] Many who adopt other approaches to textual criticism believe that God has preserved his Word. But the emphasis of the Byzantine priorists is that he did so *in all ages*. Pickering, in particular, seems to imply that the original text is not just the text of the majority of manuscripts extant today. It would have been the majority text in any era since the New Testament was written.

Most New Testament textual critics are reasoned eclectics who affirm the general priority of the Alexandrian text. In that view, the Alexandrian text was changed by copyists over centuries to become the Byzantine text. This Byzantine text essentially became the text used by the church for over a thousand years. Then, scholars succeeded in restoring the text (mostly) to its original condition. Many who adopt this approach believe that God has preserved his Word. They might insist that the New Testament was preserved *through* the ages, but they might be hesitant to affirm that it was "kept pure *in* all ages," depending on the degree of purity one has in mind. In contrast, Robinson and Pierpont assert, "Yet the original Greek New Testament text has been preserved by ordinary means with a remarkable degree of accuracy in almost all manuscripts, through the unregulated dissemination and transmission of the New Testament documents."[10] And they deny that the purpose of textual

---

from the autograph" (Robinson and Pierpont, *The New Testament in the Original Greek: Byzantine Textform 2005*, 546).

8. Robinson and Pierpont, *The New Testament in the Original Greek: Byzantine Textform 2005*, xxi. The statement is a reference to section I.VIII of the Westminster Confession which states "The Old Testament in Hebrew . . . and the New Testament in Greek . . . being immediately inspired by God, and by his singular care and providence kept pure in all ages, are therefore authentical." For an explanation of the statement and a defense of its consistency with modern textual criticism, see B. B. Warfield, *The Westminster Assembly and Its Work* (New York: Oxford University Press, 1931), 236–51. He argued: "It admits of no denial that they explicitly recognized the fact that the text of the Scriptures had suffered corruption in process of transmission, and affirmed that the 'pure' text lies therefore not in one copy, but in all, and is to be attained not by simply reading the text in whatever copy may chance to fall into our hands, but by a process of comparison, i.e. by criticism" (p. 239).

9. Wilbur N. Pickering, "An Evaluation of the Contribution of John William Burgon to New Testament Textual Criticism" (ThM Thesis, Dallas Theological Seminary, 1968), 90.

10. Robinson and Pierpont, *The New Testament in the Original Greek: Byzantine Textform 2005*, xxi (see also v).

criticism is the "restoration or recovery of an 'original' text long presumed to have been 'lost.'"[11]

Byzantine priorists also object that the standard method of establishing the text is too speculative, and its results too uncertain. When one accepts that the original text is a consensus-based text, establishing the original text is a "clear and simple task" even though the task still requires "diligent labor, careful research, and a systematic methodology."[12] The standard method, on the other hand, is plagued by "the hazards of subjective speculation" since it often appeals to "favored individual manuscripts, local texts, minority regional texttypes," and "subjective internal criteria."[13] Such a text is subject to constant revision.

Byzantine priorists also object that the standard critical editions "adopt an amalgam of individual readings."[14] Rule 9 proposed by Kurt Aland stated: "Variants must never be treated in isolation, but always considered in the context of the tradition. Otherwise there is too great a danger of reconstructing a 'test tube text' which never existed at any time or place."[15] Robinson in particular has argued that the standard method does exactly what Aland (a reasoned eclectic) prohibited. Like scientists mixing chemicals over a burner in a laboratory to create a new substance different from any in the natural world, critics select readings from many different texts and assemble them together to create a text that is sometimes different from every single manuscript even over short stretches of text or single verses.

Resources

The most important edition of the Byzantine text today is *The New Testament in the Original Greek: Byzantine Textform* compiled and arranged by Maurice Robinson and William Pierpont.[16] The primary source used for the creation of the edition was the apparatus in the Greek text edited by Hermann Freiherr von Soden.[17] Von Soden valued the Byzantine text (which

---

11. Robinson and Pierpont, *The New Testament in the Original Greek: Byzantine Textform 2005*, vii.
12. Robinson and Pierpont, *The New Testament in the Original Greek: Byzantine Textform 2005*, xxii.
13. Robinson and Pierpont, *The New Testament in the Original Greek: Byzantine Textform 2005*, xxii–xxiii.
14. Robinson and Pierpont, *The New Testament in the Original Greek: Byzantine Textform 2005*, xxiii.
15. Kurt Aland and Barbara Aland, *The Text of the New Testament: An Introduction to the Critical Editions and to the Theory and Practice of Modern Textual Criticism*, trans. Erroll F. Rhodes, 2nd ed. (Grand Rapids: Eerdmans, 1989), 281.
16. The most recent is Maurice Robinson and William Pierpont, *The New Testament in the Original Greek: Byzantine Textform 2018* (Nürnberg: VTR Publications, 2018). This edition lacks the detailed defense of Byzantine priority that appeared in pre-2016 editions since it is now available in Maurice Robinson, "The Case for Byzantine Priority," *TC* 6 (2001).
17. Robinson and Pierpont, *The New Testament in the Original Greek: Byzantine Textform 2005*, x. The data in Von Soden was confirmed (or corrected) by use of several other sources.

he called the Koine text) more highly and followed it more closely than any previous modern critical edition. This was the result of an important principle in von Soden's text-critical method. He divided texts into three major groups and adopted the reading supported by two of the three groups.

Von Soden also identified about seventeen different subgroups within the Byzantine text type. He regarded the readings in the manuscripts represented by a bold *K* as the consensus form of the Byzantine text. Robinson and Pierpont followed the readings in von Soden's *K* text when possible. When the *K* text was divided, they followed *K*[x], the dominant component in the *K* group. They used other critical editions to supplement von Soden's work and found that "these full collation results tend to confirm the Byzantine group evidence presented in von Soden's early twentieth-century apparatus."[18]

Objections

Westcott and Hort acknowledged that the Byzantine text was current in the second half of the fourth century and could be traced to an ancestor that was as old or even older than the oldest manuscripts available to them (before the discovery of the papyri).[19] However, they inferred that the Byzantine text must have been later than the Western and Alexandrian texts for several reasons. First, the Byzantine text frequently conflated the two readings of the Alexandrian and Western texts in cases in which they differed.[20] One of the eight examples offered is Mark 9:49. Important Alexandrian witnesses read, "for every [person] will be salted with fire." Important Western witnesses read, "for every sacrifice will be salted with salt" (which, Westcott and Hort argued, interpreted the Alexandrian reading in light of Leviticus 7:13). But Byzantine witnesses read, "for every person will be salted with fire, and every sacrifice will be salted with salt." This reading seems to have resulted from a scribe finding both the Alexandrian and Western readings in his exemplars and choosing to give both in his copy.

Westcott and Hort also argued that no church fathers appear to quote the distinct readings of the Byzantine text prior to the Council of Nicaea.[21] Finally, they found that internal evidence (examination of what scribes most likely would have changed and authors would most likely have written) consistently showed the Byzantine text to be secondary.[22] They concluded: "It follows that all distinctively Syrian [Byzantine] readings may be set aside at once

---

18. Robinson and Pierpont, *The New Testament in the Original Greek: Byzantine Textform 2005*, ix.
19. Westcott and Hort, *Introduction to the New Testament in the Original Greek*, 92.
20. Westcott and Hort, *Introduction to the New Testament in the Original Greek*, 93–107.
21. Westcott and Hort, *Introduction to the New Testament in the Original Greek*, 107–15. Westcott and Hort defined distinct readings as those not supported by other ancient forms of the text (i.e., not shared by Sinaiticus, Vaticanus, or Bezae).
22. Westcott and Hort, *Introduction to the New Testament in the Original Greek*, 115–17.

as certainly originating after the middle of the third century, and therefore, as far as transmission is concerned, corruptions of the apostolic text."[23]

More recently, Gordon Fee argued that "this text-form [Byzantine] is completely unknown by any of the evidence up to AD 350, the earliest evidence being in some fourth-century church fathers, then late in the fifth century in portions of Codices W and A."[24] Wallace likewise insisted that "as far as the extant witnesses reveal, the MT [Majority Text] did not exist in the first three centuries."[25] Isolated Byzantine readings appear in some of the earliest manuscripts, but none of these manuscripts preserve a *pattern* of specific Byzantine readings.

Byzantine priorists respond that the few texts that have survived from the early period may not be representative of the state of the text at this period. They argue that, since all the papyri were found in Egypt, they likely represent the local text of Egypt rather than representing the form of the text that circulated throughout the rest of the Greek-speaking world. The problem with this claim is that the papyri not only include texts from the Alexandrian cluster (as the argument appears to assume) but also include texts of the Western text type (e.g., P^{38} P^{48} P^{69}) and possibly even a few ancestors of what would later become the Byzantine text-form that exhibit some of the tendencies of the later Byzantine text.[26]

Daniel Wallace has offered several other major critiques of the Majority Text approach. First, he noted that the doctrine of preservation (at least when this requires that the pure text will be accessible to Christians at every age) lacks biblical support.[27] Second, he has argued that "as far as the extant MSS reveal, the Byzantine text did not become a majority until the ninth century (although historically it most likely became a majority several centuries earlier), and even then 'majority' must be qualified: there are almost

---

23. Westcott and Hort, *Introduction to the New Testament in the Original Greek*, 117. The qualification "distinctively" is important. The argument was that the reading of the Byzantine text should be rejected when the Byzantine text is not supported by another textual group.
24. Gordon Fee, "The Majority Text and the Original Text of the NT," in *Studies in the Theory and Method of New Testament Textual Criticism*, SD 45, eds. Eldon J. Epp and Gordon D. Fee (Grand Rapids: Eerdmans, 1993), 184.
25. Wallace, "Majority Text Theory: History, Methods, and Critique," in *The Text of the New Testament in Contemporary Research: Essays on the Status Quaestionis*, 2nd ed., NTTSD, eds. Bart D. Ehrman and Michael W. Holmes (Leiden: Brill, 2012), 731. Note, however, that though the Alands insisted that the Byzantine text did not receive its final form until around 300, an "undoubtedly early tradition" formed its foundation. The Alands admitted the existence of one or more papyri that *might* be ancestors of what would later become the Byzantine text-form. This possibility prompted them to call for more research into these papyri (Aland and Aland, *The Text of the New Testament*, 23n50).
26. See Aland and Aland, *The Text of the New Testament*, 23n50.
27. Daniel Wallace, "Inspiration, Preservation, and New Testament Textual Criticism," *GTJ* 12 (1992): 21–50.

twice as many Latin MSS as there are Greek, and, to my knowledge, none of them belongs to the Byzantine text."[28] He added that no ancient version was based on the Byzantine text until the Ethiopic and Gothic versions at the end of the fourth century, and the earliest church figure to use the Byzantine text was the heretic Asterius of Antioch in the fourth century.[29] Therefore, to argue that the Byzantine text existed in the first three centuries is an argument from silence. Thus, the Majority Text theory is based on possibilities rather than probabilities.[30] Third, he argued that, although internal evidence can sometimes be subjective, internal evidence is at times sufficient to lead to conclusions about readings that are objectively verifiable. In these cases, the Majority Text almost always has an inferior reading.[31] Although MT theorists and Byzantine priorists often point to the subjectivity of internal evidence, they essentially admit the legitimacy of the standard approach when they resort to it in cases in which no reading has a clear majority or they reject a majority reading in favor of a minority reading. Although some Byzantine priorists have claimed to consider the evidence of the traditional canons of textual criticism (including internal evidence) in evaluating readings, Wallace charged that so far no scholar has produced a textual commentary that presents the evidence for these decisions. Wallace considers this "a tacit admission that the traditional text really is indefensible on internal grounds, which, in turn, is a concession that internal evidence is not altogether subjective."[32]

Summary

The Byzantine Priority theory asserts that the original reading is generally the reading preserved in the vast majority of surviving manuscripts. The consensus readings are found in manuscripts consistently belonging to the Byzantine text type. This view is based largely on the premise of "normal transmission" in which the strong consensus of extant manuscripts for any variant unit is presumed to preserve the original reading. This theory, however, is affirmed by a small minority of textual scholars since internal evidence generally confirms the inferiority of the Byzantine text and the Byzantine text does not represent the majority of extant witnesses until the ninth century. On the other hand, although most scholars reject Byzantine priority, many exhibit a new appreciation for individual Byzantine readings.[33]

---

28. Wallace, "The Majority Text Theory," 727–28.
29. Wallace, "The Majority Text Theory," 727–28.
30. Wallace, "The Majority Text Theory," 728–29.
31. Wallace, "The Majority Text Theory," 735. A similar argument was used earlier by Michael Holmes. It was also foundational to the approach of Westcott and Hort.
32. Wallace, "The Majority Text Theory," 737.
33. See the description of attitudes toward the Byzantine text in Question 12.

REFLECTION QUESTIONS

1. What is the greatest strength of the Byzantine Priority theory?

2. What is the greatest weakness of the Byzantine Priority theory?

3. Do any of the criticisms raised by Byzantine Priority theorists against the standard view seem unfair?

4. Do any of the criticisms raised by advocates of the standard view against the Byzantine Priority theory seem unfair?

5. What other evidence is needed to help you decide between the two views?

How Do Most Scholars Decide Between Readings of Different Manuscripts?

The vast majority of scholars engaged in New Testament textual criticism today use an approach called "reasoned eclecticism." Similar to the adjective "eclectic" mentioned earlier, the noun "eclecticism" is likewise derived from the Greek verb ἐκλέγομαι ("to select" or "to pick out something"). The term indicates that the scholar is selecting readings from different texts in order to restore the original text. The adjective "reasoned" is intended to distinguish this method from another method called "thoroughgoing eclecticism" (also sometimes called rational criticism, radical criticism, rigorous criticism, or consistent criticism) in which the scholar places far more weight on internal evidence than external evidence.[1] Reasoned eclecticism, on the other hand, seeks to balance the findings of external and internal evidence.

External Evidence

Prefer a Reading That Is Demonstrably Early

Samuel Tregelles argued that the only proof that a reading was truly ancient (and thus a legitimate candidate for the original reading) was its discovery in an ancient document.[2] For this reason, a reading that is not attested

---

1. Internal evidence refers to the clues found in the variant readings themselves. External evidence refers to all other evidence.
2. Samuel P. Tregelles, *An Account of the Printed Text of the Greek New Testament: with Remarks on Its Revision upon Critical Principles* (London: Samuel Bagster, 1854; repr., Cambridge: Cambridge University Press, 2013), 175. Tregelles was influenced by the principles that Griesbach articulated in his *Prolegomena to the Greek Testament* (I.lxii). This preference for the ancient witnesses was also a hallmark of the work of Carl Lachmann

in ancient manuscripts should not generally be adopted as the original reading regardless of the internal evidence that may support it. It is true that late manuscripts sometimes preserve very early readings. For example, we saw in Question 9 that 1739 is a manuscript that dates to the tenth century. However, the manuscript is likely a copy of a text from the famous library of Caesarea that predates the year 400. Its text of the epistle of Romans is essentially a text known and used by Origen in the first half of the third century.[3] But, despite a few such exceptions, generally the earlier the witness to a particular reading, the better. Unfortunately, this principle is not always as helpful as it may seem. In some cases, variant readings may be of equal antiquity as far as can be proven from the extant witnesses.[4]

Prefer Witnesses Judged to Be Trustworthy on Other Grounds

Consider the quality of witnesses that support a particular reading. Westcott and Hort are famous for their dictum that "KNOWLEDGE OF DOCUMENTS SHOULD PRECEDE FINAL JUDGMENT UPON READINGS."[5] These scholars argued that some textual questions can be decided definitively based on internal evidence alone. Manuscripts that consistently preserve the obviously correct reading in these cases are likely trustworthy elsewhere too. The reliability of a manuscript can be determined, in part, from the number of singular readings (appear in only one early manuscript), sub-singular readings (appear in only one early manuscript and in late manuscripts, early versions, or citations by early church fathers),[6] or nonsense readings in the manuscript. If few of these exist in the manuscript, the scribe was clearly careful. If a large number of these exist, the scribe who produced the manuscript was probably careless, and the manuscript should be viewed with greater caution. On the other hand, a skilled scribe does not guarantee a reliable text. A careful scribe could produce an almost perfect copy of a bad exemplar. Quality involves more than the lack of careless mistakes. True quality involved both faithful copying and a reliable exemplar.

---

and Constantine Tischendorf. For these scholars, ancient witnesses included Greek manuscripts and early church citations from the fourth to ninth centuries.

3. Günther Zuntz correctly pointed out that "the text of Origen" was not a "fixed entity" since his writings sometimes support one reading or another depending on the text available to him at the moment (*The Text of the Epistles: A Disquisition up the Corpus Paulinum* [British Academy, 1953; repr., Eugene, OR: Wipf and Stock, 2007], 92).

4. See, for example, Charles Quarles, "Matthew 16.2b–3: New Considerations for a Difficult Textual Question," *NTS* 66 (2020): 228–48.

5. B. F. Westcott and F. J. A. Hort, *Introduction to the New Testament in the Original Greek with Notes on Selected Readings* (1882; repr., Peabody, MA: Hendrickson, 1988), 31. This was one of only two principles so important for their methodology as to be printed in all caps.

6. These definitions are derived from Westcott and Hort, *Introduction to the New Testament in the Original Greek*, 230.

Prefer Readings That Have a Wide Geographical Distribution of Witnesses

Wide distribution suggests that the reading significantly predates the witnesses that support it. If fourth-century witnesses from all over the world contain a particular reading, that reading likely existed several generations of copies prior to these early witnesses. Since it is unlikely that these witnesses all relied on the same exemplar, the reading can likely be traced back at least several generations of copies to a much earlier shared ancestor. Unfortunately, we do not know for certain where some of our earliest Greek manuscripts (much less their exemplars) were produced. Thus, an understanding of geographical distribution must depend largely on the readings in the ancient versions and New Testament quotations in the early church fathers.

In the past, many reasoned eclectics argued that a consideration of the text types supporting various readings is important to the evaluation of the external evidence. Two different views have been popular. Scholars like Metzger, Ehrman, and the Alands have argued that one should prefer readings in what is generally recognized as the earliest and most reliable text type (Alexandrian) and should avoid readings found only in the inferior Byzantine text type.[7]

Other scholars have argued that no one text type should be favored over another. Instead, the textual critic should prefer readings supported by multiple text types or the larger number of text types.[8] This second approach was championed by Harry Sturz, who argued that three major text types should be given equal weight in text-critical decisions. He wrote: "Individual readings supported by a concensus (sic) of the major text types should be considered as (1) heavily attested by external evidence and (2) preserved from very early in the second century."[9]

Some reasoned eclectics combine these two approaches. For example, Greenlee wrote: "If the text types are considered individually, the Alexandrian is generally the most reliable single text, although it sometimes contains a 'learned' correction. At the same time, a reading which is supported by good

---

7. Bruce Metzger and Bart Ehrman, *The Text of the New Testament: Its Transmission, Corruption, and Restoration*, 4th ed. (Oxford: Oxford University Press, 2005), 305–6; Kurt Aland and Barbara Aland, *The Text of the New Testament: An Introduction to the Critical Editions and to the Theory and Practice of Modern Textual Criticism*, trans. Erroll F. Rhodes, 2nd ed. (Grand Rapids: Eerdmans, 1989), 335–37.
8. This approach seems to have been pioneered by Griesbach. Vincent wrote: "In deciding on a reading he relied chiefly on the evidence furnished by the union of families. The agreement of the Western and Alexandrian he regarded as particularly important, often decisive" (*A History of the Textual Criticism of the New Testament* [London: Macmillan, 1899]), 101–2). For recent supporters, see Harry Sturz, *The Byzantine Text Type and New Testament Textual Criticism* (Nashville: Thomas Nelson, 1984), 129–31; David Alan Black, *New Testament Textual Criticism: A Concise Guide* (Grand Rapids: Baker, 1994), 35; Amy Anderson and Wendy Widder, *Textual Criticism of the Bible*, rev. ed. (Bellingham, WA: Lexham Press, 2018), 156.
9. Harry Sturz, *The Byzantine Text Type and New Testament Textual Criticism*, 129–31.

representatives of two or more text types may be preferable to a reading supported by one text type exclusively."[10]

However, since scholars are increasingly rejecting or questioning the traditional text types, they play little if any role in text-critical decisions for some reasoned eclectics. Analysis involving the traditional text types does not play a role, for example, in the new Coherence-Based Genealogical Method that is being used in the reconstruction of the initial text in the Editio Critica Maior and future editions of the NA and UBS Greek New Testament. The one guideline for the restoration of the text related to traditional text types is Guideline 5: "The priority of a majority reading [Byzantine text] is indicated if it is linguistically more difficult or contextually less suitable and thus atypical of the majority text."[11] The theory is that, when the Byzantine text contains readings that do not match the normal characteristics of that text, the reading must predate the development of the Byzantine text. The principle implies that Byzantine readings will otherwise be regarded as secondary.

Internal Evidence

Reasoned eclectics divide internal evidence into two subcategories: intrinsic evidence and transcriptional evidence. Intrinsic evidence focuses on the question, "What was the author most likely to have written?" Transcriptional evidence focuses on the question, "What was the ancient scribe most likely to have changed in the process of copying the text?"

Intrinsic Evidence

An examination of intrinsic evidence entails research of the normal grammar, vocabulary, style, and theology of a book or corpus (like the epistles of Paul). Good exegetes normally excel in this area of research especially if they have studied a particular book intensively for a prolonged period. Not surprisingly, the discussions of text-critical issues in commentaries on the Greek New Testament often focus primarily on intrinsic evidence since that is generally the area in which commentators are most knowledgeable.

Sometimes discussions of intrinsic evidence overlook two drawbacks of overemphasizing this category of evidence. First, sometimes the assessment of the grammar and style of an author varies from one text type to another or one manuscript to another. For example, the Byzantine or Majority text is sometimes characterized by a preference for consistency in vocabulary that is not found in the Alexandrian text.[12] For another example, Matthew normally

---

10. Harold J. Greenlee, *Introduction to New Testament Textual Criticism*, rev. ed. (Grand Rapids: Baker Academic, 2012), 114.
11. See Gäbel, Hüffmeier, Mink, Strutwolf, and Wachtel, "The CBGM Applied to Variants from Acts—Methodological Background," *TC* 20 (2015): 3.
12. Charles L. Quarles, "ΜΕΤΑ ΤΗΝ ΕΓΕΡΣΙΝ ΑΥΤΟΥ: A Scribal Interpolation in Matthew 27:53?" *TC* 20 (2015): 6.

uses singular verbs with neuter plural nouns that are impersonal but plural verbs with neuter plural nouns that are personal. But, in Codex W, the gospel of Matthew almost always uses singular verbs with neuter plural nouns regardless of whether they are personal or impersonal. Apparently, the scribe who copied Codex W adapted the grammar of the gospel of Matthew to suit his own personal preferences.[13] Consequently, an analysis of an author's style should consider how other text-critical decisions affect the analysis. If one just does a computer search for a particular construction in a particular critical edition, he may get different results than if he conducted the same search in another edition. Conducting the search in two or more texts and comparing the results is generally the wisest approach.

Second, New Testament authors did not always employ consistent grammar, style, vocabulary, or even spelling. Modern readers may have never noticed, for example, that Matthew spells the word Jerusalem two different ways: Ἱεροσόλυμα and Ἱερουσαλήμ. When he uses the form Ἱεροσόλυμα, he sometimes treats it as feminine singular and at other times as neuter plural. And one finds this variety of usage in Matthew in both critical texts that largely follow the Alexandrian text and those that are based on the Majority text. If the scholar operates with an iron-clad rule that a single author must use grammar, style, and vocabulary consistently, he may be imposing that consistency on the text based on his modern expectations.

Still, intrinsic evidence is often immensely helpful in deciding between various readings. For example, several scholars of the eighteenth and nineteenth centuries have argued that Matthew 27:52–53 is an early scribal interpolation, and this theory was recently revived.[14] The argument for this view is based on the alleged absence of references to the passage in the early church fathers in the second and third centuries. However, several features characteristic of Matthew appear in this passage. These include repeated use of the divine passive and Matthew's favorite vocabulary.[15] Some are so subtle that it is unlikely that an ancient scribe would have spotted these features and been capable of imitating Matthew's style so well. The unanimous testimony of our ancient manuscripts and these stylistic features combine to build a case overwhelmingly in favor of the genuineness of these verses.[16]

Transcriptional Evidence

An examination of the transcriptional evidence considers scribal practices and the kinds of errors that scribes were most prone to make. Several different

---

13. Charles Quarles, "Matthew 27:52–53 as a Scribal Interpolation: Testing a Recent Proposal," *BBR* 27, no. 2 (2017): 75.

14. Craig A. Evans, *Matthew*, NCBC (Cambridge: Cambridge University Press, 2012), 466.

15. Charles L. Quarles, "Matthew 27:52–53: Meaning, Genre, Intertextuality, Theology, and Reception History," *JETS* 59 (2016): 271–86.

16. Quarles, "Matthew 27:52–53 as a Scribal Interpolation," 57–76.

kinds of errors of sight, hearing, and memory were discussed in Question 3. One of the most common errors that scribes made was haplography (an accidental skip in the text). This error usually resulted from parablepsis ("looking from one side [to the other]"). As a scribe's focus shifted from the exemplar to the copy and then back to the exemplar, their gaze sometimes landed on the same word or series of letters that was previously copied but at a different place in the exemplar. This was an especially easy mistake to make in instances of homoeoteleuton ("similar ending of lines"). One of the clearest examples of haplography due to parablepsis in a case of homoeoteleuton (isn't that a mouthful) is the very odd reading in Codex Vaticanus at John 17:15: "I am not praying that you take them from the evil one."[17] Other texts read: "I am not praying that you take them from the world, but [I am praying] that you keep them from the evil one." Notice that the verse contains two instances of the construction "them from the" (αὐτοὺς ἐκ τοῦ). After copying "I am not praying that you take them from the . . . ," the scribe's eyes jumped from the first "them from the" to the second, resulting in the accidental omission of the second occurrence of the construction and all the words that appeared in between ("the world, but that you keep them from the"). We will see in a moment that a generally recognized rule of textual criticism is "the shorter reading is to be preferred." However, one clear exception to this is in cases in which accidental omission due to homoeoteleuton may have occurred.

Scholars have developed several general guidelines for making text-critical decisions. Here are a few of the more helpful principles:

- **The reading more difficult for the scribe is to be preferred.** This principle stems from the pattern that scribes generally tried to remove difficulties from the text rather than create them. John Albrecht Bengel suggested this principle in 1734 and has been affirmed by most textual critics ever since. It must, however, be properly qualified since it does not mean that one should prefer readings that are so difficult as to be practically impossible. We discussed "nonsense" readings that are automatically dismissed in Question 6. In instances in which variants result from the intentional scribal change, the original reading is most often the one that is difficult on the surface but, after all factors are considered, makes perfect sense.
- **The reading unlike parallel passages is to be preferred.** Scribes tended to make parallels more alike rather than dissimilar.
- **The reading that includes rarer vocabulary and awkward grammar should be preferred.** Scribes sometimes smoothed out the text in hopes of helping the reader better understand its message.

---

17. See Metzger and Ehrman, *The Text of the New Testament*, 253.

- **The reading that best explains the appearance of the other variants is to be preferred.** Many text critics since Constantine Tischendorf have argued that this is the most important principle. The reading that seems to be the common denominator in other readings is a strong candidate for the original reading. For example, in Questions 3 and 5, we looked briefly at the major variant unit in 1 Timothy 3:16 that has three possible readings: ὅς, θεός, and ὅ. We can explain how both "God" (θεός) and "which" (ὅ) could be directly derived from "who" (ὅς). In majuscule script, the OC (who) closely resembled the nomen sacrum ΘC ("God"). And the masculine relative pronoun ὅς could have been changed to the neuter relative ὅ by a scribe who thought that the intended antecedent was the neuter noun "mystery" (μυστήριον). But θεός could not have been directly derived from ὅ or vice versa. We can diagram the possible development of the variants thusly:

"Who"	"God"	"Which"
ὅς	θεός	ὅ

Since the variant "who" seems to be the direct source of the other variants, it is probably the original reading.

Not a Mechanical Approach

Although laying out these steps might help readers grasp important elements of the text-critical method, it runs the risk of giving the impression that the process of making text-critical decisions is mechanical. However, when they seek to follow the steps, they will often find that some steps do not really apply in certain situations. They will also find that many textual problems are unique and require a unique approach. In some cases, external evidence will be decisive. In others, internal evidence will be decisive. In still others, the balance of both categories of evidence will be key. Sometimes evidence not directly related to any of the steps above will be vital.[18]

---

18. Elsewhere I argue that evidence from the Eusebian apparatus is a critical factor in restoring the original text. The apparatus in manuscripts of Matthew demonstrates that two major readings are of equal antiquity and that the shorter reading was intentionally created by

A. E. Housman wrote a famous essay on textual criticism in which he claimed that the most important tools for the task are "reason and common sense."[19] He insisted that textual criticism

> is not susceptible of hard-and-fast rules. It would be much easier if it were; and that is why people try to pretend that it is, or at least behave as if they thought so. Of course you can have hard-and-fast rules if you like, but then you will have false rules, and they will lead you wrong; because their simplicity will render them inapplicable to problems which are not simple, but complicated by the play of personality.[20]

He added that a textual critic seeking the original reading is "like a dog hunting for fleas. If a dog hunted for fleas on mathematical principles, basing his researches on statistics of area and population, he would never catch a flea except by accident. They require to be treated as individuals; and every problem which presents itself to the textual critic must be regarded as possibly unique."[21]

Summary

Reasoned eclectics do not follow a single text type but attempt to restore the original readings of the New Testament by selecting them from a variety of witnesses. Like thoroughgoing eclectics, they give attention to internal evidence. Internal evidence includes intrinsic evidence suggesting what the author was most likely to have written and transcriptional evidence suggesting what changes a scribe was most prone to make. Unlike thoroughgoing eclectics, reasoned eclectics also emphasize the importance of external evidence including the age, geographical distribution, general quality of texts as well as (sometimes) the text type to which they belong. However, reasoned eclecticism cannot be reduced to a mechanical process. The approach must often be adapted and expanded based on the uniqueness of a particular textual question.

---

scribes whose exemplars actually contained the longer reading (Quarles, "Matthew 16.2b–3," 234–37).

19. A. E. Housman, "The Application of Thought to Textual Criticism," *Proceedings of the Classical Association* 18 (1922): 67–84.
20. Housman, "The Application of Thought to Textual Criticism," 68.
21. Housman, "The Application of Thought to Textual Criticism," 69. See also the comments of Günther Zuntz, *The Text of the Epistles: A Disquisition upon the Corpus Paulinum* (London: Oxford University Press, 1953; repr. Eugene, OR: Wipf and Stock, 2007), 12–13.

REFLECTION QUESTIONS

1. In what sense are critical editions of the Greek New Testament "eclectic"?

2. What factors are considered in evaluating external evidence?

3. What factors are considered in evaluating intrinsic evidence?

4. What factors are considered in evaluating transcriptional evidence?

5. Why did Housman compare a text critic's search for the original reading to a dog hunting for fleas?

The Practice of Textual Criticism

What Are the Differences Between the Major Editions of the Greek NT Today?

G reek students often ask, "Which edition of the Greek New Testament is the best?" The answer to that question depends largely on the purpose for which the Greek New Testament will be used. The best option might be one edition if the purpose is devotional reading, another if the purpose is detailed exegesis, and still another if the purpose is detailed text-critical research. This chapter will introduce readers to recent editions of the Greek New Testament and their different apparatuses.

Nestle-Aland Edition

The origin of this edition may be traced back to 1898 when Eberhard Nestle first published his *Novum Testamentum Graece*. Nestle's approach was simple. The text was based on the three respected scholarly editions by Tischendorf, Westcott and Hort, and Weymouth (soon replaced by Weiss). If the editions differed, Nestle adopted the text agreed upon by two of these editions and relegated the minority reading to the apparatus. Beginning with the thirteenth edition (1927), Nestle's son Erwin added a critical apparatus that identified the readings from manuscripts, early versions, and quotations in the early church fathers. However, the apparatus was based on information derived from earlier critical editions and was not verified until the mid-1950s when Kurt Aland began checking the primary sources to correct errors in the apparatus.

With the twenty-sixth edition (1979), the editors abandoned the approach of largely following the readings supported by the majority of other critical editions. Instead, the editorial committee embraced the task of making its own text-critical decisions based on the members' evaluation of the internal and external evidence. The committee had access to a richer store of external evidence than was available to earlier editors, due to the discovery of early papyri and other manuscripts in the twentieth century.

The twenty-eighth edition was published in 2012. This edition contains the same text as the twenty-sixth and twenty-seventh editions except in the Catholic letters. The editors adopted the text established in the Editio Critica Maior (ECM) of the Catholic letters. The ECM was based on a new approach called the Coherence-Based Genealogical Method (see Question 20). The apparatus of the entire edition was corrected and revised in order to make it easier to use.

The apparatus of the NA[28] lists significantly more variants than any of the other current single-volume editions. The reading of all consistently cited witnesses is identified in the apparatus unless the witness has a lacuna or the reading is unclear at that point.[1] In order to keep the size of the edition manageable, the apparatus does not list all significant witnesses or all known variants. A task of such enormity is reserved for the ECM that will be a massive multivolume set.[2] The purpose of the Nestle-Aland text is primarily to provide the user with "the basis for studying the text and evaluating the most important variants."[3] Important variants have a positive apparatus (giving evidence supporting the reading in the text) and a negative apparatus (identifying other variant readings and their support). In cases in which the editors are confident that they have restored the initial text, but variant readings may be helpful for interpreting the text or understanding its history, only a negative apparatus appears.

In addition to important Greek manuscripts, the apparatus normally cites the evidence of the earliest versions that were made directly from the Greek text. These are the Latin, Syriac, and Coptic versions. Other versions like the Armenian, Georgian, Gothic, Ethiopic, and Old Church Slavonic versions are rarely cited and only when they are especially important for a particular reading. Quotations from the early church fathers are treated if they meet certain conditions. First, evidence must demonstrate that the writer intended to quote precisely the text available to him. Second, the source must belong to the eighth century or earlier. Third, evidence must indicate that the extant manuscripts of the patristic writing have not altered the original wording to conform it to the developing textual tradition.

The apparatus is more difficult to use than those in other handbook editions. The user must learn the meaning of and preferably memorize a handful of critical signs, pay special attention to the symbols that separate variant units and those that separate variants (| and ¦ respectively), and learn about a dozen

---

1. NA[28], 48*.
2. So far, the first four volumes have appeared: the gospel of Mark, Parallel Pericopes, the Catholic Letters, and Acts.
3. NA[28], 55*.

abbreviations (mostly Latin). The fonts used in the apparatus are significantly smaller than those used for the main text. Fortunately, the NA[28] is available in a large print edition, which is much easier on the eyes even though it is a bit more cumbersome to carry. Students may want to use the regular edition for classes and church but purchase the large print edition to keep on the desk for intensive study.

United Bible Society Edition

The United Bible Society edition was first published in 1965 in order to assist Bible translators throughout the world. Beginning with the third edition, the text has been essentially identical to the text used in the then-current NA edition (UBS[3]=NA[26]; UBS[4]=NA[27]; UBS[5]=NA[28]). The UBS[5] text is identical to the NA[28] except for some differences in punctuation and capitalization.

The editors stated that the purpose of the edition is "to enable its readers to read, understand, and translate the New Testament in its original language in as competent and skilled a manner as possible."[4] This edition treats approximately 1,438 variant units, significantly fewer than the NA[28]. However, the apparatus gives more evidence in a clearer format than the NA[28]. The apparatus gives the evidence of all papyri extant for a given passage. It gives the evidence of all majuscules belonging to categories I–IV of Aland's categorization (all categories except the Byzantine text).[5] Byzantine manuscripts as a group are identified with the abbreviation *Byz* rather than identifying them individually. All minuscules belonging to Aland's categories I and II (manuscripts of special importance for reconstructing the original New Testament) are included in the apparatus as well as ten manuscripts from category III.[6] Evidence is given in the following order: (1) papyri, (2) majuscules, (3) minuscules, and (4) lectionaries.

Unlike the NA[28] in which the evidence for the preferred reading is given last, the UBS[5] lists evidence for the preferred reading first (which is a more intuitive ordering). The UBS[5] gives more evidence from ancient versions: Latin, Syriac, Coptic, Armenian, Georgian, Ethiopic, and Old Church Slavonic. The UBS[5] also offers "as complete a survey as possible of the Fathers through the mid-fifth century, because the citations of these authors are of the greatest importance for reconstructing the original text of the New Testament."[7] The apparatus also identifies the variants on which the text of several English,

---

4. UBS[5], 1*.
5. See Kurt Aland and Barbara Aland, *The Text of the New Testament: An Introduction to the Critical Editions and to the Theory and Practice of Modern Textual Criticism*, trans. Erroll F. Rhodes, 2nd ed. (Grand Rapids: Eerdmans, 1989), 317–37.
6. No minuscules belong to category IV. Minuscules from category V are identified by the abbreviation *Byz*.
7. UBS[5], 37*.

French, Spanish, and German translations are based when these differ from the preferred text in the UBS[5] (although this is rare). The UBS[5] also includes a discourse segmentation apparatus.

Another important feature of the UBS[5] is the use of a grading system by which the editors express their degree of confidence in the variant selected for the text. The editors explain:

- The letter A indicates that the text is certain.
- The letter B indicates that the text is almost certain.
- The letter C, however, indicates that the Committee had difficulty in deciding which variant to place in the text.
- The letter D, which occurs only rarely, indicates that the Committee had great difficulty in arriving at a decision.

Additionally, the diamond ◊ is used to express the highest level of uncertainty. It appears in cases in which the Committee was unable to make a decision based on the evidence presently available. Additionally, double brackets ([ ]) surround lengthier readings that are widely recognized as later additions to the original text that have been important in the history of the church. This system enables the busy exegete to concentrate his efforts in establishing the text on the variant units about which other seasoned text critics have expressed the greatest doubt.

The table below compares the apparatus of the NA[28] with that of the UBS[5] on the variant unit in John 1:18, so readers can see the difference in detail. The material highlighted in the table appears in one apparatus but not the other.

Comparison of the Apparatuses for John 1:18
NA[28] — 18 ⸂ ο μονογενης θεος 𝔓[75] ℵ[1] 33; Cl[pt] Cl[exThd pt] Or[pt] ¦ ο μονογενης υιος A C[3] K Γ Δ Θ Ψ f[1.13] 565. 579. 700. 892. 1241. 1424 𝔐 lat sy[c.h]; Cl[pt] Cl[exThd pt] ¦ ει μη ο μονογενης υιος W[s] it; Ir[lat pt] (+ θεου Ir[lat pt]) ¦ *txt* 𝔓[66] ℵ* B C* L sy[p.hmg]; Or[pt] Did [8]

---

8.   Barbara Aland, Kurt Aland, Johannes Karavidopoulos, Carlo M. Martini, and Bruce M. Metzger, eds., *Nestle-Aland Novum Testamentum Graece*, 28th ed. (Stuttgart: Deutsche Bibelgesellschaft, 2012).

	Comparison of the Apparatuses for John 1:18
UBS[5]	{B} μονογενὴς θεός 𝔓[66] ℵ* B C* L syr[p, hmg] geo[2] Origen[gr 2/4] Didymus Cyril[1/4] // ὁ μονογενὴς θεός 𝔓[75] ℵ[2] 33 cop[bo] Clement[2/3] Clement[from Theodotus 1/2] Origen[gr 2/4] Eusebius[3/7] Basil[1/2] Gregory-Nyssa Epiphanius Serapion[1/2] Cyril[2/4] // ὁ μονογενὴς υἱός A C[3] W[supp] Δ Θ Ψ 0141 *f*[1] *f*[13] 28 157 180 205 565 579 597 700 892 1006 1010 1071 1241 1243 1292 1342 1424 1505 *Byz* [E F G H] *Lect* it[a, aur, b, c, e, f, ff2, 1] vg syr[c, h, pal] arm eth geo[1] slav Irenaeus[lat 1/3] Clement[from Theodotus 1/2] Clement[1/3] Hippolytus Origen[lat 1/2] Letter of Hymenaeus Alexander Eustathius Eusebius[4/7] Serapion[1/2] Athanasius Basil[1/2] Gregory-Nazianzus Chrysostom Theodore Cyril[1/4] Proclus Theodoret John-Damascus; Tertullian Hegemonius Victorinus-Rome Ambrosiaster Hilary[5/7] Ps-Priscillian Ambrose[10/11] Faustinus Gregory-Elvira Phoebadius Jerome Augustine Varimadum REB BJ // μονογενὴς υἱὸς θεοῦ it[q] Irenaeus[lat 1/3]; Ambrose[1/11vid] // ὁ μονογενής vg[ms] Ps-Vigilius[1/2] [9]

The NA[28] treats significantly more variant units. This variant unit is the thirteenth in the gospel of John to be treated in the NA[28], but only the fifth to be treated in the UBS[5]. On the other hand, the UBS[5] provides significantly more information regarding the readings of the minuscules, ancient versions, and church fathers (not only by listing more fathers but by providing more precise statistics on their various uses). In this case, it also lists one variant not mentioned in the NA[28] apparatus.[10]

The value of the UBS[5] is enhanced by a complementary volume that explains the basis for the textual decisions made by the Committee. This *Textual Commentary* will be discussed in greater detail in Question 17.

Society of Biblical Literature Edition

The Greek New Testament: SBL Edition (SBLGNT) was created primarily to make a recent critical text of the Greek New Testament widely available without cost. However, an equally important benefit of the edition was providing an alternative to what has become recognized as "the standard text," the text shared by the NA and UBS editions. The Preface states:

> The standard text is viewed by some of those who use it as a "final" text to be passively accepted rather than a "working"

---

9. Barbara Aland, Kurt Aland, Johannes Karavidopoulos, Carlo M. Martini, and Bruce Metzger, eds., *The Greek New Testament*, 5th rev. ed. (Stuttgart: Deutsche Bibelgesellschaft, 2014).

10. Note also the discrepancy between the two editions regarding the reading ὁ μονογενὴς θεός in Sinaiticus (ℵ). The NA[28] ascribes this reading to the first corrector, but the UBS[5] to the second corrector.

text subject to verification and improvement. For example, the exegetical habits of some scholars and students seem to reflect a belief that all the important text-critical work has already been completed, that one can more or less equate the standard Greek New Testament with the "original" text. With a mindset such as this, it is not surprising that entire commentaries have been written that simply take the standard text as printed and scarcely discuss textual matters.[11]

The SBLGNT serves, in part, to "remind readers of the Greek New Testament that the text-critical task is not finished."[12] This is a valuable and immensely important contribution. The production of alternative critical editions will hopefully prevent the standard text from becoming enshrined as a new "textus receptus" whose readings are no longer subject to challenge.

The text of the SBLGNT differs from the standard text in at least 540 variant units. The text compared the editions by Westcott and Hort, Samuel Tregelles, Robinson and Pierpont, and the Greek Text behind the New International Version. When all four editions agreed, the reading was tentatively accepted. However, the editor, Michael Holmes, carefully evaluated all readings. He chose readings not supported as the text in any of these editions for fifty-six variant units. Such readings are identified in the apparatus as "Holmes." The apparatus does not list Greek manuscripts, ancient versions, or early church fathers who support the various readings. Instead, it identifies the modern edition that supports a particular variant (NA, NIV, RP, TR, Treg, WH). The apparatus treats more than 6,900 variant units.

Tyndale House Edition

This recent edition (THGNT) "aims to present the New Testament books in the earliest form in which they are well attested."[13] The editors, Dirk Jongkind and Peter Williams, originally planned to produce a light revision of the edition produced in the nineteenth century by Samuel Prideaux Tregelles. Tregelles emphasized the oldest evidence in his effort to reconstruct the earliest attested form of the New Testament books. Likewise, except in cases in which this is unfeasible (such as the Book of Revelation for which few early manuscripts are extant), the editors have chosen readings that appear in multiple manuscripts of which at least one dates to the fifth century or earlier.

A significant number of manuscript discoveries have been made since the time of Tregelles. Reliance on the 137 papyri and other finds resulted in such thorough changes to Tregelles's edition that the planned revision soon

---

11. SBLGNT, vii–viii.
12. SBLGNT, viii.
13. THGNT, vii.

became a completely new edition. These early witnesses have enabled scholars to analyze early scribal habits to a degree not possible in Tregelles's era.

This new knowledge about early scribal habits led the editors to prioritize transcriptional evidence in making text-critical decisions. However, rather than merely considering scribal tendencies in general, the editors attempted to keep in mind the tendencies of the individual scribes who produced particular manuscripts. They explained: "The observation of general scribal habits needs to be informed by the study of the tendencies of individual manuscripts or groupings of related manuscripts."[14]

The apparatus is relatively brief since the editors saw the text itself rather than the apparatus as the edition's most important contribution. The apparatus was primarily intended to show the basis for the editors' textual decisions. Since the edition emphasizes "directly verified antiquity," that is, the readings of the earliest extant manuscripts, the apparatus focuses on the evidence of the papyri and the majuscules. The apparatus identifies several kinds of variants:

1. Variants that were in the eyes of the editors extremely close contenders for consideration for the main text. In some cases, the editors were in doubt as to the correct decision. These are marked by a diamond.
2. Variants that have high exegetical importance.
3. Select variants that illustrate scribal habits.[15]

Jongkind has written *An Introduction to the Greek New Testament* that extensively explains the method employed in making textual decisions.[16] The editors have also promised a future textual commentary that will explain the rationale for individual textual decisions.

Summary

The recent publication of two new critical editions of the Greek New Testament will hopefully prevent assumptions that the text of the NA/UBS is to be equated with the original text and that no serious text-critical work remains to be done. However, of the four recent editions, the NA treats many more variant units than any other, and the UBS, though it restricts the number of variant units it treats, supplies significantly more evidence for the various readings. These two editions will remain the most important "hand editions" for text-critical research.

---

14. THGNT, 507.
15. THGNT, 515.
16. Dirk Jongkind, *An Introduction to the Greek New Testament* (Wheaton, IL: Crossway, 2019).

REFLECTION QUESTIONS

1. What are the strengths and weaknesses of the NA[28] as a tool for textual criticism?

2. What are the strengths and weaknesses of the UBS[5] as a tool for textual criticism?

3. What are the strengths and weaknesses of the SBLGNT as a tool for textual criticism?

4. What are the strengths and weaknesses of the THGNT as a tool for textual criticism?

5. How is the NA[28] different from the original Nestle edition?

What Are the Most Helpful Tools for Studying Textual Differences?

In addition to the critical hardcopy editions of the Greek New Testament, scholars have a wealth of other resources to assist them in making text-critical decisions. What are these tools, and how do they assist in the restoration of the original Greek New Testament?

Textual Commentaries

A textual commentary is a helpful supplement to a critical apparatus. Although the critical apparatus usually lists important witnesses that support specific variants, a textual commentary explains the reasons that the editors evaluated the various readings as they did and why they concluded that a specific reading was original.

Bruce Metzger wrote the commentary that complements the UBS edition (though the most recent edition of the commentary is based on the fourth edition of the UBS rather than the fifth).[1] He based the commentary on the voting record of the committee members and thorough notes from the committee's deliberations. In cases in which a member strongly disagreed with the committee's final decision, the commentary explains the reasons for the member's dissent and even identifies him by his initials.

In addition to the variant units treated in the UBS[4], the commentary treats about six hundred other variant units. Most of these are from Acts since this book poses special challenges to the textual critic. The textual commentary

---

1. Bruce Metzger, *A Textual Commentary on the Greek New Testament*, 2nd ed. (Stuttgart: Deutsche Bibelgesellschaft, 1994). Perhaps a note here on Roger L. Omanson's adaptation and partial revision of Metzger's work would be useful? Roger L. Omanson, *A Textual Guide to the Greek New Testament: An Adaptation of Bruce M. Metzger's "Textual Commentary" for the Needs of Translators* (Stuttgart: Deutsche Bibelgesellschaft, 2006).

has a very helpful introduction that summarizes the criteria used to make textual decisions, describes the major text types, and gives a panoramic view of the history of the transmission of the New Testament text.

Philip Comfort has also written a helpful textual commentary that contains more detailed descriptions of important New Testament manuscripts and contains a discussion of *nomina sacra* (sacred names) that early scribes often wrote in a special way.[2] Both commentaries are invaluable tools. Most introductions to New Testament textual criticism explain the methodology of reasoned eclecticism in detail but give relatively few examples of the application of that method. Metzger's textual commentary gives over two thousand explanations of the decisions of some of the world's most respected textual critics as they attempted to restore the original text. Thus, these tools are not only helpful reference tools that should be consulted on a particular variant unit, but reading through these commentaries enables students to learn the methodology of reasoned eclecticism by following the model of skilled mentors.

Editio Critica Maior

The goal of the ECM is to provide "the full range of resources necessary for scholarly research in establishing the text and reconstructing the history of the New Testament text during its first thousand years."[3] The volume on Acts presents all the variants that appear in the 183 manuscripts selected for the edition. It also includes variants that appear in the citations by the Greek church fathers. The ECM presents the evidence for variants from the four most significant early versions, the Latin, Coptic, Syriac, and Ethiopic, as well as evidence from the Armenian, Georgian, and Old Church Slavonic versions where these exist in reliable editions. The ECM includes supplementary studies that explain textual decisions, describe the textual character of the manuscripts of the book or corpus, and explain the role of the text of each manuscript in the transmission of the New Testament text.

Since most textual variations involve only a few manuscripts, the ECM often presents only a negative apparatus. A negative apparatus only lists witnesses that differ from the reading in the base text. A positive apparatus, which presents complete evidence for the base text, is offered only when fifteen or more witnesses differ from the base text.

The ECM offers the most detailed evidence from the largest number of witnesses currently available in any critical edition. The primary line text

2. Philip Comfort, *A Commentary on the Manuscripts and Text of the New Testament* (Grand Rapids: Kregel, 2015).
3. Holger Strutwolf, Georg Gäbel, Annette Hüffmeier, Gerd Mink, and Klaus Wachtel, eds. *Acts of the Apostles*, vol. 3 of *Novum Testamentum Graecum: Editio Critica Maior* (Stuttgart: Deutsche Bibelgesellschaft, 2017), 1.1:18*.

of the ECM was established using a new approach called the Coherence-Based Genealogical Method. This method is discussed in Question 20. The volumes on Mark, Acts, the Catholic Epistles, and selected parallel pericopes in the Synoptic gospels are currently available. When complete, the ECM will comprise six volumes:[4] I. Synoptic gospels; II. gospel of John; III. Acts; IV. Catholic Letters; V. Pauline Letters; and VI. John's Apocalypse. The order of the volumes is based on the order of the books in most Greek manuscripts.

CNTTS Apparatus

The Center for New Testament Textual Studies (CNTTS) at New Orleans Baptist Theological Seminary has developed an extensive critical apparatus. Although the apparatus was based on information gleaned from other critical editions, the CNTTS has committed to verifying the information drawn from other works by collations of ancient texts by members of the CNTTS research team. The most recent update of the database contained more than twenty thousand pages. Thus, this apparatus is currently more thorough than any printed apparatus on the entire New Testament.[5]

The apparatus is packed with helpful information, more than can be summarized here. For example, it classifies different types of variants. It indicates whether a particular variant is or is not helpful for tracing relationships to other texts. It also identifies the variant as an addition, omission, replacement, transposition, or a nonsense reading, and whether it may have resulted from homoeoteleuton (confusion due to similar endings of lines or words) or homoeoarcton (confusion due to similar beginnings of lines or words). Best of all, the database is fully searchable. For example, a simple search can locate all examples of nonsense readings.

The digital apparatus has other very helpful features. Although a user of the critical hardcopy editions must flip back to the front matter to see details about the various witnesses in the apparatus, simply placing the cursor over a witness in the CNTTS apparatus will immediately open a window giving important details about the witness such as the witness's siglum, Gregory-Aland number, probable date, current location, Aland category, and text type. If the reading is a scribal correction, the note identifies the approximate time that the correction was made. Unless the user has all of these details memorized, this feature can help save time in researching text-critical issues.

---

4. Each of these volumes is, in fact, a multivolume work. For example, the "volume" on Acts consists of four large volumes.
5. Only volumes on individual New Testament books or sections of the New Testament in series like the Editio Critica Maior and the International Greek New Testament Project have more extensive apparatuses.

Institute for New Testament Textual Research Website

The website of the Institut für Neutestamentliche Textforschung (INTF)[6] offers free online utilities that are indispensable for advanced text-critical research. Users can access the Kurzgefasste Liste, the official registry of known New Testament manuscripts. The online list often includes recent discoveries that may not appear in print editions. The website also provides tools that enable users to see how closely related texts are for the New Testament books and corpora already treated in existing volumes of the ECM.[7] Users who wish to consult transcriptions or images of New Testament manuscripts may do so in the NTVMR (NT virtual manuscript room). Some of the available images are high-resolution color images, though some are from black-and-white microfilm. The VMR is continually improving and more resources are being constantly added. The VMR provides tools for transcribing and indexing texts and access to the rich store of information in the Amsterdam Database of New Testament Conjectural Emendation.[8] The VMR has enabled scholars without direct access to manuscripts to make important contributions to the field of textual criticism. Due to the willingness of the INTF to make their resources widely available, anyone with the necessary skills and an internet connection can engage in textual research.

Center for the Study of New Testament Manuscripts Website

The Center for the Study of New Testament Manuscripts[9] makes high-resolution digital photographs of the extant manuscripts of the Greek New Testament, so these can be preserved and made available to scholars doing textual research around the world. Although images of many New Testament manuscripts from black-and-white microfilms are available elsewhere, many of these are difficult to read and features such as erasures and corrections may be impossible to spot. The photographs of manuscripts available through CSNTM are far clearer and more legible. Users can also access images of old books that are important for textual research such as the editions of the Greek New Testament by Erasmus, Robertus Stephanus, Theodore Beza, John Mill, Samuel Tregelles, and Hermann Freiherr von Soden.

Summary

Many new digital resources are available that have the potential to revolutionize New Testament textual criticism. In just seconds from the comfort of their offices, twenty-first-century researchers can access resources

---

6. http://egora.uni-muenster.de/intf/index_en.shtml.
7. These tools are associated with the links to "Genealogical Queries" and "Manuscript Clusters."
8. https://ntvmr.uni-muenster.de/nt-conjectures.
9. www.csntm.org.

that previous generations of scholars could only access by traveling across the world to hundreds of different libraries. Now anyone who desires to contribute to the task of improving our editions of the Greek New Testament has the necessary resources at their fingertips.

REFLECTION QUESTIONS

1. Which of the tools discussed provides the most detailed apparatus for the Book of Acts?

2. Which of the tools discussed provides the most detailed apparatus for the Gospels and the Epistles of Paul?

3. Which of the tools best explains the reasoning behind the textual decisions in the UBS Greek New Testament?

4. Which tools offer high-resolution color photographs of many important New Testament manuscripts?

5. Which tool enables users to determine how closely the texts of many manuscripts are related to each other in certain New Testament books?

Should the Ending of Mark (16:9–20) Be Included in Our Bibles?

One of the best known, lengthiest, and most difficult textual questions relates to the ending of the gospel of Mark. Four different major variants appear in the ancient Greek manuscripts and early versions.

- **Short ending**—Two of the earliest manuscripts end the gospel with Mark 16:8.

- **Longer ending**—The vast majority of manuscripts add Mark 16:9–20.

- **Intermediate ending**—Eight other manuscripts preface the longer ending with these words: "And they briefly announced all the things that they were commanded to those who were around Peter. And after these things, Jesus himself sent out through them, from the east and to the west, the holy and incorruptible proclamation of eternal salvation. Amen."

- **Longer ending plus the Freer logion**—Finally, one early Greek manuscript inserts additional material in the longer ending (between 16:14 and 15).

This discussion will examine some aspects of the external and internal evidence for the various options using reasoned eclecticism.

External Evidence

Date of the Readings

The two oldest manuscripts of the Greek New Testament that contain the entire gospel of Mark are Codex Vaticanus and Codex Sinaiticus. Both manuscripts (as well as twelfth-century minuscule 304) end the gospel with Mark 16:8.[1] The only manuscript to contain the intermediate reading (without the longer reading) is a manuscript of the Old Latin text (*k*, Codex Bobbiensis). However, the intermediate ending also appears in a marginal note on one manuscript of the Harclean version of the Syriac translation. The oldest extant manuscripts to include the longer reading are A, C, D, and W, which all date to the fifth or sixth century. The oldest manuscript to contain the combination ending is 083 (sixth or seventh century).[2] The only Greek manuscript to insert the additional material (called the Freer logion) between 16:14 and 15 is W (fifth century).[3] However, Jerome claimed that this additional material was found "especially in Greek manuscripts" (*Against Pelagius*, 2.15).

Both Eusebius of Caesarea (early fourth century)[4] and Jerome (early fifth century)[5] state that nearly all copies of Mark available to them, including the most accurate copies, ended at 16:8. This would be straightforward evidence for the greater antiquity of the short ending except for a significantly earlier reference to the longer reading in Mark by Irenaeus (*Against Heresies* 3.10.5;

---

1. The scribe who copied Mark in Vaticanus may have been aware of the existence of the longer ending. This could explain why he left an entire column blank at the end of Mark rather than beginning the next book at the top of the very next column as he does throughout the entire NT. Although similar gaps appear after Nehemiah, Daniel, and Tobit, good reasons exist for the blank column in all three cases. See the explanations offered in James Snapp, Jr., *Authentic: The Case for Mark 16:9–20* (n.p., 2022), 8–9. For differing opinions on this, compare J. Keith Elliott, "The Last Twelve Verses of Mark: Original or Not?," in *Perspectives on the Ending of Mark: Four Views*, ed. David Alan Black (Nashville: B&H Academic, 2008), 83, to Daniel B. Wallace, "Mark 16:8 as the Conclusion to the Second Gospel," in *Perspectives on the Ending of Mark*, 16–18. The text of the ending of Mark in Sinaiticus is on a replacement leaf in which scribe D (probably the scribe who supervised the copying process) has replaced the work of scribe A with his own work. Scribe D was probably aware of the longer ending, but chose not to include it. See Elliott, "Last Twelve Verses of Mark," in *Perspectives on the Ending of Mark*, 84–85.
2. The combined ending also appears in 019, 044, 099, 579, 2937, 1422, and *l*1602. Two catena manuscripts, 1422 and 2937 include the shorter ending and contain passages discussing the presence of the longer ending in some manuscripts. See the Virtual Research Environment of the MARK16 Project (https://mark16.sib.swiss).
3. The Freer logion consists of an additional eighty-eight words.
4. *Quaestiones Ad Marinum* 1.1. Eusebius stated that "more or less all the copies" (σχεδὸν ἐν ἅπασι τοῖς ἀντιγράφοις) lacked the longer ending. For the Greek text and an English translation, see Roger Pearse, ed., *Eusebius: Gospel Problems and Solutions* (Ipswich: Chieftain, 2010), 96–97.
5. Jerome's comment is largely borrowed from Eusebius, but his knowledge of manuscripts apparently led him to agree with Eusebius's earlier observation.

late second century) and the probability that the copy of Mark used by Tatian in his Diatessaron around 170 contained the longer ending.[6] One might conclude that the longer reading predates the short ending by more than a century. However, the situation is a bit more complicated.

The only evidence that one would expect in this early period for the short ending is silence regarding the content of 16:9–20. However, failure to refer to the longer ending does not necessarily mean that a writer was unaware of the longer ending. Clement of Alexandria, for example, never quotes or clearly alludes to Mark 16:9–20. On the other hand, he seldom quotes other portions of Mark so there is no reason to expect him to cite the longer ending, even if his copy contained it. Origen's silence may be more telling. By a direct appeal to the details of Mark 16:9, Origen could have forcefully and persuasively rebutted one of Celsus's specific objections to the resurrection of Jesus.[7] Origen's failure to appeal to Mark 16:9 in response to Celsus's argument suggests that Origen's text of Mark ended at 16:8 and he was not aware of the longer ending.[8]

An argument from silence is necessarily weak but, in this case, the argument should not be flippantly dismissed because such silence is the only evidence that can be offered to support the absence of a particular passage from the text of a writer who was unaware of an alternative reading.[9] In any event, the fact that Vaticanus, Sinaiticus, and the many manuscripts referred to by Eusebius supported the short ending suggests that the reading can be traced back to the time of Irenaeus since the reading was so widespread by the early third century. Thus, most scholars are convinced that the short ending and the longer ending both existed in the second century.

Some scholars have claimed that some manuscripts (e.g., 137, 138, 264, 1221, 2346, 2812) that contain the longer reading mark this reading with asterisks or obeli to express their opinion that the reading was a scribal

---

6. Robert Stein wrote, "The early attestation of this ending (*Epistle of the Apostles* 9–10 [mid-2nd century]; Tatian's *Diatessaron*; Irenaeus, *Adv. Haer.* 3.10.5; possibly Justin Martyr, Apology 1:45) suggests that the longer ending was composed early in the 2nd century" ("The Ending of Mark," *BBR* 18 [2008]: 82). However, the modest amount of parallel material between the longer ending and the Ep. Apos. and Justin's *1 Apol.* is not sufficient to argue confidently that these sources were familiar with the longer ending. The lost text of the *Diatessaron* is notoriously difficult to reconstruct from the extant resources. Nevertheless, it is highly probable that Tatian used a copy of Mark that contained the longer ending when he produced his harmony around AD 170.
7. Origen, *Against Celsus*, 2.60.
8. Snapp suggests that Origen shows awareness of the longer ending of Mark in *Philocalia* 5 (*Authentic*, 58–59). However, the parallels between the two texts seem far too weak to substantiate this suggestion.
9. For a similar observation, see David Parker, *The Living Text of the Gospels* (Cambridge: Cambridge University Press, 2006), 136–37.

addition.[10] However, these scholars apparently misunderstood the purpose of these marks. These marks (at least in these specific manuscripts) either serve to refer to a note in the margin[11] or to signal a new lectionary reading.[12] The notes in 137, 138, and 2812 associated with the mark are drawn from the explanation for the inclusion of the longer reading in Victor of Antioch's commentary on Mark. The note explains that although the longer reading is absent in most copies (since some scribes thought the passage to be spurious), the *majority* of *accurate* copies (judged by their resemblance to a Palestinian exemplar) include the passage.[13] In other words, the symbols denote the very opposite of what some scholars have claimed!

A small cluster of about a dozen manuscripts (mainly in family 1) add a note after Mark 16:8 which says, in its fullest form: "In some of the copies, the evangelist finishes here, and so does the canon list of Eusebius of Pamphilius. But in many manuscripts, these things are also contained."[14] Three of the manuscripts (20, 215, 300) add a final sentence to the note stating, "But in the ancient manuscripts, it all appears intact."

Geographical Distribution

A few manuscripts of the earliest versions support the 16:8 ending. One Sahidic Coptic manuscript (sa 1 [fifth century), one Old Syriac manuscript (Syrus Sinaiticus [third or fourth century]), and the Armenian version of Mark end at 16:8. Interestingly, some of the Armenian manuscripts contain the longer reading but place it at the end of Luke or of John, suggesting that this portion of narrative circulated independently of the gospel of Mark.[15] Most scholars recognize the Old Latin version preserved by Codex Bobbiensis

---

10. Metzger, *Textual Commentary*, 103; Dan Wallace, "Mark 16:8 as the Conclusion to the Second Gospel," 26.
11. Sometimes the associated commentary is a page or two after the related text so the special mark was very important for signaling the connection.
12. The sigla in 264, 1221, and 2346 are clearly lectionary markers. The work of James Snapp was particularly helpful in examining these marks. I verified his claims by consulting photographs of the pertinent manuscripts.
13. For a translation and critical text of the scribal note, see John W. Burgon, *The Last Twelve Verses of the Gospel according to Mark Vindicated against Recent Critical Objectors and Established* (Oxford: James Parker, 1871), 65, 288–90. My understanding of the note is slightly different from Burgon's since I treat the adjective πλεῖστος as superlative rather than elative.
14. In minuscule 1, the text of Mark ends at 16:8 and the longer ending appears in the form of an appendix. Similarly, in 1582, the use of a line of decorative marks indicates that the gospel ends after 16:8. This formal ending is followed by the scribal note and 16:9–20. However, other manuscripts in family 1 (118 and 131) lack the note and treat the longer ending as part of the gospel of Mark.
15. Ernest C. Colwell, "Mark 16.9–20 in the Armenian Version," *JBL* 55 (1937): 369–86.

(*k*; [fourth century])[16] as a witness to the short ending too since its intermediate ending was clearly added by someone who felt that the 16:8 ending was inadequate but who was either unaware of or rejected the authenticity of the longer ending (16:9–20). Although another Old Latin manuscript, Codex Vercellensis (*a* [fourth century]) is missing the leaf that contained the ending of Mark, the missing portion probably did not have sufficient space for the longer ending.[17] The original text of Mark in this MS probably either ended at 16:8 or had the intermediate ending like Bobbiensis.

Strong versional evidence supports the longer ending as well. However, the manuscripts of these versions are generally later than those supporting the Mark 16:8 ending. Several Sahidic Coptic (357L),[18] Syriac (Peshitta [fifth century] and Harklean [early seventh century] versions), and Old Latin manuscripts (*aur* [late eighth century], *c* [twelfth century], *l* [eighth century], *n* [fifth century], *q* [sixth or seventh century]) include the longer ending (or portions of it). The versional evidence shows that both the 16:8 ending and the longer ending were early and widely distributed even in the earliest period, but provides some modest evidence that the 16:8 ending is earlier.

The external evidence supporting the intermediate ending, the combination ending, and the Freer logion is weak. The short ending and the longer ending are the most likely candidates for the original reading. Thus, the exploration of internal evidence will focus mainly on these two options.

Internal Evidence

Transcriptional Probability

Textual critics have long held that scribes were more likely to add material than to omit it. Recent research has served to challenge this principle by pointing out important exceptions. However, these exceptions are usually cases of accidental omission of text rather than intentional omission. Some early Christians were so afraid of potentially rejecting inspired truth that, when they encountered several possible readings, they tended to accept them all. Eusebius referred to those who adopted that approach to the ending of Mark.[19] Scribes were aware of the short ending found in some manuscripts

---

16. J.-C. Haelewyck, the editor of the critical edition of the Old Latin text of Mark, considers Bobbiensis to preserve the oldest form of the Latin text. See Holger Strutwolf et al., eds., *The Gospel According to Mark*, ECM 1.2/2, 58.

17. C. H. Turner, "Did Codex Vercellensis (*a*) Contain the Last Twelve Verses of St Mark?" *JTS* 29 (1927–28): 16–18.

18. Several other Sahidic Coptic manuscripts (9, 14La, 102v, 121v, 474) combine the intermediate and longer endings. The longer ending is also supported by 15L, 134, and 333L.

19. In *Ad Marinus* 1.1, Eusebius explained that some readers of Mark would reject the long ending that was absent from "almost all copies" as "extraneous" and "superfluous." However, he added (1.2): "Another view, from someone diffident about athetizing [rejecting as

and the longer ending found in others and decided to include the longer ending, often with a marginal note mentioning the differences in the manuscripts known to them. This is clearly the option chosen by the scribes who ended the gospel with Mark 16:8 and then added the long ending as an appendix (1, 1582). This also appears to have been the approach of the scribes who produced the family 1 MSS that introduce the longer ending with the shorter form of the scribal note. The shorter form of the note mentioned the differences in the manuscripts of Mark without defending the greater antiquity of the longer reading.

Although some scholars have suggested that scribes intentionally omitted 16:9–20 because of a perceived contradiction with other resurrection accounts in the Gospels, this is unlikely. Eusebius shows that the resurrection accounts can be reconciled. Although he mentions that some dismiss 16:9–20, the primary reason was its absence in the vast majority of manuscripts. Perceived contradiction with the other Gospels was only additional evidence that the account was not authentic. Furthermore, the text that some had trouble reconciling to the others was really Matthew 28:1, a text misunderstood by some as implying that Jesus rose "on the evening of the Sabbath" rather than "after the Sabbath." If Matthew 28:1 contradicts Mark 16:9, it would also contradict Luke 24:1 and John 20:1. Thus, dispensing with Mark 16:9 would not fix the supposed discrepancy. The best way to resolve the apparent (and it was merely apparent) contradiction was to change Matthew 28:1, but no known texts make the necessary clarification to the ὀψέ in Matthew.[20]

Others have suggested that scribes objected to elements of the longer ending such as the references to casting out demons, speaking in tongues, taking up serpents and drinking poison unharmed, healing the sick, and confirming the gospel through miracles, and this prompted them to delete the passage. This suggestion has not been supported by evidence. First, scribes could easily omit only verses 16 and 17, which contained the objectionable content, and retain the rest of the passage so that the resurrection appearances and commissioning of the disciples were preserved. Second, the very portion of the longer ending that modern scholars find objectionable seems to have been the favorite part of the early church fathers. Quotations of the longer reading frequently come from those very verses! Vincentius referred approvingly to 16:15–18 in 256. The Acts of Pilate quoted 16:15–18. Aphrahat

---

spurious] anything at all in the text of the gospels, however transmitted, is that there is a twofold reading, as in many other places, and that both are to be accepted; it is not for the faithful and devout to judge either as acceptable in preference to the other" (Pearse, *Eusebius of Caesarea, Gospel Problems and Solutions*, 99).

20. A few MSS (L Δ and several minuscules) change the σαββάτων (gen. pl.) to σαββάτῳ (dat. sg.) but this heightens the problem. The dative would apparently be an example of a dative of time so that the construction ὀψέ σαββάτῳ would mean "late on the Sabbath" or "in the evening on the Sabbath."

quoted 16:16–18 in a sermon in 337. The Apostolic Constitutions quoted 16:17–18 in 380. Scholars defending the longer ending are unable to point to a single ancient author who specifically objects to the content of these verses.

Scribes appear to have had a tendency to add the longer ending. This becomes most apparent in manuscripts L (eighth century), Ψ (ninth or tenth century), 099 (seventh century), and 083 (sixth or seventh century). In these manuscripts, the longer ending follows the intermediate ending. The two endings clearly arose independently of each other since earlier witnesses have one reading or the other rather than both, and because the endings seem contradictory.

Wallace has pointed out that manuscripts that include both the longer and intermediate ending consistently place the longer ending after the intermediate ending even though this creates tension in the narrative. The tension emerges since, in the intermediate ending, Mary announces Jesus's resurrection to the disciples and the resurrected Jesus commissions them to proclaim the gospel from the East to the West. However, in the longer ending, Mary announces Jesus's resurrection to the disciples, but they respond with disbelief. Wallace correctly observes that the two endings would make more sense if the intermediate ending followed the longer one and served as a concluding summary.[21] Oddly, no witnesses use this approach. This suggests a scenario in which the gospel of Mark originally circulated with the short ending, then scribes added the intermediate ending, then others later added the longer ending which they found in other manuscripts.

Since the intermediate ending is an obvious attempt by later scribes to supply an appropriate ending to 16:8, these manuscripts can be taken as lending support to the 16:8 ending. These manuscripts show that, in some cases, scribes added the longer ending when copying an exemplar that lacked it. If this occurred with texts containing the intermediate ending despite the tension it introduced, it likely occurred even more frequently for exemplars that ended at 16:8.

Intrinsic Probability

Scholars have noted several problems that raise doubts that Mark wrote 16:9–20 as the conclusion of his gospel. First, the narrative in 16:9–20 does not seem to flow from the preceding narrative. It seems odd that Mary Magdalene should be formally introduced by Mark in what amounts to the *last* reference to her in his gospel. Mary Magdalene was explicitly mentioned in 15:40, 47; and 16:1. However, only in 16:9 is the reader informed that this was the woman from whom Jesus cast out seven demons. By contrast, Luke shares this detail about Mary Magdalene, as one would expect, in his *first* mention of her in Luke 8:2. This seems to imply that the longer ending was created by

---

21. Wallace, "Mark 16:8 as the Conclusion to the Second Gospel," 25–26.

someone familiar with Luke 8:2 and then added to Mark's gospel. Similarly, Mark 16:7 (and 14:28) sets the reader up for appearances of the resurrected Jesus in Galilee. However, the appearances that are described in 16:9–20 all occurred in Jerusalem or its vicinity.

Second, the longer ending contains some linguistic features that are not found elsewhere in Mark's gospel. For example, the verb θεάομαι is used twice in the longer ending (16:11, 14) but nowhere else in Mark. Mark prefers other verbs for sight such as ὁράω (50x), βλέπω (15x), and θεωράω (7x). Mark 16:12 uses the adjective ἕτερος, its only occurrence in Mark. The use of ὕστερον in Mark 16:14 has no parallel elsewhere in this gospel. Other *hapax legomena* (words not used elsewhere in Mark) include πενθέω, μορφή, ἕνδεκα, παρακολουθέω, ὄφις, θανάσιμος, βλάπτω, ἀναλαμβάνω, συνεργέω, βεβαιόω, and ἐπακολουθέω.[22]

More importantly, other words appear elsewhere in Mark but always with a different sense. For example, Mark used the noun κτίσις in 10:6 and 13:19. In both those instances, however, the noun refers to the act of creation rather than to a "creature," a "created being" as in 16:15. The unusual features include grammatical issues too. For example, Mark 16:14 is the only passage in the New Testament in which a characteristic ("their unbelief and hardness of heart") is rebuked. Although Mark 15:32 also uses the verb "rebuke" (ὀνειδίζω), a person rather than a characteristic or action is the object of the rebuke. Although Mark uses ἅπας three times in his gospel (1:27; 8:25; 11:32), each of these occurrences function as a substantive (instead of modifying a noun). Only in 16:15, does the word function as an adjective. Mark strongly prefers πᾶς as an adjective (29x). Mark 13:10 contains a statement similar in sense to 16:15 but uses different vocabulary and grammar. Mark does not elsewhere use the expression ἔχω καλῶς (16:18) to refer to healing even though he records numerous healing miracles.[23] The combined title and name "the Lord Jesus" does not appear in Mark outside of 16:19 either. Although none of these examples by themselves would necessarily preclude Markan authorship of the passage, the frequency of non-Markan expressions in the passage builds a strong cumulative case that Mark 16:9–20 was not the original ending of this gospel or penned by the same evangelist who wrote Mark 1:1–16:8. Wallace stated bluntly: "There is not a single passage in Mark

---

22. Admittedly, the concentration of *hapax legomena* in these verses is not high enough to preclude Markan authorship. Mark contains 635 *hapax legomena* in its 353 verses, an average of approximately 1.8 per verse or 5.6 per one hundred words. However, the *hapax legomena* are not evenly distributed and some portions of the gospel have concentrations almost as high as 16:9–20. The concentration of *hapax legomena* in the intermediate ending, however, does seem to preclude Markan authorship. That ending contains ten *hapax legomena* in a single verse.

23. The use of the verb ἔχω to refer to one's health condition is characteristic of Matthew (4:24; 8:16; 9:12), not Mark.

1:1–16:8 comparable to the stylistic, grammatical, and lexical anomalies in 16:9–20."[24]

Not all of the supposed differences from the Markan style are as persuasive as the examples above. For example, among the "most important features that are peculiar to the longer ending or are alien to Mark 1:4–16:8," Elliott lists the use of σημεῖα in 16:17, 20. He claims that the plural form of this noun is "not found in Mark in the sense of miracles or wonders."[25] This is puzzling since σημεῖα appears in Mark 13:22 to refer to miraculous signs, and the singular form appears another four times (8:11, 12 [2x]; 13:4). He also claims that ἀπιστέω used in 16:11 and 16 is "non-Markan."[26] This is technically accurate, but since Mark used the related noun ἀπιστία (6:6; 9:24) and the related adjective ἄπιστός (9:19), his use of the verb would not be at all surprising. Elliott lists the use of ἐκεῖνος, a pronoun occurring five times in the longer ending (16:10, 11, 13 [2x], 20), as another non-Markan feature.[27] However, ἐκεῖνος does appear to be used as a pronoun in Mark 4:20 and 7:20, even though this usage is not nearly as common as the use of ἐκεῖνος as an adjective (20 out of 22 occurrences in 1:1–16:8). Elliott also points to the unusual expression, "they will lay hands on the sick" (ἐπὶ ἀρρώστους χεῖρας ἐπιθήσουσιν), in 16:18. A similar expression in 6:5 uses the bare dative without the preposition as do most other references to laying hands on a person (5:23; 7:32; 8:23). Only Mark 8:25 uses the preposition ἐπί for the expression, but there the object of the preposition is in the dative case rather than the accusative used in 16:18.[28] On the other hand, Mark 10:16 uses ἐπί with the accusative to refer to laying hands on children. Even though this text uses the verb τίθημι (rather than ἐπιτίθημι), the example suggests that the construction in 16:18 is not inconsistent with Mark's style.

The longer ending has several features that seem to reflect a different theology than the rest of the gospel. For example, Mark 5:34 and 10:52 emphasize that faith is a prerequisite for salvation. Mark 16:16 seems to imply that baptism is also a condition for salvation. Elliott mentions one feature of the longer ending that seems to conflict with Mark's theological stance. He argues that "the teaching that believers will be granted miraculous powers and that signs would prove the truth of the preaching is against Mark 8:11–13."[29] However, the statements are not irreconcilable since Mark 8:11–13 was addressed to a group of people who had already witnessed multiple signs and requested another sign as part of a dispute with Jesus. However, other differences that Elliot lists are indisputable:

---

24. Wallace, "Mark 16:8 as the Conclusion to the Second Gospel," 30.
25. Keith Elliott, "The Text and Language of the Endings to Mark's Gospel," *TZ* (1971): 260.
26. Elliott, "The Text and Language of the Endings to Mark's Gospel," 259.
27. Elliott, "The Text and Language of the Endings to Mark's Gospel," 258.
28. Elliott, "The Text and Language of the Endings to Mark's Gospel," 261.
29. Elliott, "The Last Twelve Verses of Mark," 92.

"Tongues" are nowhere else in our Gospels. Drinking poison without harm is nowhere else in the New Testament; this detail seems to belong better in the New Testament apocrypha. The picking up of snakes differs from Luke 10:19 [in which snakes and scorpions are trampled underfoot]. Some of these anomalies can be argued over but cumulatively they tell against Markan authorship.

Some of these differences are even more pronounced than this brief summary indicates. For example, the earliest text of the longer ending likely claimed that believers will speak in new tongues (γλώσσαις λαλήσουσιν καιναῖς).[30] Although the New Testament contains numerous references to speaking in tongues or in different kinds of tongues, no other New Testament text refers to speaking in *new* tongues. The adjective "new" gives the impression that these are not the ordinary human languages related to the tongues gift in Acts 2.[31]

This internal evidence suggests that the longer ending was an early scribal addition. Early scribes likely assumed that the short ending was far too abrupt to have been the original conclusion of the gospel of Mark. The gospel ended without recording any resurrection appearances of Jesus. It ended merely with an angelic announcement to the women that left them afraid. It also ended with the particle γάρ, and this was an odd way of ending a book. Although one study located more than 1,500 examples of sentences ending in γάρ,[32] only one other ancient book is claimed to have ended in this way (Plotinus, *Ennead* 5.5).[33] However, the claim appears to be mistaken. Plotinus did not originally end his book with γάρ. His pupil Porphyry rearranged sections of Plotinus's original work and the final γάρ is the result of Porphyry's careless transposition.[34] Likely, scribes assumed that the ending of the gospel had been lost. This was a reasonable assumption since, once a book was in codex form (as opposed to a scroll), the beginning and ending of the book were usually most vulnerable to damage or loss.[35] A scribe probably sought to solve the problem of the abrupt ending by appending an account that was already circulating

---

30. This is the reading in the UBS[5], NA[28], RP, and SBLGNT. The THGNT omits the adjective. The agreement of A and W is strong external evidence for the inclusion of the adjective. Codex C is the only Greek manuscript prior to the eighth century that omits it.
31. BDAG uses the glosses "unknown, strange, remarkable" with "the connotation of the marvelous or unheard-of" for Mark 16:17.
32. Steven Cox, *A History and Critique of Scholarship concerning the Markan Endings* (Lewiston: Mellen, 1993), 149–57, 223–28.
33. P. W. van der Horst, "Can a Book End with a ΓΑΡ? A Note on Mark XVI.8," *JTS* 23 (1972): 121–24.
34. N. Clayton Croy, *The Mutilation of Mark's Gospel* (Nashville: Abingdon, 2003), 48–49.
35. Croy, *The Mutilation of Mark's Gospel*, 137–63.

independently.[36] If a scribe had composed the account specifically to complete Mark's gospel, one would have expected the composition to fit the preceding material better. For example, the expected customized ending would describe Jesus's post-resurrection meeting with the disciples in Galilee, a meeting that was mentioned in Mark 14:28 and 16:7. The appearance described in Mark 16:14 seems to have occurred in Jerusalem, rather than in Galilee.

Although scribes appear to have thought that the original ending of Mark was lost, this does not mean that 16:8 could not have been the original ending. As one reads the gospel of Mark, he is immediately struck by the recurrence of terms like "amaze," "astonish," "awestruck," and "fear." Mark uses five Greek verbs (ἐκπλήσσω [5x], θαμβέω [3x], ἐξίστημι [4x], ταράσσω [1x], and φοβέω [11x]) with striking frequency, usually to describe people's reaction to Jesus.[37] Mark intends for his gospel to inspire this same amazement in his readers. Thus, Mark may have intended to bring this theme to a climax in the final verse of his gospel. The terror of the women who heard the angel's announcement of Jesus's resurrection at the empty tomb were then gripped with terror and their inability to speak to anyone because of their fear both suit this prominent theme of the gospel quite well. Nevertheless, most scholars are convinced that 16:8 does not serve as a proper ending of the book and the original ending was lost very early.[38]

Although most scholars are convinced that Matthew and Luke used Mark to write their own gospels, the Evangelists do not appear to have known a copy of Mark that continued beyond 16:8. The resurrection narratives of the other two Synoptics occasionally have some overlap with the contents of the longer ending of Mark, but the material shared by Matthew is not shared by Luke and vice versa. Although Matthew and Luke often share material in Mark prior to the resurrection narratives, only one or the other (or neither) shares material in the longer ending of Mark. In other words, although the other portions of the Synoptic gospels show signs of Markan priority, the resurrection narratives better support Markan posteriority (if one includes 16:9–20 in Mark). Thus, it is not likely that Matthew and Luke had access to a copy of Mark that contained the longer ending. Instead, the author of the longer ending of Mark seems to have been familiar with the events already described in the resurrection accounts of Matthew and Luke.[39]

---

36. This theory has some support from the fact that four Armenian manuscripts place the longer ending in other places—the end of Luke, the end of John, or as an Appendix after the title "According to Mark" at the end of Mark's gospel. See Ernest Colwell, "Mark 16.9–20 in the Armenian Version," *JBL* 55 (1937): 378. This may suggest that the account was a free-floating tradition.

37. Mark 1:22, 27; 2:12; 4:41; 5:15, 20, 33, 42; 6:2, 50, 51; 7:37; 10:24, 26, 32; 11:18; 15:5, 44; 16:8.

38. R. T. France, *The Gospel of Mark*, NIGTC (Grand Rapids: Eerdmans, 2002), 671–73.

39. One detailed study concludes that the author of the longer ending knew and borrowed from all four canonical Gospels and the Book of Acts. See Kelhoffer, *Miracle and Mission*,

Summary

Ancient manuscripts of the gospel of Mark end the gospel in four different ways. The endings most worthy of consideration as the original are the short ending (16:8) and the longer ending (16:9–20). The longer reading is very early since it was known by Irenaeus at the end of the second century. However, Eusebius's statement that the majority of Greek manuscripts ended Mark at 16:8 and the testimony of the two earliest majuscules suggest that the short reading is at least as old. Thus, the decision between the two endings must be made primarily on the basis of the internal evidence. Both scribal tendencies and Markan style suggest that the longer ending is a scribal addition. Probably, the gospel of Mark originally ended at Mark 16:8, or the original ending was lost very early. However, this probability is nowhere close to certainty! While both the opinions of some scholars who write on this topic and the "A" rating given in the UBS[5] for the short reading seem too confident,[40] it is reasonable to conclude that the short ending is the best choice among the possible options.

REFLECTION QUESTIONS

1. Why do textual critics usually rule out the intermediate and combination endings as serious candidates for the original ending of Mark?

2. Why do textual critics usually rule out the possibility that the Freer logion was part of the original ending?

3. What is the most persuasive evidence supporting the originality of the longer ending?

4. What is the most persuasive evidence supporting the originality of the short ending?

5. Which reading do you support and why?

137–54, 473–74. For much briefer arguments, see F. F. Bruce, "The End of the Second Gospel," *EvQ* 17 (1945): 180–81; and France, *Mark*, 686–88.

40. The restraint shown by the editors of the THGNT at this point seems wise: "The end of the Gospel of Mark poses a unique set of questions, and the issue has a long history within Christian scholarship. As editors, we did not see it as our task to commit ourselves to any particular solution to the problem" (Dirk Jongkind, *An Introduction to the Greek New Testament* [Wheaton, IL: Crossway, 2019], 81).

Should John 7:53–8:11 (the Woman Caught in Adultery) Be Included?

Another substantial variant unit is John 7:53–8:11. The episode is known to scholars as the *Pericope Adulterae* (PA). This is the account in which the scribes and Pharisees attempted to entrap Jesus by bringing an adulteress to him and asking him to decide her fate. Since the passage was printed in the Textus Receptus and translated in the King James Version, millions accept the account as a part of Holy Scripture. Many cherish the account because it provides assurance that Jesus will forgive even the immorality of those who are repentant. Sinners understandably cling to the comforting words, "Neither do I condemn you" (8:11). They may be alarmed, even angered, to see many modern translations bracket this text with a brief explanation such as "The earliest manuscripts do not include 7:53–8:11." How dare they tamper with the Scriptures so irresponsibly! In fact, this treatment is the result of an effort to treat the Scriptures responsibly. Compelling evidence supports the claim that this account was not a part of the original gospel of John.

External Evidence

The earliest manuscripts of the Greek New Testament are almost unanimous in supporting the exclusion of the PA. Only two papyri of this portion of John have survived: P⁶⁶ (200) and P⁷⁵ (early third century). Neither of these two earliest witnesses contains the PA. The two earliest majuscules, ℵ and B, also lack the account. Although the fifth-century majuscules A and C are missing the leaves that contained this section of John, given the general consistency in the number of letters per line and lines per column, one can calculate that these manuscripts did not contain enough room on the missing leaves to have included the PA. The passage is also absent from other majuscules and minuscules including L N T W Δ Θ Ψ 0141 33 157 1241 1333[1] 1424 as well as many lectionaries and ancient versions.[2]

Some of the manuscripts that do contain the PA (E Λ S 28 and several lectionaries) mark it with asterisks or obeli, symbols sometimes used by ancient scribes to indicate that a passage is suspected to be a later addition. Minuscule 1 places it at the end of the gospel of John with a lengthy note that explains that the scribe omitted the passage from its normal position after John 7:52 since it did not appear in the ancient manuscripts or the writings of the fathers such as John Chrysostom, Cyril of Alexandria, or Theodore Mopsuestia. Approximately fifty-eight manuscripts include the PA but place it in other locations in the gospel of John or even in another gospel entirely.[3] For example, minuscule 225 places it after John 7:36. The family 13 manuscripts put the text after Luke 21:38. These different placements of the account give the initial impression that the PA was an independently circulating tradition and that some ascribed its authorship to John and others to Luke. However, this theory faces two problems. First, Chris Keith has recently gathered evidence suggesting that the placement of the PA "in *some* of its alternative positions" was due to the influence of lectionary readings of the Gospels, not theories of the account's origin.[4] Second, these alternative positions of the PA only occur in manuscripts dating to the tenth century or later.[5]

The only manuscript of the Greek New Testament prior to the seventh century to contain the PA is Codex D, a fifth-century text. However, this majuscule is famous for expanding the New Testament by adding new material (though no other additions match the PA in length). The Book of Acts in Codex D is nearly 10 percent longer than in the standard text due to additional material. The presence of the passage in this particular manuscript alone out of all the major majuscules gives the impression that the account may be an independently circulating tradition that the scribe of D (or an earlier ancestor) chose to add to John.

---

1. A later scribe added the PA on a blank page preceding the gospel of John. The inserted text was taken from lectionary 1755, a twelfth-century manuscript. See Maurice Robinson, "The Source of the Pericope Adulterae Insertion in GA 1333," *Evangelical Textual Criticism Blog*, September 26, 2018, https://evangelicaltextualcriticism.blogspot.com/2018/09/maurice-robinson-source-of-pericope.html.
2. Majuscules L and Δ leave blank spaces for the PA indicating that they were aware of its existence.
3. Chris Keith, "The Initial Location of the Pericope Adulterae in Fourfold Tradition," *NovT* 51 (2009): 214.
4. Keith, "The Initial Location of the Pericope Adulterae in Fourfold Tradition," 222–31 (italics original). Robinson has suggested that all the relocations were due to lectionary influence ("Preliminary Observations Regarding the Pericope Adulterae Based upon Fresh Collations of Nearly All Continuous-Text Manuscripts and All Lectionary Manuscripts Containing the Passage," *Filologia Neotestamentaria* 13 [2000], 45).
5. Keith, "The Initial Location of the Pericope Adulterae in Fourfold Tradition," 225.

The witnesses that lack the PA come from a wide range of geographical regions. The PA is absent in some early Old Latin manuscripts (a f l q). It is also absent in manuscripts of versions from the East including Syriac (Sinaitic and Curetonian from the third and fourth centuries as well as the Peshitta from the first half of the fifth century and the Harclean version from 616), Armenian, Georgian, and Slavonic versions. It was also absent from manuscripts of the early versions in Egypt including the Sahidic, Proto-Bohairic, Bohairic, and Achmimic Coptic texts. This same wide geographical distribution is supported by the text found in the earliest fathers of the church in both the East and the West. The text was not present in the New Testament text used by the Greek fathers Origen (d. 253/54), Chrysostom (d. 407), Theodore of Mopsuestia (d. 428), Cyril of Alexandria (d. 444), nor in the text used by the Latin fathers Tertullian (d. after 220) and Cyprian (d. 258).

The earliest Greek father to refer to manuscripts containing the PA appears to have been Didymus (d. 398).[6] The earliest Latin church fathers to refer to the PA were Ambrosiaster (d. 384), Ambrose (whose text of John contained the pericope at its traditional location; d. 397), Jerome (the Vulgate, translated by 384, contained the pericope at its traditional location); Pacian (d. before 392), and Rufinus (d. 410).

The external evidence stands squarely against the PA as an original part of the gospel of John. Metzger did not exaggerate when he claimed, "The evidence for the non-Johannine origin of the pericope of the adulteress is overwhelming."[7]

Internal Evidence

The absence of this text in our earliest manuscripts of John is sufficiently strong that only the most impressive internal evidence in favor of John's inclusion of the PA could shift the balance of evidence. However, internal evidence supporting this pericope is quite weak. Most scholars are convinced that the internal evidence weighs decisively against John's inclusion of the PA in his gospel.

Intrinsic Evidence

Several features of the PA seem inconsistent with John's normal style. One of the most unusual stylistic features in the PA is the large number of verbs with the

---

6. Didymus claims that the account could be found "in certain Gospels," by which he was likely referring to the gospel of John and the Gospel of the Hebrews also mentioned by Eusebius as containing this story. See Bart Ehrman, "Jesus and the Adulteress," *NTS* 34 (1988): 24–44.
7. Bruce Metzger, *A Textual Commentary on the Greek New Testament*, 2nd ed. (Stuttgart: Deutsche Bibelgesellschaft, 1994), 187.

κατά prefix. Six such verbs appear in the span of just twelve verses.[8] However, not a single κατά-prefix verb appears outside of the PA in the gospel of John. John Punch notes that this is "admittedly odd" but suggests that the prefix was demanded by the unusual context and necessary to communicate "the intensity of the proceedings."[9] Although the gospel of John refers elsewhere to the Pharisees (19x), John 8:3 is the only reference to the "scribes" in this gospel. Jesus's opponents in the gospel of John are typically described as the Pharisees or "the chief priests and Pharisees" (John 7:32; 11:47, 57; 18:3). The phrase "the scribes and Pharisees" seems to be borrowed from one of the Synoptic gospels.[10] These are only two examples of several stylistic features that are unusual in John's gospel.

Punch argues that examining only the differences between the PA and the rest of the gospel of John without also examining their similarities is a poor methodology that may lead to unjustifiable conclusions. He is certainly correct in this observation. However, half of the examples given by Punch of Johannine features in the PA (use of διδάσκαλε; reference to Moses; use of the vocative γύναι) are features that he admits are not uniquely Johannine. He offers two primary examples of features unique to John: reference to stoning (8:59; 10:32; 11:8) and use of the expression μηκέτι ἁμάρτανε (5:14). Punch claimed, "The Synoptics are full of controversial stories and even references to Jesus's opponents' desire to kill him, but it is only John who makes reference to stoning."[11] Yet this claim is an overstatement. Although the Synoptics do not use the precise verb used in John to refer to stoning (λιθάζω), they do repeatedly refer to stoning using another verb (λιθοβολέω), which was commonly used in the LXX to refer to stoning.[12] The most that can be concluded is that the PA uses the Johannine term rather than the Synoptic term to refer to stoning. Even this claim is complicated by text-critical issues, and a good possibility exists that the original reading of the PA used λιθοβολέω instead of λιθάζω.[13]

---

8. The data related to internal evidence analyzed by John Punch and discussed here is derived from the form of the PA found in the double bracketed text of the UBS5. However, significant variation occurs in the text of the PA. An analysis of the internal evidence of von Soden's μ⁵ and μ⁶ texts printed as the main text and marginal text respectively in Maurice Robinson and William Pierpont, eds., *The New Testament in the Original Greek: Byzantine Textform* (Southborough, MA: Chilton, 2005), 247–48 would yield significantly different results. For example, the μ⁵ text contains five κατά prefix verbs and the μ⁶ text contains three (with a total of four occurrences since one verb is used twice).
9. John Punch, "The Piously Offensive Pericope Adulterae," in *The Pericope of the Adulteress in Contemporary Research*, LNTS 551, eds. David Black and Jacob Cerone (London: Bloomsbury T&T Clark, 2016), 15.
10. Matthew 5:20; 12:38; 23:2, 13, 15, 23, 25, 27, 29; Mark 2:16; Luke 5:21; 6:7; 11:53.
11. Punch, "The Piously Offensive Pericope Adulterae," 17.
12. See Matthew 21:35; 23:37; Luke 13:34; and the variant reading in Mark 12:4.
13. The preferred text in Robinson and Pierpont uses λιθοβολεῖσθαι, but the marginal text uses λιθάζειν. The earliest Greek manuscript of the PA, Codex D, uses λιθάζω, but even earlier

The use of the expression μηκέτι ἁμάρτανε in 8:11 is much more impressive, at least initially, since the only parallel to this construction is in John 5:15. But just as one must not ignore similarities when examining differences, one must not ignore differences when examining similarities. The odd redundancy in the earliest witnesses to the PA, "Go, and from now on sin no longer" is unlike John. The expression "from now on" (ἀπὸ τοῦ νῦν) is not used elsewhere in John and is redundant due to the adverb μηκέτι ("no longer") that is a close synonym. This prepositional phrase is found elsewhere in the Gospels only in Luke (1:48; 5:10; 12:52; 22:18, 69; cf. Acts 18:6; 2 Cor. 5:16).[14]

Maurice Robinson has more skillfully demonstrated that the PA has vocabulary, syntax, and style that fits well with the rest of the gospel of John.[15] However, Larry Hurtado has shown that the presence of Johannine features in the PA does not necessarily support John's authorship of the PA. Johannine features appear in other documents, like P. Egerton 2, even though John clearly did not write it. Readers of John's gospel who were heavily influenced by its theology and style naturally exhibited Johannine features in their writing.[16]

Although one can find evidence from features of the PA both supporting and raising doubts about John's composition of the narrative, an analysis of how the PA fits in the narrative flow of this section of John yields clearer results. The PA seems to disrupt the unity of John 7 and 8. Chapter 7 ends with Nicodemus's mention that proper court procedure was not being used with Christ since he had not been given the opportunity to testify on his own behalf (7:51). In 8:12 and following, the Pharisees argue that Jesus's testimony is not valid. In 7:52, the Pharisees rejected Jesus because of his Galilean origin, but, in 8:14, Jesus claimed that the Pharisees did not understand his true (heavenly) origin. Furthermore, John 7:35 indicates that Jesus was teaching in the temple on the final day of the Feast of Tabernacles. The statement "I am the light of the world" (8:12) is best understood in this same time and place. However, when the pericope of the adulteress is included, the close

---

Latin manuscripts were based on a Greek text that used λιθοβολέω (a k). Internal evidence is difficult to assess. One could argue that λιθάζω is the more difficult reading also since the LXX text to which the scribes and Pharisees referred (Deut. 22:21) used λιθοβολέω and since the later verb more closely approximates the expression used in 8:7. On the other hand, one could argue that an attentive scribe later noticed John's preference for λιθάζω and conformed the PA to John's style after its incorporation into the Gospel of John.

14. Punch's claim that the PA contains Johannine symbolism and dualism are unpersuasive. The arguments that the PA contains Johannine irony and a Johannine aside are stronger ("Piously Offensive Pericope Adulterae," 19–20).

15. Maurice Robinson, "A Johannine Tapestry with Double Interlock," in *The Pericope of the Adulteress in Contemporary Research*, 115–45.

16. Larry Hurtado, "Where from Here?" in *The Pericope of the Adulteress in Contemporary Research*, 154–55.

connections between John 7 and John 8:12–14 are disrupted by the chief priests and Pharisees returning to their homes, Jesus proceeding to the Mount of Olives, then the entire group returning to the temple the following day when the Feast of Tabernacles has concluded.

Transcriptional Evidence

One principle for text-critical decisions is that the shorter reading is to be preferred.[17] Tommy Wasserman has correctly argued that this principle supports the view that the PA is an early scribal addition to John.[18] He demonstrates that early texts sometimes added significant amounts of new material, and Codex Bezae and the Old Latin Gospels were particularly prone to this. These happen to be our earliest manuscripts that support the inclusion of the PA in John.[19]

Ambrose referred to the PA at least nine times in his writings and specifically states that the account was found in the gospel of John (Epistle 26). A work attributed to Ambrose considers the claim that Christ made a mistake by freely forgiving the adulteress. However, the author protests: "It is not right that this should enter our thoughts."[20] A few years later Augustine (d. 430) argued that husbands had deleted the PA from some manuscripts of the gospel of John because they were afraid that "liberty to sin with impunity is granted their wives."[21] However, Augustine qualified his comment with the phrase "as I believe," which indicates that this was his suspicion rather than a charge about which he had any direct knowledge. Augustine's suspicion seems to be unfounded. Although the early church certainly opposed adultery, it generally celebrated the forgiveness and transformation of repentant adulteresses

---

17. For qualifications to this rule, see Question 14. Based on the approach of the church fathers to textual variants, deletion of a large pericope like the PA seems highly unlikely. Jennifer Knust argued, "Nevertheless, a careful review of patristic attitudes toward deletion and textual correction (διόρθωσις) strongly suggests that outright expulsion of the passage is highly unlikely, if not impossible" ("'Taking Away From': Patristic Evidence and the Omission of the *Pericope Adulterae* from John's Gospel," in *The Pericope of the Adulteress in Contemporary Research,* 67).

18. Tommy Wasserman, "The Strange Case of the Missing Adulteress," in *The Pericope of the Adulteress in Contemporary Research*, 41–46.

19. Wasserman, "The Strange Case of the Missing Adulteress," 47–58. The story is mentioned by eleven different fourth- and fifth-century Latin authors as well. See Jennifer Knust and Tommy Wasserman, "Earth Accuses Earth: Tracing What Jesus Wrote on the Ground," *HTR* 103 (2010): 416–22. For an extensive scholarly discussion of the account, see Jennifer Knust and Tommy Wasserman, *To Cast the First Stone: The Transmission of a Gospel Story* (Princeton, NJ: Princeton University Press, 2019).

20. Punch incorrectly asserts that Ambrose suggests that "it is right that some might think this" ("The Piously Offensive Pericope Adulterae," 26). He appears to have misunderstood the expression: "*Fas non est ut hoc veniat in sensus nostros.*"

21. Augustine, *On Adulterous Marriages*, 2.7 (FC 27).

and prostitutes (Matt. 21:31–32; James 2:25; Heb. 11:31; Justin Martyr, *2 Apol.* 16:2; Mart. Pet. 33–38).[22]

Although most scholars recognize that the PA was not a part of the original gospel of John, many suspect that the account is based on a historical tradition. Metzger argues that the account "has all the earmarks of historical veracity."[23] Eusebius seems to have known this account (though not as a part of the gospel of John) and to have attributed it to Papias: "And he [Papias] relates another story of a woman, who was accused of many sins before the Lord, which is contained in the Gospel according to the Hebrews."[24] Eusebius does not claim that Papias drew the account from the Gospel of the Hebrews. Papias and the Gospel of the Hebrews may have independently derived the account from earlier sources. Eusebius preserves Papias's claim that he received the traditions he recorded from associates of the apostles. A probable allusion to the content of the story appears in Protevangelium of James 16:3 (150–200) and another possible allusion in P. Egerton 2 (mid-second century). A clear reference to the PA appears in Didymus the Blind's (c. 331?– 398) commentary on Ecclesiastes. Didymus claims that the account could be found "in certain Gospels." This likely includes the Gospel of the Hebrews and possibly the gospel of John.[25]

Summary

Although the story of the woman caught in adultery is both powerful and beautiful, the oldest extant manuscripts of the Greek New Testament lack it. The only Greek manuscript prior to the eighth century to contain the text is Codex Bezae, which is generally known for its tendency to add new material. Some of the late manuscripts that do contain the text place it at other locations in John or even in Luke. The account contains features that seem uncharacteristic of John's writing style. Furthermore, the account seems to disrupt the flow of John's narrative. Although the account is clearly early and possibly historical, it does not appear to have been an original part of the gospel of John.

---

22. Knust, "'Taking Away From,'" 68. Knust offers persuasive evidence undermining the more recent scholarly claim that Origen was the culprit responsible for expunging the pericope from John's gospel (pp. 79–88).

23. Metzger, *Textual Commentary*, 188.

24. Eusebius, *Eccl. Hist.* 3.39.10. This was at least how Rufinus interpreted the statement. In his Latin translation of Eusebius, Rufinus identified this woman accused of many sins as "an adulterous woman, who was accused by the Jews before the Lord." See Knust, "'Taking Away From,'" 66.

25. See Bart Ehrman, "Jesus and the Adulteress," *NTS* 34 (1988): 24–44.

REFLECTION QUESTIONS

1. What is the most persuasive evidence supporting the originality of the PA?

2. What is the most persuasive evidence supporting the early addition of the PA?

3. Which reading do you support and why?

4. Should the PA be included in modern translations? If so, how should it be presented?

5. Should pastors base an expository sermon on the PA? Why or why not?

What Are the Most Recent Advances in New Testament Textual Criticism?

In 1973, Eldon J. Epp delivered an important lecture at the Society of Biblical Literature that criticized a "twentieth-century interlude" in New Testament textual criticism.[1] He pointed out that critical editions still printed essentially the 1881 text of Westcott and Hort. Furthermore, no real progress had been made in the quest to understand the early history of the New Testament text or in the evaluation of the established readings in the standard critical editions. He also lamented the "return of the Textus Receptus" in pseudo-scholarship.[2]

Epp's lecture ended on a more encouraging note. He saw a few "hopeful signs" that the discipline might begin to make progress. Among these were (1) quantitative measurement of manuscript relationships and (2) the use of computers in text-critical research.[3] These two hopeful signs have merged into what is widely regarded as the most important advancement in New Testament textual criticism in recent decades: the Coherence-Based Genealogical Method (CBGM).

The Genealogical Method

Westcott and Hort pointed out that since all New Testament texts ultimately descended from the autographs, they are all related in a great "genealogical tree of transmission."[4] Their second emphatically stated principle is "ALL TRUSTWORTHY RESTORATION OF CORRUPTED TEXTS IS

1. Eldon J. Epp, "The Twentieth-Century Interlude in New Testament Textual Criticism," in *Studies in the Theory and Method of New Testament Textual Criticism*, SD 45, eds. Eldon J. Epp and Gordon D. Fee (Grand Rapids: Eerdmans, 1993), 83–108.
2. Epp, "The Twentieth-Century Interlude in New Testament Textual Criticism," 84–100.
3. Epp, "The Twentieth-Century Interlude in New Testament Textual Criticism," 101–108.
4. B. F. Westcott and F. J. A. Hort, *Introduction to the New Testament in the Original Greek with Notes on Selected Readings* (1882; repr., Peabody, MA: Hendrickson, 1988), 40.

FOUNDED ON THE STUDY OF THEIR HISTORY, that is, of the relations of descent or affinity which connect the several documents."[5] In other words, textual critics need to reconstruct the family tree of texts by determining which texts are most closely related to each other and how.

Westcott and Hort argued that scholars can identify texts that are closely related to each other by their number of shared readings: "The process depends on the principle that identity of reading implies identity of origin."[6] When two manuscripts agree on the "great bulk" of readings, this agreement "may at once be taken as certain evidence of a common origin."[7]

Westcott and Hort acknowledged that the ability to construct a genealogy of texts was hampered by two factors: accidental coincidences and mixture. Accidental coincidences occurred when two (or more) different scribes independently made the same change to a text. This occurred very rarely except in cases in which the alteration was "very plausible and tempting," that is, when the agreement was the result of a common transcriptional error. Mixture occurred when a scribe occasionally consulted another manuscript in addition to his primary exemplar and thereby combined readings from two different ancestries. Mixture would make it more difficult to identify the primary ancestor(s) of the text in the copy.[8] Texts that were the product of mixture could be recognized by the presence of "conflate" readings, that is, readings that blended two different variants drawn from two different exemplars. Most variants could not be conflated since the conflation would not make any sense in context. Thus, the presence of conflate readings in just a few variant units of a manuscript generally implied that mixture had occurred in many other variant units as well.[9]

Westcott and Hort argued that, once a genealogy of New Testament texts from the available manuscripts had been developed, this genealogy would become the most important evidence for the evaluation of variant readings. The genealogy would enable scholars to dismiss readings that only emerged late and thus could not have been derived from the autograph. The "only safe order of procedure" in textual criticism was to prefer "the reading suggested by a strong genealogical presumption," i.e., the reading supported by witnesses closest to the autograph in the family tree of manuscripts.

Unfortunately, Westcott and Hort were unable to produce such a family tree. The genealogies that appear in their *Introduction to the New Testament in the Original Greek* are only hypothetical and used to illustrate the logic of their argument. Scholars in the nineteenth century lacked the resources

---

5. Westcott and Hort, *Introduction*, 40.
6. Westcott and Hort, *Introduction*, 46.
7. Westcott and Hort, *Introduction*, 46.
8. Westcott and Hort, *Introduction*, 46–52.
9. Westcott and Hort, *Introduction*, 48–52.

necessary to construct such a genealogy. However, recent advancements have finally made this goal achievable. The vision of Westcott and Hort is the goal of the Coherence-Based Genealogical Method.

The Coherence-Based Genealogical Method

Tommy Wasserman and Peter Gurry define the CBGM as "a method that (1) uses a set of computer tools (2) based in a new way of relating manuscript texts that is (3) designed to help us understand the origin and history of the New Testament text."[10] Although Westcott and Hort sometimes referred to the genealogy of texts and of documents, the CBGM is focused exclusively on the relationships of texts. A text refers to the specific readings that appear in a manuscript rather than the artifact itself. The basic purpose of the method is to identify the readings of the "initial text." This is the reconstructed text (not the text that appears in a single extant manuscript) from which all the other extant texts descended.

The first step of the method involves determining how closely texts are related as indicated by their levels of agreement. Using the data from the Editio Critica Maior volumes, the CBGM determines how frequently texts agree out of all the variant units that they both contain. For example, in the Book of Acts, Codex Vaticanus and Codex Sinaiticus agree on 6,801 out of 7,387 variant units or in 92.067 percent of variant units. This high level of agreement indicates a close relationship between the two texts. They are clearly derived from the same ancestor probably only a few generations of copies back.

The level of agreement between two texts is referred to as *pre-genealogical coherence*. The data is pre-genealogical because it does not show which text is earlier or later in the genealogy of texts. Identifying a group of relatives is only a first step in constructing a family tree. To complete the genealogy, one must determine how texts are related, i.e., which are parents, siblings, cousins, etc. Pre-genealogical coherence indicates *that* the two texts are related and shows *how closely* they are related. It does not, however, indicate *how* they are related.

The second step involves determining genealogical coherence. The researcher examines all the variant units on which the two closely related witnesses disagree looking for variant units in which it is fairly obvious which reading is prior to the other. For example, in the Book of Acts, Codex Vaticanus and Codex Sinaiticus have different readings in 586 variant units. Vaticanus has the prior reading 328 times. Sinaiticus has the prior reading 192 times. In fifty-two variant units, the researchers were unable to determine which reading was prior. In fourteen variant units, the two texts had readings that seem to be unrelated to each other, i.e., neither reading was apparently derived from the other. Since Vaticanus has the prior reading in 63 percent

---

10. Tommy Wasserman and Peter J. Gurry, *A New Approach to Textual Criticism: An Introduction to the Coherence-Based Genealogical Method* (Atlanta: SBL, 2017), 3.

of the instances in which the prior reading can be determined, it is probably closer to the initial text than Sinaiticus is.

After determining which texts are most closely related and how they are related, a general textual flow can be composed. This "textual flow" shows the earliest text, its immediate descendants, their descendants, and so forth. Here is the top portion of the general textual flow for the Book of Acts.

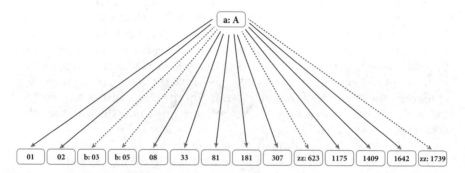

The CBGM offers solutions to the two major problems that Westcott and Hort identified that prevented construction of an accurate genealogy of texts: accidental coincidences and mixture. The architects of the CBGM use the expressions "multiple emergence" and "coincidental agreement" to refer to scribes independently making the same error in their respective copies so that they agreed on a reading even though the agreement was not drawn from a shared ancestor. They use the term "contamination" to refer to what Westcott and Hort called mixture. Contamination results from a scribe occasionally consulting another exemplar with different readings from his primary exemplar.

Ordinarily, witnesses that share the same reading should form a coherent chain. Each witness should have derived its reading from one of its close relatives. However, if there are breaks in the coherence chain, that is, if witnesses that are not closely related share the same reading, this suggests that the shared reading is a result of multiple emergence or contamination. Multiple emergence is more likely in cases in which the reading can be explained as a common accidental error. Contamination is more likely in other cases.

The Impact of the CBGM

The application of the CBGM is changing and will continue to change the text of the standard critical editions of the Greek New Testament, the Nestle-Aland text and the UBS text. The method resulted in changing the reading of thirty-three passages in the NA[28] and UBS[5] compared to the previous editions. Some of these changes impact the meaning of the passages, and some are also theologically significant. For example, the text of Jude 5 in the previous editions read, "although the Lord ([ὁ] κύριος) once saved his entire people out of the land of Egypt." However, the NA[28] and UBS[5] read, "Although Jesus ('Ιησοῦς) once saved his entire people out of the land of Egypt." The revised reading affirms Jesus's identity as the Lord who accomplished the exodus. Jude 4 identifies Jesus as "our Lord." Jude 5 demonstrates the "Lord" has its highest sense. It functions not merely as a title of authority, but as a name of deity. As future volumes of the Editio Critica Maior are produced and the application of the CBGM continues, new changes will come to other passages in other books and corpora of the New Testament.

Summary

Although the CBGM can be difficult to understand, it essentially fulfills the vision of Westcott and Hort. The CBGM seeks to construct a genealogy of texts. This method has been applied to the Catholic Letters, Acts and Mark and will ultimately be applied to the entire New Testament. The method has the potential to improve the accuracy of the critical editions of the Greek New Testament.

REFLECTION QUESTIONS

1. What were the signs that Eldon Epp saw suggesting that the field of textual criticism could make real progress at the end of the twentieth century? Was his prediction correct?

2. How did Westcott and Hort believe scholars could identify closely related manuscripts?

3. How does the CBGM fulfill the vision of Westcott and Hort?

4. What two obstacles to constructing a genealogy of texts did Westcott and Hort face in using their second great principle of textual criticism? How does the CBGM address these two obstacles?

5. How is the CBGM changing standard critical editions of the Greek New Testament?

The Canon of the New Testament

Definitions and Theories of Canon

How Should We Define the Term "Canon"?

"Canon" has been variously defined over the centuries. For most Christians, it is just another name for the Bible. Scholars, though, vigorously contest how we should define the canon. The primary debate is whether "canon" is a list of *authoritative books* or an *authoritative list* of books. The former leaves room for adjustment; the latter does not. The maddening subtlety and nuance of the question reflects the field of study itself. To be frank, to study the NT canon is to stare into the mists of history. These mists dispel only occasionally to show bits and pieces regarding the question of canon. For example, in the second century, we have no record of any discussion about forming a NT canon. Yet, by the end of that century, it is clear much of the NT canon is firmly set.[1] Thus, Bruce Metzger could note: "Nothing is more amazing in the annals of the Christian Church than the absence of detailed accounts of so significant a process."[2]

For the most part, the existing evidence for the canon is known. Agreement on how to interpret those lines of evidence is not forthcoming.[3] Most of this disagreement comes from the development and role of interpretive models that are based on foundational assumptions. So, the result is a mass of secondary literature often in disagreement regarding the same pool of evidence.

We will begin our exploration of the topic by briefly describing and evaluating the different models. In the following question, we will explain our model in more detail. Similar overarching principles define three primary

---

1. Joseph Verheyden, "The New Testament Canon," in *The New Cambridge History of the Bible; Vol. 1 From the Beginnings to 600*, eds. James Carleton Paget and Joachim Schaper (Cambridge: Cambridge University Press, 2013), 398.
2. Bruce Metzger, *The Canon of the New Testament: Its Origin, Development, and Significance* (Oxford: Oxford University Press, 1987), 1.
3. John Barton, *Holy Writings, Sacred Text: The Canon in Early Christianity* (Louisville, KY: Westminster John Knox, 1998), 1.

191

models: Extrinsic, Magisterial, and Intrinsic models. Within the models, we will group similar approaches as "definitions." An individual's theory will be called an "expression."

The Extrinsic Model

For scholars promoting an extrinsic model, the canon was chosen by a natural, historical process. Advocates differ on the particulars, but all see an entirely human process. Some would call it "community-driven" because the community chose the canon. We divide them into four subgroups: Historical-Critical, Exclusive, Functional, and Criteria of Canonicity.

Historical-Critical

Advocates of this approach employ rationalism to theological and biblical studies. They aim to uncover assured results on unassailable premises.[4] The man often hailed as the father of the movement,[5] J. S. Semler, addressed canon as one of his major areas of research and laid the foundation for those to follow. He defined "canon" as the Jewish and Christian list of divinely inspired books. Because the early church did not settle the debate until later, he denied the inspiration of all the books.[6] For Semler, rather than all the Scripture being God's Word, the Bible merely contained God's word, and his reasoned judgment could locate it.[7] His unassailable premise was that the canon came into existence in the fourth century, culminated by conciliar declarations.

In the centuries to follow, advocates like Wrede would call on Semler to deny the inspiration of all the Scriptures.[8] His understanding of the historical process of canonization (deliberation and dispute) led him to declare the canon was a fourth-century determination by the bishops of the day, whose authority he did not recognize.[9] Modern proponents say something similar.[10] Contemporary critics like Bart Ehrman use this interpretation of the evidence to advocate that the canon

---

4. D. A. Carson, "Systematic Theology and Biblical Theology," in *New Dictionary of Biblical Theology*, eds. T. Desmond Alexander and Brian S. Rosner (Downers Grove, IL: InterVarsity Press, 2000), 92.
5. W. G. Kümmel, *The New Testament: The History of the Investigation of Its Problems*, trans. McLean Gilmor and Howard C. Kee (London: SCM Press, 1973), 62.
6. Johann Salomo Semler, *Abhandlung von Freier Untersuchung des Canon*, ed. Heinz Scheible, Texte zur Kirchen- und Theologiegeschichte, Heft 5 (Gütersloh: Mohn, 1967), 20–21.
7. Semler, *Abhandlung*, 13.
8. William Wrede, "The Task and Methods of 'New Testament Theology,'" in Robert Morgan, William Wrede, and Adolf Schlatter, *The Nature of New Testament Theology: The Contribution of William Wrede and Adolf Schlatter*, Studies in Biblical Theology, 2nd Series 25 (London: SCM Press, 1973), 69.
9. Wrede, "Task and Methods," 70–71. Wrede did no independent investigation but cited Semler.
10. See Heikki Räisänen, *Beyond New Testament Theology*, 2nd ed. (London: SCM, 2000), 187.

was produced as a weapon against their opponents.[11] Thus, it was an ancient and arbitrary process. These scholars proposed the Scriptures were "selected" centuries after the founding of Christianity and centuries before the modern reader. In short, it is an obsolete authority not applicable to modern Christians.

Exclusive

The Exclusive approach focuses on the closing of the canon. Most follow the lead of A. C. Sundberg.[12] They maintain that "canon," defined as a list of books that one must not reduce or enlarge (an authoritative list), is a late theological development. Their historical reconstruction suggests the early church had no concept of canon. They base this on a sharp distinction between "scripture" and "canon." "Scripture" is defined merely as an authoritative document. In contrast, "canon" is a fixed list of authoritative books. This distinction is key to the definition. Geoffrey Hahneman notes, "Once a distinction is made between scripture and canon, the idea of a New Testament canon does not appear applicable until the fourth century."[13]

They defend this definition of canon on purely historical grounds. Thus, the creation of canon is sometimes referred to as a "fourth century" or a "patristic" achievement.[14] If so, it is a human achievement, i.e., purely historical and humanly explainable. In this sense, it largely agrees with the historical-critical expression. The major break with that definition is that, in some expressions, the decision of the fourth- and fifth-century church is a binding achievement and not seen as an arbitrary development. For some, it does leave open the possibility of adjusting the canon. At stake, along with the other problems, is whether the early church had conflicting and contradictory authorities.

Functional

The functional (or "inclusive") approach grew out of Brevard Childs's development of canonical criticism. For him, there was little difference between "scripture" and "canon."[15] As soon as a community considered a book as "Scripture," it functioned as canon.[16] In this view, he echoed Harnack and Zahn from the

---

11. Bart D. Ehrman, *Lost Christianities: The Battles for Scripture and the Faiths We Never Knew* (New York: Oxford University Press, 2003), 246.
12. A. C. Sundberg, "Towards a Revised History of the New Testament Canon," in *Studia Evangelica IV, Texte und Untersuchungen Zur Geschichte Der Altchristlichen Literatur* 103 (Berlin: Akademie-Verlag, 1968).
13. Geoffrey M. Hahneman, *The Muratorian Fragment and the Development of the Canon* (Oxford: Clarendon, 1992), 129–30.
14. Craig D. Allert, *A High View of Scripture? The Authority of the Bible and the Formation of the New Testament Canon* (Grand Rapids: Baker Academic, 2007), 145, 175.
15. Brevard Childs, "On Reclaiming the Bible for Christian Theology," in *Reclaiming the Bible for the Church*, eds. Carl E. Braaten and Robert W. Jenson (Grand Rapids: Eerdmans, 1995), 9.
16. Michael J. Kruger, *The Question of Canon: Challenging the Status Quo in the New Testament Debate* (Downers Grove, IL: IVP Academic, 2013), 35.

early twentieth century.[17] Ultimately, the community determined the canon, and for Childs, that was the Western Church. Later scholars often refer to the period before closing as "canon 1" and after "canon 2," or something similar.[18]

A functional canon departs from the exclusive definition by considering a local community's list canon, at least for that community. This is not to say that the canon was in a final form. Sanders calls "relevance and adaptability" the primary trait of a canon.[19] A community may adopt a different canon than others, but it makes sense to the community since the process is entirely human. Over time and distance, that canon evolves. Thus, "canon" is considered a list of authoritative books rather than an authoritative list. The major problem is that it is difficult to affirm any fixed nature for the canon under some expressions.

Criteria of Canonicity

Scholars holding to this approach maintain that a series of external and internal criteria guided the church's adoption of the canon. While their benchmarks are not uniform, advocates employ a similar process.[20] Some evangelicals hold to this view as historical reconstruction and validation of the NT canon. Non-evangelicals typically merely describe the historical process.[21] The result is a historical reconstruction of the development of the canon.

Harry Y. Gamble is representative of those who hold to a purely historical expression.[22] He suggests the church over the centuries unevenly applied five criteria to determine the canon. First, it must have apostolicity (i.e., direct authorship by an apostle, indirect connection to an apostle, or be apostolic in content).[23] Second, it must have catholicity (that is, relevancy to the whole church).[24] Third, a work must conform to "the rule of faith" (Latin: *Regula Fidei*) or that which is within Christian orthodoxy.[25] Fourth, a book should demonstrate traditional usage (widespread and early use).[26] And fifth, it must

---

17. Kruger, *The Question of Canon*, 35.
18. First coined by Gerald T. Sheppard, "Canon," in *Encyclopedia of Religion*, ed. Lindsay Jones (Detroit: Thomson Gale, 1987), 3:64. For a recent variation, see Christoph Markschies, *Christian Theology and Its Institutions in the Early Roman Empire: Prolegomena to a History of Early Christian Theology* (Waco, TX: Baylor University Press, 2015), 193–94.
19. James A. Sanders, "The Issue of Closure in the Canonical Process," in *The Canon Debate*, eds. James A. Sanders and Lee Martin McDonald (Peabody, MA: Hendrickson, 2002), 259.
20. See, e.g., F. F. Bruce, *The Canon of Scripture* (Downers Grove, IL: InterVarsity Press, 1988), 255–69; Metzger, *Canon*, 252–54; and Arthur G. Patzia, *The Making of the New Testament: Origin, Collection, Text and Canon* (Downers Grove, IL: InterVarsity Press, 1995).
21. Michael J. Kruger, *Canon Revisited: Establishing the Origins and Authority of the New Testament Books* (Wheaton, IL: Crossway, 2012), 74.
22. Harry Y. Gamble, *The New Testament Canon: Its Making and Meaning* (Philadelphia: Fortress, 1985), 67–72.
23. Gamble, *New Testament Canon*, 68.
24. Gamble, *New Testament Canon*, 69.
25. Gamble, *New Testament Canon*, 70.
26. Gamble, *New Testament Canon*, 71.

show inspiration to be in the NT canon. For most, inspiration is a late-arriving criterion where they also applied the inspiration of the Jewish Scriptures to the NT. Ultimately, it is a standard attributed after the book is canonized and used to reject heretical works.[27]

Response

Because canon is a historical question, the different advocates have produced valuable research. Some are goldmines of information. However, definitions dependent on historical reconstructions all have the same general problem: the sample size of early Christian works is limited. Markschies gives a chilling assessment of the state of affairs: "85 percent of the texts from the second century whose existence we know about has been lost—and this quantity presumably forms only a rather small percentage of the sources that once existed in their entirety."[28] The unavoidable conclusion is that we have less, likely much less, than 15 percent of the Orthodox Christian literature of the second century. Some of the known missing literature (like Justin's *Against Marcion*) surely would significantly impact our understanding of the NT canon. The problem is not that we cannot know anything but that "absence of evidence" quickly becomes "absence of existence" in some of these historical reconstructions, skewing the results toward underlying assumptions.[29]

Magisterial Model

The Roman Catholic and Orthodox churches understand the church selected the canon. The title comes from the Latin "magisterium," which means the teaching authority of the catholic church. They extend that authority to the selection of the canon.[30] Thus, we call the approach the magisterial model. Both Roman Catholics and Orthodox Churches ascribe to similar definitions.

Roman Catholic

The modern Roman Catholic approach to canon began with the council of Trent (a counter-reformation effort). The fourth session (April 8, 1546) presumably addressed the *sola scriptura* of the reformers. "The Decree on the Canon of Scripture" presented Scripture as a coequal source of revelation with the traditions of the church (the rulings of the church on manners and doctrines). They included an OT and NT canon list: "lest any doubt should

---

27. Gamble, *New Testament Canon*, 72.
28. Markschies, *Christian Theology and Its Institutions*, 21.
29. Levi Baker, "New Covenant Documents for a New Covenant Community: Covenant as an Impetus for New Scripture in the First Century" (PhD diss., Southeastern Baptist Theological Seminary, 2022), 276.
30. Kruger, *Canon Revisited*, 39.

arise."[31] They showed no interest in the authentication of the NT canon other than the church's authority. Most notably, Trent canonized the Latin Vulgate that included the books of the OT Apocrypha and limited correct interpretation to the Magisterium.

The current Roman Catholic position on the canon was adopted in 1964 at the Vatican II council. The official document, *Dei Verbum*, builds on the declaration of Trent. It affirmed the same sources of revelation. Regarding the canon, the Magisterium, interpreting the tradition, has the privilege of authenticating the canon. [32]

Orthodox

Although the separation of Byzantium from Rome occurred well before Trent, the Orthodox Church took a similar position. Orthodox theologian Eugen Pentiuc affirms that the Greek Orthodox Church has "never defined its position on the scriptural canon in any ecumenical or Pan-Orthodox council."[33] Instead, they lean on the councils before 1054 and the church's tradition. The latter is defined as the Holy Spirit's ongoing involvement in the church.[34] Geffert and Stavrou describe the result:

> [T]he Eastern Orthodox insist that Scripture grew out of the church; the church did not grow out of Scripture. The same is true of patristic writings, say the Eastern Orthodox. The church and its councils decided which were valid and which were inadequate or heretical. Thus Scripture and patristics bear whatever authority the church, acting under the influence of the Holy Spirit, ascribes to them.[35]

As a result, Roman Catholic and Orthodox theologians claim the authentication of the canon comes from a mixture of the nature of the books and the nature of the church.

Response

Both the Roman Catholic and Orthodox Churches affirm the inspiration and trustworthiness of the Scriptures. This sets them apart from the previous models. However, the role they assert in the canonical process undermines the

---

31. *The Doctrinal Decrees and Canons of the Council of Trent: Transl. from the First Edition Printed at Rome, in 1564* (New York: American Protestant Society, 1845), 5–6.
32. *Dei Verbum*, 8.
33. Eugen J. Pentiuc, *The Old Testament in Eastern Orthodox Tradition* (New York: Oxford University Press, 2014), 109.
34. See Pentiuc, *The Old Testament in Eastern Orthodox Tradition*, 143.
35. Bryn Geffert and Theofanis George Stavrou, *Eastern Orthodox Christianity: The Essential Texts* (New Haven, CT: Yale University Press, 2016), 5.

independence of the word of God. For example, in theory, the Magisterium of the Roman Catholic Church could adjust the canon. Trent exercised this privilege when they added the Apocrypha to the OT canon. Previously the books had a less-than-solid position in Christian life and belief.

Catholic apologist Peter Kreeft made the following analogy: Church and Scripture "are not two rival horses in the authority race, but one rider (the Church) on one horse (Scripture). The Church as writer, canonizer, and interpreter of Scripture is not another source of revelation but the author and guardian and teacher of the source, Scripture."[36] In this analogy, it is hard to overlook the fact that a horse with a rider typically has a bit in its mouth.

Ultimately, there is an inescapable and disturbing aspect of the expression that exercises at least some kind of authority over the word of God. The same is true of the Orthodox position, although they rely more on the ancient councils to close the canon.

Summary

We could place the models covered here in the category "community determined" because a community (however defined) selects the NT canon.[37] The difference is that advocates of the Magisterial model insist on the role of the Holy Spirit in the process. In the Extrinsic model, no such activity is necessary. While we affirm the community's value and part in the canonical process, we disagree that the community's proper role was canonizer. If the community's job is selection, we often have the problems stated above: an obsolete authority, an adjustable canon, and a canon without the highest authority. Each difficulty undermines the canon as the Word of God. In the following question, we address a model that proposes the role of the community is recognition rather than selection. We feel this model reflects the early church's theology and what we can see of the historical process.

REFLECTION QUESTIONS

1. What is the difference between the terms "models," "definitions," and "expressions?"

2. Why is the concept of canon at stake in extrinsic models?

---

36. Peter Kreeft, *Fundamentals of the Faith: Essays in Christian Apologetics* (San Francisco: Ignatius, 1988), 275–76.
37. See John C. Peckham, *Canonical Theology: The Biblical Canon, Sola Scriptura, and Theological Method* (Grand Rapids: Eerdmans, 2016), 3–4.

3. What is the danger of assuming that the evidence never existed, since we don't have existing evidence?

4. What is the central critique of the Magisterial model?

5. What are the three problems about the canon resulting from the Extrinsic and Magisterial models?

What Is the Intrinsic Model?

In the previous Question, we explored the Extrinsic and Magisterial models. We call the remaining model the Intrinsic model because the authority of the NT does not derive from any external authority (like councils or synods). Instead, the NT is the result of divine activity. Therefore, the authority that makes it Scripture is inherent in these books. The reformers referred to the phenomenon as *autopistie* or "self-authenticating." They first articulated the model in response to the Council of Trent (1545–1563) based on the Roman Church's declaration that the Magisterium had the authority to select the canon of Scripture.

The Intrinsic Model

Before the Council of Trent, the authority of the canon was stated rather than defended among the early reformers.[1] After Trent, vindication became necessary, and the Lutherans began specifically supporting the canon. Ultimately, Martin Chemnitz wrote the primary defense of the canon in *Examen Concilii Tridenti* (1578). Chemnitz saw the authority of Scripture as causative and normative.[2] "Causative" is the inherent power of the Word of God working faith in the hearers. "Normative" authority flows from causative authority and is the power of Scripture to set the norms for its doctrine and practice.[3] As to the proof of the canonicity, the appeal is to the Holy Spirit as the author, the early church (who had more evidence of authenticity), and the testimony of Scripture itself.[4]

---

1. See, e.g., the Augsburg confession of 1530 in Philip Schaff, *The Creeds of Christendom: With a History and Critical Notes*, 6th ed. (Grand Rapids: Baker, 1993), 3:97.
2. Fred Kramer, "Chemnitz on the Authority of the Sacred Scripture: An Examination of the Council of Trent," *Springfielder* 37 (1973): 165.
3. Heinrich Schmid, *The Doctrinal Theology of the Evangelical Lutheran Church* (Minneapolis: Augsburg, 1961), 51–62.
4. Martin Chemnitz, *Examination of the Council of Trent*, trans. Fred Kramer (St. Louis: Concordia, 1971), 1:176.

Leading the French wing of the Reformation, John Calvin also affirmed that the church could not determine the canon. He argued the writings of the prophets and the preaching of the apostles were the church's foundation.[5] Thus, the doctrine, wherever it is found, predates the church. Furthermore, the canon itself is self-authenticating. For Calvin, we do not build up faith in Scripture through argument. Those rational proofs, however, do have a place as "secondary aids."[6] Instead, the believer has the resources to recognize the canon since God is its author, it contains his words (substantiated by the prophets and apostles refraining from boasting of their abilities), and it is validated for the believer by the Spirit.[7]

Both supporters and critics have interpreted Calvin's appeal to the Spirit as the only grounds for the authentication of the Scriptures.[8] Quite early, this basis was attacked as "circular reasoning" because the Spirit reveals the inspiration.[9] However, John Murray has shown that Calvin addressed the witness of the Spirit as only the means the individual Christian has confidence.[10] Instead, the Reformed view is that the Scripture's divine nature attests to their authority, but its persuasion is a different work of God.[11]

In 1557, Calvin made an extensive response to the Council of Trent in which he addressed in more detail the objective evidence for the Scripture's self-authentication.[12] In his rejection of the Apocrypha (and the Vulgate), we can distill three dimensions of self-authenticity: (1) agreement with the rest of Scriptures; (2) widespread evidence of reception by the people of God; and (3) literary evidence of its divine nature.

First, he proposed the addition of the Apocrypha would be a source of doctrines he calls "dregs": purgatory, worship of saints, "satisfactions, exorcisms, and whatnot."[13] The implication is that if the books genuinely show these doctrines, they are self-defeating because they disagree with the Scriptures. Thus, the mark of the Spirit would be theological agreement ("harmony").

---

5. Calvin, *Institutes* 1.7.1–2, 5.
6. Calvin, *Institutes* 1.8.13.
7. Calvin, *Institutes* 1.7.4.
8. See the discussion in John Murray, "Calvin and the Authority of Scripture," in *The Collected Writings of John Murray* (Carlisle, PA: Banner of Truth, 1982), 4:184. Theodor Zahn (Die bleibende Bedeutung des neutestamentlichen Kanons für die Kirche [Leipzig: A. Deichert, 1898], 27–47) also made the accusation.
9. Martin Becanus, "De circulo Calvinistico, contra Paraeum. Cum appendice," *Opuscula theologica*, I, Münster 1610, 386–418.
10. Murray, "Calvin and the Authority of Scripture," 183–90.
11. See Herman Ridderbos, *Redemptive History and the New Testament Scriptures*, 2nd rev. ed., Biblical and Theological Studies, trans. H. D. Jongste and Richard B. Gaffin, Jr. (Phillipsburg, NJ: P&R, 1988), 9.
12. John Calvin, "Canons and Decrees of the Council of Trent with the Antidote," in *John Calvin, Tracts and Letters*, trans. Henry Beveridge (Carlisle, PA: Banner of Truth, 2009, repr. 1851), 67–77.
13. Calvin, "Canons and Decrees of the Council of Trent with the Antidote," 68.

Second, he notes the lack of early consensus regarding those books; they were added "without the consent of the early church."[14] He found this somewhat of a trump card to the actions of Trent. He notes that Jerome and Rufinus had an explicit category for these books—useful but less than Scripture.[15] He, therefore, valued the testimony of the early church in identifying the canon.

Third, the text itself does not show the marks of divinity. For example, the book of Maccabees concludes with a plea for forgiveness if the author got anything wrong. Calvin could not imagine the Spirit inspiring such a fear: "How very alien this acknowledgment from the majesty of the Spirit."[16] Thus the work is self-falsifying.[17] On the other hand, the books of Scripture do no such thing.

Modern Expressions

Michael Kruger's 2012 treatment is one of the latest expressions of the Reformed position.[18] Kruger, like Calvin, affirms that if the canon is the Word of God, humans cannot authenticate it: "For the canon to be the canon it must be self-authenticating."[19]

However, he distances himself from a typical Reformed position by organizing the conversation around the providential acts of God that allow us to recognize the canon. He calls this an epistemic environment. The providence of God has created an environment whereby we have access to the books, the books bear the divine qualities of canon, and the work of the Spirit overcomes the noetic effects of sin in the believer, enabling recognition. Thus, the environment is composed of three elements, and all three are necessary for confidence that a book is canonical.

The first component is providential exposure.[20] Here, the church must possess the books in the first place. More than a mere truism, the necessity of exposure limits the number of books that can be considered to those that have a continual witness throughout the church's history. We know of now-lost prophetic and apostolic works. That they are lost is evidence that God did not intend them to be in the canon of Scripture. We must consider this an act

---

14. Calvin, "Canons and Decrees of the Council of Trent with the Antidote," 70.
15. Calvin, "Canons and Decrees of the Council of Trent with the Antidote," 70.
16. Calvin, "Canons and Decrees of the Council of Trent with the Antidote," 71.
17. He goes no further in "Canons and Decrees of the Council of Trent with the Antidote," but in the *Institutes*, he lists the apostolic tone—not boasting in their eloquence, thoughts that couldn't come from humans, antiquity, inarguable miracles, and fulfilled prophecy as other such evidence (Calvin, *Institutes*, 1.7.4; 1.8).
18. Michael J. Kruger, *Canon Revisited: Establishing the Origins and Authority of the New Testament Books* (Wheaton, IL: Crossway, 2012).
19. Kruger, *Canon Revisited*, 89.
20. Kruger, *Canon Revisited*, 95–97.

of God's providence. Even if we found them, their historic absence from the church disqualifies them.

The second component is that these books must show the divine attributes of canon. This component is essentially a refinement of the self-authenticating model expressed by Calvin (and other reformers). The divine qualities (including beauty, efficacy, and harmony) are objectively clear. Still, the means of recognizing them is through the regenerating and confirmatory activity of the Spirit in the individual. The corporate reception of the books overcomes a stubborn individualism (possible in any believer) regarding the books.[21] Even Luther could not remove James from the canon.

The apostolic origin of the NT anchors the books in history and in an appropriate authority delegated by Christ. The apostles were entrusted with the gospel representing Christ (see Luke 10:16). Thus, "the apostles are the link between the redemptive events themselves and the subsequent announcement of those events."[22] Although this appeal involves historical evidence, these are not independent of the other components.

The third component, the witness of the Holy Spirit, recalls the affirmation of the Reformation creeds. The discussion of the other two components had to include a dialogue of the role of the Holy Spirit, for he is the supervisor of all these matters. However, the spiritual element in the environment also includes preservation, inspiring the apostles to write with divine qualities, and the confirmation in the believer's heart.

Criticism and Response

Lee Martin McDonald criticized the intrinsic position in six arguments. First, several NT books have a long history of dispute (e.g., the minor General Epistles [GE]).[23] And second, some books, later rejected, achieved scriptural status at certain places.[24] Thus, the authority wasn't self-evident to all. However, for these arguments to be defeaters of self-authentication, the result must be that humans would be infallible in the matter if the Spirit were involved. Experience and Scripture tell us this is not so.

His third argument is that no NT author claims to be writing Scripture (except possibly Revelation).[25] McDonald's assumption is that awareness of scripture-writing is essential for the intrinsic view to be correct. The NT books

---

21. Kruger, *Canon Revisited*, 103–108.
22. Kruger, *Canon Revisited*, 109.
23. John J. Collins, Craig A. Evans, and Lee Martin McDonald, *Ancient Jewish and Christian Scriptures: New Developments in Canon Controversy* (Louisville, KY: Westminster John Knox, 2020), 106.
24. Collins, Evans, and McDonald, *Ancient Jewish and Christian Scriptures*, 106.
25. Collins, Evans, and McDonald, *Ancient Jewish and Christian Scriptures*, 106.

were merely occasional documents for him and others in the exclusive camp. They were neither Scripture nor canon in their writing or earliest reception.[26]

Because Question 36 contains a more detailed treatment of the topic, we will only summarize it here. It certainly cannot be affirmed that the apostles and their followers had a concept of a twenty-seven-book NT canon, and we know of no modern scholar who does.[27] The minimum argument is that the writers as apostles or those approved by apostles had and were aware of the highest level of authority, even Christ's authority.[28] This authority expressed in writing cannot be much different than Scripture in the mind of the one wielding the authority.[29]

What is more, the underlying thesis of the critique may be unnecessary. Put another way, if we grant that the writers of the NT had no intention of writing Scripture, does that by definition invalidate the thesis? The early church surely could recognize the providence of God in circumstances and his influence on the apostolic response apart from specific apostolic awareness.

Fourth, McDonald argues that the proponents confuse the authority of the gospel message for the literature written and then transpose it to all the NT books.[30] However, the claims for apostolic authority in the NT go well beyond references to the gospel. For example, in places like 1 Corinthians 11 and 12–14, Paul lays down the norms for public worship as the apostle of Christ, not merely as implications of the gospel.

The fifth argument is that the claim to inspiration in these writings is not sufficient to claim a scriptural status is undoubtedly correct.[31] Simply because an author claims inspiration does not make it Scripture. However, if an apostle makes the claim, it unquestionably suggests a Scripture-like authority was being wielded.

McDonald finally argues that the public reading of Paul's letters in the churches was not equivalent to the Jewish practice of reading Scripture.[32] This is possibly true in the references in the NT but not necessarily so. It is true that very shortly afterward, they were. Given the intentional Scripture-like composition noted above, it is entirely possible that within the life of the apostles, the church was reading their works as Scripture. Ultimately, the arguments against self-authentication are not compelling.

---

26. Lee M. McDonald, *The Formation of the Biblical Canon* (London: Bloomsbury T&T Clark, 2018), 1:12–15.

27. McDonald mistakenly accuses Kruger of this. Cf. Michael J. Kruger, *The Question of Canon: Challenging the Status Quo in the New Testament Debate* (Downers Grove, IL: IVP Academic, 2013), 120 (and *Canon Revisited*, 184) and Collins, Evans, and McDonald, *Ancient Jewish and Christian Scriptures*, 116.

28. Kruger, *The Question of Canon*, 153.

29. Kruger, *The Question of Canon*, 121–22.

30. Collins, Evans, and McDonald, *Ancient Jewish and Christian Scriptures*, 106.

31. Collins, Evans, and McDonald, *Ancient Jewish and Christian Scriptures*, 110.

32. Collins, Evans, and McDonald, *Ancient Jewish and Christian Scriptures*, 113.

Summary

The intrinsic model affirms the NT canon is self-authenticating. The environment of the reception of these books is availability, demonstrating the divine attributes, and witnessed by God's Spirit. We affirm the NT presents all these matters. Moreover, as we progress, we will see that the evidence about the NT canon in the existing sources reflects an organic, natural recognition. This is what we would expect given the nature of these books and the environment provided by God. Furthermore, it more closely fits the theology of the early church regarding Scripture. The upshot, then, is that the church did not *select* the canon but *recognized* what God had done in these books.

REFLECTION QUESTIONS

1. What was the impetus for the Reformed expression of the intrinsic model?

2. Is the intrinsic model based solely on a subjective inner witness?

3. How many elements of the epistemic environment must be present for a book to be considered canon?

4. Does the rejection of a canonical book or the reception of a noncanonical book in history suggest the Spirit of God does not bear witness to the NT canon?

5. Did the biblical writer have to know they were writing Scripture for the intrinsic model to be correct?

Did the Ancients Have Scripture but Not Canon?

A. C. Sundberg popularized the notion in the Exclusive definition that the early church had no concept of canon (i.e., a closed list). Instead, they had authoritative literature (Scripture).[1] Many in the present academy embrace this definition.[2] In this view, the canon only occurs when the fixed collection is created. As such, the authority of the list's creators is of the highest level. As Metzger noted, the church "creates . . . [the book's] authority by collecting them and placing on the collection the label of canonicity."[3] Most see the fourth century as the critical period when this occurred.[4] This, then, is a revolutionary moment for the church.[5]

The benefits of understanding the canon's history in this way are at least twofold. First, this view attempts a consistent understanding of *graphē* ("scripture") that seeks to make sense of the use of the word with books that are not now considered canonical. Second, and related, this view does not promote books that enjoyed a local status as Scripture to canon and then must explain

---

1. A. C. Sundberg, "Towards a Revised History of the New Testament Canon," in *Studia Evangelica IV*, *Texte und Untersuchungen Zur Geschichte Der Altchristlichen Literatur* 103 (Berlin: Akademie-Verlag, 1968), 52, 54.
2. See, e.g., Craig D. Allert, *A High View of Scripture? The Authority of the Bible and the Formation of the New Testament Canon* (Grand Rapids: Baker Academic, 2007), 47–48; and Lee M. McDonald, *The Formation of the Biblical Canon* (London: Bloomsbury T&T Clark, 2018), 1:39–117.
3. Bruce Metzger, *The Canon of the New Testament: Its Origin, Development, and Significance* (Oxford: Oxford University Press, 1987), 283.
4. See, e.g., Allert, *A High View of Scripture*, 145, 175.
5. Sundberg describes it as "unequivocally the decision of the church" ("Towards a Revised History," 461).

them fading off the scene.[6] However, these "benefits" are often gained by mis-identifying Scripture in antiquity. Moreover, the theory that the fourth century was a revolutionary moment does not adequately represent the scriptural environment that is evident in the period.

Misidentifying "Scripture" in Antiquity

Proponents of the exclusive definition suggest that many works now rejected were once considered Scripture in early Christianity. Generally, this is done by flattening the term *graphē* to one meaning (i.e., as Scripture), suggesting that "reading" means to read in public worship as Scripture, and quoting a book means it had the highest authority. Upon a closer look, these conclusions are unwarranted.

Scripture-like Signifiers

The term for "scripture" (*graphē*) simply means "writing" at its most basic level. It is, however, the preferred term for Scripture in Greek. Thus, when the ancients used *graphē* (and cognates) to refer to noncanonical works, some assume those works had scriptural authority. In some cases, we are sure it has this meaning.[7] So, we cannot say that the ancients never used the word to refer to a noncanonical book as Scripture.

However, not every use of *graphē* by the ancients refers to Scripture. Depending on the context, it can mean any kind of writing, inscription, or even a drawing.[8] When the referent is to sacred writing, it is appropriate to translate it "Scripture." In other occurrences, "document" is more appropriate.[9] Moreover, between these two meanings, there is a use that signifies a writing with secondary and derivative authority.[10]

Irenaeus (c. 178–200) used *graphē* to describe the *Shepherd of Hermas* and *1 Clement*.[11] Although he twice used the word to refer to Clement's letter, "Scripture" is an inaccurate translation for both instances. He considered the letter "powerful" because it declared "the tradition which it had lately received from the apostles."[12] Bingham suggests that *graphē* here likely refers to a work

---

6. See Michael J. Kruger, *The Question of Canon: Challenging the Status Quo in the New Testament Debate* (Downers Grove, IL: InterVarsity Press, 2013), 31.

7. E.g., citations in the *Apostolic Fathers* include twenty-nine noncanonical works (twenty-two in *Barnabas* and *2 Clement*). Not all twenty-nine are cited as Scripture but some certainly are.

8. BDAG, 206; Timothy L. Swinson, *What Is Scripture? Paul's Use of Graphe in the Letters to Timothy* (Eugene, OR: Wipf & Stock, 2014), 178.

9. See, e.g., Eusebius, *Hist. eccl.* 3.25.4.

10. These terms "secondary and derivative" are from D. Jeffrey Bingham, "Senses of Scripture in the Second Century: Irenaeus, Scripture, and Noncanonical Christian Texts," *The Journal of Religion* 97 (2017): 26–55.

11. See, *Adv. Haer.* 4.20.2 and 3.3.3.

12. Irenaeus, *Adv. Haer.* 3.3.3; ANF 1:416.

that falls short of "Scripture" and whose authority is secondary and derivative to the apostles, at most clarifying and putting boundaries to their teaching.[13]

His use of the same word to describe *Hermas* is less clear. Some moderns follow Eusebius and claim Irenaeus received *Hermas* as Scripture because in one of four allusions he cited it as *graphē*.[14] However, that may be a hasty conclusion. Only *Adv. Haer.* 4.20.2 is an actual quote. The rest are best seen as allusions. Moreover, each of the four referenced the same passage, Mandate 1:1.[15] Additionally, the reference at 4.20.2 is followed by three biblical passages that produced the order of Hermas, Malachi, Paul, then Jesus. It looks like a progression to the ultimate authority, placing *Hermas* lowest on that list.[16] That Mandate 1:1 was frequently mentioned in antiquity, particularly by those refuting heresy,[17] suggests a popular and elegant expression of biblical theology. So then, in Irenaeus, Mandate 1:1 was a summary of biblical theology but did not have the stand-alone authority. Bingham's terms of secondary and derivative authority seem to apply well.

This secondary and derivative authority of certain books became fixed in later years and still employed descriptors reminiscent of the canon. One of the more straightforward examples is Athanasius, a fourth-century bishop of Alexandria. His canon list of 367 is our twenty-seven-book NT canon. Yet despite the list, he cited *Wisdom* and *Sirach* elsewhere with near-canonical terms.[18] For some, this is evidence that Athanasius treated them exactly like the canonical Scriptures.[19]

However, Athanasius had a well-defined place for both *Wisdom* and *Sirach*. The festal letter mentioned above not only defined the biblical canon but also has a list of books for new converts. These were "appointed by the Fathers,"[20] profitable to be read, but not canonical. For Athanasius, then, *graphē* (and similar descriptors) was not exclusive to the canonical Scriptures. Thus, his letter described Christian books in three categories: canonical, catechetical (also "useful"), and apocryphal (the invention of heretics).[21] This taxonomy was common and lasted into the Renaissance.[22]

---

13. Bingham, "Senses of Scripture in the Second Century," 52–53.
14. See, e.g., M.C. Steenberg, "Irenaeus on Scripture, *Graphe*, and the Status of *Hermas*," *St Vladimir's Theological Quarterly* 53 (2009): 29–66. The citation is Irenaeus, *Adv. Haer.* 4.20.2.
15. He cites it four times in his extant writings (*Adv. Haer.* 1.22.1; 2.30.9; 4.20.2; and *Dem.* 4).
16. Carolyn Osiek, *Shepherd of Hermas: A Commentary*, Hermeneia (Philadelphia: Fortress, 1999), 5.
17. Osiek, *Hermas*, 103.
18. See, e.g., *Contra Arianus* II, 47 (PG 26, col. 245–48) and *Epistula Encyclica* 3.
19. A. C. Sundberg, "The Old Testament of the Early Church," *HTR* (1958): 51, 223.
20. Athanasius, *Ep. Fest.* 39.6.
21. François Bovon, "Useful for the Soul: Christian Apocrypha and Christian Spirituality," in *The Oxford Handbook of Early Christian Apocrypha*, eds. Andrew Gregory and Christopher Tuckett (Oxford: Oxford University Press, 2015), 185.
22. Bovon, "Useful for the Soul," 186.

With this taxonomy of Christian literature as both ancient and enduring, phenomena otherwise considered markers of canonicity should be scrutinized. For example, it is true that these works occasionally appear in biblical codices but were not incorporated into the traditional NT. Instead, works like *Hermas* and *1 Clement* appear after Revelation, a spot appropriate for such works.[23]

Public Reading

If an ancient report notes that a book was read in the church, does that signify a liturgical reading as Scripture? The most famous example regards Serapion, a late second-century bishop in Syrian Antioch. Some in the church at Rhossus had been reading the *Gospel of Peter*, a matter of dispute in the church. To quell the disagreement, Serapion let it be read, considering it to be a trifling (not having read it himself). Thus, some modern canon scholars, interpreting it as liturgical reading, assume the church at Rhossus received the pseudepigraphal gospel as Scripture.[24]

The assumption is highly unlikely. The society of the Greco-Roman world valued writing but especially loved the public reading/performance of these works. They enjoyed multiple venues, both public and private, for such reading.[25] So then, while it may be true that literacy rates were low,[26] communal reading was prime-time education and entertainment (only one reader was necessary).[27] So much so, Brian Wright suggests, "virtually all literature during this time period was composed to be read communally."[28]

The Christians of this period not only attended secular public reading events but had a variety of private and liturgical opportunities to read letters, books, and poetry to each other.[29] It is certain that reading groups existed outside of formal worship opportunities and that they read more than biblical texts. In fact, the appetite for reading was the likely impetus for the large number of apocryphal works in antiquity.

---

23. See John D. Meade, "Myths about Canon: What the Codex Can and Can't Tell Us," in *Myths and Mistakes in New Testament Textual Criticism*, eds. Elijah Hixson and Peter J. Gurry (Downers Grove, IL: InterVarsity Press, 2019), 253–77.

24. McDonald, *Formation*, 1:68.

25. William Shiell, *Reading Acts: The Lector and the Early Christian Audience*, Biblical Interpretation Series 70 (Leiden: Brill, 2004), 116–17.

26. Harry Gamble, "Literacy, Liturgy, and the Shaping of the New Testament Canon," in *The Earliest Gospels: The Origins and Transmission of the Earliest Christian Gospels—the Contribution of the Chester Beatty Gospel Codex P*[45], JSNTSupp 258, ed. Charles Horton (London: T&T Clark, 2004), 30.

27. Larry W. Hurtado, *Destroyer of the Gods: Early Christian Distinctiveness in the Roman World* (Waco, TX: Baylor University Press, 2016), 108.

28. Brian J. Wright, *Communal Reading in the Time of Jesus: A Window into Early Christian Reading Practices* (Philadelphia: Fortress, 2017), 60.

29. Wright, *Communal Reading*, 4.

Serapion was almost certainly referring to private communal reading. The event led to his own book that denounced the *Gospel of Peter*.[30] The event in no way suggests the *Gospel of Peter* was received as Scripture by the church at Rhossus and certainly not by her bishop.

The conclusion, then, is that we cannot consider a community to be receiving a work as Scripture simply because the source refers to reading it. Not all reading by Christians was liturgical.

Citing an Authority

The early Christians quoted both pagan and Christian literature. For some scholars, these citations suggest there was no closed canon or a broader local canon.[31] The citation of nonbiblical literature is undeniable. The most prolific example is Clement of Alexandria in the late second century. From what we can tell, he was one of the most well-read men in antiquity. His extant works appeal to pagan, Jewish, and Christian literature around eight thousand times, a third of which are pagan sources.[32] Based on his use of these sources, Metzger concluded that he did have a canonical core, but "on the whole one can say that, so far as his understanding of Scripture was concerned, he had an 'open' canon."[33]

Nobody suggests Clement would consider *all* those books as Scripture. Certain citations, however, have been presented as evidence of a broader set of Gospels.[34] The prime example is his citation of the *Gospel to the Egyptians*. He quotes the apocryphal work, but the context denies any affirmation of it. In *Stromata*, Clement merely notes those who appeal to that Gospel misunderstand it (3.6.45).[35] In his final word on it (3.13.91–93), he criticized a certain Julius Casinos's support of a "godless opinion" on three grounds. First, Julius cited the *Gospel of the Egyptians*, not one of the four Gospels "handed down to us." Second, Julius misunderstood the saying he quoted. Third, he misrepresented Paul. The citation is a magnificent example of displaying the baseless argument of an opponent, not an affirmation of the *Gospel to the Egyptians*.

The Scripture discernable from Clement's extant writings includes the Four Gospels, fourteen letters of Paul (including Hebrews), 1 Peter, 1 John, and Revelation.[36] To this, we can likely add an allusion to 2 Peter as well.[37]

---

30. Eusebius, *Hist. eccl.* 6.12.2.
31. See, e.g., MacDonald, *Formation*, 2:79 and John Barton, *A History of the Bible: The Story of the World's Most Influential Book* (New York: Viking, 2019), 263. For a lengthy defense of this position, see C. E. Hill, *Who Chose the Gospels? Probing the Great Gospel Conspiracy* (Oxford: Oxford University Press, 2010), 81–82.
32. Metzger, *Canon*, 131.
33. Metzger, *Canon*, 135.
34. McDonald, *Formation*, 2:280.
35. See also *Strom.* 3.10.63.
36. Metzger, *Canon*, 134–35.
37. See *Quis dives Salvetur* 36.20–22.

Clement also refers to a body of literature known as "the New Testament."[38] Moreover, according to Eusebius, he wrote "brief explanations" on all the canonical Scriptures (even the disputed books, specified as Jude and the other Catholic Epistles) and the *Epistle of Barnabas* and the *Apocalypse of Peter.*[39] Clement may have a wider canon, but nothing suggests it is open. More importantly, citation, even frequent citation, does not seem to be an indication of canonical status.

To sum up, it is not enough that the work was read, received Scripture-like signifiers, or was cited. Ultimately, we know of only a few works with such local canonicity and only one with widespread popularity. To interpret *graphē* and cognates to mean the modern view of Scripture is a flattened designation that is too broad. As Chapman states, "Scripture is left vague and ill-defined: authoritative but not yet normative, religious but not yet orthodox, inspired but not yet 'closed.' Rarely asked, in fact, is whether the distinction between canon and Scripture does full justice to the historical phenomenon of *Scripture. . . .*"[40]

A Fourth-Century Revolution?

If scholars have been overstating what the ancients considered Scripture, it adjusts how we view the fourth-century environment. A revolutionary moment requires the period to be radically different than the previous ages. However, what we see is more of a status quo than an upheaval. The fourth-century councils with canon lists merely affirmed what the fathers passed down to them.[41] There is no evidence of debate, sorting, or sifting. McDonald, largely an advocate of Sundberg's thesis, agrees and does not ascribe to a moment of canonization. He states, "No single individual made a declaration on the matter that everyone accepted."[42] He ultimately concludes that the recognition of the canon as a closed list of books *broadly* happened in the late fourth century.[43] We contend that when we decline the maximalist position of what constituted Scripture, the fourth century does not look so different than the previous 150 years.

So how would we describe the status of the canon at that time? Hebrews and Revelation had challenges to remove them from the canon. It would be another hundred years before the Syrian church received the lesser General

---

38. See, e.g., *Strom.* 5.1.
39. Eusebius, *Hist. eccl.* 6.14.1.
40. Stephen B. Chapman, "The Canon Debate: What It Is and Why It Matters," *Journal of Theological Interpretation* 4 (Fall 2010): 273–94.
41. See Question 25.
42. John J. Collins, Craig A. Evans, and Lee Martin McDonald, *Ancient Jewish and Christian Scriptures: New Developments in Canon Controversy* (Louisville, KY: Westminster John Knox, 2020), 127.
43. Collins, Evans, McDonald, *Ancient Jewish and Christian Scriptures*, 127.

Epistles (2 Peter, 2–3 John, and Jude). The most protracted holdout would be the Greek church regarding Revelation. Still, however, the majority affirmed our twenty-seven-book NT canon. The period, then, was an era when there was a general consensus in the face of ongoing hesitation regarding certain books. It raises a significant question: if this is the case, how is that fundamentally different from the same realities a century (or more) earlier or even today? The brute fact is that universal consensus has never occurred, nor is forthcoming.[44] If the fourth century brought a revolutionary moment, nobody seemed to notice, and people lived their faith as they had always done.

Summary

When investigating the term *graphē*, we found it had a broad semantic domain. It was undoubtedly used in a few places to indicate the author's belief a book was Scripture, but it also was used more broadly. So, the term (and its cognates) do not automatically suggest the reference was Scripture in the modern sense. Furthermore, because communal reading was common, not every reference to reading referred to a liturgical reading. Finally, just because a work was cited, it does not mean it was cited as Scripture. Altogether this evidence suggests fewer works were considered Scripture than often proposed. This evidence indicates that the status in the fourth century (basic consensus with dissenting voices) was similar to what appeared centuries earlier. Thus, it is unnecessary to suggest a divide between "canon" and "scripture."

REFLECTION QUESTIONS

1. When a writer believes a noncanonical book was Scripture, does that mean he has no concept of canon?

2. If a writer introduced a work with *graphē*, does that always suggest it was considered Scripture?

3. How does the fact of widespread communal reading affect our understanding of statements about reading books in antiquity?

4. Can a writer cite a work without that book being considered Scripture?

5. How different from earlier generations was the scriptural environment of the fourth century?

---

44. Chapman, "Canon Debate," 283–84.

Did the Early Christians Have an Old Testament Canon?

When and how the Hebrew Bible was canonized is not exactly our topic. The question is more precisely about the situation in the first century. At stake is whether "canon" was a theological concept for the early believers. If there is no early concept of a finite list of sacred books, it was imposed later. This leaves open the implications of the exclusive and magisterial models noted earlier. Namely, what is the relevancy, adjustability, and authority of the church over the canon?

Old Testament scholars can be grouped into two major camps regarding the OT canon: maximalists and minimalists.[1] The maximalists set the closure of the OT canon in the second century BC.[2] In this opinion, the Christian church had not only a canon consciousness, but a closed OT canon. Minimalists set the canon between the late second to fourth centuries AD. Most who hold to a minimalist opinion follow the lead of A. C. Sundberg. He suggested that between AD 30–70, Judaism had a closed collection in the Law and Prophets but another category, the Writings, was still undefined.[3] Sundberg described this phenomenon as "as scripture on the way to canon."[4] This undefined category is proposed as a canonical practice by the early Christians, so they had "scripture" but not canon. If true, the early Christians

---

1. Stephen Dempster, "The Old Testament Canon, Josephus, and Cognitive Environment," in *The Enduring Authority of the Christian Scriptures,* ed. D. A Carson (Grand Rapids: Eerdmans, 2016), 181.
2. Dempster, "Josephus" 181.
3. A. C. Sundberg, "Protestant Old Testament Canon: Should It Be Re-examined?" *CBQ* 28 (1966): 200.
4. A. C. Sundberg, "Towards a Revised History of the New Testament Canon," in *Studia Evangelica IV, Texte und Untersuchungen Zur Geschichte Der Altchristlichen Literatur* 103 (Berlin: Akademie-Verlag, 1968), 453.

received a body of Scripture with blurred edges and had no concept of canon. Moreover, there can be no NT canon until much later in the life of the church, for the ancients had no concept of canon. It is germane to our task, then, to see if there is evidence for a closed OT canon in the earliest era of Christianity.

The OT Canon Before the First Century

Given the antiquity of the literature, it is difficult to find explicit statements on the OT canon as canon, but there are some suggestive phenomena. In the narrative books of the apocrypha, Devorah Dimant located nineteen explicit quotations of the Hebrew Bible: Torah (13); Prophets (3); Writings (3).[5] Moreover, she further concluded regarding the pseudepigrapha and apocrypha that "the paucity of explicit quotations from books other than the Tora [*sic*] is striking compared with the profusion of implicit quotations and allusions from almost all the biblical books."[6] This is suggestive of a wide consensus regarding the *contents* of the OT.

The apocrypha also contain references to a *body* of sacred literature. *Sirach* (175–200 BC) contains the first known reference to the three-part OT canon we know: Law, Prophets, and Writings. The introduction of the Greek translation (by the writer's grandson) also referred to the object of comment as "The Law, the Prophets, and the others following them" and later, "the Law, the Prophets, and the other books of the Fathers," and "the Law . . . and the Prophecies, and the rest of the books." The grandfather's text refers to the faithful scribe: "On the other hand he who devotes himself to the study of the *law* of the Most High will seek out the *wisdom* of all the ancients, and will be concerned with *prophecies*."[7] The grandson's threefold reference seems reflective of the grandfather. Moreover, the content of *Sirach* cites the whole Hebrew Bible except Daniel and Esther.[8]

The OT Canon in the NT

The NT use of the OT is immense. Roger Nicole calculated that the explicit citations to the OT make up about 4 percent of the NT.[9] That number rises to 10 percent when including allusions.[10] Needless to say, we cannot make a full

---

5. Devorah Dimant, "Mikra in the Apocrypha and Pseudepigrapha," in *Mikra: Text, Translation, Reading and Interpretation of the Hebrew Bible in Ancient Judaism and Early Christianity*, ed. M. J. Mulder (Peabody, MA: Hendrickson, 2004), 385.

6. Dimant, "Mikra," 387.

7. Quotations of the apocrypha come from the RSV (italics added).

8. J. W. Miller, *How the Bible Came to Be: Exploring the Narrative and Message* (New York: Paulist, 2004), 6–7.

9. Roger Nicole, "New Testament Use of the Old Testament," in *The Right Doctrine from the Wrong Texts? Essays on the Use of the Old Testament in the New Testament*, ed. G. K. Beale (Grand Rapids: Baker, 1994), 13.

10. Nicole, "New Testament Use of the Old Testament," 14.

evaluation here. We can, however, note some particulars regarding the whole collection. Three times Jesus referred to the whole OT as "the law and the prophets."[11] This binary reference was once expanded to a tripartite reference, "everything written about Me in the Law of Moses, the Prophets, and the Psalms must be fulfilled" (Luke 24:44). Elsewhere Jesus cited all the OT but Judges, Ruth, Ezra, Ecclesiastes, Song of Solomon, Lamentations, Nehemiah, Obadiah, Nahum, Habakkuk, and Haggai.

Outside of Jesus, the writers of the NT cite the OT so much so that only six books are not explicitly cited (and they have probable allusions).[12] No apocryphal work and one pseudepigraphal work is explicitly cited. The latter is the curious case of Jude 14–15. It is not at all certain that Jude cited it as Scripture or merely an elegant description of biblical truth. Jude did feel the need to appeal to the apostles in verse 17 as the ultimate authority. What is more, in the dependent parallel passages in 2 Peter, the apocryphal references are removed. The exceptional nature of the citation makes it stand out.

In two passages, the history of Israel is rehearsed that is also illuminating. Stephen's defense in Acts 7 narrated the history of Israel. Stephen cited mostly the Pentateuch but also, Joshua, Isaiah, Jeremiah, Amos, Samuel, Kings/ Chronicles, and the Psalter. Notably, his last citation is introduced as "the book of the prophets," but quoted Psalm 11:4. This is likely not a mis-citation but a reflection of the belief that the psalter was prophetic (see Acts 2:30). We should also note that while there are plenty of such narratives to draw upon, no noncanonical work is cited.

Hebrews 11 is the second passage. The well-known "hall of faith" is a broad tour through the OT. As Eisenbaum stated, "the author was striving for broad coverage of biblical events, so as to better convey the *story* of biblical history—and that is what I think we have in Hebrews."[13] The "canon" in Hebrews 11 includes the Torah (11:3–22), Writings (11:30–35), and Prophets (11:36–37). The last division is in the preacher's summation and quite broad. References to "stoned," "sawn in two," and "killed by the sword" are most likely to Zechariah, Isaiah, and the prophets of Israel murdered by Ahab. Although "sawn in two" is a pre-Christian legend that shows up in several noncanonical works,[14] the reference is to the biblical prophet. Again, while there are noncanonical works that could provide appropriate examples of the faithful, the

---

11. Matthew 7:12; 22:40 and Luke 16:16. See also Acts 13:15 and Romans 3:21.
12. Nicole, "New Testament Use of the Old Testament," 14. These are Judges, Ruth, Song of Solomon, Ecclesiastes, Esther, Ezra, Nehemiah, and Chronicles.
13. Pamela Eisenbaum, "Heroes and History in Hebrews 11," in *Early Christian Interpretation of the Scriptures of Israel: Investigations and Proposals*, Studies in Scripture in Early Judaism and Christianity, eds. Craig A. Evans and James A. Sanders (Sheffield, England: Sheffield Academic, 1997), 395.
14. Paul Ellingworth, *The Epistle to the Hebrews: A Commentary on the Greek Text*, NIGTC (Grand Rapids: Eerdmans, 1993), 630–32.

writer used only biblical examples. Such a list is on the assumption of an OT canon. Ultimately the saturation of the OT in the NT is undeniable and telling of the status of the corpus in the first century.

The more modern versions of Sundberg's thesis have turned to identifying apocryphal allusions in the NT as part of the validation of a broad, undefined OT. A number have made large lists of such allusions.[15] McDonald admitted parallels do not always suggest the NT writers thought these books were canon, nor that all the parallels are legitimate but appeals to "cumulative effect" to support "tenuous boundaries of Scripture collections in the first century."[16]

Daniel Harrington noted two major problems with the interpretation of such lists. First, many of the proposed allusions are invalidated upon closer examination. The "allusions" may simply be background information or conceptual parallels. It is certainly reasonable to think that different people can draw similar conclusions from the same OT text. Second, even if a writer did cite a noncanonical text (and Jude 14–15 certainly did) it would not prove the book was considered canonical.[17] Harrington, then, examined the three most compelling suggested allusions (Matt. 11:25–30/*Sir.* 51; Rom. 1:18–32/*Wis.* 13–4; and Heb. 1:3/*Wis.* 7:26) and found no direct dependence.[18] Thus, the leap from possible allusions and shared themes to "tenuous boundaries of Scripture collections" is substantial. Our opinion is that the evidence of the NT does not support the idea that Israel's sacred Scripture was a broad, undefined body of literature.

The OT Canon in the First Century

There is also evidence of an OT canon among first-century Jews. The Therapeutae were a Jewish sect resembling the Essenes and practiced a monk-like life.[19] Philo, our only direct description of them, reports that their study for a sanctified life was "laws and oracles delivered through the mouth of prophets, and psalms and anything else which fosters and perfects knowledge and piety."[20] At the least, they held to a threefold division. The third section

---

15. See, e.g., David DeSilva, *The Jewish Teachers of Jesus, James, and Jude: What Earliest Christianity Learned from the Apocrypha and Pseudepigrapha* (New York: Oxford University Press, 2013) and Craig Evans, *Ancient Text for New Testament Studies: A Guide to Background Literature* (Grand Rapids: Baker, 2011), 342–409.
16. Lee M. McDonald, *The Formation of the Biblical Canon* (London: Bloomsbury T&T Clark, 2018), 1:312.
17. Daniel J. Harrington, "The Old Testament Apocrypha in the Early Church and Today," in *The Canon Debate*, ed. James A. Sanders and Lee Martin McDonald [Peabody, MA: Hendrickson, 2002), 200.
18. Harrington, "The Old Testament Apocrypha," 200–1.
19. See Craig A. Evans, "Therapeutae," in *Dictionary of New Testament Background: A Compendium of Contemporary Biblical Scholarship* (Downers Grove, IL: InterVarsity Press, 2000), 1230.
20. Philo, *Contempl.* 3.25, LCL 363:127.

referred to as "psalms" shows up in several places as the description of the third part of the Hebrew Bible, including Qumran and the NT.[21]

Finally, the Jewish historian, Josephus, at the end of the first century, made the first extant explicit claim to a closed canon. In *Against Apion* he contrasted Judaism to the Pagans:

> For we have not an innumerable multitude of books among us, disagreeing from and contradicting one another [as the Greeks have], but only twenty-two books, which contain the records of all the past times; which are justly believed to be divine; and of them five belong to Moses, which contain his laws and the traditions of the origin of mankind till his death. . . . the prophets, who were after Moses, wrote down what was done in their times in thirteen books. The remaining four books contain hymns to God, and precepts for the conduct of human life.[22]

The stated contents are significant in three areas. First, the three major sections (the Law, the Prophets, and the Hymns and precepts) sounds very much like the tripartite canon. Second, the number twenty-two was one of two numbers commonly stated for the number of OT books. The alternate number, twenty-four, was generated by separating Ruth from Judges and Lamentations from Jeremiah.[23] Both Origen and Jerome noted both listings were common among the Hebrews; twenty-two corresponded to the Hebrew alphabet.[24] Third, the enumerated contents suggest works grouped in genres rather than the rabbinic arrangement found later. Josephus's arrangement is also represented in the LXX. So then, Josephus's "list" was not idiosyncratic.[25]

Not only was the list finite, it was fixed. Josephus stated: "no one has been so bold as either to add anything to them, to take anything from them, or to make any change in them; but it becomes natural to all Jews, immediately and from their very birth, to esteem those books to contain divine doctrines. . . ."[26] Thus, in Josephus we see all the elements of a fixed canon. Moreover, he presents his case as the convention among the Jews. Lim noted Josephus could not mean every single Jew (for there are always dissenters). Instead, "if Josephus meant that most Jews in his present time at the end of the first century AD agreed on

---

21. See 4QMMT. It reads "the Book of Moses [and] the book[s of the Pr]ophets and of Davi[d...]" (J. C. T. Barrera, "Origins of a Tripartite Old Testament Canon," in *The Canon Debate*, 130).
22. Josephus, *C. Ap.* 1:8. Translation from *The Works of Flavius Josephus*, new updated ed., trans. William Whiston (Peabody, MA: Hendrickson, 1987), 776.
23. Timothy H. Lim, *The Formation of the Jewish Canon*, AYBRL (New Haven: Yale University Press, 2013), 27.
24. Lim, *Formation of the Jewish Canon*, 47.
25. Dempster, "Josephus," 189.
26. Josephus, *C. Ap.* 1:8 (Whiston, *Josephus*, 776).

the canon, then that would have been a credible generalization."[27] It is beyond unlikely that this was a recent phenomenon in the late first century. Instead, he calls on an agreement that likely predated him for more than a hundred years.

Finally, *4 Ezra* 14:44–46 also described a list of twenty-four books for "the worthy and the unworthy" (i.e., public consumption). He added another seventy to be reserved for "the wise." The content of the seventy works is unknown and, as a secret collection for the illuminated, it hardly takes the role of canon, for they were meant to remain secret.[28] The twenty-four are clearly a numeration of the Hebrew Bible. But because the allusion is all that the writer notes, he assumes that his readers would recognize it from the number alone. This implies it is a long-standing cultural phenomenon.

What is germane is that before the first century an OT canon seems fixed in the minds of most Jews. While sectarian groups or academic guilds might have different opinions, by and large the canon is fixed for mainstream Judaism. Early believers received this canon without question.

Summary

Although there was a robust body of noncanonical literature, some highly respected, there is little to no indication that these were considered canon in earliest Christianity or mainstream Judaism of late antiquity. The evidence suggests that the OT canon was fixed by the second century BC at the latest. So then, Christianity did not receive a canon with vague borders but one well defined in the minds of most. They not only had a canon-consciousness—they also had a canon.

REFLECTION QUESTIONS

1. What is the significance of Judaism having a canon with vague borders to the study of the NT canon?

2. How is Josephus's statement on the OT canon significant?

3. What was the significance of the numbers 22 and 24 regarding the OT canon?

4. What is the assumption of the NT regarding the OT canon?

5. What do we make of the NT's allusions to noncanonical work?

---

27. Lim, *Formation of the Jewish Canon*, 49.
28. Karel van der Toorn, *Scribal Culture and the Making of the Hebrew Bible* (Cambridge, MA: Harvard University Press, 2007), 262.

Did the Early Church Councils Decide the Canon?

Throughout the history of the church, the leaders of the churches met to decide critical matters of faith and practice. Perhaps the most famous is the Council of Nicaea (325) that defined the orthodox position on the divinity of Christ, resulting in the famous Nicene Creed. Local gatherings were known as "synods," while gathering from across the empire are more properly called "ecumenical councils." Their rulings are listed as "canons."

The idea that the biblical canon was decided by these meetings has been somewhat of an "urban legend." It still shows up from time to time in writing. These are usually from popular-level works.[1] Occasionally, however, some academic works come close to the same idea. Sundberg, for example, considered the councils as a key evidence in a "stage" of canonization that begins with Eusebius.[2] His comments on the OT canon suggest a similar place for the NT canon: "The Old Testament canonical list was substantially settled in the West with the councils in North Africa at the end of the fourth and the beginning of the fifth century."[3] Likewise, Barton suggests the outer edges of the NT canon are from the life and teaching of Jesus to "the series of fourth- and

---

1. Dan Brown suggested that the canon was determined and significantly updated at the Council of Nicaea (*The Da Vinci Code* [New York: Doubleday, 2003], 234). The Council, however, never discussed the matter. Instead, this first ecumenical council presupposed the NT Scriptures, including the four canonical Gospels, as the arbiter of all disputes (see B. F. Westcott, *A General Survey of the History of the Canon of the New Testament*, 7th ed. [Cambridge: Cambridge University Press, 1896], 438).

2. A. C. Sundberg, "The Making of the New Testament Canon," in *The Interpreter's One-Volume Commentary on the Bible*, ed. Charles M. Laymon (Nashville: Abingdon, 1971), 1224.

3. A. C. Sundberg, "The Bible Canon and the Christian Doctrine of Inspiration," *Journal of Bible and Theology* 19 (1975): 357.

fifth-century conciliar decisions which settled all but a few marginal uncertainties about the contents of the New Testament."[4]

Most do not consider the councils as decisive for closing the canon, even those employing an exclusive definition of canon (who tend to emphasize the significance of the council lists).[5] Jens Schröter expresses it well, "the New Testament was never officially agreed upon and declared to be binding by a synod of the ancient church."[6] Instead of binding proclamations, these councils represent the local opinions regarding the Scriptures that were, echoing Sundberg, setting the stage for closing the canon. Primarily what the councils provide is significant evidence for suggesting that the fourth century was a revolutionary period for canonization by those who see a strict distinction between "scripture" and "canon."

It is correct that there is no indication of sorting, sifting, deliberating, choosing, or establishing the canon of Scripture in the councils' lists. Moreover, evidence of any sort of an atmosphere for closing the canon does not seem to be evident. Instead of pointing forward, the councils clearly point backwards to an existing consensus that had been in place for a long time.

The Purpose of Church Councils

The local bishops of the early church often met to decide matters of conflict. None of the earliest gatherings could be called "universal" in the sense of worldwide. "Universal," then, in the ancient references indicates churches within the same district.[7] These seem to be rather common for Tertullian (late second to early third century) who mentions that "councils are gathered out of every church."[8] Those who downplay the significance of the council's lists tend to point out the local nature of the synods.[9]

The topics of the earliest synods were generally heresy and the date of Easter (the "Quartodeciman" controversy).[10] Tertullian (c. 210) noted that the *Shepherd of Hermas* was rejected as apocryphal and pseudepigraphal by

---

4. John Barton, *Holy Writings, Sacred Text: The Canon in Early Christianity* (Louisville, KY: Westminster John Knox, 1998), 1.

5. See Harry Y. Gamble, "The New Testament Canon: Recent Research and the Status Quaestionis," in *The Canon Debate*, eds. James A. Sanders and Lee Martin McDonald (Peabody, MA: Hendrickson, 2002), 233.

6. Jens Schröter, *From Jesus to the New Testament: Early Christian Theology and the Origin of the New Testament Canon* (Waco, TX: Baylor University Press, 2013), 250.

7. See Mark Edwards, "Synods and Councils," in *The Cambridge History of Christianity*, ed. Augustine Cassiday and Frederick W. Norris (New York: Cambridge University Press, 2007), 367.

8. Tertullian, *Jejun.* 3.6.

9. See, e.g., Bart D. Ehrman, *Lost Scriptures: Books That Did Not Make It into the New Testament* (Oxford: Oxford University Press, 2003), 341.

10. See Karl Joseph von Hefele, *A History of the Councils of the Church: From the Original Documents* (Edinburgh: T&T Clark, 1883), 1:77–85.

numerous early councils.[11] He made no other appeal to the decisions of councils regarding Scripture. No other early church Father appealed to a council regarding Scripture.

Only three of the known ancient councils officially mention the canon of Scripture. Of these three lists, one is doubtful (Laodicea), perhaps added later; another gives the appearance of an afterthought (Hippo-Regius), and the third contains the only original composition out of the three (Carthage).

The Synod of Laodicea

The first, the Synod of Laodicea, was a local meeting of less than thirty bishops around 360.[12] As such, it is representative of the Greek-speaking church, although there are Latin and Syriac translations. It survives in an ancient summary of the individual rulings called "canons." Of particular interest, canon LIX states, "No psalms composed by private individuals nor any uncanonical books may be read in the church, but only the Canonical Books of the Old and New Testaments."[13] We should note here that the term "canonical" is used assuming a status for these books already in place.

Reading the rest of the canons of the synod, we find that the bishops had more to say about the relationship between worship and Scripture. Canon XVI states, "The Gospels, the Apostle (Paul's epistles) and the other Scriptures are to be read on the Sabbath."[14] The reader, a layman who is to read the Scripture of the day (called the "lection"), and likely other matters for the congregation, plays a quasi-official role (Canon XVIII and XIX), likely due to the sacred nature of his reading. So, at Laodicea we see an understanding of the Scriptures as an *existing* set of documents that is woven into the worship life of the church. The ruling does not permit reading other works as the lection in worship because they are not canon.

A list of OT and NT books only appears in a Greek version of the synod. The NT list is our present canon minus Revelation (not unusual for the Eastern Greek Churches). The list does not appear in the Syriac and Latin translations. Since a removal of a canon list is far less likely, it is more likely to have been added later and does not represent the synod itself.[15]

---

11. Tertullian, *Pud.* 10 (ANF 4:85).
12. For more information, see Edmon L. Gallagher and John D. Meade, *The Biblical Canon Lists from Early Christianity: Texts and Analysis* (Oxford: Oxford University Press, 2017), 129–34; and B. F. Westcott, *A General Survey of the History of the Canon of the New Testament*, 7th ed. (Cambridge: Cambridge University Press, 1896), 439–47.
13. NPNF 2.14:158.
14. NPNF 2.14:148.
15. Virtually all agree. See Westcott, *Canon*, 505; and Bruce Metzger, *The Canon of the New Testament: Its Origin, Development, and Significance* (Oxford: Oxford University Press, 1987), 210.

The Council of Hippo-Regius

The first council to have a canonical list was the Council of Hippo in North Africa (c. 393). It was part of a series of meetings held in the North African Church. In all, there were eighteen meetings that ultimately formed the *African Code*.[16] The code was very influential and was ultimately incorporated into the Eastern Church as well. The canons (rulings) are somewhat of a rolling list, with later synods either modifying or accepting the previous canons.[17]

Outside of the canons incorporated in the later code, the actual rulings are lost. A summary of the council of Hippo was read at the third council of Carthage (another in this series of meetings), of which a reconstructed and disputed text remains.[18] The thirty-sixth canon of that summary begins, "Besides the canonical Scriptures, nothing shall be read in the church, under the title of 'divine writings.' The canonical books are: . . ." This is followed by a list of the OT books (including some of the Apocrypha) and the present twenty-seven-book NT. The only oddity being Paul listed as thirteen epistles, immediately followed by "one Epistle of S. Paul to the Hebrews."[19] The canon closes with this comment, "Concerning the confirmation of this canon [i.e., the ruling], the transmarine Church shall be consulted. On the anniversaries of martyrs, their acts shall also be read."[20]

Although we do not have a complete copy of the canons of this synod, we do know a good bit about the meeting itself. First, Augustine was in attendance, and he described it as "a Plenary Council of all Africa at Hippo Regius."[21] He was invited to give an address even though he was ordained the previous year. His message is preserved for us as "On the Faith and the Creed."[22] In that message he makes no mention of the status of the biblical canon. Instead, his topic is a commentary on the Nicene Creed through biblical interpretation. His later statements on the council are just as silent on the matter. Thus, it is not possible to affirm that Augustine, as one scholar states, "threw his weight behind Athanasius' list and pushed its acceptance."[23]

Furthermore, we have his letter to Bishop Aurelius that refers to the council. There he noted the purpose of the council was "to bring healing to the many carnal blemishes and disorders which the African Church is

---

16. NPNF 2.14: 438.
17. See Charles Joseph Hefele, *A History of the Councils of the Church from the Original Documents*, trans. and ed. Henry Nutcombe Oxenham (Edinburgh: T&T Clark, 1876), 2:441–42.
18. See Hefele, *History*, 396.
19. Hefele, *History*, 400.
20. Hefele, *History*, 400.
21. Augustine, *Retract.*, 1.16.
22. See NPNF 1.3: 322.
23. Ehrman, *Lost Scriptures*, 341. Augustine did consider the canon "definitively closed" (Augustine, *Civ.* 22.8). It is not likely he was referring to the council at Hippo.

suffering in the conduct of many."[24] From all appearances, a determination to close the canon seems nowhere on the minds of these men. Instead, the life and practice of the church is the focus. Thus, regarding the worship of the church, nothing but the divine Scriptures should be read in the lection of the church apart from a special allowance for the acts of the martyrs on the day of their death. It seems, at least for the North African Church, the assumption was that the canon of Scriptures was already set and affirmed in the council.

The Third Council of Carthage

In 397, the Third Council of Carthage read the previous affirmations and adopted them.[25] Some textual observations are required before we evaluate the ruling. The text appears very much like the Hippo-Regius canon except for a couple of matters. The strange reference to Hebrews at Hippo is edited to read "one epistle of the same to the Hebrews." Such a correction of a clumsy expression is certainly understandable (and lends credence to the originality of the Hippo version as we have it). E. J. Jonkers's version of the text ends after the list of NT books.[26] John Dominic Mansi's text (seventeenth century) makes a note that an ancient copy concludes with the same admonition to consult the transmarine church that appears in the Hippo-Regius ruling.[27]

The last three sentences, as it appears in the *African Code*, read, "Let this be made known also to our brother and fellow-priest Boniface, or to other bishops of those parts, for the purpose of confirming that canon. Because we have received from our fathers that those books must be read in the Church. Let it also be allowed that the Passions of Martyrs be read when their festivals are kept." This note cannot be original to the council of 397 for Boniface's succession was in 418. Obviously, these sentences were adapted to the situation of the writing of the *African Code* (419). It is the opinion here that the Hippo-Regius Council was read at the third Carthaginian council and adopted as is. However, the reading appearing in the *African Code* that appealed to the Scriptures as "received from our fathers" does represent the general attitude regarding the canon of Scripture. It does not suggest a dawning awareness of a closed canon. Instead, closure is the status of these books in the church for a lengthy period of time.

Summary

All things considered, the early councils were not about the business of selecting a canon but already recognized a set of books as canonical. Nor was

---

24. Augustine of Hippo, "Letters of St. Augustin," in NPNF 1:239.
25. See Metzger, *Canon*, 314–15 and Westcott, *Canon*, 448–49.
26. E. J. Jonkers, ed., *Acta et Symbola Conciliorum Quae Saeculo Quarto Habita Sunt,* Textus Minores 19 (Leiden: E. J. Brill, 1954), 136.
27. Giovan Domenico Mansi and Philippe Labbe, ed., *Sacrorum Concilioru: Nova Et Amplissima Collectio* (Graz: Akademische Druck- u. Verlagsanstalt, 1759), 3:891.

their recognition only a matter of local importance alone (although their authority likely was) for the Eastern and Western Churches made similar rulings. The Carthaginian Church felt it was a universal matter; they recommended the ruling to read only canonical Scriptures to the church at Rome as well.

The fact that so few council leaders were known to address the canon of Scripture is noteworthy. In his *History of the Councils of the Church*, Hefele covers the church councils and synods to c. 429 in two volumes, detailing 104 known meetings. Only three councils address the canon. So then, while the period up to the fourth century has been described a prolonged fight over the canon,[28] in the place where we would expect to see such debates—the rulings of the councils—there is virtual silence. And what is more, they addressed it as a previously existing list that should be the lections of the church. The canon lists of the councils, then, are not evidence of a revolutionary period of canonization but a reactionary response to progressive standards in the churches.

REFLECTION QUESTIONS

1. What are the three councils/synods that mention the canon of Scripture?

2. Why are they not considered to be closing the canon?

3. Is it significant that they were local and not empire-wide?

4. Why can we not say that Augustine at the council of Hippo-Rhegius pushed for the ratification of the canon list?

5. What is the significance that only three councils list the books of Scripture?

---

28. Bart D. Ehrman, *Lost Christianities: The Battles for Scripture and the Faiths We Never Knew* (New York: Oxford University Press, 2003), 245.

What Led Christians to Recognize Contemporaneous Writings as Scripture?

The NT itself recognizes contemporaneous works as Scripture (2 Peter 3:15, Paul's letters and 1 Tim. 5:18, Luke's gospel).[1] What is more, as early as we can tell, the early believers were virtually never without new Scripture alongside the OT. For example, the earliest collection of Christian writings outside of the NT (the so-called "Apostolic Fathers") cite the present NT at least 151 times (and the OT 187 times). Many of these citations are introduced as "Scripture" or other Scripture-like introductions like, "it is written."[2] Regardless of whether one sees a sharp distinction between "Scripture" and "canon," as in the extrinsic model, the phenomenon of new Scriptures is certainly evident in earliest Christianity. The present question asks what would lead the early believers to add to their body of religious literature? Some have suggested the answer is a response to a second-century crisis (like Marcion's truncated canon).[3] Markschies calls it an emergency-brake model.[4] But that discussion is more about a closed list rather than the impetus for receiving Scripture that, given the NT witness, greatly predated Marcion. Others have suggested that the need for Christian Scripture to be read in the church's

---

1. See Question 35 for details.
2. See, e.g., *2 Clem.* 2:1–6 for the NT as "Scripture;" the *Ep. Barn.* 4:11 uses "it is written" of Matthew 22:14.
3. See Jason B. BeDuhn, *The First New Testament: Marcion's Scriptural Canon* (Salem, OR: Polebridge, 2013).
4. Christoph Markschies, "The Canon of the New Testament in Antiquity," in *Homer, the Bible, and Beyond: Literary and Religions Canons in the Ancient World,* eds. Margalit Finkelberg and Guy G. Stroumsa (Leiden: Brill, 2003), 176.

lectionary was the impetus.[5] We agree this ritual use of texts indicates they were recognized as Scripture. It is not clear that this was the stimulus for receiving these works as Scripture. Instead, we suggest the impetus for receiving new Scriptures is best found in the internal theological convictions of the earliest believers. These convictions are the authority of Jesus and the apostles, the inauguration of the new covenant, and prophetic apostolic fulfillment.

The Authority of Jesus and the Apostles

From the earliest periods, Christians placed the highest authority in Jesus and his words because he is the Son of God.[6] Thus, it is no surprise that the earliest believers collected and treasured his teachings.[7] It cannot be said, however, that the early believers were indiscriminate regarding the sources of the oral tradition or devalued the written word. From the earliest moments, Christianity was producing written teaching and recording the words of Jesus.

The early church also embraced the concept that Jesus had appointed his disciples as apostles. As his emissaries, he commissioned them with his own authority to speak in his name and to be his witnesses. From the beginning, writing was a major part of their ministry, using literature to assert their authority while absent. As the church lost the living voice of the apostles, their writings became even more valuable. But their reception as Scripture was not an added authority. As N. T. Wright notes, they did not merely write about establishing the kingdom, the Scriptures "were, and were designed to be, part of the *means whereby that happened*, and whereby those through whom it happened could themselves be transformed into Christ's likeness."[8] The NT, then, bears "an internal authority by which these relatively few writings validate themselves as divine and as canon."[9]

We commonly call it "apostolicity," but this is more of an internal and theological principle than merely an external criterion. Ultimately their expression of the words and teaching of Jesus (or by men validated by apostles, e.g., Mark and Luke) as his appointed emissaries bears a second layer of authority that was viewed as Christ's extended authority. Dunn suggests this two-layer authority was already in place in the first thirty years of Christianity.[10]

---

5. For a modern proponent, see Tomas Bokedal, *The Formation and Significance of the Christian Biblical Canon: A Study in Text, Ritual, and Interpretation* (London: Bloomsbury, 2014), 237.
6. See, e.g., James D. G. Dunn, "How the New Testament Canon Began," in *From Biblical Criticism to Biblical Faith*, eds. William H. Brackney and Craig A. Evans (Macon, GA: Mercer University Press, 2007).
7. See Bruce Metzger, *The Canon of the New Testament: Its Origin, Development, and Significance* (Oxford: Oxford University Press, 1987), 3.
8. N. T. Wright, *The Last Word: Scripture and the Authority of God—Getting beyond the Bible Wars* (New York: Harper Collins, 2005), 51.
9. Wright, *The Last Word*, 229.
10. Dunn, "How the NT Canon Began," 137.

Inauguration of the New Covenant

At its inception, Christianity was a Jewish sect, and a common assumption is that Christianity's Jewish roots precluded the early church from even contemplating new Scriptures. For example, Adolf von Harnack suggested the OT was a "formidable obstacle" to a new collection, particularly since Christians interpreted the OT Christologically: "Christians already possessed in [the OT] a foundation document for that new thing which they had experienced."[11] C. F. Evans agrees: "[W]hat eventually took place was precisely what in the earliest days of the Church could hardly have been conceived, namely, the creation of a further Bible to go along with that already in existence."[12]

However, it is likely that it was precisely the Jewish theological matrix that was a major stimulus for recognizing new literature as Scripture. This stimulus is involved in the Jewish understanding of the relationship between covenant and covenant documents. The premise is that in Judaism covenants also included covenant documents. So that even the Sinai covenant was not merely a verbal agreement, but was accompanied by the tables of the law and the book of the covenant (Exod. 12–26).

The relationship between covenant and covenant documents is well established in the Ancient Near East (ANE) and the OT.[13] At Sinai, the stone tablets are the covenant documents that are then placed in the ark of the covenant. The description of the Sinai covenant and its recensions (Exodus-Leviticus, Deuteronomy, and Joshua 24) is remarkably similar to the fourteenth-century-BC Hittite suzerain-vassal treaties.[14] Thus, there is a strong connection between canon and covenant. So much so, the name of the books themselves is called *diathēkē*. A word commonly translated, "testament," it is more properly "covenant."

We see this in the OT when it (or portions of it) was called "the book of the covenant" (see Exod. 24:7; Deut. 29:20; 31:9, 26; 2 Kings 23:2, 21;

---

11. Adolf von Harnack, *The Origin of the New Testament*, trans. J. R. Wilkinson (New York: Macmillan, 1925), 6, 31.

12. C. F. Evans, "The New Testament in the Making," in *From the Beginnings to Jerome*, vol. 1, *The Cambridge History of the Bible*, eds. P. R. Ackroyd and C. F. Evans (Cambridge: Cambridge University Press, 1970), 234.

13. For representative research that compares formal and conceptual correspondences between biblical covenant documents and ANE treaties, see Kenneth Kitchen and Paul Lawrence, *Treaty, Law and Covenant in the Ancient Near East*, 3 vols. (Wiesbaden: Harrassowitz, 2012) and John Walton and Harvey Walton, *The Lost World of the Torah: Law as Covenant and Wisdom in Ancient Context* (Downers Grove, IL: IVP Academic, 2019), 46–53. The foundational essay was by George E. Mendenhall, "Covenant Forms in Israelite Tradition" *BA* 17 (1954): 49–76. For the most recent treatment, see Levi Baker, "New Covenant Documents for a New Covenant Community: Covenant as an Impetus for New Scripture in the First Century" (PhD diss., Southeastern Baptist Theological Seminary, 2022).

14. K. A. Kitchen, *On the Reliability of the Old Testament* (Grand Rapids: Eerdmans, 2003), 320.

2 Chr. 34:30). This is likely because these texts are the documents regarding the history, enactment, and living within the covenant established by God. Moreover, repeatedly in the OT, the covenant was renewed. These renewals added documents to Israel's Scripture.[15] The point was for the worship of the people of God.[16]

Later, second temple literature often connected "Scripture" to "covenant" and referred to the Hebrew Bible as "covenant" or "book of the covenant."[17] Thus, there is a theological precedent that with the inauguration/renewal of the covenant, they anticipated new documents. Consequently, the early Jewish expansion of the church likely would have expected new covenant documents with the inauguration of the covenant.

Prophetic Apostolic Fulfillment

The second theological principle is found in Jesus's interpretation of the prophets. C. E. Hill makes the compelling case that the canon was the fulfillment of a prophetic, eschatological expectation.[18] From this perspective, the rise of the NT canon was inevitable as the OT fulfillment.[19]

He first notes that Jesus's statement in Luke 24:47 ("repentance and forgiveness of sins should be proclaimed in his name to all nations, beginning from Jerusalem") is an allusion to Isaiah 2:2–3 ("for out of Zion shall go the law, and the word of the Lord from Jerusalem"). This seems to be the foundation for Jesus's claim that the prophets predicted the preaching of the gospel. It is repeated in Acts 1:8.[20] Acts, then, shows the progress of the fulfillment of both Jesus's command and Isaiah 2:2 and is "a critical part of the Scriptural foundation for the apostolic mission."[21]

The NT writers interpreted Isaiah 2:2 (and other Isaianic texts) to declare that an inherent aspect of the latter days was a new revelation about the Messiah from God. This message was propagated by the apostles' preaching

---

15. After Sinai (Exod. 19–24), the covenant is renewed with explicit mention of new writings at Exodus 34, Deuteronomy 29–30, and Joshua 24. See, also, the renewals at 2 Kings 11:17–18, and Ezra 10:1–5.

16. Scott W. Hahn, "Canon, Cult and Covenant," in *Scripture and Hermeneutics Series 7: Canon and Biblical Interpretation*, eds. Craig G. Bartholomew, et al. (Grand Rapids: Zondervan, 2006), 211.

17. See, e.g., 1 Maccabees 1:56–57; 2:48; Sirach 24. The concept can be seen in 2 Baruch which likely presents itself as a covenant renewal and thus written to be a covenant document. See Mark Whitters, "Baruch as Ezra in *2 Baruch*" *JBL* 132 (2013): 569–84.

18. C. E. Hill, "God's Speech in These Last Days: The New Testament Canon as an Eschatological Phenomenon," in *Resurrection and Eschatology: Theology in Service of the Church, Essays in Honor of Richard B. Gaffin Jr.*, eds. L. G. Tipton and J. C. Waddington (Phillipsburg, NJ: P&R, 2008), 203–54.

19. Hill, "God's Speech in These Last Days," 207.

20. Hill, "God's Speech in These Last Days," 210.

21. Hill, "God's Speech in These Last Days," 211.

ministry. It cannot refer to an oral gospel alone. For, in time, the apostles began to write from the standpoint of their divine commission.[22]

The early church clearly interpreted the passage in the same way. Hill notes that Justin Martyr states:

> And that it [Isa. 2:2–3] did so come to pass, we can convince you. For from Jerusalem there went out into the world, men, twelve in number, and these illiterate, of no ability in speaking: but by the power of God, they proclaimed to every race of men that they were sent by Christ to teach to all the word of God.[23]

To this, we can add Irenaeus (*Adv. Haer.*, 4.34.4), Clement of Alexandria (*Protr.*, 1), Tertullian (*Adv. Jud.*, 3; *An.*, 3; *Marc.*, 3:21, 4:1), Origen (*Cels.*, 5.33), and Cyprian (*Test.*, 1.10). Often, in these the gospel through the apostles is referred to as a new law coming out of Jerusalem.

Michael Kruger incorporates Hill's thesis into an even broader eschatological framework that led to the expectation of new Scriptures in early Christianity.[24] He argues three facets of this eschatological dimension. First, Christianity and Second Temple Judaism embraced an eschatological expectation of a new age that included a view of the "story of the Old Testament books as incomplete."[25] Thus, it is not a stretch to assume this promised completion of a written work would also be written.[26] Second, the source of these yet-fulfilled promises, the OT, shows "a tight connection between God's major redemptive acts and God's new installments of revelation."[27] Thus, Christians might naturally expect a new deposit of Scripture given the magnitude of the event.[28] His third facet expands Hill's thesis regarding the prophetic fulfillment of the OT accompanied by a "new divine message" to include Deuteronomy 18:18, Isaiah 11:1; 61:1–2, as well as 2:2–3.[29] All these together suggest the early church interpreted the OT to predict new Scripture as part of the eschatological fulfillment in Christ.

---

22. Hill, "God's Speech in These Last Days," 218.
23. Justin Martyr, *1 Apol.* 39 (ANF 1: 175–176).
24. Michael J. Kruger, *The Question of Canon: Challenging the Status Quo in the New Testament Debate* (Downers Grove, IL: InterVarsity Press, 2013), 49–57.
25. Kruger, *The Question of Canon*, 50.
26. Kruger, *The Question of Canon*, 51–52.
27. Kruger, *The Question of Canon*, 53.
28. Kruger, *The Question of Canon*, 53
29. Kruger, *The Question of Canon*, 54. Kruger also includes the relationship between covenant inauguration/renewals and Scripture, and the authority of the apostles (see above) to form a threefold impetus for new Scripture like the view espoused here.

Summary

We suggest three theological convictions led the earliest Christians to embrace contemporaneous documents as Scripture. First, the conviction that Jesus possessed the highest level of authority and extended that to his apostles led the early church to value the writings of the apostles far more than other writings. Second, the early Jewish believers would expect that with the inauguration of the new covenant, correlating Scripture would be forthcoming. And third, the eschatological/prophetic fulfillment of the OT virtually demands new Scripture. Although the ultimate recognition of the canon's limits is later, the process by which the recognition occurs is theological and belongs most strongly to the earliest expansion of Christianity.

REFLECTION QUESTIONS

1. Why is it that the "emergency brake" model falls short of describing the impetus for new Scriptures in earliest Christianity?

2. Does the reading of the NT books in the early church stimulate the recognition of new Scripture or is it simply evidence of recognition?

3. What are the theological convictions that led to the recognition of the canon?

4. How does the inauguration of the new covenant inspire the early church to look for new Scripture?

5. What OT verses suggest there would be new Scripture in the new age?

Did External Pressure Play a Part in Recognizing the Canon?

Scholars occasionally speculate about forces outside the church that might have influenced the contents of the NT. In the present question, we investigate four of the most cited factors. Two are Roman emperors, and two are heretical movements. Ultimately the question is not whether these influenced the church, but whether they had such an effect that the church responded with decisions about its Scripture.

Imperial Pressure

Two fourth-century emperors are the substance of this inquiry. Diocletian (c. 242–312) instituted the last and greatest state persecution of Christians. The son of his successor, Constantine (c. 272–337) ended the persecution and eventually converted to Christianity. Although their approach to Christianity could not be more different, both are said to have influenced the selection and closing of the NT canon.

Diocletian

"The Great Persecution," as Christians called it, was partly hostility against the Scriptures. Shortly before Easter 303, Diocletian issued an edict that (1) burned all church buildings, destroyed copies of Scripture and liturgical books, confiscated all property, and banned all meetings, and (2) removed all legal protections for Christians and enslaved members of the imperial civil service.[1] Three more edicts in the next year were designed to further ban Christianity. The persecution lasted until 313 when the Eastern Empire under

---

1. G. E. M. de Ste. Croix, "Aspects of the 'Great' Persecution," *HTR* 47 (1954): 75–76.

the leadership of co-emperors Constantine and Licinius published an edict granting religious freedom and restoration of property.[2]

The liturgical books were surrendered quickly, but believers made several attempts to protect the Scriptures. At least in one report, the clergy claimed the readers had the codices; and they would not reveal their names.[3] We know of at least one bishop who hid his Scriptures and turned over the "recent heretics'" writings.[4] Unfortunately, often the report was that the clergy either surrendered Scripture, sacrificed to idols, or suffered death.

The empire's confiscation and burning of the Scriptures is said to be the matter that influenced canonization. The assumption is that when the soldiers knocked at the door, decisions on what was worth risking your life for likely crystalized canonicity in the church.[5]

Although sensible, this is little more than a what-must-have-been argument. Furthermore, it only imagines two categories to choose from: canonical versus noncanonical. While we can rightly imagine some hesitating over a document regarding canonical status, we can just as well imagine persecution forcing other judgments. For example, perhaps one faced a "canon-within-the-canon" crisis. That is, perhaps one would relinquish the GE but risk one's life over the Four Gospels. An individual's prior opinions certainly played a part as well. For example, Eusebius likely would have given up a copy of 2 Peter and the Apocalypse (both he deemed noncanonical) without reservation. In such a toxic soup of terror, angst, and regret, it is hard to imagine a single clear response arose regarding the Scriptures.

There is also the matter of the response of the church. Those church leaders who willingly handed over the Scriptures in the persecution were labeled *traditores* ("traitors") for their collaboration, for their crime was treason (*traditio*).[6] The act became a consistent and divisive point of contention in church life through the fourth century and beyond.[7] Not only was that clergyman considered to have committed an unforgivable sin, but it disqualified all those ordained by him.[8] For our purposes, we note that such an indignant response to handing over the Scriptures by clergy belies any large-scale

---

2. Lactantius, *Mort.* 48. 2–12.

3. See J. Stevenson and W. H. C Frend, eds. *A New Eusebius: Documents Illustrating the History of the Church to AD 337* (Grand Rapids: Baker Academic, 2013), 287–89.

4. Mensurius, the Bishop of Carthage. See W. H. C. Friend, *Martyrdom and Persecution in the Early Church* (New York: Anchor, 1967), 372.

5. See Bruce Metzger, *The Canon of the New Testament: Its Origin, Development, and Significance* (Oxford: Oxford University Press, 1987), 106–7; and Lee M. McDonald, *The Formation of the Biblical Canon* (London: Bloomsbury T&T Clark, 2018), 2:99.

6. Michael Gaddis, *There Is No Crime for Those Who Have Christ: Religious Violence in the Christian Roman Empire*, The Transformation of the Classical Heritage 39 (Berkeley: University of California Press, 2005), 40.

7. See Frend, *The Early Church*, 139–55.

8. Gaddis, *There Is No Crime*, 40.

indication of canonical uncertainty. Instead, these were particularly a "people of the book."

Furthermore, the church in the West did not suffer as the church in the East from the persecutions.[9] The effect of any canonical implications would be limited to those regions where the crisis occurred. Therefore, the results regarding the canon would have been negligible.

Constantine

David Dungan has proposed that Constantine the Great was ultimately the source of the canon.[10] Dungan follows Sundberg's thesis fairly closely but deviates in that he sees the declaration of the canon must also have the power to enforce it. Thus, it is not the late fourth/early fifth century that is critical but the early part of the fourth century, alongside a newly favorable empire.[11]

Dungan sees the canon of the NT in three stages, Constantine is the last stage in two movements. His *Edict against the Heretics* led to the confiscation of their books.[12] And, more importantly, Constantine ordered fifty copies of the Scriptures to be produced by Eusebius to be placed in the churches of the imperial capital. For Dungan and others, the order implies which books were to be included.[13] No one would dare deviate after that time.

Ultimately, there is no direct evidence that Constantine dictated the contents of the NT canon. Instead, there is the implication for something already fixed. For example, the letter requesting copies of the Scriptures goes into details on the production, materials, craftsmen, and even how the books are to be sent to Constantinople. Yet, there was no word of the contents. This implies that the contents were part of the shared presupposition pool between Eusebius, Constantine, and likely the Western Church. Constantine's order also makes no mention of the practice of churches beyond Constantinople. At this time, the Syrian church still held to a twenty-two-book NT canon and did so for centuries afterward. The order does not seem to have standardization in mind.

Heresy

Another external pressure on the selection of the canon is said to come from heresy. Early on the church was faced with those claiming Christianity but not sharing core beliefs. Some of these movements presented alternate views that are said to influence the formation of the NT canon. Two of the most common are treated below.

---

9. Frend, *The Early Church*, 142.
10. David L. Dungan, *Constantine's Bible: Politics and the Making of the New Testament* (Minneapolis: Fortress, 2007).
11. Dungan, *Constantine's Bible*, 3.
12. Dungan, *Constantine's Bible* 121; Eusebius, *Vit. Const.* 3.63–66.
13. Dungan, *Constantine's Bible*, 122. See also, Burton Mack, *Who Wrote the New Testament? The Making of the Christian Myth* (San Francisco: Harper San Francisco, 1995), 287.

Marcion

Marcion was one of the earliest named heretics in Christianity. Very little biographical information about him is known for sure.[14] Born into a Christian home in Pontus, Marcion developed two influential matters: (1) an unusual theological paradigm and (2) a fortune in the shipping business. He eventually migrated to Rome and joined the church with a donation of 200,000 sesterces (worth about $400,000 in modern terms).[15]

Likely influenced by a man named Cerdo,[16] Marcion rejected the belief that the God of the OT was the same as the NT. Instead, the former was lower and less worthy than the latter. Thus, he set out to remove any vestige of the OT from Christianity and its books. What remained was an edited version of Luke and a ten-letter version of Paul (likewise edited). Sometime around 144, he was excommunicated (with the return of the donation!).[17] He was the head of his own congregation until his death sometime before 161.[18] His movement lasted at least into the fourth century.[19]

Several have suggested that Marcion had a primary role in the formation of the NT canon.[20] Harnack, for example, declared that Marcion was "the creator of Christian Holy Scripture."[21] While the degree of his influence is debated, they all agreed that his canon was the first to which the church began to form a canon consciousness.

Many among present scholarship follow suit.[22] The spectrum of Marcion's influence is said to have been immense. Some suggest Marcion's actions required the church to do something that it would not have done otherwise

---

14. For a good summary, see Paul Foster, "Marcion: His Life, Works, Beliefs, and Impact," *ExpTim* 121 (2010): 269–80.
15. Calculated on the assumption of sesterces being worth one quarter of a denarius (the dollar amount is subject to modern inflation!). Peter Lampe calculated it to be worth half the net worth of a Roman of the equestrian order, or a fifty-hectare piece of land—a mid-sized farm or a large house in Rome (Peter Lampe, *From Paul to Valentinius: Christians at Rome in the First Two Centuries*, trans. Michael Steinhauser [Minneapolis: Fortress, 2003], 245).
16. See, e.g., Irenaeus, *Adv. Haer.* 1.27.1–2; 3.4.3.
17. For the return, see Tertullian, *Marc.* 4.4.5. For the amount, see Tertullian, *Praescr.* 30.
18. Clement of Alexandria, *Strom.* 7.17.106.
19. Epiphanius, *Pan.*, 42.1–2.
20. See, e.g., Adolf von Harnack, *The Origin of the New Testament*, trans. J. R. Wilkinson (New York: Macmillan, 1925), 23–24; E. J. Goodspeed, *The Formation of the New Testament* (Chicago: University of Chicago Press, 1926), 126; and William Barclay, *The Making of the Bible* (London: Lutterworth, 1961), 81.
21. Adolf von Harnack, *Marcion: The Gospel of the Alien God* (Durham, NC: Labyrinth, 1990), 112.
22. E. g., see, Hans von Campenhausen, *The Formation of the Christian Bible* (Philadelphia: Fortress,1972), 148; and Jason B. BeDuhn, *The First New Testament: Marcion's Scriptural Canon* (Salem, OR: Polebridge, 2013).

in establishing a canon.[23] Burton Mack is representative: "Marcion of Sinope triggered the explosion" that would culminate in the New Testament.[24] Some go further and suggest that Marcion's was the first continuous gospel upon which canonical Luke was based,[25] and/or it led to the canonization of the OT,[26] Acts,[27] rediscovering and prioritizing Paul in the canon,[28] the production of the Pastorals,[29] the preference for the codex format,[30] and quite a bit more. At least one author suggests the entirety of Matthew, Mark, and Luke were written based on Marcion's Gospel.[31] Others suggest an influence, but not to such a degree.[32]

John Barton rightly defends two major reasons for backing off Marcion's canonical influence on the church. First, Marcion aimed to *exclude* books, suggesting an existing corpus.[33] Marcion's stated reason for rejecting works was that the apostles regressed into Judaism.[34] Thus, the books were rejected from a list of apostolic works.

Barton further notes that if the church responded to Marcion with their own NT, we would expect to see the citation of the books increase after him.[35] We do not. Using the statistical analysis of Franz Stuholhofer,[36] he affirms that the central core of the NT was cited extensively and consistently before *and* after Marcion. Thus, Barton concludes that Marcion "was rejected and anathematized, but not paid the compliment of being imitated, not even in the sense that the church felt constrained to produce a rival 'New Testament' as a response to his truncated one."[37]

---

23. See, e.g., John Knox, *Marcion and the New Testament: An Essay in the Early History of the Canon* (Chicago: University of Chicago Press, 1942), 31; and Barclay, *Making of the Bible*, 81.
24. Mack, *Who Wrote the New Testament?* 253.
25. See, e.g., Joseph B. Tyson, *Marcion and Luke-Acts: A Defining Struggle* (Columbia: University of South Carolina Press, 2006), 79–120.
26. Harnack, *The Origin of the New Testament*, 4–6, 30–31; Knox, *Marcion and the New Testament*, 30–31, 159.
27. Knox, *Marcion and the New Testament*, 114–39, 160.
28. BeDuhn, *The First New Testament*, 28.
29. David Trobisch, "Who Published the New Testament?," *Free Inquiry* 28.1 (2007): 30–33.
30. John W. Miller, *How the Bible Came to Be: Exploring the Narrative and Message* (Mahwah, NJ: Paulist Press, 2004), 73.
31. Markus Vinzent, *Christ's Resurrection in Early Christianity: And the Making of the New Testament* (Farnham, England: Routledge, 2011), 88.
32. Metzger, *Canon*, 126; and F. F. Bruce, *The Canon of Scripture* (Downers Grove, IL: InterVarsity Press, 1988), 145.
33. John Barton, "Marcion Revisited," in *The Canon Debate*, ed. James A. Sanders and Lee Martin McDonald (Peabody, MA: Hendrickson, 2002), 342.
34. Based on the encounter between Peter and Paul in Galatians 2. See Tertullian, *Marc.* 1.20.
35. Barton, "Marcion Revisited," 343.
36. Franz Stuhlhofer, *Der Gebrauch der Bibel von Jesus bis Euseb: Eine statistiche Untersuchung zur Kanongeschichte* (Weppertal: Brockhaus, 1988).
37. Barton, "Marcion Revisited," 344.

This conclusion is also supported by internal evidence. From what we can tell, Marcion did not rework, revise, or add any significant content to his Bible. Instead, he tended to simply remove any positive reference to Judaism or the OT. Regarding Paul's letters, Schmid notes, "the only certain textual alterations by Marcion based on the extant evidence are omissions, and it is only in Galatians, Romans, and Colossians where more extensive omissions are found."[38] His view of Marcion's Gospel is similar. It demonstrates both reduction of the four-Gospel collection and textual emendation.[39]

The actual impact of Marcion was less about canon formation and more likely the challenge of a heretical group that looked much like the church. Thus, the depiction of Marcion as a major impetus for the formation of the canon is unlikely to be accurate. As Barbara Aland notes, "One can hardly name a single element, either in dogma or in the development of the canon, that without him would not have been introduced or that would have been different."[40]

Montanism

Montanism was a movement that arose in the late second century in Phrygia. Named for their founder, Montanus, they emphasized a new charismatic revelation.[41] They referred to themselves as "the New Prophecy" or simply "the Prophecy."[42] They were not particularly theological opponents of the church.[43] So we are not surprised to find some notable converts and sympathy among the orthodox.[44] Although ultimately condemned, for a time they enjoyed a place at the fringe of orthodoxy.

Two matters have led scholars to assign Montanism an important role in canonization. First, Hippolytus of Rome noted they recorded their

---

38. Ulrich Schmid, *Marcion und sein Apostolos: Rekonstruktion und Historische Einordnung der Marcionitischen Paulusbriefausgabe, Arbeiten zur Neutestamentlichen Textforschung*, bd. 25 (Berlin: De Gruyter, 1995), 282.
39. Ulrich Schmid, "Marcion's Evangelium und die neutestamentlichen Evangelien: Rückfragen zur Geschichte und Kanonisierung der Evangelienüberlieferung," in *Marcion's und seine kirchengeschichte Wirkung/Marcion and His Impact on Church History*, ed. Gerhard May and Katharine Greschat (New York: de Gruyter, 2002), 67–79.
40. Barbara Aland, "Marcion–Marcionism," in *Encyclopedia of Ancient Christianity*, ed. Angelo Di Berardino (Downers Grove, IL: IVP Academic, 2014) 2:677–78.
41. On Montanism, see William Tabbernee, *Fake Prophecy and Polluted Sacraments: Ecclesiastical and Imperial Reactions to Montanism*, Supplements to Vigiliae Christianae (Leiden: Brill, 2007).
42. See Eusebius, *Hist. eccl.* 5.19.2 (from Serapion) and 5.16.14 (from an anonymous source) for the respective terms.
43. See Hippolytus, *Haer.* 8.12 who notes their orthodoxy regarding creation, God, and Christ.
44. K. L. Carroll, "The Earliest New Testament," *BJRL* 28 (1955): 50.

prophecies and highly valued them.[45] For some, the period of canonization begins here as a reaction against Montanism.[46] However, not every Montanist embraced these writings. Tertullian, who became a Montanist late in his ministry, certainly did not embrace any new Scripture. Whatever they made of these books, their vague statements fall short of new Scripture.

Second, the Montanist prophets closely associated themselves with the Spirit. Montanus not only claimed that he was the Lyre (a musical instrument) the Spirit played but he also claimed to be the Johannine Paraclete.[47] Some assert this new revelation provoked the church to insist that binding revelation came from the time of Jesus and the apostles.[48] This is hard to maintain in the face of known responses. For example, Eusebius records the words of an apologist writing against the heresy. When asked to write against the Montanists, he hesitated lest he seemed to "be adding to the writings or injunctions of the word of the new covenant of the gospel, to which no one who has chosen to live according to the gospel itself can add and from which he cannot take away."[49] This report, contemporaneous with Montanus (virtually the definition of canon) assumes rather than proposes a canon.

Summary

No doubt the first three centuries of Christianity saw several forces that could have played an influence on the church's reception of the NT. Likewise, it is without question that the external forces did have a major effect on the church's self-identity. In every community, there are such environmental elements that may shape its expression and sharpen its beliefs.

However, regarding the NT canon, hostile forces cannot be demonstrated to have shaped the recognition process on a large scale. Ultimately both the great persecution and the heretical forces were either too late, too local, or misinterpreted to have had a major influence. Instead, we see a people already committed to preserving the Scriptures, often with their lives. This does not suggest large-scale canonical uncertainty.

Likewise, those friendly forces embodied in Constantine's embracing of Christianity certainly affected the church. However, it does not seem to be about the business of selecting Scripture. Ultimately, we conclude that while external pressure is often called upon to explain the formation of the NT canon, those forces had little to no effect.

---

45. Hippolytus, *Haer.* 8.12.
46. Adolf von Harnack, *Origin of the New Testament*, 133. See also van Campenhausen, *Formation*, 231–32 and Goodspeed, *Formation*, 109–30.
47. See Eusebius, *Hist. eccl.* 5.14.1.
48. Goodspeed, *Formation*, 67, 78–79.
49. Eusebius, *Hist. eccl.* 5.16.3 (LCL 1:473).

REFLECTION QUESTIONS

1. What was different about the great persecution from earlier hostilities?

2. Why would the great persecution be said to influence the recognition of the NT canon?

3. Why would Constantine's order of fifty Bibles influence the contents of the NT canon?

4. What does Marcion's canon say about the shape of the NT in the mid-second century?

5. Why would Montanism's embracing of a spontaneous revelation affect the shape of the NT canon?

Were There Other Orthodox Books That Nearly Made It into the Canon?

The short answer to the present question is "no" if we define "Nearly made it into the canon" should be defined as an orthodox work demonstrating widespread acceptance as much as the least attested book in the NT. If so, no ancient work even comes close. That is not to say that no noncanonical books were received as Scripture in local communities in the early period. The phenomenon is undeniable. In the first three centuries, the church fathers cited some noncanonical works as Scripture and noted certain "others" receiving books that were not accepted by the church at large.[1]

However, these kinds of citations do not seem to be a lingering issue much beyond the second century. To defend this opinion, we must identify what is genuinely a candidate from among the large body of Christian writings in the target period. Second, we will note orthodox works that apparently had advocates in isolated communities. And finally, we will examine the evidence for the *Shepherd of Hermas*, the only ancient book with any serious claim for the position.

Limitations

Just because a document was in a biblical genre does not suggest the church ever received it as canonical. In his chapter on works with temporal or local canonicity, Metzger described the different kinds of works early Christians produced: Gospels, Acts, Apocalypses, and, to a lesser extent, epistles, together known as the Christian Apocrypha.[2] The assumption seems to be that the existence of these works meant they were considered Scripture by

---

1. See, e.g., Eusebius, *Hist. eccl.* 3.25.5.
2. Bruce Metzger, *The Canon of the New Testament: Its Origin, Development, and Significance* (Oxford: Oxford University Press, 1987), 165–250. The term "apocrypha" is used today to

the communities that produced or read them. The evidence suggests, on the whole, they did not.

Without a doubt, the early Christians and their unorthodox counterparts were industrious. The *Decretum Gelasianum* (sixth century) cites a series of received works (including the twenty-seven-book NT), councils, and ecclesiastical writers but concludes with a list of banned books that includes sixty-two entries (mostly apocryphal Gospels and Acts).[3] The two-volume *Early Christian Greek and Latin Literature* reports on hundreds of works.[4] Even these likely underrepresent the scope of Christian appetite for reading and writing literature.

R. A. Coles noted that classical Greek literature at Oxyrhynchus was likely "three times the quantity of classical Greek literature to be found on the shelves of the university libraries of today."[5] Evans rightly suggests that the same phenomenon is likely true of Christian literature of the day.[6] We have lost more books than we even know. Only a tiny minority of the books we know are ever said to have had a local canonicity. When considering the amount of what the ancients surely produced, that ratio shrinks considerably.

Of the extant works, we should exclude nonorthodox works. We know heretical groups composed their own documents and considered them Scripture. Irenaeus lists the *Gospel of Truth*, the *Gospel of Judas*, and knows "an unspeakable number of apocryphal and spurious writings."[7] Eusebius rejects the Gospels of *Peter*, *Thomas*, and *Matthias*, for the ancients ignore them.[8] Because of its discovery in the Nag Hamadi Library, the most famous is the *Gospel of Thomas*. Scholars debate if *Thomas* was composed by a Gnostic.. But it was undoubtedly embraced by Manichaeism (a Gnostic Sect).[9] Their adoption of it was certainly a significant point in the nearly immediate rejection by the orthodox.[10] The *Gospel of Ebionites* belonged to a group that denied the deity of Christ. As the work of a heretical group, it would never be considered by the church at large. Among Gentile Christians, the *Gospel*

refer to ancient religious works not in the canon of Scripture regardless of orthodoxy or not. The ancients used the word to describe heretical documents.

3. Wilhelm Schneemelcher, *New Testament Apocrypha*, trans. R. McL. Wilson (Louisville, KY: Westminster/John Knox, 1991), 1:38–40.

4. Claudio Moreschini and Enrico Norelli, *Early Christian Greek and Latin Literature: A Literary History*, 2 vols., trans. Matthew J. O'Connell (Peabody, MA: Hendrickson, 2005).

5. R. A. Coles, "Oxyrhynchus: A City and Its Texts," in *Oxyrhynchus: A City and Its Texts*, Graeco-Roman Memoirs 93, eds. A. K. Bowman, et al (London: Egypt Exploration Society, 2007), 9..

6. Craig Evans, "The Christian Apocrypha," in *Ancient Jewish and Christian Scriptures: New Developments in Canon Controversy* (Louisville, KY: Westminster/John Knox, 2020), 166.

7. Irenaeus, *Adv. Haer* 3.11.9; 1.31.1; 1.20.1 (ANF 1:344).

8. Eusebius, *Hist. eccl.* 3.25.6.

9. Schneemelcher, *New Testament Apocrypha*, 112.

10. See Hippolytus, *Haer.* 5.2.

of the Egyptians was a Greek Gospel produced in Egypt by the Encratites (a Gnostic sect).[11] We noted earlier Clement's encounter with the Encratite Julius Casianus denouncing it. We know of no orthodox writer who embraced it. Works like these never had an extensive hearing among the Orthodox and were never serious candidates for inclusion in the canon.

We should also exclude the entertainment works or those filling in historical gaps with assumptions of what must have been. We noted earlier that several apocryphal works were possibly written for communal reading, not as a biblical addition. The apocryphal Acts have long been discussed as influenced by the Greco-Roman novel, an entertainment media.[12] Most seem to have been produced to fill in historical gaps and show examples of Christian morality. Likewise, infancy gospels like the *Protevangelium of James* and the *Infancy Gospel of Thomas* also existed to fill in the gaps regarding the events around the early life of Jesus. Although highly influential on catholic piety later, neither was considered Scripture.

Finally, we should exclude works that were late compositions. We suggest that works must be early to be considered canonical. For example, in the Latin MS tradition, the pseudepigraphal *Epistle to the Laodiceans* shows up often.[13] Gregory the Great (540–604) affirmed its canonicity and influenced later writers.[14] Although some were convinced, it comes too late to be a serious contender. The church at large was never going to receive it. By anyone's account, works after the fourth century were not serious canonical candidates.

Orthodox Works with a Local Canonicity

Gospels

We know of two Gospels received by Jewish-Christian communities in the early period. The *Gospel of the Nazareans* was written before 180. It is thought to be a version of or an adaptation of the gospel of Matthew in Aramaic. In antiquity, it was known as "the Jewish Gospel." Although scholars debate its contents, it is reasonably sure that it was "used by Jewish Christians in the time of Jerome."[15] The second is the *Gospel of the Hebrews*. It was probably from Jewish Christians in Egypt, written in the second century; it did not last beyond their disappearance.[16] We only have scattered quotations of

11. Moreschini and Norelli, *Early Christian Greek and Latin Literature*, 63–64.
12. Moreschini and Norelli, *Early Christian Greek and Latin Literature*, 1:154–55.
13. Metzger, *Canon*, 183.
14. J. K. Elliott, *The Apocryphal New Testament: Apocryphal Christian Literature in an English Translation* (Oxford: Clarendon Press, 1993), 544.
15. Jörg Frey, "Texts about Jesus: Noncanonical Gospels and Related Literature," in *The Oxford Handbook of Early Christian Apocrypha*, eds. Andrew Gregory and Christopher Tuckett (Oxford: Oxford University Press, 2015), 24.
16. Frey, "Texts about Jesus," 23.

these Gospels in the church fathers (none affirming their canonicity).[17] At best, Christian theologians considered these and other Gospels as secondary sources of information about Jesus and his teaching.[18]

Epistles

Three pre-Constantinian epistles are sometimes claimed to have had local canonicity. The oldest two are *1 Clement* and the *Epistle of Barnabas* (both likely first-century compositions). We have already argued that *1 Clement* was esteemed for its proximity to the apostles. Its authority was not inherent but secondary to and derivative from the apostles.

The *Epistle of Barnabas* is probably the most serious contender of these excluded works. It enjoyed a long and respected career among the orthodox. Metzger assessed it as "on the fringe of the canon."[19] Clement, Origen, and Jerome are among the Orthodox who appreciated it.[20] However, both Origen and Jerome have canon lists that do not include it.[21] Clement cited it often.[22] According to Eusebius, Clement wrote "brief explanations" of the entire NT, including the *Apocalypse of Peter* and the *Epistle of Barnabas*.[23] This might be considered an expanded canon list. If so, Clement had a larger canon than that which is affirmed by the church today. However, Clement's citation of Barnabas included disagreements with the work.[24] Whatever the depth of early appreciation, Barnabas slipped off the scene—by the time of Athanasius, it was not even in the intermediate category.[25]

Third Corinthians was probably written sometime in the second century.[26] Although it was often part of the *Acts of Paul*, it was likely a composition by someone other than that author.[27] Most quarters of Christianity rejected the letter as pseudonymous. However, some evidence exists that the Syrian exegete Ephraim received it.[28] The letter found its most ardent supporters in the Armenian Church starting in the fifth century. But by the

---

17. For a list of the fragments, see Moreschini and Norelli, *Early Christian Greek and Latin Literature*, 59–61.
18. Jens Schröter, "Formation of the NT Canon and Christian Apocrypha," in *The Oxford Handbook of Early Christian Apocrypha*, 171.
19. Metzger, *Canon*, 188.
20. Jerome, *Vir. ill.* 6; Origen, *Princ.* 3.2.4; *Cels.* 1.63.
21. Origen, *Hom. Jes. Nav.* 7.1; Jerome, *Epist. 53* 9.2–6.
22. Clement of Alexandria, *Strom.* 2.6.31; 2.7.35; 2.15.67; 2.18.84; 2.20.116; 5.8.51–52; 5.10.63.
23. Eusebius, *Hist. eccl.* 6.14.1.
24. Metzger lists *Paed.* II.X.3 and *Strom.* II.XV.67 (*Canon*, 135).
25. See Athanasius, *ep. Fest.* 39.7.
26. Moreschini and Norelli, *Early Christian Greek and Latin Literature*, 28.
27. Moreschini and Norelli, *Early Christian Greek and Latin Literature*, 28.
28. Vahan Hovhanessian, *Third Corinthians: Reclaiming Paul for Christian Orthodoxy*, Studies in Biblical Literature 18 (New York: Peter Lang, 2000), 11.

seventh century it was losing favor, although it continued to have supporters for quite some time.[29]

Apocalypses

The Muratorian Fragment expressly declared that the *Apocalypse of Peter* was considered Scripture in the author's community but acknowledged others did not receive it.[30] Written c. 125–50, it is the other book that Clement of Alexandria considered canonical (according to Eusebius). Although appreciated early, it had limited staying power. Ultimately, the church deemed it heretical.[31]

The *Shepherd of Hermas*

Among all the works of the NT Apocrypha, only the *Shepherd of Hermas* enjoyed a relatively widespread reception. In particular, from what we can tell, no other noncanonical writing was as popular as *Hermas* in the pre-Constantinian empire.[32]

Not only was it cited often, but the MS evidence for *Hermas* is better in the earlier periods than for many canonical books. There are eleven fragments/copies that appear in the second/third centuries.[33] Surprisingly this is better than every canonical book before Constantine, except Matthew (14) and John (17). It was not until the fifth century that copies of Mark outpaced *Hermas* in the MS tradition.[34] That does not suggest *Hermas* was more popular than canonical books. Most were found in the trash heaps of Oxyrhynchus. Given the Christian reticence for disposing Scripture, we could interpret the evidence to suggest *Hermas* was less respected than the canonical Scriptures.[35]

Moreover, these MSS appear in both codex and roll formats. The rolls are at a higher rate than with canonical works (about 36%), with two on reused rolls. That two are on unused rolls suggests a position outside of the canon for at least the producers of the texts. As Bagnall states, "for the canonical

29. Hovhanessian, *Third Corinthians*, 15–16.

30. MF 72–73.

31. Jan N. Bremmer, "Orphic, Roman, Jewish and Christian Tours of Hell: Observations on the Apocalypse of Peter," in *Other Worlds and Their Relation to This World: Early Jewish and Ancient Christian Traditions*, eds. Tobias Nicklas, Joseph Verheyden, Erik M. M. Eynikel, and Florentino Garcia Martinez (Leiden: Brill, 2010), 306.

32. Carolyn Osiek, *Shepherd of Hermas: A Commentary*, Hermeneia (Philadelphia: Fortress, 1999), 1.

33. Roger S. Bagnall, *Early Christian Books in Egypt* (Princeton, NJ: University of Princeton Press, 2009), 42–48.

34. Malcom Choat and Rachel Yuen-Collingridge, "The Egyptian Hermas: The Shepherd in Egypt before Constantine," in *Early Christian Manuscripts: Examples of Applied Method and Approach*, eds. Thomas J. Kraus and Tobias Nicklas, Texts and Editions for New Testament Study (Leiden: Brill, 2010), 196.

35. See Evans, "The Christian Apocrypha," 165–66.

scriptures there is no parallel for this practice."[36] This and other format issues suggest many of these are private copies (i.e., not intended for liturgical settings).[37] We should note several more factors play into the survival of manuscripts than mere popularity, but the numbers are impressive.

As noted above, the Fathers of the period frequently cited it with and without caveats. The first suggestion that some received it as canonical is in the Muratorian Fragment. It states,

> The *Pastor*, moreover, did Hermas write very recently in our times in the city of Rome, while his brother bishop Pius sat in the chair of the Church of Rome. And therefore it also ought to be read; but it cannot be made public in the Church to the people, nor *placed* among the prophets, as their number is complete, nor among the apostles to the end of time.[38]

Pius served c. 140–154, making the date of *Hermas* relatively fixed. For the author of the fragment, the recent writing alone was enough to place it in a position of limited reception (read, but not like the prophets or apostles). This is remarkably similar to the book's place in the third and fourth century in the intermediate category.

About fifty years later, Tertullian also makes an interesting claim regarding the deliberation over *Hermas*: it was "habitually judged by every council of Churches (even of your own) among apocryphal and false (writings)."[39] Although his take on *Hermas* is hostile, the fact that second-century councils rejected it should not be considered a fabrication. This suggests, along with the MSS evidence, that *Hermas* fell well short of being included in the NT. Ultimately, the popularity of *Hermas* did not make it canonical but in a premier place alongside *Wisdom* and *Sirach* in the intermediate category.[40]

Summary

Christians have always been particularly bookish people. The earliest periods saw an enormous amount of literary production. The early church sincerely appreciated quite a number of these works, some to the point of local canonicity. None of these found widespread or lengthy support among the churches. A few found a spot just short of canon in the intermediate category.

In terms of the debate about the canon, there was very little debate about books *excluded* from the canon. Most were quickly rejected if ever considered.

---

36. Bagnall, *Early Christian Books in Egypt*, 42.
37. Bagnall, *Early Christian Books in Egypt*, 199.
38. ANF 5:604 (MF 74–81).
39. Tertullian, *de Pud.* 10.12; ANF 4:85.
40. Explicitly stated in Athanasius *ep. Fest* 39.7.

What we see is that the more lingering debate was about the books *included* in the canon—that is, whether some books in the canon should have been given that status (like Hebrews, Revelation, and the minor GE).

REFLECTION QUESTIONS

1. Why would we exclude nonorthodox works from consideration for canonicity?

2. Why were most of the apocryphal Acts never considered canon?

3. What is the significance of the intermediate category when considering this question?

4. What was the most popular noncanonical book among ancient Christians?

5. Did any book almost make it into the NT canon?

What Books in the Present Canon Were Disputed and Why?

M ost canon scholars agree that a "core NT canon" was fixed in churches by the late second century.[1] This core included the Four Gospels, thirteen letters of Paul, Acts, 1 Peter, and 1 John but may embrace more. However, some books were more disputed and for a much longer time.

The disagreement can be seen in the early fourth century in Eusebius's *Church History*. He noted three categories of NT books: received, disputed, and spurious. The received books, "according to the tradition of the Church," are "true, genuine, and accepted."[2] The disputed books "are not canonical but disputed, yet nevertheless are known to most of the writers of the Church."[3] This includes 2 Peter, 2–3 John, James, and Jude. The spurious books are orthodox but not to be considered canonical. These include works like the *Shepherd of Hermas*.[4] Ultimately, the list is only his opinion, for he admits others have a different list of "received" books.

The disputed books are Hebrews, Revelation, 2 Peter, Jude, and 2–3 John. The first two were the victims of attempts to remove them from the canon. The last group, sometimes called the "Antilegomenon," had lingering doubts for various reasons.

Efforts to Remove Books from the NT Canon

We can classify the doubts about Hebrews and Revelation in this category because they both received early and widespread affirmation. It was only later

---

1. See, e.g., John Barton, *A History of the Bible: The Story of the World's Most Influential Book* (New York: Viking, 2019), 261.
2. Eusebius, *Hist. eccl.* 3.25.6.
3. Eusebius, *Hist. eccl.* 3.25.6.
4. Eusebius, *Hist. eccl.* 3.3.6.

that they fell into disfavor. This disfavor was not so much an indication of "canonical softness" but a result of the theological environment that developed in various regions.

Revelation

Even though the book was written in the late first century, Revelation enjoyed an early and widespread acceptance. Virtual contemporaries like Papias, the *Epistle to Diognetus*, and Justin Martyr affirm it.[5] In the late second century, Irenaeus, the Muratorian Fragment, Hippolytus, and Clement of Alexandria cite it approvingly and often.[6] In the third century, Tertullian, Origen, and Cyprian, among others, confidently mention it.[7] Michael Kruger examined the evidence and rightly suggested that the acceptance of Revelation is more substantial than many books considered core canon at the close of the second century.[8] The issue, of course, is the dissenting voices.

Kruger notes the first hint of dissatisfaction was a presbyter in Rome named Gaius who is likely to have rejected it, although it is not certain.[9] Dionysius of Alexandria (Origen's successor) objected to Johannine authorship (but not its inclusion in the NT as sometimes implied).[10] Famously, in the list cited above, Eusebius placed the book in both the received and spurious categories (skipping "disputed" altogether). It is unclear the extent of Eusebius's doubt about the book.[11] Several canon lists from the Eastern Church excluded Revelation. That dispute ultimately was not resolved until the seventeenth century.[12] Thus, the "dissatisfaction" is evident but not as strong as often proposed.

Kruger suggests two primary reasons for the rejection of the Apocalypse in the East. First, the accusation that Cerinthus forged the book is likely to have cast lingering doubts on the book.[13] Second, chiliasm (belief in the

---

5. See Papias *Frag.* 14 (Irenaeus, *Adv. Haer.* 5.33.3–4, and the statement of Andrew of Caesarea in his Commentary on Revelation [*Frag.* 10; PG 106: 224, 418]); *Diog.* 12; and Justin Martyr, *Dial.* 81 and 116.
6. See, e.g., Irenaeus, *Adv. Haer.* 1.26.3 and *Epid.* 38 and 39; Hippolytus, *Haer.* 6.12; and Clement of Alexandria, *Strom.* 6.13.
7. See, e.g., Tertullian, *De Paenitentia*, 8; Origen, *Princ.* 1.2.10; and Cyprian, *Eleem.* 14. For more, see Michael Kruger, "The Reception of the Book of Revelation in the Early Church," in *Book of Seven Seals: The Peculiarity of Revelation, Its Manuscripts, Attestation, and Transmission*, eds. Thomas J. Kraus and Michael Sommer, WUNT 363 (Tübingen: Mohr Siebeck, 2016), 161–67.
8. Kruger, "The Reception of the Book of Revelation," 173.
9. Eusebius, *Hist. eccl.* 3.28.2; see Kruger, "The Reception of the Book of Revelation," 167.
10. Eusebius, *Hist. eccl.* 7.25.1–4.
11. Eusebius, *Hist. eccl.* 3.25; Kruger "The Reception of the Book of Revelation," 169.
12. See the summation in Edmon L. Gallagher and John D. Meade, *The Biblical Canon Lists from Early Christianity: Texts and Analysis* (Oxford: Oxford University Press, 2017), 279.
13. Gallagher and Mead, *The Biblical Canon Lists*, 173.

millennium) is another issue that seems to be the weightier theological issue.[14] We may add a third factor: the staying power of tradition. The enduring commitments of a faith community to what was handed down to them surely propagated lingering doubts. We can see this commitment in the modern liturgy that omits Revelation.[15]

Ultimately, the dissenting voices did not win the day. We should not perceive the journey as a struggle to gain acceptance into the canon, given the history. Instead, the book of Revelation survived an attempt to remove it from the canon.[16]

Hebrews

The dispute about Hebrews is, in many ways, a mirror image of Revelation. Both have early and strong attestation. Theological issues rather than early use seem to be the problem in both books. However, the geography is reversed. The East virtually never doubted Hebrews. The West did throughout the third century and into the fourth.

In the Apostolic Fathers, the citation of Hebrews is conspicuous, with ten discreet citations. This list does not include the obvious and pervasive use of Hebrews by *1 Clement* (even having a list of the faithful like Hebrews 11).[17] Later second-century authors who attest to Hebrews include Justin Martyr,[18] Irenaeus,[19] the *Epistula Apostolorum*,[20] Clement of Alexandria,[21] Hippolytus.[22] Theophilus and Athenagoras likely cite it as well.[23] These works show no hesitancy regarding the epistle.

---

14. Opposition to some form of chiliasm is expressly mentioned by Gaius and Eusebius. For Gaius see *Hist. eccl.* 3.28.2. Eusebius's opinion can be found in his critique of Papias for holding the doctrine in *Hist. eccl.* 3.39.12–13.

15. Gallagher and Mead, *The Biblical Canon Lists*, 279.

16. Kruger seems to agree: "doubts about its apostolic authorship were sufficient (at least in the minds of many) to remove it from the canon despite its long and respected pedigree" ("The Reception of the Book of Revelation," 173).

17. *First Clement* 9–10. The use of Hebrews was also noted by Eusebius, *Hist. eccl.* 3.38.1–3.

18. *Apology* 1, 12/Hebrews 3:1 (Jesus as apostle); *Apology* 46, 56, 79, 130/Hebrews 3:5 (faithful servant Moses); *Apology* 34/Hebrews 8:7 (new covenant proving the old obsolete)/ Hebrews 9:13 (blood of goats, sheep, and ashes of red heifer).

19. See Jeffrey Bingham, "Irenaeus and Hebrews," in *Christology, Hermeneutics, and Hebrews: Profiles from the History of Interpretation*, eds. J. C. Laansma and Daniel Treier, LNTS 423 (London: T&T Clark, 2012), 48–73. See also Eusebius, *Hist. eccl.* 5.26.1.

20. Technically, the *Epistula Apostolorum* belongs to the Apocryphal writings. It alludes to 1:1 and 8:11/§3; 19; and 51.

21. According to *The Index of Biblical Quotations in Early Christian Literature* (accessed online at biblindex.mom.fr, July 21, 2020) verses in Hebrews are cited/alluded to 106 times in his extant works.

22. Hippolytus, a disciple of Irenaeus (c. 170–235), cites Hebrews eleven times in his extant works.

23. See Theophilus, *Autol.* 2.25, 31 and Athenagoras, *Leg.* 10.

In the same period, we start to get glimpses of issues in the West. The Muratorian Fragment listed only thirteen epistles of Paul and made no mention of the book of Hebrews. Eusebius reported that Gaius of Rome mentioned only thirteen epistles of Paul in his book against Proclus (a Montanist promoting new Scripture).[24] Later, Tertullian noted that Hebrews was "more generally received than that apocryphal 'Shepherd' of adulterers" (i.e., *Hermas*).[25] However, he made no explicit statement that others contested it; otherwise, he was a firm advocate of the book (although citing Barnabas as the author).[26] Likewise, Origen considered Hebrews as Scripture, mentioning it more than two hundred times. However, he is the first known writer to note that some contested it.[27]

We see more hints of doubt in the West in the later third century and early fourth, but the book's affirmation is still evident. For example, Theognostus of Alexandria (c. 260)[28] and Alexander, Bishop of Alexandria (ca 321), affirm it.[29] Meanwhile, Hebrews continued to be well represented in the East;[30] most canon lists of the period include the letter.[31]

The hints for rejection are mostly an unexpected silence. For example, Cyprian, bishop of Carthage (200–258), left a rather large corpus to examine. He cited the entirety of the NT, except Philemon, James, 2 Peter, 2 and 3 John, Jude, and Hebrews.[32] He never addressed the canonicity of these letters.

In the fourth and fifth centuries, some textual evidence regarding the Old Latin Bible suggests that Latin Christians (mainly in North Africa) were suspicious of Hebrews. The most suggestive evidence includes (1) Ambrosiaster's commentary on the Pauline Letters (c. 366–84) that does not include Hebrews,[33] (2) the *Speculum*, a testimonia list, c. 400, that does not cite Hebrews, 3 John,

---

24. Eusebius, *Hist. eccl.* 6.20 (also 3.3.4). Eusebius goes on to note that "seeing that even to this day among the Romans there are some who do not consider it to be the Apostle's" (LCL 265, 2:67).

25. Tertullian, *Pud.* 20.1–5.

26. See, e.g., Tertullian, *Adv. Jud.* 9/Hebrews 4:12; *Adv. Jud.*, 14/Hebrews 13:10–13. He ascribes the letter to Barnabas (*Pud.* 20.1). This ascription to Barnabas appears several times after Tertullian. See E. A. de Boer, "Tertullian on 'Barnabas' Letter to the Hebrews' in *Pud.* 20.1–5," *VC* 68 (2014): 243–63.

27. Metzger, *Canon*, 138.

28. Quoted in Athanasius, *On the Decrees of the Nicene Council*, sec. xxv.

29. Alexander, *Epistles on the Arian Heresy*, I.12/Hebrews 1:3; II.3/Hebrews 13:8; 11:10.

30. See, e.g., Methodius of Olympus, *Symp.* 4.1/Hebrews 1:1; *Symp.* 5:7/Hebrews 10:1, 11:10; *Symp.* 9:5/Hebrews 4:14.

31. Gallagher and Meade, *Canon Lists*, 39.

32. See Michael Fahey, *Cyprian and the Bible: A Study in Third-Century Exegesis*, BGBH 9 (Tübingen: Mohr Siebeck, 1971), 40–41.

33. H. A. G. Houghton, *The Text of the Early Latin New Testament: A Guide to Its Early History, Texts, and Manuscripts* (Oxford: Oxford University Press, 2018), 25, 171. However, note that *AN Paul*, an anonymous commentary on Paul, c. 397, does (Houghton, *Text of the Early Latin New Testament*, 27).

or Philemon,[34] (3) Pelagius's commentary on the Pauline Epistles, c. 406–11, does not include Hebrews,[35] (4) Codex Boernerianus (a ninth-century Old Italian MS of Paul's writings) that does not contain Hebrews, and (5) the Mommsen List (no later than 365—likely Donatist), which is the only Latin NT list that certainly excludes Hebrews.[36]

Eusebius, Jerome, and others from the fourth and fifth centuries indicate some rejected the epistle.[37] The writers who address the source of the issue cite similar issues to Revelation. For example, Philastrius, writing c. 384, notes four reasons for dispute about the book: (1) authorship issues; (2) style issues; (3) in Hebrews 3:2 the Old Latin reads "*factum Christum*" ("Christ was made"); and (4) the issue of repentance is "because of Novatian."[38] The latter issue was a long-standing dispute with those who refused to receive those who lapsed in the face of persecution (i.e., the Novatians and sometimes Donatists—groups not considered heretics but schismatics).

The fifth-century heresiologist Epiphanius noted the issue with Hebrews 3:2 was a dispute with the Arians. They made use of the statement while simultaneously rejecting the book.[39] Thus, the major problem with the book seems to be more about internal questions regarding theological disputes with both schismatics and heretics. The combination of authorship issues and theological debates (both internal and external) created an environment that can explain the situation in North Africa and some in Rome.

Jerome gives the opinion of the church at large for both Hebrews and the Apocalypse :

> It is of no great moment who the author [of Hebrews] is, since it is the work of a churchman and receives recognition day by day in the churches' public reading. If the custom of the Latins does not receive it among the canonical Scriptures, neither, by the same liberty, do the churches of the Greeks accept John's Apocalypse. Yet we accept them both, not following the custom of the present time but the precedent of early writers, who generally make free use of testimonies from both works. And this they do not as they are wont on occasion to quote from apocryphal writings, as indeed they

---

34. Houghton, *Text of the Early Latin New Testament*, 38.
35. Houghton, *Text of the Early Latin New Testament*, 171.
36. Gallagher and Meade, *The Biblical Canon Lists*, 39. The other two are the Muratorian Fragment and the defective list in Codex Claromonatanus.
37. See, e.g., Eusebius, *Hist. eccl.* 6.20.3 and 6.13.6. On Jerome, see below.
38. Philastrius, *Haeresis Quorumdam de Epistola Pauli ad Hebraeos*, LXXXIX (PL 12:1200B).
39. Epiphanius, *The Panarion of Epiphanius of Salamis, Books II and III: De Fide*, NHMS 79, 2nd rev. ed., trans. Frank Williams (Boston: Brill, 2013), 364.

use examples from pagan literature, but treating them as canonical and ecclesiastical works.[40]

Thus, given widespread early support and recent objections, Jerome felt in no way compelled to reject either Revelation or Hebrews. Therefore, the best characterization of the phenomena around these books is that they survived an attempt to remove them from the canon.

Other Books with Lingering Questions
The remaining books of the NT that had ongoing issues are the minor GE (the Antilegomena): James, 2 Peter, 2–3 John, and Jude. The Syrian Church contested these books through the sixth century and beyond.

James
It is difficult to identify early allusions to the Epistle of James because so much of it echoes traditional material.[41] L. T. Johnson suggests *1 Clement* and *Hermas* cited James.[42] We also think *Barn.* 9:9[43] and Irenaeus cited it.[44] As noted above, Eusebius claimed Clement of Alexandria wrote "brief explanations" on all the NT, including the GE.[45] The first known citation by name is from Origen (who also includes it in his canon list).[46] A third-century papyrus of James dated near the time of Origen shows signs of use in public reading (i.e., in the Scripture portion of the liturgy) and corroborates that Origen was not unique in this.[47]

Eusebius is the first to record that it was disputed (as far as we know). The issue seemed to be a lack of early citation and suspicion of being pseudepigrapha.[48] However, Eusebius did not hesitate to cite the book as from "the holy apostle."[49] Jerome also reported the suspicion of forgery by some, but he

---

40. Jerome, *Ep. 129* (to Dardanus) c. 414.
41. Douglas J. Moo, *The Letter of James*, PNTC (Grand Rapids: Eerdmans, 2000), 3. But see L. T. Johnson's critique of overstating this: "Such an extensive and intensive range of similarities forces the question, 'where does this come from if not from James?' With such an obvious source available, it seems poor method to invoke instead something so vague as 'common traditions,' particularly when these specific points of resemblance are precisely 'uncommon'" (Luke Timothy Johnson, *The Letter of James*, ABC [New York: Doubleday, 1995], 128).
42. Johnson, *James*, 77–79, 128; and *Brother of Jesus, Friend of God: Studies in the Letter of James* (Grand Rapids: Eerdmans, 2004), 52–60.
43. Aída Besançon Spencer, *A Commentary on James*, Kregel Exegetical Library (Grand Rapids: Kregel Academic, 2020), 26.
44. Irenaeus, *Adv. Haer.* 4.16.2.
45. Eusebius, *Hist. eccl.* 3.3.1.
46. Origen, *Comm. Jo.* 19.6; *Hom. Jos.* 7.1.
47. See Spencer, *James*, 25.
48. Eusebius, *Hist. eccl.* 2.23.24–25.
49. Eusebius, *Comm. in Psalmos C*, 5.

accepted it.[50] From the time of Origen forward, James is cited frequently and approvingly. It is ubiquitous by the early fifth century.[51]

The remaining evidence of questions regarding James is the omissions in the Mommsen List and the Muratorian Fragment. But this omission too is difficult to speak of in certainties, for the former said nothing and the latter is incomplete. Moreover, it is virtually impossible to find someone outside of the Syrian Church who rejects the book directly in the earliest periods.

So then, we find the book in the extant literature, but not clearly so in the major writers of the second century. We know of some anonymous rumbles of discontent. We also know at the end of the second and beginning of the third centuries James is cited unapologetically by Clement and Origen. So then, Moo's contention is likely correct: James was more neglected than rejected in the West.[52]

2 Peter

The lingering doubts about 2 Peter are first extant in Origen (who had no doubts himself).[53] Eusebius rejected 2 Peter, openly declaring it not to be "encovenanted."[54] He does note others found it useful and "studied with the other Scriptures."[55] He is, in fact, careful not to place it in the rejected books.[56] Amphilochius's list notes that "it is necessary" to accept James, 1 Peter, and John, "but some receive" also 2 Peter, 2–3 John, and Jude.[57] The terminology of "necessary" and "some" falls short of advocacy and closer to "undisputed" and "disputed." Jerome also noted some rejected it as pseudepigrapha but affirmed it himself.[58] Ultimately, unlike James, 2 Peter had both named and unnamed opponents.

The reasons for doubt are not often mentioned in antiquity but were probably twofold. First, there are clear linguistic differences between 1 Peter and 2 Peter. Jerome mentioned the phenomenon specifically.[59] Second, the earliest church fathers do not widely cite the book. Eusebius seems to allude to this issue to form his opinion.[60] Most of the extant literature in the earliest periods have only allusions to the letter (but these are better than usually admitted).

---

50. Jerome, *Vir. ill.* 2. Jerome's statement is the Letter "is claimed by some to have been published by someone else under his name, and gradually, as time went on, to have gained authority" (NPNF 3:361). One should assume the opinion that it gained authority "gradually" (lit. "little by little") was the opinion of those who thought it forgery.
51. Johnson, *James*, 138.
52. Moo, *James*, 4.
53. Origen, *Comm. Jo.* 5.3.
54. Eusebius, *Hist. eccl.* 3.3.1, 5.
55. Eusebius, *Hist. eccl.* 3.3.1.
56. Gene L. Green, *Jude and 2 Peter*, BECNT (Grand Rapids: Baker, 2008), 141.
57. Amphilocius of Iconium, *Iambi ad Seleucum*, 310–15.
58. Jerome, *Epist.*, 53.9; *Vir. ill.* 1.
59. Jerome, *Vir. ill.* 120.11.
60. Eusebius, *Hist. eccl.* 3.3.1,4; 3.25.3–4.

2–3 John

The larger Johannine epistle (1 John) was never doubted in antiquity. The two minor epistles have a different history. Along with the others mentioned, the Syrian church also rejected these epistles. The earliest extant confirmation of all three letters (from Origen) is also the first statement of doubt about them: John "left also an epistle of very few lines and, it may be, a second and a third, for not all say that these are genuine."[61] Eusebius also notes the epistles were disputed and may have been written by another John and not by the apostle.[62] Jerome likewise notes that some claimed they were the work of another presbyter but makes no mention of doubts about the inclusion of the letters.[63] He states his opinion they were authentic in later letters.[64]

C. E. Hill has identified an impressive register of citations/allusions from the earliest periods.[65] *Hermas* likely referenced 2 John or possibly 3 John (employing the phrase "walking in the truth").[66] The Muratorian Fragment listed three epistles.[67] Irenaeus identified a quote from 2 John as the apostle's. He cited 1 and 2 John as "the epistle" of "His disciple." The suggestion is that he considered 1 John and 2 John as some sort of unity. Third John 9 may be alluded to in *Adv. Haer.* 4.26.3.[68] By the time of Origen, citations become more frequent.

The question is, what circumstances led to the suspicion and by whom? The lack of citational evidence is likely more due to their brevity than anything else. Furthermore, we again find dissenting voices apart from the Syrian church difficult to find. The enduring myth of more than one John in Ephesus possibly explains the supposition that another presbyter wrote them.

Jude

Doubts about the book of Jude were not evident until Origen made a relatively mild notation "if anyone should add the Epistle of Jude."[69] On the other hand, he had no hesitation describing the book as "filled the healthful words of heavenly grace."[70] Then Eusebius,[71] Didymus,[72] and Jerome[73] mentioned doubts but affirmed the book themselves. Again, the Syrian church is the only group we can identify that rejected the letter.

---

61. Origen, *Comm. Jo.* 5.3.
62. Eusebius, *Hist. eccl.* 3.24.18; 3.25.2.
63. Jerome, *Vir. ill.* 9; 17.
64. Jerome, *Epist.* 53, 107.
65. C. E. Hill, *The Johannine Corpus in the Early Church* (Oxford: Oxford University Press, 2004).
66. *Herm. Mand.* 3.4.
67. Hill, *Johannine Corpus*, 136.
68. Hill, *Johannine Corpus*, 99.
69. Origen, *Comm. Matt.* 17.30.
70. Origen, *Comm. Matt.* 10.17 (ANF 9:424).
71. Eusebius, *Hist. eccl.* 3.25.3.
72. PG 39.1811–18. See also Didymus, *Comm. Zach.* 5.
73. Jerome, *Vir. ill.* 4.

Many writers affirmed the book by the late second century.[74] Tertullian is so confident of Jude that he's willing to accept 1 Enoch on its testimony.[75] A brief commentary of Clement of Alexandria survives, as well his numerous citations.[76] However, before this period, quotations of Jude are "scant and shadowy."[77] But since 2 Peter 2 uses it as *imitatio*,[78] its antiquity and use in the churches from the earliest periods should be undoubted.

The only stated reason for any dispute is Jude's citation of apocryphal works.[79] Didymus addressed the issue as well. These doubts are a late reaction given the fairly impressive early attestation. If we had more early second-century attestation, we might classify it as an attempt to remove it from the NT canon.

Three matters should be evident from the investigation above. First, Origen's statements are usually the first we know about any doubts about these books. In his extant works, he makes no major defense but indicates that some disputed them. These were, therefore, not debates but sidenotes. He was likely speaking from the majority opinion while respecting the view of his dissenting brothers.

Second, 2 Peter is the only book of which we definitively know individuals who denied the canonicity of a book. The linguistic differences in the face of a diverse group of pseudepigrapha claiming Peter as author seems to be the significant issue. We know of no individuals advocating the removal of any of the other minor GE.

And third, the Syrian's church rejection of these epistles is likely the primary source for the Fathers noting the dispute about specific books. We should not perceive their preference for a twenty-two-book NT canon as broad canonical uncertainty. Their opposition goes well past the period most would say the canon is closed. Therefore, it makes little sense to say their previous opposition was evidence of canonical uncertainty.

Summary

When we compare these books to the candidates in the previous chapter, we see a significant divide. For example, there are far more extant rejections of *Hermas* than 2 Peter. Regarding the canon lists in Greek and Latin, the earliest surviving list includes them without hesitation.[80] As seen earlier, the three

---

74. See, e.g., Irenaeus, *Adv. haer.* 4.36.4.
75. Tertullian, *Cult. fem.* 2.13.
76. Clement of Alexandria, *Adumbr.* 2.
77. Charles Bigg, *The Epistles of St. Peter and St. Jude*, ICC (New York: Scribners, 1909), 308.
78. See Green, *Jude and 2 Peter*, 161–62. *Imitatio* (or *Mimesis* in Greek) is the rhetorical device of paying homage to an earlier writer by appropriating and adapting his writing to a present condition.
79. Jerome, *Vir. ill.* 4.
80. Origen, *Hom. Jos.* 7.1 (c. AD 225).

early councils/synods that address the NT canon list them. The Mommsen list (see above) is the only Latin list that registers doubt about these epistles. No extant list after the Muratorian Fragment places an intermediate or heretical book in a canonical position. Eusebius and Amphilocius are the last Greek lists (early fourth century) to note a dispute over the Antilegomena. In sum, there are more questions regarding these books than any other canonical book, but their inclusion is far more robust than any "rejected" book.

REFLECTION QUESTIONS

1. Why can it be said that only Revelation and Hebrews were books that survived attempts to remove them from the NT canon?

2. Why can't the dispute about Jude be characterized as an attempt to remove it from the canon?

3. Why does Origen often seem to be the first to note a dispute, and what do we make of it?

4. Why are 2 and 3 John not mentioned very often in the extant literature?

5. Why is it so challenging to find citations of James in the patristic literature?

The Physical Evidence
of Canon

Is It Important That the New Testament Circulated in a Codex?

In the early period of Christianity, a revolution in formatting books began to happen. Rather than rolls, more people began producing books in codices. The codex is essentially the modern book format, pages bound on one edge with writing on both sides whereas rolls are continuous sheets written on one side. This revolution began in the late first century at the latest.[1] Previously, the codex had been mainly for reference works and travel editions of the classics.[2] By the fourth century, it was the preferred format. How and why this happened is a mystery, but Christians and their Scriptures were at the forefront of this puzzle.

Christian Books and Scripture

Using the Louvain Database of Ancient Books (LDAB), we calculate that less than one percent of second-century non-Christian classical texts (only twelve) are codices. In the third century, the percentage jumps to a little over 10 percent (108/1036). By the fourth, 60 percent are codices (394/655). A similar search for Christian texts shows that 71 percent (5/7) second-century MSS are codices, in the third 66 percent (76/114) are codices, and in the fourth 74 percent (207/281) are codices. Remarkably, the rate is consistent for Christian works throughout the era but exponentially rising in non-Christian works. A format revolution had taken place, and Christians were way ahead of the larger world, particularly for their Scriptures. Regarding the canon, it is

---

1. Larry W. Hurtado, "The Earliest Evidence of an Emerging Christian Material and Visual Culture: The Codex, the *Nomina Sacra* and the Staurogram," in *Text and Artifact in the Religions of Mediterranean Antiquity: Essays in Honour of Peter Richardson*, eds. Stephen G. Wilson and Michel Desjardins (Waterloo, ON: Wilfrid Laurier University Press, 2006), 272.
2. See the summary in Matthew Nicholls, "Parchment Codices in a New Text of Galen," *Greece and Rome* 57 (2010): 380.

noteworthy that all the Christian biblical texts (not on reused materials) are codices.

Caveats

We should see the adoption of the codex as significant, but we should also be careful about the conclusions we draw. We should first note that no "one-size-fits-all" explanation covers the phenomenon. Diversity of all kinds existed throughout the period, and we should expect it to be manifested in this investigation as well. In particular, there are at least three general phenomena that we should consider.

First, handwritten copies are more subject to individual adaptation than modern publishing. A given scribe might feel free to rearrange the order of the books, to include an unusual book, or only make a copy of a book in a corpus. We should expect a certain amount of variation, adaptation, and imagination. These should always be compared to the larger pattern. More often than not, these stand out because of their uniqueness.

Second, some MSS were miniatures produced for private consumption. These productions were not designed to be the authorized edition of the Scriptures to be read in the churches. People purchased them for personal needs or interests. Their size (defined as less than 10 cm wide[3]) easily shows a private purpose for these books.

Third, virtually all books are codices after the fourth century.[4] Thus, a codex after this period is far less likely to be in the format because of its association as a sacred book.

There Was No Conscious Attempt to Create a Format Revolution

Christians did not create the codex, nor imposed it on the wider world. The classical texts that exist might have equally been the possession of believers and pagans. Furthermore, they produced literature that was not in the codex format. For example, LDAB 2459, a page from Irenaeus (of professional quality) dated 200–250, is a roll. Clearly, Christians did not exclusively use the codex.

The Codex Was Not Reserved for Scripture

We should not conclude that early Christians reserved the codex format for their Scriptures alone. For example, LDAB 1094 and 1095 are codex fragments of *Hermas*. The format does not tell us that the work was considered Scripture in the modern sense. The text is so fragmentary that all we know is that it was a codex. As previously noted, though, they seem to be produced for

---

3. Eric Gardner Turner, *The Typology of the Early Codex*, The Haney Foundation Series 18 (Eugene, OR: Wipf and Stock, 2010), 22, 29.
4. LDAB database reports only twenty-two rolls in the fifth through eighth centuries.

private use (i.e., not for public reading). One cannot suggest that a Christian book was considered Scripture simply because it was in the codex format.

Not Every Book Found in a "Biblical" Codex Was Considered Scripture

Some have suggested that a work appearing in a codex with canonical books indicates a canonical status for all the books bound. Keith Elliott, for example, proposed *Hermas*, the *Epistle of Barnabas*, and *1–2 Clement* were considered canonical because they appear in two early codices.[5] These conclusions are oversimplified. For example, the books appearing in the codices represent the secondary and derivative works mentioned earlier. Conspicuously, they appear after Revelation, i.e., outside of the canonical books. Given their intermediate status, the location makes perfect sense. They are no more canon than notes in a modern study Bible.

Other MSS that have noncanonical works bound with canonical are extant. Some are examples of the educational system of the day (i.e., practice exercises by students).[6] These are clearly not intended for the public reading of Scripture but still attest to the text of the NT and demonstrate the value of the book(s). Others are written for private use, gathering documents for personal reasons.[7] We can make no canonical implications by biblical texts appearing with works like these.

At least two codices assembled with noncanonical works are more puzzling. P[72] (1–2 Peter, Jude) appears in the famous Bodmer Miscellaneous Codex (BMC).[8] The codex is a pastiche of disparate texts including the *Nativity of Mary*; *3 Corinthians*; *Odes of Solomon 11*; the Epistle of Jude; Melito of Sardis's *Peri Pascha*; a fragment of a liturgical hymn; the *Apology of Phileas*; Psalms 33–34; and finally, 1 and 2 Peter. It is usually dated to the third century. Scholars frequently cite it as an example of noncanonical literature bound with canonical Scripture that either proves the codex has no scriptural implications[9]

---

5. J. K. Elliott, "Manuscripts, the Codex and the Canon," *JSNT* 19 (January 1997): 105–23. See also Lee M. McDonald, *The Formation of the Biblical Canon* (London: Bloomsbury T&T Clark, 2018), 2:235.
6. See, e.g., LDAB 2763. It contains a page of mathematical exercises in Greek, then John 10:8–30 in Coptic.
7. See e.g., LDAB 8942 (the *Vindobonesis*). A pastiche of works with parts of Matthew 26–28 in a miniature codex. Myriam Despineux concludes, "It cannot be compared to the collections of canonical texts. Those were official, public, whereas the Vindobonensis—see its format—seems to have been produced on a private initiative, for private use" ("Une version Latine Palimpseste du Ve siècle de l'Évangile de Nicodéme [Vienne, ÖNB 563]," *Scriptorum* 42 [1988]: 180).
8. See T. Wasserman, "Papyrus 72 and the Bodmer Miscellaneous Codex," *NTS* 51 (2005): 137–54. Only the biblical text is called P[72].
9. John D. Meade, "Myths about Canon: What the Codex Can and Can't Tell Us," in *Myths and Mistakes in New Testament Textual Criticism*, eds. Elijah Hixson and Peter J. Gurry (Downers Grove, IL: InterVarsity, 2019), 269.

or that all these works were considered Scripture.[10] Some have described it as "the exception that proves the rule."[11] None are the best interpretation of the manuscript.

There is a growing consensus that the BMC had its origins in a liturgical context, i.e., a document for a worship service. Christian worship in late antiquity featured a Scripture reading followed by an exhortation.[12] Some indications are that at least 1–2 Peter are included as the Scripture portion of a liturgy. Within the MS, only 1 and 2 Peter contain marginal content summaries.[13] The origins are debated, but only these epistles had the gravitas for marginal notes. Next, much of the rest of the MS has connections to 1 Peter or 2 Peter. For example, Psalms 33 and 34 are likely included because 1 Peter cited Psalm 33. Likewise, both *Peri Pascha* and *The Nativity* allude to 1 Peter.[14] Jude, of course, has powerful affinities with 2 Peter. Finally, the twin themes of righteous suffering and right doctrine are evident throughout the collection. These themes suggest the selection of the other material was due to their relationship to 1–2 Peter.

A similar MS found in the same context may also indicate its liturgical use. Crosby-Schøyen (C-S) Codex MS 193 is comparable in size and content, suggesting a similar usage. It is a Coptic MS of 1 Peter, Psalm 33–34, and *Peri Pascha*. Pietersma and Comstock make a compelling case that it was an Easter lectionary.[15] C-S MS 193 is a far more attractive presentation than BMC (a "less polished presentation"[16]). This suggests a liturgical setting (notice the more traditional order of Scripture-exhortation) for the document. Instead of showing all these works as Scripture, the codices were special preparations for an Easter liturgy.

Once we consider these caveats, a remarkable pattern emerges for an uncontrolled canonization. From the earliest period, the preferred format for Christian scriptures was the codex. Using the LDAB database, we find only four Christian biblical MSS that were not in the codex format, and these were

---

10. James Charlesworth, "Ruminating on the Canonical Process in Light of Bodmer Papyrus Anthology (P72)," in *"Noncanonical" Religious Texts in Early Judaism and Early Christianity*, eds. Lee Martin McDonald and James H. Charlesworth, T&T Clark Jewish and Christian Texts Series (New York: T&T Clark, 2012), 114.

11. Michael J. Kruger, *Canon Revisited: Establishing the Origins and Authority of the New Testament Books* (Wheaton, IL: Crossway, 2012), 246.

12. See, e.g., Justin Martyr, *Dial.* 67.

13. See D. G. Horrell, "The Themes of 1 Peter: Insights from the Earliest Manuscripts (the Crosby-Schoyen Codex Ms 193 and the Bodmer Miscellaneous Codex Containing P72)," *NTS* 55 (2009): 511.

14. Wasserman, "P72," 147.

15. See Albert Pietersma and Susan Comstock, "Two More Pages of Crosby-Schoyen Codex MS 193: A Pachomian Easter Lectionary?" *Bulletin of the American Society of Papyrologists* 48 (2011): 27–46.

16. Horrell, "Themes," 521.

all written on the back of other works (i.e., reusing material).[17] Hurtado sums it up well: "In the surviving evidence, we do not see an evolution in Christian preference with incremental stages but an appropriation of the codex that appears to have been as thorough as it was early."[18] He further notes that this is a convention, not legislation.[19]

But it is more than that—they are transmitted *together* in codices. As Dormandy says, "there is nothing even resembling an alternate Bible."[20] No noncanonical gospel is ever combined with one of the four in Greek. Likewise, none is found with a canonical gospel in a meaningful way in other languages. Therefore, "there may be *other gospels*, but there is no other gospel collection."[21]

Roger Bagnall concludes:

> In sum, when making private copies on used papyrus, early Christians behaved just like anyone else, using the blank backs, but otherwise, when not recycling, they put Scripture into codices but homilies and the like into book rolls, as if they were normal literary texts. The codex was thus not so much adopted generally by the early Christians for their books production; rather, the Christians adopted the codex as the normative format of deliberately produced public copies of scriptural texts.[22]

So "codex" does not always mean "Scripture," but it is standard for Scripture not privately copied to be in the codex format beginning in the late first century.

Why the Preference?

The origins of the codex occur without comment by the ancients, and it is beyond our ability to reconstruct confidently these origins. That the Fathers made no mention of the format suggests it was already a tradition in the earliest periods. However, in the vacuum, several suggestions have been made. Parker lists four common reasons but only the fourth has canonical implications: more room. Only the codex could easily contain all four

17. These are P[12], P[18], P[13], and P[22].
18. Hurtado, "Earliest Evidence," 272.
19. Hurtado, *The Earliest Christian Artifacts: Manuscripts and Christian Origins* (Grand Rapids: Eerdmans, 2006), 61.
20. Michael Dormandy, "How the Books Became the Bible: The Evidence for Canon Formation from Work-Combinations in Manuscripts," *TC* 23 (2018): 22.
21. Dormandy, "How the Books Became the Bible," 22.
22. Roger S. Bagnall, *Early Christian Books in Egypt* (Princeton, NJ: Princeton University Press, 2009), 76–78.

gospels or the letters of Paul.[23] In response, Hurtado appeals to the fact that many of the extant second-century gospel texts only include a single gospel to suggest this is not the case.[24] However, all but one (P[66]) are either too fragmentary to tell or were likely originally Four-Gospel codices.[25] Regardless, there is a more plausible explanation for the origin of the Christian preference for the codex.

The evidence suggests the switch to codex was no gradual accommodation but a long-standing convention that overtook an even longer-standing tradition, the roll. Furthermore, the codex's invention and the codex's adoption for Scripture are not necessarily the same thing.

The earliest attestation of any collection of NT Scriptures comes in 2 Peter 3:15–16, where Peter refers to Paul's letters on equal terms with the "rest of the scriptures" (i.e., the OT).[26] Therefore, the publication of these letters was early and predated the gospel of John by several decades. By extension, the published edition of Paul's letters predates the Four-Gospel codex. It is here that we should look for the origins of the Christian preference for the codex. We see such an indication in the Pastoral Epistles.

In 2 Timothy 4:13, Paul requests Timothy, "When you come, bring the cloak that I left with Carpus at Troas, also the books, and above all the parchments." "Books" (*biblia*) would refer to rolls. Writers in Paul's day used the term "parchments" (*membranas*) to refer to "notebooks, account books, memoranda, first drafts of literary works, and other writings not intended for the public."[27] It was also the word for a parchment codex. Since there was a specific term for a parchment roll (*diphtherai*), Paul's *membranas* is likely a parchment codex as it is distinct from the rolls. The ancient practice of copying and retaining letters lends itself to a growing collection by Paul in the codex format. This technology enabled the owner to add texts over time and bind different texts together with ease.

The codex technology was also better suited to collect Paul's letters in a single volume. According to Gamble, to include Paul's letters in a single roll, the roll had to exceed twenty-four meters (almost eighty feet).[28] Rolls are known to reach a length of fifteen to twenty meters. Rolled up, an eighty-foot

23. D. C. Parker, *An Introduction to the New Testament Manuscripts and Their Texts* (Cambridge: Cambridge University Press, 2008), 17.
24. Hurtado, *Earliest Christian Artifacts*, 70.
25. Of the latter, see P[75] and P[45].
26. This assessment does not require Petrine authorship or a pre-AD 70 date, although both are affirmed here. See Andreas J. Köstenberger, L. Scott Kellum, and Charles L. Quarles, *The Cradle, The Cross, and the Crown: An Introduction to the New Testament*, 2nd ed. (Nashville, TN: B&H, 2016), 856–63.
27. C. C. McCown, "The Codex and Roll in the New Testament," *HTR* 34 (1941): 222.
28. Harry Gamble, *Books and Readers in the Early Church: A History of Early Christian Texts* (New Haven, CT: Yale University Press, 1995), 47.

roll would produce cylinders about 41.8 cm (16.457 in.) in diameter, the size of some automobile rims.[29] To prevent such a monstrosity, size determined the number of volumes (rolls) a book contained.[30] The codex, however, could handle it easily in a manageable edition.

All things considered, the codex collection seems to originate with Paul's letters published as a codex either by him or his close followers. As D. C. Parker sums it up:

> [T]he peripatetic nature of Paul's activity, the fact that the first Christian reference to codices comes in a letter attributed to him, and the practical requirements of a collected copy provide an attractive group of ideas explaining the causes of the phenomenon that early Christianity adopted the codex and that in time this adoption led to its popularisation.[31]

However, something more than "popular" is going on here. Subsequent NT collections were also put into codices, although they almost certainly previously existed as rolls. After the publication of Paul's letters, the Four Gospels are collected, reformatted, and published together. The same is true for the rest of the NT. Nothing survives that suggests the previous circulation of these books in other formats. Moreover, Christians received the OT from Judaism in rolls and reformatted it into codices. Such recasting of authoritative texts calls for something more than convenience or popularity and certainly something more meaningful. Christians were putting their Scripture in a format that was a visual symbol.

Summary

Far from being a preference, the codex was a visual symbol of Christian Scripture. What is more, the MSS suggest the codex is only one ubiquitous feature among many that marked Christian Scripture. Several editorial/visual features are common to all the manuscripts that are difficult to explain apart from an archetype. These include the arrangement of the books in the codex, the grouping of books together, uniform titles for the books, and other visual items. These will be the subject of the following question regarding the canon's arrangement and other visible markers.

---

29. See Hurtado, *Earliest Christian Artifacts*, 67.
30. See e.g., Pliny the Younger's description of his uncle's (the elder) works (*Ep.* III.5). *Throwing the Javelin from Horseback* is in one roll, while *the Natural History* is in 37 (LCL 55:173–75).
31. Parker, *Introduction*, 19.

REFLECTION QUESTIONS

1. Why is it not possible to say Christians invented the codex format?

2. Should every Christian book appearing in a codex be considered Scripture?

3. When did the Christian preference for Scripture in a codex begin?

4. Why did the Christians prefer the codex?

5. Why is it significant that Christian versions of the OT are in codices?

QUESTION 31

What Unique Visual Features of the Biblical MSS Mark Them as Scripture?

In 1998, Larry Hurtado suggested the codex format was one of three features of a "material and visual culture." The other two were what is known as the *nomina sacra* (abbreviations of the divine names in Christian MSS) and the staurogram (a kind of *nomina sacra* that wrote tau (τ) and rho (ρ) of "cross" (σταυρός) and "crucify" (σταυρόω) as one combined letter (Ⲣ), representing a crucified man).[1] The staurogram, while early (see P[45], P[66], and P[75]), had no staying power, suggesting something local. The other features were not merely traditional but were physical/visual features that marked the MS as different from other books in early Christianity. Two of these (the codex format and the *nomina sacra*) are so pervasive and early that they should be seen as something more authoritative in origins.

In 2000, David Trobisch published a bold thesis that the NT was a published book by the mid-point of the second century.[2] While much of his theory remains unproven (including the impetus and the ultimate editors) in terms of the physical characteristics, he was on to something. He rightly suggested that the MSS of the NT show an editorial concept. His theory includes the codex and *nomina sacra* but also consists of the individual groupings of books in separate codices, the titles of the individual biblical texts, and the order of the books within the codices.[3] To this evidence, the Fathers' reference to the collections should be added.

---

1. Larry Hurtado, "The Earliest Evidence of an Emerging Christian Material and Visual Culture: The Codex, The *Nomina Sacra*, and the Staurogram," in *Text and Artifact in the Religions of Mediterranean Antiquity: Essays in Honour of Peter Richardson*, eds. Stephen G. Wilson and Michel Desjardins (Waterloo, ON: Wilfrid Laurier University Press, 2006).
2. David Trobisch, *The First Edition of the New Testament* (Oxford: Oxford University Press, 2000).
3. See, particularly, Trobisch, *First Edition*, 11–46.

In all, ancient Christians gathered the NT documents and copied them in a format and style that allowed someone to know what they had the moment they held it in their hands. We will examine the phenomenon of each visual and material marker in the present question.

The Circulation of the Books

The evidence from multibook MSS and literary statements reveal that the NT circulated in four collections. These are the Four Gospels, Acts-GE, Pauline Epistles, and Revelation. These are addressed in the following chapters more fully. An introduction to the phenomenon is suitable for the present discussion.

The MSS dating from the late second through the fourth century shows remarkable content and format consistency. Of course, handwritten copies tend to vary in one matter or another, but a pattern emerges when examined across the spectrum. First, the NT did not tend to circulate in complete Bibles like we have today. This is most easily seen in the description of the MSS in the UBS[5] Greek NT. The editors marked the contents of the listed MSS as "e" (Gospels), "ac" (Acts-GE), "p" (Paul), and "r" (Revelation). These abbreviations are helpful because the contents of the MSS generally fall into these groups.

The Four-Gospel codex is well attested in the extant MSS. From about the beginning of the third century forward, MSS (like P[45]) appeared as a four-Gospel codex. More fragmentary collections like P[75] (also third century) that contains Luke and John (in that order) also suggest a four-gospel codex. Of course, some early Gospel MSS are of single Gospels. Some are so fragmentary that we cannot tell the original contents of the codex. Others are clearly single-Gospel texts.[4] Anything from affordability to the replacement of a worn-out codex could explain the existence of such texts. What is noteworthy is that they do not independently present themselves. They carry the visual markers noted above: the codex format, and the *nomina sacra*, but more importantly, the title pattern distinguishes them in reference to the other Gospels. That is, "according to John" identifies it from other Gospels.[5] The result is that the variety in the gospel MSS are still related to this group of four.

Early MSS of Acts are common enough, as well as a good number of the GE. Only a few can be determined to be multibook MSS, though. Some fragments like GA0166 (450–550) that include the end of Acts and the beginning of James are quite suggestive of the collection of Acts-GE but not conclusive. Before the seventh century, three MSS in Syriac place Acts with their accepted

---

4. E.g., P[66] (John) begins with page 1, thus no works preceded it.
5. See Richard Bauckham, *Jesus and the Eyewitnesses*, 2nd ed. (Grand Rapids: Eerdmans, 2006), 303.

GE, as does one text in Latin, although none have all eight books.[6] The first MS of the complete collection dates to the seventh century.[7] However, both codex *Vaticanus* and codex *Sinaiticus* (fourth-century pandects—whole Bibles) have Acts followed by the GE. But *Vaticanus* has the group following the Gospels and *Sinaiticus* following Paul. This suggests that the great codices (or their exemplars) were copied from these individual codices. Thus, well before 325, Acts and the GE were circulating together.[8]

The MSS evidence regarding the Pauline letter collection is early and impressive. The most remarkable copy is P[46], an incomplete (the ending past 1 Thessalonians is lost) yet robust second-century copy of Paul's letters. Hebrews is always in the Pauline corpus. Virtually all copies of Paul's letters are from this collection of fourteen epistles.

Finally, the book of Revelation is a bit of an oddity with its circulation. It may show up in any of the other four codices or, after 611, individually attached to a commentary by Andrew of Caesarea.[9] This searching for a secure position is over when the complete NT and the Pandects (OT and NT) are produced: Revelation is always at the end of the biblical books (only rarely followed by the "useful" books).

The following chapters will contain an investigation of these collections more fully. We can see here, though, certain books were transmitted together because of their similarity. This similarity manifests in several layers. One such grouping is by genre. Gospels are grouped together, letters form two collections, and the apocalypse is relatively independent. They are similar in that they are specifically Christian and apostolic. Another type of grouping is by author: Paul and the "Pillars" (i.e., James, Peter, and John). We should particularly note that it tends to be just these works gathered together. For example, no canonical gospel is ever bound with a noncanonical gospel.[10] Likewise, no apocryphal letter appeared in either Greek NT letter collection in antiquity. It is indisputable that these documents circulated together because they were considered Scripture in contrast to other works.

The "Titles" of the Collections

The earliest table of contents for a Greek Bible is found in codex *Alexandrinus* (fifth century). More than merely listing the books, the scribe categorized the books under collective titles followed by the individual books.

---

6. For the Syriac, see LDAB 116029; 117832, 116069. For the Latin see, LDAB 7746.
7. D. C. Parker, *An Introduction to the New Testament Manuscripts and Their Texts* (Cambridge: Cambridge University Press, 2008), 283.
8. Trobisch makes the case that the fourth and fifth century arrange all the books of the NT in a similar pattern demonstrating a common archetype (*First Edition*, 24).
9. See, J. K. Elliott, "The Distinctiveness of the Greek Manuscripts of the Book of Revelation," *JTS* 48 (1997): 116–17.
10. J. K. Elliott, "Manuscripts, the Codex, and the Canon," *JSNT* 63 (1996): 107.

The entire NT is referred to as *hē kainē diathēkē* ("the new covenant"). The other titled groupings are *euaggelia d* ("Gospels four"), *katholikai z* ("Catholics seven"), *epistolai paulou id* ("epistles of Paul 14").[11] Acts and Revelation appear on their own.

This is nearly exactly like the earliest canon lists. Cyril of Jerusalem's canon list (c. 350) is arranged in the same way, except he omitted Revelation.[12] Athanasius named the same categories in the same order in 367.[13] The Synod of Laodicea categorized the books exactly the same way. More than a list, these appear to be collections.

These collection titles are also mentioned in the early church fathers. The term "Gospels" is ubiquitous, as is the "letters of Paul." The latter, however, is sometimes referred to as "the Apostle."[14] Without a doubt, this is an old convention: Irenaeus typically refers to Paul when he uses "apostle" without naming the individual disciple. Sometimes he does so without ever naming that it is Paul. He merely writes, "the apostle says . . ."[15] Other ancient writers do so as well.[16] Since Marcion called his edited version of Paul "*apostolikon*," it might be he was appropriating the contemporary references to the Pauline corpus.

The ancients also referred to the collection of the GE. The late second-century Muratorian Fragment possibly mentions the epistles of John (at least two) and Jude as "reckoned among the Catholic *epistles*."[17] Clement of Alexandria referred to Jude as a catholic epistle.[18] Eusebius referred to the collection six times (although he disputes the entire contents) in his church history.[19] Origen uses the term to refer to the group several times.[20] Later writers before Nicaea do so as well.[21]

---

11. See the description by W. Andrew Smith, *A Study of the Gospels in Codex Alexandrinus: Codicology, Paleaeography, and Scribal Hands* (Leiden: Brill, 2014), 64–68.
12. Cyril of Jerusalem, *Catechesis* 4.36.
13. Athanasius, *Ep. Fest.* 39.
14. In his conversion account, Augustine describes picking up "codicem apostoli" ("the codex of the apostle") meaning Paul (Aug., *Conf.* 8.12.29).
15. Irenaeus, *Adv. Haer.* 1.1.1.
16. *Diogn.* 12; see also Ireanaeus's reference to "the Traditions of the Elders" at *Adv. Haer.* 5.36.1–2 (also Papias *Frag.* 5.2).
17. MF 69. The Latin says "habentur in catholica," lit. "are held in the catholic." Since the Catholic Church was mentioned a few lines above, the reference might be to the church and not the epistles (Metzger, *Canon*, 386).
18. Clement of Alexandria, *Frag.* 2.1.
19. Eusebius, *Hist. eccl.* 2.23.25; 4.23.1; 6.14.1; 6.25.5; 7.25.7; 7.25.10.
20. See, e.g., Origen, *Comm. Jo.* 1.23, 2.18, 6.18.
21. See, e.g., Dionysius of Alexandria (cited in Eusebius, *Hist. eccl.* 6.24 and 25) and Peter of Alexandria, *Ep. Can.* Canon XI.

The significance of this collective nomenclature is that the ancients were naming collections of books as Scripture. These collections were not merely mental arrangements but physical entities that they referred to as a whole.

The Titles of the Books

It has been suggested in the past that the Gospels were originally anonymous. Usually this is affirmed because the books do not name the author. Most no longer consider this a viable option. Few modern books name the author in the text but on the apparatus (the spine or introduction pages). Ancient books were similar only that the names of the books (with the author) were given on a tag called a *"sitybus"* or *"syllabus"* attached to the end of the roll. When converted to a codex, this is transferred to the end of the books. It is beyond unlikely that these books had no titles. But are the titles we have original?

The Four Gospels are each expressed as "according to . . ." with the name of the author. For example, in Greek, *Euangelion Kata Maththaion* is the earliest form of "The Gospel according to Matthew." Each of the other canonical Gospels bears this form of the title with *Kata* and the author. Modern scholars often deny the authorship implications in favor of vague connections to the person named.[22] The ancients would not recognize such a process.

Hengel's proposal makes better sense. The naming convention of the Gospels is indeed unusual, but it is not without precedence. The competing versions of the Greek OT were referred to with *kata* plus the translator's name. Specifically, Aquila's version is *Kata Akyla*, Symmachus's—*Kata Symmachon*, Theodotian's—*Kata Theōdotina*, and the Seventy's—*Kata Hebdomēkonta* (abbr. LXX). The terminology is appropriate for identifying the different versions. However, it is important to remember that while there are different translators there is still only one OT. Early Christians used the singular "gospel" in a similar vein because there is only one gospel of Christ.[23] Thus, the titles present the Gospel as interpreted by their authors. What is remarkable is that there are no known competing titles for these Gospels in either the MSS or the Fathers' statements.

The rest of the NT is perhaps less remarkable but equally consistent. The Pauline collection entitles the letters according to their destination: "to the Romans," "to the Philippians," etc. This is consistent throughout every MS that is complete enough to include titles.[24] This format is also true of the disputed epistle to the Hebrews. Other letters in the NT (GE) follow the more

---

22. See, e.g., Donald Hagner, *Matthew 1–13*, WBC (Dallas: Word, 1993), lxxvi.
23. Martin Hengel, *The Four Gospels and the One Gospel of Jesus Christ: An Investigation of the Collection and Origin of the Canonical Gospels*, trans. John Bowden (Harrisburg, PA: Trinity Press International, 2000), 3.
24. See, e.g., P[46].

conventional genitive construction: "from" John, Peter, James, and Jude. If more than one letter is given, it is numbered alphabetically, "*a, b,* or *g.*" It is noteworthy that this enumeration is consistent across both letter collections. So, it is "Corinthians A or B" and "From Peter A or B." Revelation is always the Apocalypse "of John" even though the text is introduced with *Apokalypsis Iēsou Christou* ("the Revelation of Jesus Christ").

The significance is a standardization that appears in all the MSS when possible. Given that these Gospels and letters were produced independently and published before the collection of the Four-Gospel codex, such a uniformity suggests *at the very least* that the canonical edition was a runaway bestseller that obliterated even the knowledge of any previous titles.

The Order of the Books Within the Codices

In multibook MSS, the four Gospels generally demonstrate the order of Matthew, Mark, Luke, and John. Metzger lists eight other sequences: most after the fourth century.[25] One of the more known competitors to the current order is the Old Latin order of Matthew, John, Luke, and Mark. This order is also reflected in a few Greek MSS (e.g., W, D, and likely P[45]). Skeat suggested the Old Latin order was ultimately replaced by Jerome.[26] It is generally assumed this is a preference for apostles over apostolic men. However, the great majority of MSS have the Greek order so familiar to us.[27]

The Pauline Collection is known to have seventeen different sequences in the MSS.[28] The earliest are generally organized according to length. They include Romans, 1–2 Corinthians, Galatians, Ephesians, Philippians, Colossians, 1–2 Thessalonians, Hebrews, Pastoral Epistles, and Philemon.[29] Much of the divergence of order regards the book of Hebrews. While it is always found in the Epistles of Paul, the position tends to migrate within the codex, especially early on, ultimately landing toward the end of the codex. For example, most contain Hebrews between the letters to churches and individuals (i.e., between 2 Thessalonians and 1 Timothy). However, two early MSS (P[46] and P[13]) place Hebrews after Romans, suggesting an order based on length. At least eight other positions are known for Hebrews in the Pauline corpus. The collection has certain minor deviations in order beyond the book of Hebrews, but the general pattern holds in the multibook MSS.

25. Bruce Metzger, *The Canon of the New Testament: Its Origin, Development, and Significance* (Oxford: Oxford University Press, 1987), 296–97.
26. T. C. Skeat, "Irenaeus and the Four-Gospel Canon," in *The Collected Biblical Writings of T.C. Skeat*, ed. Keith Elliott, Supplements to Novum Testamentum (Leiden: Brill, 2004), 76.
27. Edmon L. Gallagher and John D. Meade, *The Biblical Canon Lists from Early Christianity: Texts and Analysis* (Oxford: Oxford University Press, 2017), 296.
28. Metzger, *Canon*, 298.
29. Metzger counts nine uncials and sixty minuscules with this order (*Canon*, 298).

The MSS of Acts and the GE do appear in the second through third centuries, but they are too fragmentary to disclose an order. As stated above, though, the pandects of the fourth century (which are not directly related to one another) do give the same order for the books. They are arranged as Acts, James, 1–2 Peter, 1, 2, and 3 John and Jude. This is apparently the early order. It is also attested in two of the earliest Greek canon lists.[30] Eusebius's reference to James as the "first of the epistles called Catholic" is likely a reference to the oldest order.[31] There are at least six other orders known, several dating to the fourth century. Most alternate orders place Peter at the head of the list.[32] It is noteworthy that the older order is the same as Paul mentioned these men in Galatians 2:9, except Jude does not appear.[33]

In sum, the NT MSS do show an early order of books within the circulation units mentioned above. Even in the divergent sequences in the centuries that followed, no book wandered out of its original circulation unit (granting an exception to Revelation). The best example of this is the order of Athanasius's list (c. 367) compared to the great codices of the fourth and fifth centuries. It is the exact order as found in the extant portions of Vaticanus and the entirety of Alexandrinus. The books within the circulation units are the same order as Sinaiticus. For our purposes, the early order is significantly stable to suggest it to be part of the visual and material culture of the NT.

The *Nomina Sacra*

The ancient MSS of Christian Scripture contain abbreviations of references to God or Jesus (the four earliest and most common are "Jesus," "Christ," "Lord," and "God"). In antiquity, abbreviations were relatively common. Coins and inscriptions often employ them to save space. Space-saving, however, was not a particular concern for those writing MSS. Instead, they functioned as a mark of piety that likely had its roots in Judaism as a concept (i.e., the reverence for the name of God).[34] As such, it is an overtly theological expression.

The system of abbreviation, however, is entirely Christian.[35] They appear with a horizontal line drawn above the letters to indicate the word. The

---

30. These are the lists of Cyril and Athanasius (Gallagher and Meade, *Biblical Canon Lists*, 115 and 123).
31. Eusebius, *Hist. eccl.* 2.23.25.
32. P[54], a late fourth-century fragment of James 2:16–18, 22–26; 3:3–4, has the page numbers 29 and 30 (Comfort, *Text of the Earliest NT MSS*, 1:344). This is likely attesting to a collection with the Petrine Epistles first.
33. Trobisch, *First Edition*, 60. Paul refers to the "pillars" of "James and Cephas and John."
34. See Larry Hurtado, *The Earliest Christian Artifacts: Manuscripts and Christian Origins* (Grand Rapids: Eerdmans, 2006), 104–5.
35. Colin H. Roberts, *Manuscript, Society, and Belief in Early Christian Egypt: The Schweich Lectures of the British Academy* (London: Oxford University Press, 1979), 34. See also Hurtado, *The Earliest Christian Artifacts*, 101.

abbreviation features either the first letter and the inflected ending (determined by context), a suspension of the word (i.e., the first two letters), or both. For example, "Jesus" could be written as $\overline{I\Sigma}$, $\overline{IH}$, or $\overline{IH\Sigma}$.[36] The four earliest are God ($\overline{\Theta\Sigma}$), Lord ($\overline{K\Sigma}$), Jesus ($\overline{I\Sigma}$), and Christ ($\overline{X\Sigma}$). As time progressed, the number of the *nomina sacra* grew to fifteen such words.[37]

Their antiquity, however, is undisputed. There is likely a reference to the *nomina sacra* in the *Epistle of Barnabas* and Clement of Alexandria;[38] otherwise, no ancient writer mentions the convention. Roberts rightly suggests that such a taking-for-granted indicates great antiquity. Furthermore, the appearance in both orthodox and heterodox writings suggests the convention predates the theological distinctions.[39]

The use of the *nomina sacra* outside of Christian circles is extremely rare.[40] So much so, it is virtually sure that a document containing them is Christian. The abbreviations appear in nonbiblical Christian documents but not consistently—even within individual documents.[41]

Such is not the case in biblical MSS. They are ubiquitous. Not every MS is consistent in the application or use of the convention. Some MSS use different methods of abbreviation. Others occasionally write the word out in full.[42] However, the use in biblical MSS nearly always appear when expected.

What is more, we can track this phenomenon from the earliest MSS. For example, the earliest fragment of the NT (P[52]) does not have any of the four major words extant but likely had a form of *nomina sacra* in the immediate context.[43] Another of the earliest MSS, P[90] (c. 170), almost certainly exhibits the *nomina sacra*. Roberts maintained this kind of evidence suggests they "belong to the earliest stratum of the Christian faith and may well be contemporary with the first authorized or authoritative Christian writing."[44]

---

36. Roberts, *Manuscript, Society, and Belief*, 26.
37. For a listing, see Bruce Metzger, *Manuscripts of the Greek Bible* (Oxford: Oxford University Press, 1981), 36–37.
38. See Roberts, *Manuscript, Society, and Belief*, 35–36. *Ep. Barn.* 9.8 and Clement of Alexandria, *Str.* 6.11.
39. Hurtado, "Material and Visual Culture," 278. Roberts notes that Gnostic MSS do employ the *nomina sacra* but do not extend it to words denoting their own conceptions of divinity suggesting a firm convention predating them (*Manuscript, Society, and Belief*, 43).
40. Roberts, *Manuscript, Society and Belief*, 32–33.
41. Lincoln Blumell noted that by the seventh century all private Christian use disappeared (*Lettered Christians: Christians, Letters, and Late Antique Oxyrhynchus* [Leiden: Brill, 2012], 51).
42. Trobisch, *First Edition*, 12.
43. Hill and Hurtado suggest it is more probable the abbreviation was used (C. E. Hill, "Did the Scribe of P[52] Use the *Nomina Sacra*? Another Look," *NTS* 48 [2002]: 587–92; Larry Hurtado, "P[52] [P. Rylands GK. 457] and the Nomina Sacra: Method and Probability," *TynBul* 54 [2003]: 1–14).
44. Roberts, *Manuscript, Society, and Belief*, 46.

The ubiquitous and early appearance in biblical MSS of the more common *nomina sacra* suggests a visual symbol of theology/piety that influenced all following biblical MSS. Moreover, the convention, like the adoption of the codex format, replaced the practice in any earlier copies. Skeat suggests that such activity takes "a degree of organization, of conscious planning, and uniformity of practice among the Christian communities which we have hitherto had little reason to suspect."[45] In other words, we cannot explain the saturation of the *nomina sacra* without a version of the biblical text with tremendous authority that stamped a visual marker of theology for all future texts.

Summary

Along with the codex format, at least four other phenomena contribute to the visual and material culture of the NT MSS. These are the circulation of the books in four codices; the uniform "titles" of the collections; the uniform titles of the individual books; the order of the books within the codices; and the *nomina sacra*. The fact that other ancient Christian literature virtually never appears within the collections nor demonstrates some of these features consistently (codex, *nomina sacra*) marks these features as particularly belonging to Christian Scriptures. This binding together and marking of the texts must have been very early.

REFLECTION QUESTIONS

1. What were the signs of the material and visual culture of early Christians?

2. How many noncanonical gospels appear bound with canonical Gospels?

3. What do the titles of both collections and books signify?

4. How does the *nomina sacra* suggest a very early publication of the NT?

5. How persistent was the order of the books?

---

45. T. C. Skeat, "Early Christian Book Production: Papyri and Manuscripts," in *The Cambridge Companion to the Bible*, ed. G. W. H. Lampe (New York: Cambridge University Press, 1969), 2:72.

How Early Was the Four-Gospel Codex?

In the previous question, we noted the normal circulation of the Gospels in the Four-Gospel codex. D. C. Parker began his study of the Four Gospels with a memorable statement, "The Four Gospels, the Tetraevangelium, is *the* book of Christianity—not four books, but one codex."[1] Our question is, "how early?" We must first investigate when the four Gospels were received as Scripture to answer the question. And then, how early was the term "gospel" used to refer to a book. Comparing the two tracks will help identify a probable period for the production of the codex.

The Reception of the Four Gospels

The collection of the earliest Christian works, *The Apostolic Fathers*, cites the Gospels fifty-six times, some expressly referred to as Scripture. These early works do contain allusions to unidentifiable and noncanonical books. Notably, these cluster in *2 Clement* and the *Epistle of Barnabas* (arguably some of the earliest works in the collection) though not exclusive to these books.

A little later, the *Epistula Apostolorum* (an early second-century anti-Gnostic pseudepigraphal letter) also attests to a fourfold Gospel.[2] It clearly made use of Matthew, Mark, and Luke,[3] but the use of John is, according to Darrell Hannah, "well nigh overwhelming."[4] Since the author did not defend the authority of these works but merely assumed it, we can surmise the

---

1. D. C. Parker, *An Introduction to the New Testament Manuscripts and Their Texts* (Cambridge: Cambridge University Press, 2008), 311.
2. See Charles E. Hill, "The Epistula Apostolorum: An Asian Tract from the Time of Polycarp," *Journal of Early Christian Studies* 7 (1999): 1–53.
3. Darrell Hannah, "The Four-Gospel 'Canon' in the *Epistula Apostolorum*," *JTS* 59, no. 2 (2008): 611–18.
4. Hannah, "The Four-Gospel 'Canon,'" 610.

Epistula Apostolorum was not creating a canon. This suggests, at a minimum, a local convention or consensus in the decades before 140.

About the same time, Justin Martyr famously noted that the "memoirs of the apostles" were read alongside the "prophets" in the church.[5] He is clear that these are read in a liturgical setting, placing these works on the same level as the OT. Justin also cited all four Gospels[6] and seemed to embrace the idea that the gospel of Mark contains the memoirs of Peter.[7]

Some theorize that Justin was citing a harmony in his works, for his citations are often conflations.[8] While there is no extant MS or ancient reference to such a harmony, we know his disciple Tatian did select, harmonize, stitch together, and sometimes rewrite verses and phrases from the four into a continuous narrative.[9] Whether Tatian intended a harmony or a new gospel is debated and perhaps unprovable.[10] For our purposes, whatever one might theorize about Tatian's motivations, his choice of sources is telling. That the *Diatessaron* extensively utilized only Matthew, Mark, Luke, and John suggests a superior status to these works than any competitors. Otherwise, out of the known options, that he chooses the four canonical Gospels would be an enormous coincidence. Nicholas Perrin observed that it belongs to the genre of "rewritten Scriptures" current in Judaism that smoothed out inconsistencies, made implicit textual correlations explicit, and offered further explication of Scripture.[11] This work was composed sometime before 170, likely between 120–160.

The most unmistakable literary evidence is from Irenaeus, the bishop of Lyons, at the end of the second century. The bishop was adamant that the Gospels are precisely four in number. He compared them to the four winds, the four angelic creatures of Ezekiel, and the four covenants of God.[12]

Several scholars have suggested that Irenaeus's argument was an attempt to limit the number of the Gospels to "these four and no more."[13] But his point

---

5. Justin Martyr, *1 Apol.* 67.
6. See, e.g., Matthew, *Dial.* 103, 105, 107; Mark, *Dial.* 106; Luke, *1 Apol.* 66, *Dial.* 103; and John, *1 Apol.* 61.4.
7. Justin Martyr, *Dial.*106.
8. W. L. Peterson, "Textual Evidence of Tatian's Dependence upon Justin's ΑΠΟΜΝΗΜΟΝΕΥΜΑΤΑ," *NTS* 36 (1990): 512–34.
9. Nicholas J. Zola, "Evangelizing Tatian: The Diatessaron's Place in the Emergence of the Fourfold Gospel Canon," *PRS* 43 (2016): 410.
10. Zola, "Evangelizing Tatian," 399.
11. Nicholas Perrin, "Hermeneutical Factors in the Harmonization of the Gospels and the Question of Textual Authority," in *The Biblical Canon*, eds. J. M. Auwers and H. J. de Jonge, BETL 163 (Leuven: University Press, 2003), 599–606.
12. Irenaeus, *Adv. Haer.* 3.11.8.
13. E.g., McDonald argues that Irenaeus was an innovator here (*The Biblical Canon: Its Origin, Transmission, and Authority*, upd. and rev. 3rd ed. [Peabody, MA: Hendrickson, 2007], 290).

was that four is the complete number. Neither more nor fewer Gospels are sufficient. He rebuked those who used only one Gospel (Ebionites/Matthew; Docetists/Mark; and Marcionites/Luke).[14] Moreover, the Valentinians' preference for John was bad enough, but their production of the *Gospel of Truth* (adding a gospel) was an audacious act. Thus, he argued for a fixed Gospel collection, neither more *nor* less. Altogether, the canonicity of the four Gospels seems firm from the first half of the second century. It raises the question, how soon was this collection a book?

"Gospel" Referring to a Book

James A. Kelhoffer investigated the term "gospel" (*euangelion*) in early Christian writings to discern how early the word was used for a book rather than proclamation.[15] He concluded that the ancients used the term for a book before Marcion, *2 Clement*, and the *Didache*. Although we do not embrace all his conclusions, Kelhoffer has made a plausible thesis that the term was a reference to Gospel materials (i.e., books).[16]

2 Clement

The preacher states, "for the Lord says in the gospel: 'If you will not keep the small thing, who will give you the great thing? For I say to you, he that is faithful in the small thing, is also in the great'" (8.5). This citation has widely been recognized as a reference to a book.

The sense is similar to Luke 16:10 and 12, but the wording differs. The second half ("he that is faithful . . .") is identical to Luke 16:10, but the first half resembles Luke 16:12 with emendation. Because of the difference and their judgments that previous references are to noncanonical works, some suppose the reference is possibly the now-lost *Gospel of the Egyptians* rather than Luke.[17]

The later church fathers often paraphrased such references (even this same text).[18] It is more likely that the preacher of *2 Clement* anticipated them and streamlined Luke 16:12 as a paraphrase.[19] Because the preacher used Luke elsewhere, there is no need to search for any source beyond the canonical

---

14. Irenaeus, *Adv. Haer.* 3.11.9.
15. James A. Kelhoffer, *Conceptions of "Gospel" and Legitimacy in Early Christianity*, WUNT 324 (Tübingen: Mohr Siebeck, 2014), 39–75.
16. Kelhoffer, *Conceptions*, 74.
17. Holmes notes the possibility as well as the similarity to Luke 16 (Michael W. Holmes, *The Apostolic Fathers: Greek Texts and English Translations*, updated ed. [Grand Rapids: Baker, 1999], 115).
18. See Irenaeus, *Adv. Haer.* 2.34.3, Hippolytus, *Haer.* 10.32, and Hilary, *Epistola Seu Libellus*, 1.
19. Martin Hengel, *The Four Gospels and the One Gospel of Jesus Christ: An Investigation of the Collection and Origin of the Canonical Gospels*, trans. John Bowden (Harrisburg, PA: Trinity Press International, 2000), 251.

Luke.[20] Thus, it is probable that "gospel" was used of a canonical book (Luke) by the year 100 or so.

The Didache

If citation of a canonical gospel as "gospel" is only probable in *2 Clement*, an earlier work leaves no doubt. The *Didache* is an ancient work on discipleship slightly longer than Galatians.[21] It likely originated sometime between 70–90.[22] In three places, it cites canonical Gospel material as "in the gospel" (Did. 8.2, 11.3, and 15.3, 4).

The most ambitious interpreters believe they can find editorial layers, including oral pre-gospel traditions.[23] Presumably, this is due to the citations introduced with "the Lord says." But since 14:3 introduces Malachi 1:11, 14 as "spoken by the Lord," the teacher is more likely following the long-standing tradition that the Bible is God speaking.

Some critics contend that Matthew and the Didachist independently used Jesus traditions.[24] Three primary objections make this unlikely. First, the Didachist calls his source a "gospel," so it is a narrative text whatever the source. Second, the cited texts elsewhere are consistently only Matthean. As far as we know, the Didachist's gospel includes only material found in canonical Matthew. Finally, the traditions come from the finished version of Matthew's gospel.[25] Thus, many scholars do not doubt that these references are to Matthew's gospel.[26] Therefore, by the late first century "gospel" was a term used to describe the book of Matthew.

---

20. Christopher J. Tuckett, "2 Clement and the New Testament," in *Intertextuality in the Second Century*, ed. Jeffrey Bingham and Clayton Jefford (Leiden: Brill, 2016), 29.

21. William Varner, *The Way of the Didache: The First Christian Handbook* (New York: University Press of America, 2007), 8–11.

22. Varner, *The Way of the Didache*, 4. Others suggest a date as early as AD 50 (Clayton Jefford, "Didache," in *The Cambridge Companion to the Apostolic Fathers*, eds. Michael F. Bird and Scott D. Harrower, Cambridge Companions to Religion [New York: Cambridge University Press, 2021], 249) and as late as 150 (Aaron Milavec, *The Didache: Faith, Hope and Life of the Earliest Christian Communities, 50–70 C. E.* [New York: Newman Press, 2003]).

23. See, e.g., Jens Schröter, "Jesus Tradition in Matthew, James, and the Didache: Searching for Characteristic Emphases," in *Matthew, James, and Didache: Three Related Documents in Their Jewish and Christian Settings*, eds. Huub van de Sandt and Jürgen Zangenberg, SBL Symposium Series 45 (Atlanta: SBL, 2008), 239.

24. John W. Welch, "From the Sermon on the Mount to the Didache," in *The Didache: A Missing Piece of the Puzzle in Early Christianity*, eds. Jonathan A. Draper and Clayton N. Jefford (Atlanta: SBL, 2015), 336.

25. C. M. Tuckett, "The Didache and the Writings that Later Formed the New Testament," in *The New Testament and the Apostolic Fathers: The Reception of the New Testament in the Apostolic Fathers*, eds. Andrew Gregory and Christopher Tuckett (Oxford: Oxford University Press, 2005), 127.

26. See, e.g., B. H. Streeter, *The Four Gospels* (London: Macmillan, 1924), 507–11; J. M. Court, "The Didache and St. Matthew's Gospel," *SJT* 34 (1981): 109–20; and Hengel, *Four Gospels*, 64.

Ignatius of Antioch

A few decades later, Ignatius of Antioch (c. 107–108) likely referred to written gospels in his letters as "gospel." C. E. Hill listed five places he used "gospel" to refer to the following "Scriptural Categories" expressed by Ignatius in his letters: Scripture (*Phld.* 5.1–2, 9.1–2; and *Smyrn.* 5.1, 7.2).[27] Some suggest these references are proclamations rather than written texts.[28] However, in *Smyrn.* 5.1, the accompanying references are not to the prophets but to "prophecies" and the "law of Moses," which are written texts. These contrast with "the gospel" and "individual suffering." Gundry suggests that including human suffering identifies "gospel" as nontextual.[29] In response, we note two essential matters. First, none of the references to "gospel" elsewhere include any nontextual element. Second, the opponents were Docetics, who denied Christ's human suffering. For Ignatius, Christian suffering is a continuation of Christ's suffering. Thus, the lone inclusion here is appropriate. As Hill put it, in this environment, suffering is alone in its nontextual witness against their doctrine as "the odd one out."[30]

The identification of these gospels is made difficult by Ignatius's circumstances. Writing in custody, traveling to Rome, it is not likely he had books to reference directly.[31] However, it is virtually sure he knew the gospel of Matthew.[32]

The Apology of Aristides

In the next decade, the *Apology of Aristides* was presented to Hadrian in about the year 125.[33] In it, the Athenian philosopher referred to the story of Jesus: "This is taught in the gospel, as it is called, which a short time was preached among them; and you also if you will read therein, may perceive the power which belongs to it."[34] Thus, while the gospel is something preached, it may be read, and is therefore a written text.

---

27. C. E. Hill, "Ignatius, 'the Gospel', and the Gospels," in *The New Testament and the Apostolic Fathers: Trajectories Through the New Testament and the Apostolic Fathers*, eds. Andrew Gregory and Christopher Tuckett (Oxford: Oxford University Press, 2005), 269, 284.

28. See W. R. Schoedel, *Ignatius of Antioch: A Commentary on the Letters of Ignatius of Antioch* (Philadelphia: Fortress, 1985), 208; Charles Thomas Brown, *The Gospel and Ignatius of Antioch* (New York: Peter Lang, 2000), 1–6, 15–23.

29. R. H. Gundry, "Εὐαγγέλιον: How Soon a Book?" *JBL* 115 (1996): 324.

30. Hill, "Ignatius," 278.

31. Paul Hartog, "The Epistles of Ignatius of Antioch," in *The Writings of the Apostolic Fathers*, ed. Paul Foster (London: T&T Clark, 2007), 103.

32. Hartog, "Epistles of Ignatius," 104. See *Ign. Smyr.* 1.1

33. William C. Rutherford, "Reinscribing the Jews: The Story of Aristides' Apology 2.2–4 and 14.1b–15.263," *HTR* 106 (2013): 63.

34. Aristides, *Apol.* 2.

Justin Martyr

So far, we have seen that by the first quarter of the second century "gospel" referred to both the oral proclamation and books. And not just any tale of the life of Jesus; specifically, it is used to refer to canonical gospels. To this point, the only specific canonical gospels identified are Matthew and Luke. This does not rule out other canonical gospels or noncanonical gospels, although most of the latter arrive much later.

Near the midpoint of the second century, Justin Martyr identified the "memoirs of the apostles" as "Gospels."[35] They were "drawn up by His apostles and those who followed them."[36] Hengel notes that the plurals (*apostles* and their *followers*) indicate Justin referred to no less than four Gospels.[37] As stated above, Justin cites only Matthew, Mark, Luke, and John in his extant works. So, no *less* than four are "gospels," and no *more* than four are cited. Furthermore, these are written texts as Justin "reported" Trypho saying, "I have carefully read them."[38]

Marcion and Tatian

Shortly after Marcion, Tatian constructed his *Diatessaron*. They have remarkably different places in the church's history, primarily based on their treatment of the Gospels. Hengel proposed that these two men approached the theological paradox of only one gospel but four Gospels in two different trajectories. Marcion *reduced* them to one; Tatian *combined* them into one.

It is likely that Marcion was merely reducing what was current in the church. Considering this, the title he gave his works was likely similar to the ones used by the church. According to Epiphanius, Marcion named his edited canon of Luke and Paul, "Gospel" and "Apostle."[39]

Tatian combined the church's four-gospel canon into one book. He also titled his work "Gospel."[40] It is unlikely both came up with the same title independently. It is more likely that both were imitating the church's book. If Marcion and Tatian produced what they thought were improvements to the church's texts, it would make sense that they both kept the name of the church's collection. If so, both are evidence of the Four Gospel collection in the first half of the second century. Moreover, this Four Gospel collection is named "Gospel."

---

35. Rutherford, "Reinscribing," 66.
36. Justin Martyr, *Dial.* 103.
37. Hengel, *Four Gospels,* 19–20.
38. Justin, *Dial.* 10.
39. Epiphanius, *Pan.* 42.10.1
40. See Matthew R. Crawford, "Diatessaron, a Misnomer? The Evidence from Ephrem's Commentary," *Early Christianity* 4 (2013): 365.

Irenaeus

Without a doubt, Irenaeus received only four legitimate Gospels. In *Adv. Haer.* 3.11.8, he defended its fourfold nature by comparing it to four zones of the world, four winds, and makes an analogy to Scripture's four living creatures. There can be neither more nor fewer than four. Irenaeus described the individual Gospels as four aspects of one gospel.[41]

This passage made explicit what he implicitly expressed throughout his writings. He was comfortable citing a portion from any of the four as coming from "the gospel."[42] Moreover, he preferred to use the singular "gospel" rather than the plural "gospels."[43] For example, in the conclusion of the passage above, he stated that the ancients "handed the gospel down to us."[44] Finally, he was comfortable using "gospel" in terms of the repository of the basic teachings of Christianity.[45]

Irenaeus's argument at 3.11.8 was not only theological but material as well. Skeat persuasively argued that Irenaeus's identification of the four creatures did not reference Revelation but Ezekiel. Moreover, it was both an allusion to an older work and an argument about the *order* of the Gospels. If so, he rightly concluded that it refers to a codex, for no roll could contain four Gospels.[46] Therefore, the Four-Gospel codex likely existed at least a half-century earlier than Irenaeus (c. 70), possibly earlier.

Summary

The evidence shows that the four Gospels were gathered and published before Justin's time under the title "Gospel." These are manifestly declared apostolic in their writing or by the approval of their disciples. The literary and physical evidence suggests that the fourfold Gospel codex was standard by the end of the second century.[47] By definition, the origins must be earlier, perhaps generations earlier. Thus, it appears the limits of the gospel canon are implied by the publication of the Four-Gospel codex and its overwhelming preference by the earliest believers.

REFLECTION QUESTIONS

1. How early can we tell the Four Gospels were received?

2. How early was the term "gospel" used for a book?

---

41. Irenaeus, *Adv. Haer.* 3.11.8.
42. See e.g., *Adv. Haer.* 1.7.4; 1.8.4; 3.11.1; 3.16.8; 4.29.1.
43. Hengel, *Four Gospels*, 10–11.
44. *Adv. Haer.* 3.11.9.
45. *Adv. Haer.* 3.11.7.
46. T. C. Skeat, "Irenaeus and the Four-Gospel Canon," *NovT* 34 (1992): 198–99.
47. G. N. Stanton, "The Fourfold Gospel," *NTS* 43 (1997): 316–46.

3. Did the early church fathers know of the Four-Gospel Codex?

4. What is the significance of both Marcion and Tatian calling their books "Gospel"?

5. Why do you think Irenaeus referred to a codex in his famous defense of only four Gospels?

What Is the Source and Significance of the Pauline Letter Collection?

Without a doubt, Christians have highly prized Paul's letters from the earliest periods of the church. We know it circulated in its own codex from the earliest periods, known as "the Apostle." The earliest reference to Paul's letter-writing career is 2 Peter 3:16, where Peter referred to Paul and "all his letters," explicitly calling it "Scripture." The modern mystery has been: How were his letters collected, and who did it? This question will investigate that mystery and make several suggestions about the canonical significance of our answer.

The Source of the Collection

Stanley Porter has identified six different theories regarding the Pauline Letter Collection.[1] The first is the Gradual Collection Theory ("the snowball theory"). The theory suggests the letters were slowly gathered into a collection.[2] In this view, the letters enjoyed only local circulation in the earliest periods, and then a collection grew a few letters at a time. Eventually (usually in the second century), regional collections coalesced. There are at least three reasons why this theory should be rejected. First, there is insufficient time between Paul's death and known references to a collection (see 2 Peter 3:15)

---

1. Stanley E. Porter, "When and How was the Pauline Canon Compiled?" in *The Pauline Canon*, ed. Stanley E. Porter (Leiden: Brill, 2004), 95–128. See also Stanley E. Porter, *Paul the Apostle: His Life, Thought, and Letters* (Grand Rapids: Eerdmans, 2016), 170–78; E. Randolph Richards, *Paul and First-Century Letter Writing: Secretaries, Composition and Collection* (Downers Grove, IL: InterVarsity Press, 2004), 210–11.
2. W. G. Kümmel, P. Fein, and J. Behm, *Introduction to the New Testament* (Nashville: Abingdon, 1966), 480–81; and Kurt Aland and Barbara Aland, *The Text of the New Testament: An Introduction to the Critical Editions and the Theory and Practice of Modern Textual Criticism*, 2nd ed., trans. Erroll F. Rhodes (Grand Rapids: Eerdmans, 1989), 49.

to imagine such a slow process. Second, no ecclesiastical structure exists early enough to join these regional collections.[3] And third, the contents of the collection include Philemon, but not other letters Paul was known to write. It is difficult to imagine a process only consisting of the shortest letters but no other genuine letters.

The Lapsed Interest Theory posits a rediscovery of Paul. Goodspeed and Knox proposed the theory in the first half of the twentieth century.[4] They first assert a long period of Pauline neglect. Then some individual—perhaps motivated by reading the heroic account in Acts—set out to collect the letters several decades after Paul's death.[5] Gamble rightly calls this view merely an assumption and "a romantic notion" of a search for "lost letters."[6] The theory is simply implausible.

The Composite Antignostic Theory was championed by Walter Schmithals.[7] For Schmithals, the letter collection was compiled in response to Gnosticism sometime in the 80s.[8] The most significant problems are that actual Gnosticism is much later than AD 80, and the confidence needed to build a hypothesis on purely speculative (and eccentric) views is certainly suspect.[9]

Personal Involvement Theories acknowledge that the nature of a collection suggests that a person or a group of people were involved in the publication.[10] The hallmark of these theories is that proponents name individuals rather than an abstract concept. Proposed candidates include Luke,[11] Timothy,[12] or a partially known group.[13] Most of these hypotheses are offered tentatively because proponents offer speculation based on (and often questionable) previous judgments regarding authorship, date, etc.

The Minimum Pauline Involvement Theory resembles personal involvement theories except that Paul is personally involved but only minimally. David Trobisch theorizes that Paul published Romans, 1–2 Corinthians, and

3. See Porter, *Paul the Apostle*, 171.

4. E. J. Goodspeed, *How Came the Bible?* (Nashville: Cokesbury, 1940), 59–63. See, also, J. Knox, *Philemon Among the Letters of Paul* (London: Collins, 1960).

5. E. J. Goodspeed, *New Solutions to New Testament Problems* (Chicago: University Press, 1927), 1–64

6. Harry Y. Gamble, *The New Testament Canon: Its Making and Meaning* (Philadelphia: Fortress, 1985), 37. See also James D. G. Dunn, "How the New Testament Began," in *From Biblical Criticism to Biblical Faith: Essays in Honor of Lee Martin McDonald*, eds. William H. Brackney and Craig A. Evans (Macon, GA: Mercer University Press, 2007), 133.

7. Porter, *Paul the Apostle*, 172.

8. W. Schmithals, *Paul and the Gnostics*, trans. J. E. Steely (Nashville: Abington, 1972), 239–74.

9. Porter, *Paul the Apostle*, 172.

10. Porter, "When and How Was the Pauline Canon Compiled," 109–13.

11. C. F. D. Moule, *Birth of the New Testament*, 3rd ed. rev. and rewritten, Black's New Testament Commentaries (San Francisco: Continuum, 1981), 264–65.

12. Donald Guthrie, *New Testament Introduction*, 4th rev. ed. [The Master Reference Collection] (Downers Grove, IL: InterVarsity Press, 1990), 998–1000.

13. Gamble, *New Testament Canon*, 40–41.

Galatians.[14] He assumes these letters are heavily edited (only by Paul)[15] and published to defend his practices and the offering for the poor in Jerusalem. The rest of the collection is completed in two more stages. First, Ephesians was produced as a cover letter with the addition of the longer Prison Epistles and 1–2 Thessalonians. Finally, the Pastoral Epistles and Philemon were added to complete the collection (without Hebrews). Porter rightly points out that this theory echoes F. C. Baur's four-letter hypothesis that few of any theological camp would adhere to today. If only seven letters of Paul are authentic, and the majority hold that more are genuine, the theory falls apart.[16]

The enduring contribution of Trobisch's study is the origin of letter collections in antiquity. An author typically made a copy of a letter immediately for their records, then sent the letter. We know both Cicero and Ignatius followed just such a process.[17] Paul would likely have followed suit.[18] Thus, ancient practice and Occam's razor suggest that the collection began from Paul's retained copies.

The sixth and final theory, Maximum Pauline Involvement, begins at the previous point (i.e., Paul kept copies of his letters). Paul may have mentioned his retained copies in 2 Timothy 4:13. Paul requests "the parchments" to be brought to him. "Parchments" *(membrana)* is a Latin loan word that refers to a parchment codex.[19] Thus, the content of the letter collection was likely due to Paul himself. Some of the material and visual elements mentioned in Question 31 may originate with Paul. These are the titles of the letters ("to the Romans," "to the Corinthians A," "to the Corinthians B," etc.[20]); the order of the letters; and perhaps even the origins of the *nomina sacra*.

The best interpretation of the evidence is that the letter collection comes from Paul's retained copies. That is not to say that Paul must have been the editor who published the collection. That cannot be affirmed or denied. However, if made from the retained copies, Paul or one of his close associates would have been responsible for the contents of the collection. An editor's contribution is likely limited to the consistency of titles and other standard features (like the order of the books or the *nomina sacra*). Because Peter cited multiple letters as Scripture (2 Peter 3:15) in the late 60s, we know at least some of Paul's letters were received as Scripture (i.e., equal to the OT) very

---

14. David Trobisch, *Paul's Letter Collection: Tracing the Origins* (Minneapolis: Fortress, 2000 [1994]), 5–24.
15. See, e.g., Trobisch, *Paul's Letter Collection*, 80.
16. Porter, *Paul the Apostle*, 175.
17. For Cicero, see *Att.* 1.17; 3.9; for Ignatius's letters, see *Pol. Phil.* 13:1–2. Richards, *Paul and First-Century Letter Writing*, 156.
18. Harry Gamble, *Books and Readers in the Early Church: A History of Early Christian Texts* (New Haven, CT: Yale University Press, 1995), 100–1.
19. Gamble, *Books and Readers*, 51–52.
20. Trobisch, *Paul's Letter Collection*, 22–24.

early. The remaining question revolves around how many letters were in the collection.

The Extent of the Letter Collection

Hebrews always circulated with the Pauline letter collection in the surviving Greek MSS.[21] Because it shows up in different locations in the MSS,[22] some have suggested it is a later addition to the Pauline canon.[23] However, letter collections in antiquity also contain letters not written by the authors.[24] So, while it is unlikely Paul is the author of the letter, the letter is connected to the Pauline group and, therefore, Paul. We are on reasonable grounds to understand it as a letter Paul valued and kept with his letters.

Some suggest the Pauline collection came to us in two early versions: a fourteen-letter collection containing Hebrews and the Pastorals and a ten-letter version containing only those letters to churches (a "seven-churches" edition).[25] Marcion's *Apostolikon* (with only ten letters) is said to be mildly editing this collection.[26] Thus, the suggestion is often that the "seven-churches" edition is the oldest. For some, this props up the idea that the letters to Timothy and Titus were added as a reaction to Marcion (though not all proponents reject the Pastorals).[27]

There is no MSS evidence of a ten-letter edition.[28] Instead, the primary argument comes from the existence of ancient prologues in the Latin tradition. Known as the "Marcionite Prologues," scholars suggest (1) only ten prologues are original, (2) they are not Marcionite, and, therefore, (3) they are evidence of an early ten-letter edition.[29] These conclusions have become somewhat mainstream. However, Dirk Jongkind has convincingly called these foundations into question.[30]

---

21. See, e.g., P[46], P[13].
22. Stanley E. Porter, *How We Got the New Testament: Text, Transmission, Translation*, Acadia Studies in Bible and Theology (Grand Rapids: Baker Academic, 2013), 119.
23. See, e.g., Trobisch, *Paul's Letter Collection*, 20.
24. See, e.g., Cicero's collection "Letters to Friends" contains more than seventy letters not written by Cicero and the "Letters to Marcus Brutus" contains letters by Brutus (Cicero, *Selected Letters*, Oxford World's Classics [Oxford: Oxford University Press, 2008], xv, xvi). See also the letters of Pliny the Younger that contain Trajan's replies (Pliny the Younger, *Complete Letters*, Oxford World's Classics [Oxford: Oxford University Press, 2006], 242–86 [Book 10]).
25. Nils A. Dahl, "The Origin of the Earliest Prologues to the Pauline Letters," *Semeia* 12 (1978): 233–77.
26. See, e.g., Emily Gathergood, "Papyrus 32 (Titus) as a Multi-text Codex: A New Reconstruction," *NTS* (2013): 601.
27. See Benjamin Laird, *The Pauline Corpus in Early Christianity: Its Formation, Publication, and Circulation* (Peabody, MA: Hendrickson, 2022).
28. Trobisch, *Paul's Letter Collection*, 22.
29. Dahl, "The Origin of the Earliest Prologues to the Pauline Letters," 233–77.
30. Dirk Jongkind, "On the Marcionite Prologues to the Letters of Paul," in *Studies on the Text of the New Testament and Early Christianity: Essays in Honor of Michael W. Holmes on the*

Paul indeed wrote to seven churches (Rome, Corinth, Galatia, Ephesus, Philippi, Colossae, and Thessalonica). This fact was not lost on the early church.[31] However, referring to the phenomenon is not the same as citing a collection that contained only those letters. For example, the Muratorian Fragment notes that Paul wrote to seven churches but names thirteen of Paul's Epistles (including the Pastorals). Moreover, to gain the number ten, advocates must include Philemon (ostensibly to an individual). Our opinion is that such a conjectural edition lacks significant evidence to embrace. There is, however, clear and numerous MS evidence of the traditional Pauline corpus. The only evidence we have regards a thirteen- or fourteen-letter collection where some in the Latin tradition excluded Hebrews (obviously due to the skepticism in the West).

The Significance of the Collection

Maximum Pauline involvement has at least four canonical implications. First, if the books come from Paul's retained copies, then we should not speculate about the canonicity of letters now lost. We know of two such letters. Second Corinthians 7:8 refers to a letter we call the "severe letter." It was, apparently, a scorcher meant to gain repentance. The other letter Paul mentioned in 1 Corinthians 5:4. He described at least some of the contents as "not to associate with godless people." They are gone because Paul either chose not to retain a copy or, for some reason, he lost them. Likewise, if we found a previously unknown letter of Paul, we would not consider adding it to the canon. The documents must be available to the church of all periods to be canon. Such letters would be historically significant but not canonically significant.

Second, the letter collection was not from sorting or sifting by the early church but by apostolic choice. The church, in this case, naturally receives such letters. The implication is that the church has no right to overturn the authority wielded by the apostle of Christ. We can make no legitimate canonical adjustment to the Pauline collection.

Third, the thesis makes the Pauline letter collection the earliest of the four circulation units. If Paul published them, they would date to the early second half of the first century. If close associates of Paul were responsible, no later than a decade or so seems reasonable. Although 2 Peter 3:15 possibly refers to an incomplete corpus, the final edition appears early in that period.

Finally, we could put to rest impossibly late dates for the composition of disputed books. Paul's letters were received, in full, very early. As far as we can

---

Occasion of His 65th Birthday, ed. Daniel M. Gurtner, New Testament Tools, Studies, and Documents 50 (Leiden: Brill, 2015).

31. See, e.g., the Muratorian Fragment, which states, "Paul . . . writes by name to only seven churches . . ." (MF 51).

tell, the works of the apostle were received as Scripture in the second half of the first century.

Summary

In sum, Paul's letter collection comes from his retained copies. These were either published by Paul or his close associates. From all indications, the collection was always a fourteen-letter group. However, it is not unreasonable to suggest some early adjustments. With apostolic choice at the heart of their inclusion, we have no grounds to revise any direction. We suggest that *the Apostle* was the first of the circulation units that certainly influenced the appearance of the latter units.

REFLECTION QUESTIONS

1. Why are the gradual collection theories inadequate?

2. Where did the collection of Paul's letters originate?

3. Who would have most likely published the collection?

4. Does the placement of Hebrews in the collection mean that Paul wrote it?

5. If we found a previously unknown letter of Paul, should we add it to the Bible?

How Early Did Acts-General Epistles Circulate Together?

Previously, we noted that the NT circulated in four codices (collections). Three have ample evidence of their collection status relatively early (the Four Gospels, Paul, and Revelation). Their status as Scripture was undisputed. The fourth, Acts-General Epistles (Acts-GE), is not as well attested as the rest in the early centuries but is common in the later tradition. Here we will examine what we can say about the emergence of this collection (not the composition) that form the third codex of the church's canon of Scripture. The evidence is twofold, including both the MS evidence and the allusions to the collection in the church fathers (the literary evidence). After this we will assess the significance.

Manuscript Evidence

After the sixth century, the codex containing only Acts-GE is standard (407 copies).[1] Before that time, direct MS evidence regarding the collection is generally inconclusive. While there are MSS of the individual books from the late second- and third- century, they are too fragmentary or inconclusive to say they are bound with the other books.

Several MSS do suggest a collection of sorts, but none can be stated with certainty to be in the form of Acts-GE. One of the more intriguing is a deluxe parchment codex page containing 1 Peter 5:5–13 found at Oxyrhynchus.[2] The codex obviously included previous material because it bears the page

---

1. D. C. Parker, *An Introduction to the New Testament Manuscripts and Their Texts* (Cambridge: Cambridge University Press, 2008), 283.
2. Known as GA 0206, P.Oxy. XI 1353, or LDAB 3067.

number 819 (or 829).[3] Just what that material was is impossible to say (it is too large to be only Acts, James, 1 Peter 1–5:4). Barker speculates possibly Paul's letters but notes other works might fit.[4] Thus, the evidence is inconclusive. In a similar vein, the oldest Four-Gospel codex (P[45]) also contains portions of the book of Acts. Some have cited this as evidence of significant variation in format (i.e., Acts apart from the GE).[5] It is better to say that it is inconclusive, for the GE may have once been attached to Acts but now is lost. We just don't know.[6]

On the other hand, there is no evidence that the collection did not exist. For example, the MS tradition from the earliest periods does not contain one of the GE bound with the other codex collections.[7] As shown in previous chapters, there is early solid MS evidence for these collections.

That is not to say that no evidence exists in the MSS. A significant witness to the collection is the great pandects of the early fourth century. They display the circulation units grouped together but in different orders. In other words, Acts-GE are in the order of Acts, James, 1–2 Peter, 1–3 John, and Jude in each, but the group is in different places in the MSS. This phenomenon suggests the collections had been circulating for some time before the early fourth century.

The Syrian church was isolated by language, geography, and politics from much of the rest of Christianity. Therefore, their reception of the canon followed a relatively independent route.[8] For many years, they preferred the *Diatessaron* to the Four-Gospel codex and did not receive the minor GE (2 Peter, 2–3 John, and Jude). They ultimately included them. What is more, the Syrian church is the best identification of the "some who dispute" occasionally mentioned in the church fathers.

The two oldest Syriac MSS featuring the books (fifth/sixth century) contain them in the order of Acts-GE (without the minor GE). One contains the whole Bible, but the other is only the Acts-GE codex (AKA *praxapostolos*).[9] Given the independence of the church, it is unlikely that the arrangement was

3. See Don Barker, "How Long and Old Is the Codex of Which P.Oxy. 1353 Is a Leaf?" in *Jewish and Christian Scripture as Artifact and Canon*, eds. Craig A. Evans and H. Daniel Zacharias, T&T Clark Library of Biblical Studies (London: T&T Clark, 2009), 192–202.
4. Barker, "How Long and Old," 197.
5. Parker, *Introduction*, 283.
6. David Trobisch, *The First Edition of the New Testament* (Oxford: Oxford University Press, 2000), 32–33. Trobisch notes that the GE would require only twenty pages (five sheets) to make a codex of a size that was "technically possible."
7. See Darian R. Lockett, *Letters from the Pillar Apostles: The Formation of the Catholic Epistles as a Canonical Collection* (Downers Grove, IL: InterVarsity Press, 2017), 81.
8. See David R. Nienhuis and Robert W. Wall, *Reading the Epistles of James, Peter, John and Jude as Scripture: The Shaping and Shape of a Canonical Collection* (Grand Rapids: Eerdmans, 2013), 31.
9. LDAB 115192 (=Aland-Juckel P[4]) is the whole NT. LDAB 116028 (=Aland-Juckel P[7]) only contains Acts-GE (sans minor GE) c. sixth century.

the result of cross-pollination but comes from a much earlier time closer to the original translation. The format was likely adopted from the Greek parent text rather than merely a consequence of history. If so, it is evidence that the *praxapostolos* collection predates the third century.

Ultimately, we cannot peer much deeper than the third century for physical evidence of the *praxapostolos* collection. However, afterward, the stability suggests something firmer than a third-century innovation. The literary evidence will also offer a similar conclusion.

Literary Evidence

Scholars have affirmed that individual books are certainly known and used in the early periods.[10] The present investigation will focus on evidence of the collection, not the separate books. We will start in the fourth century and move backward in time. The assumption is that the evidence in the later period is dependent on previous traditions to one degree or another.

In the fourth century, canon lists begin to appear in the records of the church in the East and the West. The seven Greek canon lists from the fourth century forward all include the entirety of the GE, with only a couple noting any dispute.[11] In particular, they generally show standardized contents, order, and terminology consistent with what we find in the MSS described above.[12] Such standardization suggests a long-standing position in the canon.

In the earliest portions of that century, Eusebius had personal doubts regarding 2 Peter and noted James, Jude, 2 and 3 John were disputed.[13] However, he certainly knows the collection and refers to it several times as "the catholic epistles."[14] He also hints at the order of the collection by referring to James as "the first" of the GE. [15] Despite Eusebius's doubts, he testified the church had received the collection. Locket notes, "If Eusebius was writing sometime before 300 and his work reflects previous tradition regarding the reception

---

10. For James, see, e.g., Luke Timothy Johnson, *Brother of Jesus, Friend of God: Studies in the Letter of James* (Grand Rapids: Eerdmans, 2004), 45–60. For 2 Peter, see Michael Kruger, "The Authenticity of 2 Peter" *JETS* 42 (1999): 645–72; John A. T. Robinson, *Redating the New Testament* (Philadelphia: Westminster, 1976), 169–99. For the Johannine Epistles, see C. E. Hill, *The Johannine Corpus in the Early Church* (Oxford: Oxford University Press, 2004), passim. For Jude, see the previous references for 2 Peter and Joseph Chaine, *Le Épitres catholiques: La Seconde Épître de Saint Pierre, Les Épitres de Saint Jean, L'Épitre de Saint Jude*, Études bibliques (Paris: Gabalda, 1939), 263–67.
11. See Amphilochius's note (Edmon L. Gallagher and John D. Meade, *The Biblical Canon Lists from Early Christianity: Texts and Analysis* [Oxford: Oxford University Press, 2017], 154).
12. Metzger noted five other sequences normally starting with Peter's epistles (Bruce Metzger, *The Canon of the New Testament: Its Origin, Development, and Significance* [Oxford: Oxford University Press, 1987], 299).
13. Eusebius, *Hist. eccl.* 3.3.1.
14. See *Hist. eccl.* 2.23.25; 4.23.1; 6.14.1; 6.25.5; 7.25.7; and 7.25.10.
15. Eusebius, *Hist. eccl.* 2.23.25.

of these letters, then we can consider the Catholic Epistles a relatively fixed canonical sub-collection at least by the close of the third century."[16] It is more than unlikely that Eusebius reports a recent innovation. Instead, the evidence suggests the collection existing as canon deep into the third century.

The earliest canon lists (broadly speaking) demonstrate an earlier reception of the collection. Origen's list is the earliest that lists the complete twenty-seven-book NT canon. Appearing in the homily on Joshua 7, the list is an application of the events at Jericho. Thus, it is not a list for the sake of setting the canon but an application of his text (assumed then to be widely held by his audience). He described the apostles and apostolic men sounding trumpets (i.e., the NT books) also destroying idolatry.[17] If the plural reference to the epistles of John includes 3 John, his list of the GE includes all seven letters and concludes with a reference to the book of Acts. In referring to 1 Peter and 1 John as "catholic," Origen's language may also demonstrate a knowledge of the collection of "catholic epistles."[18]

Origen's predecessor at Alexandria, Clement (c. 150–215), possibly knew the epistle of James, but certainly 1 Peter, 1–2 John, and Jude in his extant works.[19] Eusebius reported that Clement wrote "brief explanations" of the entirety of the NT, including the disputed books identified as "the epistle of Jude and the remaining catholic epistles."[20] And this is elsewhere independently attested by another ancient writer.[21] Clement's explanations, in a way, can function as a "canon list" without knowing the precise contents of the "explanations." Thus, given Origen's proximity to Clement (personally, geographically, and chronologically), there is no reason to doubt Clement knew of all seven GE and possibly as a unit.

Most of the Latin lists include the GE. Only the Muratorian Fragment and the Cheltenham canon (before 365) do not contain all seven. Only James

---

16. Lockett, *Pillar*, 69.
17. In times past, the list has been denounced as a creation of his Latin translator Rufinus (see, e.g., Everett R. Kalin, "Re-Examining New Testament Canon History: Pt 1, the Canon of Origen," *Currents in Theology and Mission* 17 [August 1990]: 279–81). Today, most are suggesting the list is Origen's (see Michael J. Kruger, "Origen's List of New Testament Books in Homiliae in Josuam 7.1: A Fresh Look," in *Mark, Manuscripts, and Monotheism: Essays in Honor of Larry W. Hurtado*, eds. Chris Keith and Dieter T. Roth, LSNT 528 [London: Bloomsbury, 2015], 99–117; Edmon L. Gallagher, "Origen via Rufinus on the New Testament Canon," *NTS* 62 [July 2016]: 461–76; and Lee M. McDonald, *The Formation of the Biblical Canon* [London: Bloomsbury T&T Clark, 2018], 2:282–83).
18. Lockett noted references to 1 Peter (1 Peter, *Sel. Ps.* 3; *Comm. Jo.* 6.175.9) and 1 John (*Comm. Jo.* 1.138, 2.149) (*Pillar Apostles*, 71).
19. For James, see *Strom.* 2.5; 3.6; 4.10, 18; 6.18; and 7.11. For 1 Peter, see, *Quis div.* 38. See, Clement, *Paed.* 1.6; 3.11–12 has numerous references to 1 Peter; *Strom.* 1.27; 3.6, 11, 18; 4.7, 18, 20; 6.6; *Quis div.* 23, and 38. For 1 John, see, *Quis div.* 37, 38.
20. Eusebius, *Hist. eccl.* 6.14.1.
21. Cassiodorus, *De Institutione Divinarum Litterarum*.

is missing in both lists. The omission in the former is inconclusive. It may be due to many factors, including purposeful omission and the fragmentary state of the list. The latter included the minor GE (2 Peter, 1–3 John) but with an ambiguous note.[22] The remaining Latin lists up until the early fifth century include the GE, generally as a body.[23]

Thus, Eusebius's rather offhand remarks concerning a collection existing in his day suggest tradition rather than innovation. The comments by Origen and Clement also suggest an existing tradition that would extend into the second century. Altogether, we cannot peer much past these men regarding the collection. Thus, the early third to the late second century is about as far back as we can tell. Lockett sums up the situation well, "There are hints . . . that the Catholic Epistles were received along with Acts toward the end of the canonical process which . . . found its earliest manifestation in the late second or early third century."[24] Without clear evidence for or against an earlier transmission period, we must be satisfied with such a generalization.

Other Suggestive Evidence

The relatively firm order of the books suggests a tradition set for some time and, more than likely, an intentional arrangement. The reason for the order is not particularly evident beyond subgroupings according to author. Acts is probably first due to length, but we may wonder why the order of the following GE is James, Peter, John, and Jude and its significance. A few observations are evident. First, the connection to Acts is possibly due to the authors of the letters playing prominent roles in Acts. Second, the order cannot be based on length (when counting lines, 1 John is longer than James). Third, suggestions that James was composed as an introductory letter to the collection (and therefore first) are not particularly evident.[25] Fourth, Galatians 2:9 lists James, Peter ("Cephas"), and John as "pillar apostles." This cross-reference likely had some influence on the order.[26] Altogether, it implies the antiquity of the collection (but not predating Paul) and a collection not in competition to Paul.

Another matter involves what the individual MSS can tell us. They generally follow the editorial features in the other collections. First, when titles are present, they follow the conventions that appear later (i.e., the genitive form

---

22. Gallagher and Meade, *Biblical Canon Lists*, 192.
23. Gallagher and Meade, *Biblical Canon Lists*, 235.
24. Lockett, *Pillar Apostles*, 90.
25. For proponents, see David R. Nienhuis, *Not by Paul Alone: The Formation of the Catholic Epistle Collection and The Christian Canon* (Waco, TX: Baylor University Press, 2007) and Robert W. Wall, "A Unifying Theology of the Catholic Epistles," in *The Catholic Epistles and Apostolic Tradition*, eds. Karl-Wilhelm Niebuhr and Robert W. Wall (Waco, TX: Baylor University Press, 2009), 27.
26. Lockett, *Pillar Apostles*, 102–3.

of the author). Second, they all have the *nomina sacra* where expected. Third, they are all codices (not rolls). Although, as noted above, there might be an unusual configuration, they seem to be descendants of a published edition. We can see one or more of these features even in the most fragmentary MSS.

The Significance

We have suggested that the collection of the individual books into circulation units indicates their canonical status. We have established that the first three are firmly canon by at least the midpoint of the second century. Therefore, when we propose a date for the reception of Acts-GE, we are effectively offering a date for the closing of the NT canon. The date proposed is the period *we* can affirm from the extant resources. The actual closing undoubtedly occurred much earlier. Although on different grounds, we agree with John Barton, "By the time of Origen we find that the process is more or less complete, and there is a Bible consisting of two Testaments of equal standing."[27] That is, from what we can tell, by the life of Origen (c. 184–253) the canon of Scripture is closed.

Summary

Before the production of *Vaticanus* and *Sinaiticus*, we do not have clear evidence of the Acts-GE collection in the extant MSS. But that is not to say that the collection came to exist in the fourth century or even the late third century. The fragmentary MSS show some evidence of the collection but is not fully convincing alone. When we compare the literary evidence that shows knowledge of the collection before the fourth century, more clarity emerges. We are on firm ground to suggest that the Acts-GE configuration is well established by the beginning of the third century.

REFLECTION QUESTIONS

1. Does the early MS evidence suggest Acts-GE collection did not exist?

2. Were Eusebius's doubts reflective of the church at large?

3. What do the canon lists suggest about the collection?

4. Why is the collection in the order it is?

5. What is the significance of an early date for Acts-GE?

---

27. John Barton, *A History of the Bible: The Story of the World's Most Influential Book* (New York: Viking, 2019), 251.

The Literary and
Theological Dimensions of Canon

Does the Circulation of the Book of Revelation Affect Its Canonicity?

The fourth circulation unit of the NT is the book of Revelation. However, it does not neatly fit the description "circulation unit" because its transmission is decidedly different from the other three. Revelation can be found in each of the other three units, by itself, bound with a commentary, or in a miscellaneous codex (i.e., bound with nonbiblical works). Juan Hernández rightly concluded that it is "the most peculiar and elusive of all NT writings."[1] Earlier, we described the reception of the book of Revelation as an attempt to remove a book from the NT canon. A closer look at the transmission is warranted with such a unique circulation. Although it risks oversimplification, the transmission of Revelation occurs in two streams of tradition: a biblical MSS tradition and an external stream.[2]

The Biblical MSS Tradition

The Book of Revelation survives in about 306 MSS. Parker breaks it down to seven papyri, twelve majuscules, and 287 minuscules.[3] Among the twelve plausibly pre- and Constantinian era MSS, only P^{47} among the earliest MSS contains a lengthy continuous text (essentially 9:10–17:2). Of the great

---

1. Juan Hernández, Jr., *Scribal Habits and Theological Influences in the Apocalypse: The Singular Readings of Sinaiticus, Alexandrinus, and Ephraemi*, WUNT 2/218 (Tübingen: Mohr Siebeck, 2006), 2.

2. H. C. Hoskier, *Concerning the Text of the Apocalypse: Collations of All Existing Available Greek Documents with the Standard Text of Stephen's Third Edition, together with the Testimony of Versions, Commentaries, and Fathers; a Complete Conspectus of All Authorities* (London: B. Quaritch, 1929), xxvii.

3. D. C. Parker, *An Introduction to the New Testament Manuscripts and Their Texts* (Cambridge: Cambridge University Press, 2008), 234.

fourth-century codices, only Sinaiticus is complete. All the other early MSS are particularly fragmentary.[4]

The early attestation is often described as extremely poor, but it compares well with and even better than other books of the NT. For example, in the same era (second–fourth century), the gospel of Mark is attested in Greek by P^{137}, P^{88}, P^{45}, Sinaiticus, and Vaticanus.[5] Only the fourth-century codices are complete. Likewise, Galatians is witnessed in Greek by P^{46}, Sinaiticus, and Vaticanus. Similar returns could be made on other books of the NT. All this is to say that numerically Revelation fares no worse and sometimes better than other books of the NT. In truth, the MS evidence from the era is not particularly strong for any book.

The nature of Revelation MSS varies from private, to public, to deluxe editions. Only P^{98} is a roll, but it is written on the back of a nonbiblical text, i.e., reused. However, what we see stands in contrast to what *Hermas* demonstrates (with a greater number of early MSS). Revelation never appears on an unused roll (a large percentage of *Hermas* does). And *Hermas* never appears integrated into the NT. Revelation does appear in the early MSS. As one would expect, the great codices (except Vaticanus) contain it.[6] Moreover, 0207 is a single page of a deluxe parchment codex containing Revelation 9:2–15. Written in an excellent biblical majuscule script on fine parchment, the MSS was undoubtedly made for public use.[7] Even though only one page survived, page numbers 477 and 478 suggest it was once part of a much larger codex.[8] Malik and Müller, with proper caveats, make the case that the best fit of known arrangements is the Four Gospels and Revelation.[9] As noted above, this is a format exhibited in later MSS.

From the fifth through eighth centuries, the attestation of Revelation in Greek did not increase but decreased to six MSS.[10] While unusual among

---

4. The complete list of pre-Constantinian era MSS are P^{18}, P^{24}, P^{47}, P^{85}, P^{98}, and P^{115}, *Sinaiticus*, 0169, 0207, 0308, and *Alexandrinus, Ephraemi Rescriptus* close to the era.
5. 0188 and *Beza* are close to the era.
6. *Vaticanus* is defective, excluding portions of the Pauline Epistles, Hebrews and Revelation. The rest of Hebrews and Revelation was added later as a minuscule during a restoration process. However, some marginal sigla contemporaneous with the MS continue into the minuscule of Hebrews. This suggests the supplement was produced from the damaged pages in the MS, now removed. See Edward D. Gravely, "The Text Critical Sigla in Codex Vaticanus," PhD Dissertation (Wake Forest, NC: Southeastern Baptist Theological Seminary, 2009), 57. In other words, the MS likely originally contained the apocalypse.
7. Peter Malik and Darius Müller, "Recovering the Lost Contents of Psi X 1166 (GA 0207): Codicological Reflections on a Fourth-Century *De Luxe* Copy of The Apocalypse," *JTS* 69 (2018): 92. They state, "in late fourth-century Egypt at least, this alluring work of early Christian literature played at least some part in the Christian high literary culture."
8. Malik and Müller, "Recovering," 85.
9. Malik and Müller, "Recovering," 90–92.
10. 0163, P^{85}, 0229, P^{43}, LDAB 2832 (likely an amulet).

biblical MSS, given the reluctance of the Greek church to keep Revelation in the canon, it is not surprising. Meanwhile, the MS tradition was robust outside of the Greek tradition.

The church in the West was effectively scripturally bilingual in the early period.[11] In Rome, the church was content with Greek through the second century.[12] North Africa, however, saw the first indications of a Latin text in this period, evidenced by Tertullian, although his may not have been a fixed form.[13] For the present question, they did know and use a Latin version of Revelation before the third century, as evidenced by the fixed state of the text in Cyprian.[14] Eventually, Romans transitioned from Greek to Latin for their Scriptures. By the time of Jerome, the place of Revelation had been secure for some time (if some doubt that he translated it).[15] The earliest existing texts date from the fifth century,[16] but the commentary tradition (beginning from the third century) strongly attests to it. Unlike the Greek tradition, some lectionaries included readings from Revelation.[17]

The Coptic witnesses are very fragmentary, and the earliest is from the fifth century. Parker notes, however, there are Sahidic lectionary manuscripts.[18] This suggests the reception of the book among the Copts. The Syriac attests Revelation only in the Philoxenian version (508). It also exists in the Harklean version (both versions only have one extant MS).[19] As stated previously, the Syrian church was hesitant about the book of Revelation for many centuries.

The External Stream

The second stream of transmission is outside of the biblical MS tradition. These are in the form of commentaries and miscellaneous codices. The commentaries have a copy of the book with them. A miscellaneous codex contains Revelation and unrelated nonbiblical works.

The Commentaries

Scholia, Catenas, and commentaries on Scripture are common from the earliest phases of Christianity.[20] Revelation is no exception. In the first

---

11. H. A. G. Houghton, *The Text of the Early Latin New Testament: A Guide to Its Early History, Texts, and Manuscripts* (Oxford: Oxford University Press, 2018), 7.
12. H. F. D. Sparks, "The Latin Bible," in *The Bible in the Early Church*, ed. Everette Ferguson (New York: Garland, 1993), 101.
13. Sparks, "The Latin Bible," 108.
14. Houghton, *Text of the Early Latin New Testament*, 9.
15. Sparks, "The Latin Bible," 114.
16. See, e.g., "the Fleury Palimpsest" (=VL 55).
17. VL 251, 259, 262, 271, Houghton, *Text of the Early Latin New Testament*, 181.
18. Parker, *Introduction*, 238.
19. Parker, *Introduction*, 237–38.
20. "Scholia" are comments by scholars copied into the margins of MSS; sometimes collected and published. A "Catena" is a verse-by-verse commentary compiled from ancient

thousand years of Christianity, we know of some thirty different commentaries on the book, not to mention the works now lost by Irenaeus, Origen, Athanasius, Cyril, Basil, Gregory, and Methodius, to name a few.[21] Some of Hippolytus's exegetical works on the book remain (late second century). But the earliest extant commentary is by Didymus the Blind (fourth century), mainly preserved in a scholium of a certain Cassian.[22] Next, Victorinus of Pettau in the third century drew heavily on "Papias, Irenaeus, Hippolytus, and especially Origen."[23] It was Victorinus's commentary that Jerome improved and which became popular in the West.[24] These early exegetes show no hesitancy in their reception of the book. While Didymus wrote in Greek, the early commentaries are mainly from Latin writers (Victorinus, Tyconius, and the sixth-century writer Primasius).

Sometime between 508 and 518, Oecmenius wrote a Greek commentary on Revelation.[25] Although Oecmenius was not particularly popular, Andreas of Caesarea replied in kind about a century later (c. 611).[26] The remarkable thing about Andreas is that in the extant MSS, about forty of them contain a copy of the book of Revelation. Other commentaries do as well, but not to the extent of Andreas.[27] The upshot, then, is that it creates a relatively independent stream of witnesses to the text of Revelation.

For the present investigation, the transmission with commentaries does not dispute canonicity but is an affirmation. The commentary was an attempt to understand the difficult book, that he considered canonical. Andreas himself appealed to the testimony of Gregory of Nazianzus, patriarch of Constantinople (fourth century), and Cyril of Alexandria (fifth century) for support. He also noted the ancient writers, "Papias, Irenaeus, Methodius, and Hippolytus have testified to the trustworthiness of the book."[28] Andreas himself expressly affirms the work: "We too have come to this opinion, receiving

commentators. See Frank Cross and Elizabeth A. Livingstone, eds., *The Oxford Dictionary of the Christian Church*, 3rd ed. (New York: Oxford University Press, 1997), 300 and 1468.

21. Hoskier, *Concerning the Text of the Apocalypse*, xxv.
22. P. Tzamalikos, *An Ancient Commentary on the Book of Revelation: A Critical Edition of the Scholia in Apocalypsin* (Cambridge: Cambridge University Press, 2013), ix.
23. Eugenia Scarvelis Constantinou, *Guiding to a Blessed End: Andrew of Caesarea and His Apocalypse Commentary in the Ancient Church* (Washington, DC: Catholic University of America Press, 2013), 3.
24. Constantinou, *Guiding to a Blessed End*, 4.
25. Thomas C. Oden, ed., *Greek Commentaries on Revelation: Oikoumenios and Andrew of Caesarea*, trans. William C. Weinrich, Ancient Christian Texts (Downers Grove, IL: IVP Academic, 2011), xxiv.
26. Andrew and Eugenia Scarvelis Constantinou, *Commentary on the Apocalypse*, The Fathers of the Church: A New Translation (Washington, DC: Catholic University of America Press, 2012), 16.
27. J. K. Elliott, "The Distinctiveness of the Greek Manuscripts of the Book of Revelation," *JTS* (1997): 119.
28. Oden, *Greek Commentaries*, 114.

much inspiration from these testimonies, since in certain places we make use of them."[29] Elsewhere, he directly calls the book "Scripture." Commenting on Revelation 22:18–19, Andreas stated, "The curse against those who falsify the divine Scriptures is terrible" and "we should regard the characteristics of the Scriptures as more trustworthy and venerable than Attic compositions and dialectical arguments."[30] That Andreas is in the Greek tradition suggests that they were either reaffirming the Apocalypse or the rejection was never universal in the East.

Miscellaneous Codices

Another oddity in the transmission of the book of Revelation is that it appears in several "Miscellaneous codices." That is, the text appears bound with noncanonical treatises and a hodge-podge of religious works. Some eighty-two such MSS are extant (26.4 percent of all MSS).[31] There seems to be no thorough-going relationship between the codices except the Apocalypse itself. As Malik and Müller note, "There does not seem to be any clear pattern as to the content and purpose of such compilations: quite often they seem to be (more or less) random collections."[32]

The testimony of the miscellaneous codices says little about the canonicity of Revelation. The earliest of these MSS is the tenth-century Codex Basilanus.[33] Turner speculated that the phenomenon of the composite codex was, at least for some third-century samples, the desire not to waste space.[34] This hardly explains the phenomenon of only Revelation appearing in such codices in such numbers. It is truly a mystery. However, the composition of these books occurs well after most of the churches received Revelation without question. These codices are important textual witnesses but do not impact the book's canonicity.

Summary

Previously, we noted that the seeds of dissent were placed by Dionysius of Alexandria near the midpoint of the third century. He defended a position that some other John wrote the book of Revelation. However, he accepted the book as Scripture.[35] He even wrote an interpretation of the whole book that fit his antimillenarian position to salvage it from the millenarians.[36] It would be

---

29. Oden, *Greek Commentaries*, 114.
30. Oden, *Greek Commentaries*, 206.
31. Malik and Müller, "Recovering," 83–95.
32. Malik and Müller, "Recovering," 83–95.
33. The Revelation portion is catalogued as GA 046.
34. Eric Gardner Turner, *The Typology of the Early Codex,* The Haney Foundation Series 18 (Eugene, OR: Wipf and Stock, 2010), 81.
35. Eusebius, *Hist. eccl.* 7.25.4 and 26.
36. Eusebius, *Hist. eccl.* 7.25.5.

the last known commentary until Oecumenius in the fifth century. The East, mainly protesting a physical expression of the final state, began to erode the early confidence. It was ultimately restored, but not without repercussions. These repercussions can be seen in the MS tradition. Representation as good or better than other books of the NT, then a conspicuous drop in Greek MSS until the eighth century, the absolute neglect in the lectionaries, and a wandering inclusion in the MSS afterward all are at least influenced by this doubt.

Meanwhile, in the West, they had no such distrust. Instead, it features the book consistently in the MSS, it appears in their lectionaries, and commentaries continue from the earliest periods. The Coptic versions have a similar reception (even though the early MS evidence is not robust).

Therefore, the circulation of the book of Revelation supports our thesis that the East sustained an attempt to remove the book from the canon of Scripture. It indeed lasted longer than the West's similar attempt to remove Hebrews. But it was ultimately unsuccessful. Constantinou described three broad patterns of canonization for most NT books: "overwhelmingly accepted, overwhelmingly rejected, or initially disputed then gradually accepted."[37] Revelation, however, breaks the pattern. We can best describe the reception as initially and widely accepted, gradually and locally disputed, and eventually universally restored. Like its contents, the book is *sui generis* (unique) in its transmission.

REFLECTION QUESTIONS

1. How many streams of transmission does the book of Revelation have?

2. How does the early attestation in the MS tradition fare with other books of the NT?

3. How does the commentary tradition validate the book of Revelation's canonicity?

4. What does Revelation's appearance in miscellaneous codices tell us?

5. Why did some in the East reject the book?

---

37. Constantinou, *Guiding to a Blessed End*, 15.

Did the Apostles Recognize Contemporaneous Books as Scripture?

Two passages of the NT (1 Tim. 5:18 and 2 Pet. 3:15–16) recognize contemporaneous documents or collections as Scripture on an equal plane with the OT. As one would expect, scholars both affirm and deny this interpretation. The minimum argument here is that these passages are at least from the first century and indicate the early reception of the documents mentioned. We also see good reason to affirm their apostolic origins. If so, it pushes the awareness of new Scripture being written to the earliest generation of Christians.

1 Timothy 5:18

Paul stated: "Let the elders who rule well be considered worthy of double honor, especially those who labor in preaching and teaching. For the Scripture says, 'You shall not muzzle an ox when it treads out the grain,' and, 'The laborer deserves his wages'" (1 Tim. 5:17–18 ESV). The statement has canonical implications.[1] The passage cites two passages that are both apparently under the classification of "Scripture." The first is from Deuteronomy 25:4. The second, however, cannot be found in the OT. "The laborer is worthy of his hire" is found virtually verbatim from Jesus in Luke 10:7.

Some deny that the conjunction "and" places both quotations in the classification of "Scripture." Fee, for example, argued that Luke's gospel could not have attained a written form by the writing of this letter. He then suggests it

---

1. See Michael J. Kruger, "First Timothy 5:18 and Early Canon Consciousness: Reconsidering a Problematic Text," in *The Language and Literature of the New Testament: Essays in Honor of Stanley E. Porter's 60th Birthday*, eds. Lois K. Fuller Dow, Craig A. Evans, and Andrew W. Pitts, BibInt 150 (Leiden; Boston: Brill, 2016), 680–700.

is a conflated citation much like Mark 1:2, where Isaiah is cited but Malachi is included.[2]

Two factors call his solution into doubt. First, this seems to be a stubborn insistence on a post-AD 70 date for the gospel of Luke and the assumption (in Fee's case, the possibility) that the Pastorals were forged.[3] We have defended elsewhere both an AD 62 date for Acts and that Luke, the companion of Paul, wrote it.[4] If so, Paul certainly had the opportunity to read Luke's gospel by the time of the PE. The gospel not only could have been but likely was known by Paul, especially toward the end of his career.[5]

Second, one must admit that the parallel with the prophetic quotation in Mark does not include two separate oracles joined by "and" but the conflation of multiple prophecies into one. Knight points out that more strict parallels (Matt. 15:4, Mark 7:10, Acts 1:20, Heb. 1:8, 1 Peter 2:6, and 2 Peter 2:22) combine two sources joined by "and" under one classification.[6] "Scripture" indeed describes both sources.

Others suggest that Paul cited an oral remembrance of Jesus's words. After all, such fragments, known as "agrapha," have come down to us.[7] Similarly, some suggest it was a proverb circulating in the church.[8] However, the identification *graphē* demands a *written* source. Swinson, investigating Hebrew cognates, the LXX, and contemporary usage, insists that *graphē* refers "*exclusively* to physically written or drawn material."[9] Obviously, Paul is referring to the former.

Furthermore, in the Pauline context *graphē* refers specifically to Scripture. Using the word would dismiss forms of written sources that were informal (e.g., notebooks, disconnected sayings, a collection of proverbs, etc.). For some, however, the authority is in Jesus's words, whether it comes from "Q" (one of the hypothetical sources used by Matthew and Luke) or some other

---

2. Gordon D. Fee, *1 and 2 Timothy, Titus*, rev. ed., NIBC 13 (Peabody, MA: Hendrickson, 1988), 134.
3. See, e.g., Quinn and Wacker, who use this to suggest Luke wrote the Pastorals. Jerome D. Quinn and William C. Wacker, *The First and Second Letters to Timothy: A New Translation with Notes and Commentary*, ECC (Grand Rapids: Eerdmans, 2000), 462–63.
4. Andreas J. Köstenberger, L. Scott Kellum, and Charles L. Quarles, *The Cradle, The Cross, and the Crown: An Introduction to the New Testament*, 2nd ed. (Nashville: B&H, 2016), 309–16.
5. Fee himself admitted that when Paul cited Jesus tradition, it was closer to Luke than other traditions (*1 and 2 Timothy*, 129).
6. George W. Knight, *The Pastoral Epistles: A Commentary on the Greek Text*, NIGNT (Grand Rapids: Eerdmans, 1992), 234.
7. Orenz Oberlinner made this claim (*Kommentar zum ersten Timotheusbrief* [Freiburg: Herder, 1994], 254).
8. See, e.g., Raymond F. Collins, *1 & 2 Timothy and Titus: A Commentary*, NTL (Louisville: Presbyterian, 2012), 146.
9. L. Timothy Swinson, *What Is Scripture? Paul's Use of Graphe in the Letters to Timothy* (Eugene, OR: Wipf & Stock, 2014), 93.

source.[10] But this ignores why one would cite it as "Scripture:" its authority. Witherington rightly notes the rhetorical effect of intentionally calling on Scripture assumes the reader holds the same view. It was "an inartificial proof—that is, evidence cited from a previous recognized authority, not an argument made up by the speaker."[11]

Such a rhetorical intention would rule out informal collections that both sender and receiver would not widely accept. Thus, the most plausible explanation is that Paul refers to a recently written document as Scripture on the same level as the OT. So, then, if not the gospel of Luke, what then? Except for intransigent antecedent judgments regarding the date of Luke, the authorship and date of the Pastorals, and theories of synoptic origins, one would be compelled to locate the citation with the only known document from antiquity from which it could derive. The most credible source is the gospel of Luke.

Three immediate implications are evident from this observation. First, Paul considered contemporaneous Christian documents as Scripture like the OT. Second, it should cause us to reevaluate references like 1 Corinthians 15:3–4 that appeal to Scripture. They may be referencing NT books.[12] Third, if the gospel of Luke was considered Scripture, what would Paul say about Acts?

2 Peter 3:15–16

Concluding his letter, Peter affirms, "And count the patience of our Lord as salvation, just as our beloved brother Paul also wrote to you according to the wisdom given him, as he does in all his letters when he speaks in them of these matters. There are some things in them that are hard to understand, which the ignorant and unstable twist to their own destruction, as they do the other Scriptures." The reference to "other Scriptures" is more specifically "the rest of the Scriptures" (*tas loipas graphais*). Peter undoubtedly refers to the OT, but he also includes all of Paul's letters in this classification. This leads to two significant questions.

First, to what letters does Peter refer? Minimally, it is more than one or two. It suggests a collection of some sort. It is possible that Paul's letters may have circulated in a preliminary group, given the proximity of Peter to the proposed publication of the letters.

Neyrey lists sixteen verbal parallels with Paul and four relatively uncommon themes shared by Paul and 1 Peter. Some may simply be common

---

10. See, e.g., Philip H. Towner who suggests it was referring to "various written collections of the sayings of Jesus" (*The Letters to Timothy and Titus*, NICNT [Grand Rapids: Eerdmans, 2006], 367).
11. Ben Witherington, III, *A Socio-Rhetorical Commentary on Titus, 1–2 Timothy and 1–3 John* (Downers Grove, IL: InterVarsity Press, 2006), 275.
12. Swinson, *What Is Scripture?*, 87.

Christian lexical stock; others may infer some sort of knowledge of Paul.[13] The phenomenon does not reasonably suggest the exact identification of which books he has in mind. The bottom line is that it is undoubtedly a collection the readers would know, but not necessarily the complete collection we know.

Second, when was the letter written? This question is intimately tied to 2 Peter's famous authorship issues. However, it is unlikely to be produced later than the first century, even if it was a forgery. There are several early patristic works that alluded to the letter.[14] Perhaps the earliest evidence comes from the obvious similarities to 2 Peter in the *Apocalypse of Peter* (c. 110). While some reverse the direction of dependence, the best understanding is that it knew and borrowed from 2 Peter.[15] So, then, the letter is from the first century regardless of authorship. If so, the statement in 2 Peter 3 is still a very early reception of Paul's letters as Scripture.

However, we should not dismiss Petrine authorship too quickly. Like the Pastoral Epistles, we have defended its authenticity elsewhere.[16] In sum, although it is the least well-attested book in the NT, it is better attested than all rivals. Although the style of 2 Peter is different than 1 Peter, scholars have attributed the difference to another secretary and the employment of a known style (the "grand Asian" style).[17] Furthermore, within this style variation, there are a series of subtle similarities with 1 Peter that pseudepigrapha cannot explain.[18] These and other matters lead us to conclude that the letter doesn't comfortably fit with the notion that it is a forgery.

The implication, then, is an indeterminate collection of Paul's letters was in circulation in the late 60s. Also, Peter (and his readers) received these letters as Scripture in the same sense as the OT. Moreover, it was in circulation long enough for Peter to know of those who had trouble interpreting them. Thus, the publication of this collection was not immediately before the date of 2 Peter.

These two passages demonstrate the recognition of new Scripture by the apostles. The content of which is indeterminate. However, at least some of Paul's letters and the gospel of Luke were included. Because of the connection between Luke and Acts, it is likely that they also considered Acts as Scripture.

---

13. Jerome H. Neyrey, *2 Peter, Jude: A New Translation with Introduction and Commentary*, AB 37C (New York: Doubleday, 1993), 133–34.
14. Bauckham lists possible allusions in "*1 Clem, 2 Clem, Barn.*, Aristides, Theophilus, *the Letter of the churches of Lyons and Vienne*, Irenaeus, Melito, the *Ap. John* and others" (*Jude, 2 Peter*, WBC 50 [Waco, TX: Word, 1983], 267).
15. See Bauckham, *Jude–2 Peter*, 127.
16. For a fuller defense of Petrine authorship, see, Köstenberger, Kellum and Quarles, *The Cradle, the Cross, and the Crown*, 833–39.
17. See Terrance Callan, "The Style of the Second Letter of Peter," *Bib* 84 (2003): 202–24 and D. F. Watson, *Invention, Arrangement, and Style: Rhetorical Criticism of Jude and 2 Peter*, SBLDS 104 (Atlanta: Scholars Press, 1988).
18. Michael J. Kruger, "The Authenticity of 2 Peter," *JETS* 42 (1999): 661.

Thus, the apostles affirmed a lengthy portion of the NT Scripture before the NT was completed.

Did the Apostles Know They Were Writing Scripture?

We cannot get into the minds of men long dead to determine such a specific question. On the other hand, it is certainly clear that they expected their writing to bear their apostolic authority. That is, they expected the hearers to obey their words because they were the apostles of Christ (see, e.g., 1 Cor. 14:37–38; Phil. 3:15; 1 Thess. 2:13; 1 John 1:1–5). They surely understood they held and wielded an enormous level of authority.

This authority is undoubtedly expressed in writing, intentionally shaping the practices and beliefs of earliest Christianity. In other words, they take a foundational stance. Things like the instructions for the gifts in worship (1 Cor. 14:26–40), the qualification for the officers of the church (1 Tim. 3); the process of discipline (Matt. 18:15–20) or arbitration (1 Cor. 6:1–11), and others, set the norms for corporate life. It's hard to imagine that they would not consider these ultimately binding.

Kruger points out there is virtually no difference between wielding apostolic authority in writing and Scripture, even if some in the academy hesitate to use the term. He rightly suggests the terminology is "beyond the point."[19] The point is that both the sender and recipients understood the apostolic authority and its implications. Thus, there is little semantic space between such authority and Scripture.

Moreover, some of the books seemed designed to function as Scripture. For example, few would argue that Revelation is not claiming the highest possible authority when it curses any who would add or take away from it (Rev. 22:18–19). Likewise, the Gospels were likely intended to be read in worship services.[20] We can extend that to include the bulk of the canon.[21] Bokedal concludes, "the books that came to be the Bible started off, at least in part, as books with a unique status."[22]

Summary

Both Peter and Paul referred to contemporary documents as Scripture. Moreover, these references specifically put Luke and Paul's epistles in the same category as the OT. While we cannot say that Paul would sanction Acts

19. Michael J. Kruger, *The Question of Canon: Challenging the Status Quo in the New Testament Debate* (Downers Grove, IL: InterVarsity Press, 2013), 121.
20. Martin Hengel, *The Four Gospels and the One Gospel of Jesus Christ: An Investigation of the Collection and Origin of the Canonical Gospels*, trans. John Bowden (Harrisburg, PA: Trinity Press International, 2000), 116.
21. Tomas Bokedal, *The Formation and Significance of the Christian Biblical Canon: A Study in Text, Ritual, and Interpretation* (London: Bloomsbury, 2014), 240.
22. Bokedal, *Formation and Significance*, 243.

or that Peter knew the whole Pauline canon, these references, at the very least, pave the way for much of the NT to be immediately received as canon.

REFLECTION QUESTIONS

1. How much of the NT is cited as Scripture within the NT?

2. What is the rhetorical intent of citing a work as Scripture?

3. Did the apostles know they were writing Scripture?

4. Did the citation of new Scripture invalidate the OT?

5. What is the difference between wielding apostolic authority in writing and Scripture?

How Was Scripture Used in the Churches?

From the earliest extant discussions on individual books, the use in the churches has been a factor in discussing canonicity. However, ever bookish, Christians enjoyed a broad spectrum of written materials. While all are "used," not all were considered "Scripture." Two examples from early Fathers should help frame the discussion. First, Tertullian refers to the four Gospels enjoying a "permanency of reception in the churches."[1] Few people doubt the reference is to the reception of the fourfold Gospel as Scripture on par with the OT. Second, there is a use in the church that is not on the same level. In his defense against Celsus, Origen accused Celsus of citing a book without reading it and that he was not "aware that the books which bear the name of Enoch do not at all circulate in the churches as divine."[2] This qualification admits circulation but not a scriptural status. The author of the Muratorian Fragment notes both kinds of reading when addressing the *Shepherd of Hermas*. He said, "and therefore it also ought to be read; but it cannot be made public in the Church to the people, nor placed among the prophets, as their number is complete, nor among the apostles to the end of time."[3] Thus, we must navigate the evidence between these poles of "used as Scripture" and "read" to draw canonical conclusions.

Liturgical Use of Texts

Pagan sources indicate that non-Christians were aware of Christian meetings. In some instances, their remarks on the contents of these meetings have the ring of truth. For example, the second-century satirist Lucian portrayed

---

1. Tertullian, *Marc.* 4.5.
2. Origen, *Cels.* 5.55.
3. MF 77–81.

Christians reading their sacred books to one another and giving exhortations based on them.[4] The ritual use of these texts—a liturgical use—comes in two forms: public reading as Scripture, and the foundation for preaching.

A Liturgical Pattern

The *Didache* (c. 95) gave only a few hints on the nature of public worship. It included references to the one speaking God's word (4.1), communion (14.1), and a teaching/preaching ministry (11.1, 15.1–2). A generation later, Justin Martyr described the public meeting, providing the primary evidence in the early-mid second century.[5] Christians gathered on Sunday to read the "the memoirs of the apostles" or the prophets for a set time, and then the "president" presented a sermon to advocate imitation in the life of the hearers.[6] A reference to this kind of reading is common in later works.[7] It is also commonly reported that the reading is accompanied by exhortation, like Justin's statement.

Two of the earliest extant sermons make explicit reference to the previous reading. The earliest is the so-called *2 Clement* (c. 125). At the end of his sermon, the preacher refers to it as having followed "the God of truth," i.e., reading the word.[8] The second is found in Melito of Sardis's *Peri Pascha*. The work explicitly stated that Exodus 12 had been read to his hearers (1:1). Then, a part of the sermon (11–71) explained the text.

Thus, the liturgical pattern emerges as Scripture reading then exhortation as the central elements. A Christian meeting certainly also included prayer, sometimes baptism, and communion. Typically, it was done on Sundays. In some locations, they held a daily service for instructing candidates for baptism.[9] It too featured the twofold pattern: Scripture and exhortation.

Public Reading of Scripture

With the public reading of Scripture, the one skilled in reading became an essential part of the ministry. Hippolytus put the reader on the same level as the subdeacon, yet not a part of the clergy. Specifically, the reader held an ecclesiastical office appointed by the bishop but not ordained.[10] By the time of

---

4. Lucian, *The Passing of Peregrinus*, LCL 302:13.
5. Michael J. Kruger, *Christianity at the Crossroads: How the Second Century Shaped the Future of the Church* (Downers Grove, IL: InterVarsity Press, 2018), 101.
6. Justin, *1 Apol.* 67.
7. See, e.g., Clement of Alexandria, *Str.* 6.113.3 ("by righteous hearing and divine reading") and Tertullian, *Apol.* 39.3 ("We assemble to read our sacred writings"). See also *Praescr.* 36.1–2 and *Mon.* 12.
8. *2 Clement* 19:1.
9. Hippolytus, *Apostolic Tradition*, 4.35–36.
10. *Apostolic Tradition*, 1.12.

Cyprian, this was the norm.[11] Because it is the center part of worship, we call this kind of reading "liturgical," for it is on par with the OT Scriptures and the content of the exhortation.[12]

It is likely that the early church eventually produced a system of readings, a lectionary, but no document from the earliest period has reached us. We do have many later lectionary manuscripts that the academy normally treats as a witness to the text of the NT. However, their existence is also a testimony to the book's canonical status because they were read as Scripture in the churches. It is possible lectionaries coincide with the office of the reader.[13] If so, these existed in some form from the late second century to the early third century.

Before then, it is apparent that the early churches did not rely on formal lectionaries for use in public meetings. The biblical MSS of the second century show a good bit of reading aids. These, more than likely, exist to aid in the public reading of these texts. Mispronunciation or missing a break is not particularly the concern of private reading. The primary reading aids are the relatively larger size of the texts and line spacing, the somewhat formal script (but not calligraphic), fewer ligatures, sense breaks, diaereses (noting two vowels are not a diphthong; some are rough breathing marks), punctuation points, and accents.[14] Some MSS bear formal lectionary marks. Kruger concludes that most of the NT MSS coming out of the second century "appear to be produced for the purpose of public reading."[15] The upshot then is that the evidence for this liturgical reading is found in the early MSS and the statements of the early fathers and not particularly in physical artifacts like lectionary documents that date much later. This kind of reading shows, at least in the individual location, the confidence that the book was the inspired word of God.

Sometimes patristic sources indicate that some churches liturgically read books not in the present NT canon. The Muratorian Fragment, for example, noted that they received the *Wisdom of Solomon* and the *Apocalypse of Peter*, "although some among us will not have this latter read in the Church."[16] The statement admits some do read them. We should also remember that the canon lists of the fourth century only permitted churches to read canonical

---

11. See Cyprian, *Ep.* 33.
12. Charles E. Hill, *Who Chose the Gospels? Probing the Great Gospel Conspiracy* (Oxford: Oxford University Press, 2010), 147.
13. Eric Palazzo, *A History of Liturgical Books from the Beginning to the Thirteenth Century*, trans. Madeleine Beaumont (Collegeville, MN: Liturgical Press, 2016), 84.
14. Larry Hurtado, "Manuscripts and the Sociology of Early Christian Reading," in *The Early Text of the New Testament*, eds. Charles E. Hill and Michael J. Kruger (Oxford: Oxford University Press, 2012), 58.
15. Michael J. Kruger, *Canon Revisited: Establishing the Origins and Authority of the New Testament Books* (Wheaton, IL: Crossway, 2012), 258.
16. MF 73.

books. They likely included these statements because some were reading non-approved books. History shows enough churches departing from right practice for us not to be surprised it had to be addressed. Even with these caveats, most notations of liturgical reading referred to canonical books.

Even the disputed books are known to be read as Scripture in the churches. Eusebius of Caesarea, commenting on the epistle of James, observed, "these two letters [James and Jude] have been used regularly, like the others [the GE] in most of the churches."[17] Furthermore, in his famous list of the *antilegomenon*, they are characterized as "nevertheless recognized by many."[18]

Exhortation

Only a few complete sermons survived from the earliest period. In the third century, the examples grow far more numerous. The use of Scripture is threefold in these writings. First, there is a text that is the foundation for the sermon. Second, the speaker may use Scripture to illustrate, explain, or apply the topic at hand. And finally, the preacher's expression may show the linguistic influence from specific texts (i.e., "echoes").

The foundation text of the extant sermons is always from the OT or NT. Given the lack of such material from the earliest period, we cannot say someone, somewhere, did not preach a series through *Hermas*, for example, given the respect it had in some quarters. What we can say is none appear in the extant literature coming from the third century. The evidence suggests noncanonical texts were not the foundation for most sermons.

The illustrative use is more complex, for the preacher may appreciate and cite a text whether or not he thinks it is Scripture. Such instances do not necessarily suggest canonical acceptance. Furthermore, the secondary category discussed earlier (useful but not divine) certainly appeared here. Origen, for example, cited *Wisdom* relatively often. He did not, however, place it in his canon list.[19] In like manner, Origen expressly disavowed the *Gospel of Thomas* yet used a phrase (in a mitigated way) from it to illustrate a theological point in a homily.[20]

Three homilies come from the second century. The first is the so-called *2 Clement* that expounded Isaiah 54:1. However, the author also saturated his text with other allusions to Scripture. He cited or alluded to many NT and OT books.[21] The sermon also quoted works not in the NT. The canonical works, however, significantly outpace these citations.

17. Eusebius, *Hist. eccl.* 2.23.25.
18. Eusebius, *Hist. eccl.* 3.25.3.
19. Origen, *Comm. Jo.* 19.6; *Hom. Jos.* 7.1.
20. Homily 27 in *Origen: Homilies on Jeremiah, Homily on 1 Kings 28*, FC 97 (Washington, DC: Catholic University Press, 1998), 245–59.
21. For a minimalist view, see Andrew Gregory and Christopher Tuckett, "2 Clement and the Writings That Later Formed the New Testament," in *The New Testament and the Apostolic*

Melito's *Peri Pascha* (late second century) used Exodus 12 as its base text. Similar to the other known works of Melito, *Peri Pascha* cites no NT texts but makes frequent allusions to them.[22] In modern circles, it is relatively common to assert that Melito alluded to the *Gospel of Peter* in several places.[23] However, Paul Foster disagrees and found that the "attempt to find early Patristic citations of the *Gospel of Peter* in the writings of Melito remains far from being plausible, let alone being established."[24] In contrast, most agree the Gospel tradition closest to Melito is the Johannine tradition.[25] Altogether he alluded to Matthew, John, Luke-Acts, and Paul.[26]

Clement of Alexandria wrote a homily called "Who Is the Rich Man Who Shall Be Saved?" Its base text is Mark 10:17–31. Of the three, Clement's sermon is the most easily familiar to modern Christians. Clement provided an exposition of a biblical text, followed by an appeal. He cited numerous OT and NT passages, with frequent allusions in his exposition. In some cases, he takes some liberties by placing several NT phrases on the lips of Jesus. Only a few citations cannot be identified; virtually all are scriptural.

The most interesting phenomenon is the reserve Clement shows in his citations. He was known for his breadth of knowledge and willingness to cite the broadest range of authors. Effectively all of that is gone in this sermon. It seems, in a worship context, he showed more restraint.

This early liturgical use of the NT Scriptures challenges the notion of a long-standing, free-floating oral tradition that dominated the thinking of early Christians. Instead, as Hurtado noted, "from the earliest years Christianity was a profoundly *textual* movement."[27]

Nonliturgical Use of Texts

Two more uses of texts appear in the church fathers. They were known to read works in the assembly but not as Scripture. They also were free to cite nonscriptural authorities in their own books without elevating them to scriptural status. These are classified here as "nonliturgical."

Fathers, eds. Andrew Gregory and Christopher Tuckett (Oxford: Oxford University Press, 2005), 251–92.

22. See Henry M. Knapp, "Melito's Use of Scripture in Peri Pascha," *VC* 54 (2000): 353.

23. See, e.g., Lynn H. Cohick, *The Peri Pascha attributed to Melito of Sardis: Setting, Purpose, and Sources*, Brown Judaic Studies 327 (Providence, RI: Brown University, 2000), 89.

24. Paul Foster, *The Gospel of Peter: Introduction, Critical Edition and Commentary* (Boston: Brill, 2010), 101.

25. See, e.g., Alistair C. Stewart, *Melito of Sardis, On Pascha: with the Fragments of Melito and Other Material Related to the Quartodecimians* (New York: St. Vladimir's Seminary Press, 2016), 37.

26. Knapp, "Melito's Use of Scripture," 354.

27. Larry Hurtado, "The New Testament in the Second Century," in *Transmission and Reception: New Testament Text-critical and Exegetical Studies*, eds. J. W. Childers and D. C. Parker, TS 3.4 (Piscataway, NJ: Gorgias, 2006), 26.

Reading as Exhortation

Eusebius preserved a letter by Dionysius of Corinth (c. 170) writing from the church at Corinth that gave an account of a Sunday reading of *1 Clement*.

> In this same epistle he makes mention also of Clement's epistle to the Corinthians, showing that it had been the custom from the beginning to read it in the Church. His words are as follows: "Today we have passed the Lord's holy day, in which we have read your epistle. From it, whenever we read it, we shall always be able to draw advice, as also from the former epistle, which was written to us through Clement."[28]

Quite a number have assumed "reading" here is a liturgical reading.[29] C. E. Hill notes that "your epistle" (Bishop Soter's) was also read, obviously not as Scripture but along with Clement as "occasional reading of epistolary correspondence between churches in Christian meetings for mutual encouragement."[30] Furthermore, given literacy rates, it seems rather natural that these readings of letters were as the body gathered. If so, they likely were not read as Scripture but at most as the sermon of the day.

Citation in Their Own Literature

Like modern authors, ancient Christian writers appealed to works that were not canonical in any of the contemporary definitions of the term. Modern readers should not confuse the endorsement of a propositional statement with an endorsement of the book, writer, or philosophical/religious system. Careful reading usually solves the problem.

We previously noted Clement of Alexandria's tendency to appeal to pagan, Jewish, and Christian literature. It would be reckless to assume he considered all those works as Scripture. For example, much is made of Clement's citation of the *Gospel to the Egyptians* (*Str.* 3.6.45; 3.13.91). We noted earlier that a closer look revealed he merely argued those who quote that gospel misunderstood it and should not receive it as authoritative. So yes, he cited the *Gospel of the Egyptians* but not as a canonical book.

Summary

Despite low literacy rates, Christians appreciated reading books like much of the ancient world. They produced their own and read their works to

---

28. Eusebius, *Hist. eccl.* 4.23.11 (NPNF 1:201).
29. Palazzo, *A History of Liturgical Books*, 85; Bart D. Ehrman, *Lost Christianities: The Battles for Scripture and the Faiths We Never Knew* (New York: Oxford University Press, 2003), 141–42, 175, 238.
30. Hill, *Who Chose the Gospels?*, 147.

each other (much like the rest of the ancient world). But further, they revered some of their works on the same level as the books received from Judaism. These were the content of their reading in worship and public proclamation. As Keith rightly argues, the public reading of Gospel MSS were both identity-forming and a physical symbol of that identity in the churches from the earliest periods.[31] As seen above, the church also embraced other NT books in this role. Although the canon may not have been universally solidified, the use in the churches demonstrated the highest rank for these books.

REFLECTION QUESTIONS

1. What was the pattern of early Christian worship?

2. What is the liturgical use of texts?

3. What does the production of lectionaries tell us about the NT canon?

4. What is the significance of Christian preaching of these texts?

5. Was there a nonliturgical use of texts in the church?

---

31. Chris Keith, *The Gospel as Manuscript: An Early History of the Jesus Tradition as Material Artifact* (Oxford: Oxford University Press, 2020), 201–32.

Is the Canon Closed, or Could the Church Add Books to the Canon?

In the 2002 anthology *The Canon Debate*, the late Robert Funk concluded his contribution with a call for a new NT, actually three, geared to specific audiences. The first is smaller than the present, removing matters the author deems foreign to Jesus and Paul's "original strangeness." A second, larger NT keeps the present one and includes an assortment of mostly Gnostic texts in chronological order. A third NT is for scholars. It would be much larger—in fact, a comprehensive multivolume set, each bearing "Complete" in its title. Once published, he supposed "the effect will be electric."[1] The project does not seem to have taken off yet.[2]

Eight years later, Hal Taussig, another founding member of the Jesus Seminar, published *A New New Testament*, dedicated to the memory of Robert Funk.[3] It added ten, mostly Gnostic, writings to the present NT. Added to the mix are a series of improbable dates for both the additional and original writings to give an atmosphere of chronological compatibility. The project, it seems, either wanted to correct the mistakes of the early church or redefine Christianity in what the editors deemed more likely to be appealing.

While both works present interesting concepts and views of early Christianity, neither has had traction in the academy nor the churches. Yet, the speculation of adjusting the canon is not unique to these scholars. So then, a discussion on canon must include not only *when* the canon closed but *if* it is closed.

---

1. Robert Funk, "The Once and Future New Testament," in *The Canon Debate*, eds. James A. Sanders and Lee Martin McDonald (Peabody, MA: Hendrickson, 2002), 555.
2. To date, the Jesus Seminar's Polebridge press has published four editions of *the Complete Gospels*, but does not promote it as a new NT (Robert J. Miller, ed. *The Complete Gospels*, 4th ed. [Sonoma, CA: Polebridge, 2010]).
3. Hal Taussig, ed., *A New New Testament: A Bible for the Twenty-First Century Combining Traditional and Newly Discovered Texts* (Boston: Houghton Mifflin Harcourt, 2013).

Earlier, we suggested that the impetus of the canon was essentially three-fold.[4] First, the authority of Jesus extended to his apostles was naturally recognized in the latter's writings. Second, the earliest expansion of Christianity (Jewish Christians), familiar with covenants and covenant documents, would be expecting new Scripture with the inauguration of the new covenant. Finally, prophetic fulfillment of texts like Isaiah 2 also leads to an expectation of new Scripture. These are important for the opening of the NT canon, but they are also integral to its permanent closure.

A Nontransferable Authority

In other models of canon, the authority for selecting the canon rests, at least partially, in the church. If so, the church might theoretically exercise its power to adjust the canon. Thus, Barth could affirm, "Clearly a change in the constitution of the canon, if it arises as a practical question, can take place meaningfully and legitimately only as an action of the Church, i.e., in the form of an orderly and responsible decision by an ecclesiastical body capable of tackling it."[5] Assuming an intrinsic model for the canon, the church does not have the privilege of *choosing* new Scriptures but only *recognizing* them. In other words, Christians do not have the authority to expand or reduce the canon but have the resources to recognize what God has done in providing Holy Scripture. To produce or appoint Scripture would require apostolic authority and, presumably, a living apostle.

Some modern Christians have claimed apostleship for themselves. Even in these expressions, the authority manifested by the apostles is not generally claimed.[6] Instead, most see themselves in a restorationist movement. Moreover, some make a conscious effort to distance themselves from the type of authority held by the twelve. For our purposes, none have attempted a revision of Scripture. As Wimber states, "I don't believe any of them [modern apostles] will write a new Bible or communicate anything equal with Scripture since the canon is complete."[7]

The NT writers used the term *apostolos* to describe sixteen different people.[8] It can be used in the sense of "emissary" (Christ [Heb. 3:1]), "missionary" (Barnabas [and Paul, Acts 14:14], Andronicus and Junia [Rom. 16:7]), or as the foundational office to whom Christ granted the highest level of authority (the Twelve and Paul). The Twelve seem to function much like the OT patriarchs who formed the tribes of Israel. This is evident in Revelation 22:12–14 where

---

4. See Question 26.
5. Karl Barth, "Scripture as the Word of God," in *Church Dogmatics* 1.2, trans. G. T. Thomson and Harold Knight (Edinburgh: T&T Clark 1956–1963), 478.
6. See, e.g., C. Peter Wagner, *Apostles Today* (Grand Rapids: Chosen, 2014).
7. John Wimber, "The Five-Fold Ministry," in *Vineyard Reflections, 1–12* (Anaheim, CA: Association of Vineyard Churches, 1997), 6.
8. See L. Scott Kellum, *Acts*, EGGNT (Nashville: B&H Academic, 2020), 27–28.

the gates of the New Jerusalem bear the names of the tribes and the foundation stones are inscribed with the Twelve. The foundational nature can also be seen in the replacement of Judas. They replaced him not because he died but because he was fraudulent. The apostle James, who was executed in Acts, was not replaced. The contrast suggests a singular office, not repeated in the churches.

The early church also used *apostolos* to refer to missionaries (like Barnabas in Acts 14:4), but they saw the Twelve as a *sui generis*.[9] Origen speculated that it was theoretically possible for an apostle to arise (followed by signs and proofs of the office).[10] Jerome, obviously influenced by Origen, agreed but noted that the proliferation of false church leaders included false apostles.[11] Thus, those actually claiming to be apostles were in heretical movements. For example, Mani, founder of the Gnostic sect named for him (Manichaeism), likely referred to himself as an apostle of Jesus Christ.[12]

The lack of such recognized apostolic authority made the production of new Scriptures impossible in the early church. Respected and orthodox works like *Hermas* were expressly rejected for their nonapostolic origins. In this environment, it seems impossible to suggest an adjustment to the canon is possible.

No Covenantal Expansion

Earlier it was suggested the inauguration of the new covenant was a significant impetus for recognizing contemporary works as Scripture.[13] We presented the form of the Ancient Near East covenant, with its convention of covenant documents, largely explains the growth of the OT canon. It also set the stage for the reception of the NT documents as Scripture. With the inauguration of the new covenant, the early Jewish Christians would be amicable to receiving contemporaneous writings as Scripture.

But more than just describing the impetus of the canon, it would also be a large part of affirming the canon is closed. At least two factors play a significant role in these covenantal dimensions. First, if a Jewish rabbi in the first century came along intending to set up a new covenant that replaced the previous covenant, under what conditions could those claims be validated? The most straightforward and most potent validation would be if the older covenant promised a newer one. As we defended earlier, the OT affirms a new covenant at many places; the clearest at Jeremiah 31:31–34. There is no such corresponding promise in the NT.

---

9. See, e.g., *Did.* 11.3–6.
10. Ronald E. Heine, *The Commentaries of Origen and Jerome on St. Paul's Epistle to the Ephesians*, OECS (Oxford: Oxford University Press, 2002), 174.
11. Heine, *Commentaries*, 174.
12. Jacob Albert van den Berg, et al., *In Search of Truth. Augustine, Manichaeism and Other Gnosticism: Studies for Johannes Van Oort at Sixty*, NHMS (Leiden: Brill, 2011), 241, 358–59.
13. See Question 25.

The second factor is the scope of the new covenant. The first covenant existed because of the sin of humanity. Under the new covenant, sin is eradicated (as predicted in Daniel 7); the penalty for sin is enacted or absolved in atonement, the presence of sin is eradicated in the resurrection, and the promoter of sin is ultimately cast into the lake of fire. There is no need for a further covenant regarding sin. Moreover, there seems to be no reason for a covenant renewal (as in the OT). The scope is simply too comprehensive.

Likewise, the new covenant extends to the final state of humanity. What justification is there for a newer covenant within the boundaries of the present covenant? One might argue that the situation is like that of the Sinai and Abrahamic covenants, where the former works within the latter. However, both were pointing to and fulfilled in Christ. What similar situation could work within the parameters of the new covenant? Without prior notice and theological warrant, no basis exists for a revised new covenant. Therefore, there is no basis for new Scriptures.

No Unfulfilled Prophetic Declarations

We also noted earlier that an eschatological prophetic fulfillment of the OT led early believers to receive new works as Scripture.[14] This fulfillment included an eschatological expectation of a new age that viewed the OT as incomplete; an understanding that new Scripture accompanied God's redemptive acts; and the OT oracles (like Isa. 2:2) fulfilled by a new deposit of Scripture.[15] Like the covenantal dimensions, the completion of the OT story, the finality of Christ's redemptive actions, and the fulfillment of the promise of new revelation should also figure heavily in our understanding of the closing of the canon.

When we refer to the completion of the OT, that is not to imply an incoherent book. Instead, the OT is a covenantal cliffhanger, so to speak. In particular, the prophets declared a second exodus event. Morales summarized the event as part of a pattern of sacred history declared by the prophets that included three parts: "(1) a new exodus that will lead to (2) a new relationship of consecration by covenant, which will establish (3) a new life in the land with Yahweh—a new life for both Israel and the nations in a new creation with Yahweh dwelling in their midst."[16] In turning to Christ, the believer participates in the new covenant, ultimately leading to resurrection and the final state. Thus,

---

14. See Question 26.
15. See Michael J. Kruger, *The Question of Canon: Challenging the Status Quo in the New Testament Debate* (Downers Grove, IL: InterVarsity Press, 2013), 49–57 and C. E. Hill, "God's Speech in These Last Days: The New Testament Canon as an Eschatological Phenomenon," in *Resurrection and Eschatology: Theology in Service of the Church, Essays in Honor of Richard B. Gaffin Jr.*, eds. Lane G. Tipton and Jeffrey C. Waddington (Phillipsburg, NJ: P&R, 2008), 203–54.
16. L. Michael Morales, *Exodus Old and New: A Biblical Theology of Redemption* (Downers Grove, IL: IVP Academic, 2020), 117.

believers are participating in an event underway but not complete. Morales refers to a "consummate exodus" that is coming at the return of Christ.[17]

For our purposes, we should note that the ultimate goal of the redemptive event (i.e., the final state) leaves no room for anything to be adjusted. Redemption is accomplished, applied, and completed. There are no further prophetic promises to fulfill. One can hardly imagine anything lacking in the new Jerusalem. Furthermore, the NT has no hint of an additional law in that place. Even if so, it would hardly apply to believers today. Christ achieves the eschatological prophetic fulfillment. And the NT makes no further suggestion, as did the OT prophets. If this kind of fulfillment anticipated the NT canon, it also anticipates its completion.

What If a Previously Unknown Writing Were Found?

We have noted previously that Paul wrote more letters than we have in the NT canon. What if we found one or more of those letters? Should we or could we add them to the canon?[18] What if we found authentic sayings of Jesus recorded somewhere? What if Peter had written a Gospel? What if Q were found? Metzger speculated we might consider it (in theory at least), given appropriate content and instruction not contained elsewhere.[19]

Four matters, however, suggest otherwise. First, we have established the likelihood that the Pauline letter collection comes from Paul's retained copies.[20] In Question 33, we offered this meant apostolic choice in the matter. If so, the church hardly has the authority to overturn such an expression of authority.

Second, the church has already given us a guide, especially regarding the agrapha (noncanonical sayings of Jesus). The Fathers sometimes cited these sayings, but these were never canonized.[21] In the case of a more extended treatise, the one appreciated by orthodox Christians was a supposed letter of Jesus to Abgar (King of Edessa) that promised to heal the king.[22] The letter appears in most of the languages of the empire, demonstrating the letter's popularity.[23] In this letter, Jesus's words of hope and healing were also preserved in ostraca, inscriptions, and amulets.[24] Not once was it ever considered that these should

---

17. Morales, *Exodus Old and New*, 183.
18. Barth speculated on such finds as the foundation for considering the canon "not closed absolutely" (*Church Dogmatics*, 1.2:478).
19. Bruce Metzger, *The Canon of the New Testament: Its Origin, Development, and Significance* (Oxford: Oxford University Press, 1987), 272.
20. See Question 32.
21. See Gerd Theissen and Annette Merz, *The Historical Jesus: A Comprehensive Guide* (Minneapolis: Fortress, 1998), 54–58.
22. Eusebius, *Hist. eccl.* 1.13.5.
23. Steven K. Ross, *Roman Edessa: Politics and Culture on the Eastern Fringes of the Roman Empire, 114–242 C.E.* (London: Routledge, 2001), 117.
24. Bart D. Ehrman, and Zlatko Plese, *The Other Gospels: Accounts of Jesus from Outside the New Testament* (New York: Oxford University Press, 2013), 215.

be Scripture. Any authority in these was considered Jesus's alone and not to the document. So, even if we found an authentic saying and all agreed it was from Jesus, there is no precedent to canonize it.

Third, practically, the consensus required seems exceptionally remote. At this point in history, scholars and churchmen would never agree that such a work was authentic. One can only imagine the range of opinions in dissertations, monographs, and articles produced on such a find.

Finally, recalling Kruger's criterion of availability, to add even authentic apostolic works to the NT canon would question the sufficiency of Scripture. To add the writing would suggest the lost book is necessary for the life and practice of believers. That would mean that believers had no access to a book they needed for thousands of years. Moreover, the unity believers have shared over the centuries based on the NT canon would be severely threatened. So then, both practically and theologically, any such revision presents a significant problem.

Summary

In sum, when we say the canon is closed, it is a permanent closure. Because the church has no living apostle (in the sense of the Twelve), the authority to produce or select new Scriptures passed with them. Furthermore, the factors that led to the recognition of new Scriptures no longer exist. There will be no revised new covenant or replacement covenant (none are alluded to in the NT). The prophetic promises related to the second exodus are fulfilled in Christ. And finally, any addition at this point creates complicated theological tensions. Because of these factors, there is no theological or scriptural provision for any future adjustment of the canon.

REFLECTION QUESTIONS

1. Could the church add books to the canon?

2. Why is it essential to canonical discussions that the office of apostle was limited to the Twelve?

3. How does the relationship between covenant and covenant documents signal the closing of the canon?

4. How does the eschatological prophetic fulfillment that pointed to new Scriptures also indicate the completion of the canon?

5. If we found authentic Jesus tradition, should we add that to the canon?

What Are the Theological Implications of a New Testament Canon?

The phenomenon of the NT canon carries several theological implications. An exhaustive treatment goes beyond the space allotted here. We will have to be satisfied to touch the main theological issues related to a canon of Scripture. These are inspiration, authority, and the possibility of a comprehensive theological outlook, otherwise known as biblical theology.

Canon and Inspiration

Historical-critical models reject plenary inspiration mainly due to disagreement about the canon of Scripture.[1] On the other hand, functional models often see inspiration as a criterion of canonicity recognized by believers but may diverge in different communities.[2] Between these two interpretations is a better answer. The intrinsic model affirms inspiration: not as a criterion of canonicity but its implication. As Peckham stated, "necessary but not sufficient."[3] This latter opinion better fits the biblical evidence.

The OT testifies to unknown prophetic books that did not make it into the canon.[4] This lack of canonical status does not signify that such prophecies were false but that the inspired prophecy was not for the purpose of Scripture. With their purpose accomplished, there was no reason for their continued use. Likewise, John tells us Jesus spoke an enormous amount not preserved

---

1. Johann Salomo Semler, *Abhandlung von Freier Untersuchung des Canon*, ed. Heinz Scheible. Texte zur Kirchen- und Theologiegeschichte, Heft 5 (Gütersloh: Mohn, 1967), 16, 31, 60.
2. John C. Peckham, *Canonical Theology: The Biblical Canon, Sola Scriptura, and Theological Method* (Grand Rapids: Eerdmans, 2016), 39.
3. Peckham, *Canonical Theology*, 39.
4. Peckham lists the books of Statutes (1 Sam. 10:25); Nathan, Gad the Seer (1 Chr. 29:29), Shemiah and Iddo the Seer (2 Chr. 12:15) (*Canonical Theology*, 38–39).

for us (John 21:25). Surely, this loss denies neither inspiration of the statements nor the fact of inspiration. It would suggest a different category.

That inspiration and canonicity were not wholly synonymous explain the ancients' use of the terminology. They affirmed the inspiration of the NT writings but also affirmed it for their own writings. Clement, for example, affirmed Paul's writing as "true inspiration."[5] But he also noted his letter was "through the Holy Spirit."[6] This confidence is not particularly uncommon in antiquity. At the same time, none of them were advocating their works should be Scripture. So then, works that claimed inspiration or were considered inspired were not necessarily regarded as canonical.

In the face of these expressions, they considered Scripture in another unique status. The term most related to canonical was "divine" (Lat., *divina*; Gr., *theia*) to describe that the source and substance of the Scriptures were from God.[7] They denied this status to works deemed noncanonical.[8]

This unique status is drawn from the NT's testimony regarding God's participation in the production of Scripture. Second Timothy 3:16–17 affirms that the Scriptures have God as their ultimate source and is, therefore, the source for Christian maturity. The term "inspired" (*theopneustos*) is a predicate adjective describing at least the OT (but note Paul affirmed Luke as Scripture at 1 Tim. 5:18). As Scripture, the defining characteristic is inspiration (the very breath of God).[9]

Second, the manner of the production described at 2 Peter 1:20–21 does not demand a dictation theory. Foundationally, Peter referred to Scripture and not oral proclamation (1:20 "prophecy of Scripture").[10] The passage begins with a denial that Scripture is entirely human in its source. "From someone's own interpretation" could be translated "from one's own imagination" in that the interpretation of a God-given vision (or other circumstances by extension) has no human source.[11] Instead, they spoke "from God."

Not only the source but the prime initiative was with God expressed as "carried along by the Holy Spirit." "Carried along" (*pheromenoi)* suggests passive and active participation. The active agent is the Holy Spirit; the prophet then receives the action. Without denying all the human elements involved in writing (education, vocabulary, style, historic occasion), the movement of the Spirit led the writers to express God's message. So then, the final product was exactly what God wanted and divine in both source and substance.

---

5. *1 Clem.* 47.3.
6. *1 Clem.* 63.2.
7. See, e.g., Tertullian, *de Pud.* 5, 10, and Origen, *De Princ.* 2.11.2 and 4.1.1.
8. E.g., Origen, *Adv. Celsus* 5.54.
9. For the major interpretive issues, see George W. Knight, *The Pastoral Epistles*, NIGTC (Grand Rapids: Eerdmans, 1992), 444–48.
10. Gene L. Green, *Jude and 2 Peter*, BECNT (Grand Raids: Baker Academic, 2008), 230.
11. Richard Bauckham, *Jude, 2 Peter*, WBC (Waco, TX: Word, 1983), 228–35.

Canon and Authority

Many historical-critical scholars also reject both the authority and inspiration of Scripture. For several, the canon was a late and arbitrary development of Christianity (i.e., human decisions).[12] Thus, the Scriptures have no enduring authority and (for some) were never intended to establish the norms of Christianity.[13]

However, we have seen a different view of the canon that has prophetic and theological underpinnings suggesting divine involvement. Given these divine origins, the words of Scripture are appropriately referred to as "God's words." Men speaking in the OT are often described as God speaking throughout the NT.[14] This affirmation is the recognition of God's decree to the prophets to place his words in their mouths (see Isa. 59:21; Jer. 1:9).

Evangelical scholars like Wayne Grudem have affirmed that the identification of the canon as God's Word means that "to disbelieve or disobey any word of Scripture is to disbelieve or disobey God."[15] In other words, all people must obey, for God will judge those who do not (see, e.g., Jer. 13:10). The authority of Scripture, then, is derivative from its divine source. People, especially God's people, are expected to believe and obey, for it carries the very authority of God.

Grudem also affirmed that the equation of God's word as canon means the truthfulness of Scripture is based on the very character of God.[16] Such an affirmation insists that Scripture shares God's perfection.[17] That is, since God cannot lie or speak falsely, his written word also bears this stamp of truthfulness. Irenaeus demonstrated this axiom when he referred to the Scriptures as "the body of truth" and decried others for falsely speculating about another body of truth.[18]

This connection between God and his word is the foundation for the doctrine of biblical inerrancy (i.e., without error). The *Chicago Statement of Biblical Inerrancy* began with the affirmation that God only speaks truth, and the second is that Scripture is "God's own Word."[19] Scholars affirm and deny the assertion, but some adopt a mediating position. Those scholars propose that the Scriptures are generally accurate in historical and scientific details,

---

12. James Barr, *The Bible in the Modern World* (New York: Harper & Row, 1973), 120.
13. James Barr, *Holy Scripture: Canon, Authority, Criticism* (Philadelphia: Westminster, 1983), 12.
14. See, e.g., Acts 3:21; Hebrews 1:1; 3:7, and 4:7.
15. Wayne A. Grudem, *Systematic Theology: An Introduction to Biblical Doctrine*, 2nd ed. (Grand Rapids: Zondervan Academic, 2020), 81.
16. Grudem, *Systematic Theology*, 82–84.
17. R. Albert Mohler, "When the Bible Speaks, God Speaks: The Classic Doctrine of Biblical Inerrancy," in *Five Views on Biblical Inerrancy*, eds. J. Merrick and Stephen M. Garrett (Grand Rapids: Zondervan, 2013), 39.
18. See, Irenaeus, *Adv. Haer.* 2.27.1; *Dem.* 1.
19. R. C. Sproul and Norman L Geisler, *Explaining Biblical Inerrancy: Official Commentary on the ICBI Statements* (Matthews, NC: Bastion Books, 2013), 22.

but there may be some minor, meaningless errors.[20] Thus they prefer to describe the NT's character as *infallible* rather than *inerrant*. Since the Scripture's self-attestation identifies the Bible with God so closely, even a mediating position like *infallible* seems to fall short of the implications from the association.

Generally, those rejecting canonical truthfulness in whole or in part appeal to contradictions between biblical texts or between the Bible and science/history. Both are matters of interpretation. For example, evangelical scholars have generally answered the so-called contradictions in the Bible. There are legitimate interpretations that do not create a contradiction with other texts.[21] At the very least, contradiction is not a necessary feature of Scripture. More often than not, noncontradictory interpretations are the most compelling.

Something similar exists when the Bible and science (or history) are said to conflict. Again, the issue is the interpretation of both "texts." It could be that believers have interpreted the Scriptures inadequately. For example, adding up the genealogies of the Scriptures will not generate the age of the earth. Those texts (1) do not intend to create a chronological table, and (2) have (intentional) gaps, often for literary/theological purposes (see, e.g., Matt. 1:1–17).

The secular scholars develop theories and paradigms by interpreting evidence. The interpretation of the evidence (often described as "settled science" or "fact") is, in fact, fully capable of being overturned, sometimes wiping out an alleged contradiction. For example, radical scholars alleged that the reason the Jewish leadership could not refute the resurrection by producing Jesus's corpse is the "fact" that executed criminals were never buried but left to be eaten by dogs. However, in 1968 the bones of a properly buried crucified man were found in Israel, dating near the first century.[22] As a result, the "historical fact" was overturned and the paradigm emptied of substance.[23] So then, "never" has become "rarely" and has lost its significance.[24]

---

20. Peter Jensen, *The Revelation of God*, ed. Gerald Bray, Contours of Christian Theology (Downers Grove, IL: InterVarsity Press, 2002), 198.

21. A good example is Michael Kruger's lengthy review of Ehrman's *Jesus Interrupted*. Michael J. Kruger, "Bart D. Ehrman, *Jesus, Interrupted: Revealing the Hidden Contradictions in the Bible (and Why We Don't Know About Them)*," *WTJ* 71 (2009): 502–9.

22. See J. Zias and E. Sekeles, "The Crucified Man from Giv'at ha-Mivtar: A Reappraisal," *IEJ* 35 (1985): 22–27.

23. James H. Charlesworth, *Jesus Within Judaism: New Light from Exciting Archaeological Discoveries*, ABRL (New York: Doubleday, 1988), 122.

24. John Dominic Crossan argued that one burial does not overturn the general rule and continues to deny a physical resurrection (*Who Killed Jesus? Exposing the Roots of Anti-Semitism in the Gospel Story of the Death of Jesus* [San Francisco: HarperSanFrancisco, 1995], 162). In the meantime, another crucified victim with a burial has been found in Britain. See "Crucifixion in the Fens: Life and Death in Roman Fenstanton," *British Archaeology* (January/February 2022): 18–29.

Canon and NT Theology

The concept of canon stands at the center of the nature and scope of biblical theology (particularly NT theology). J. P. Gabler launched the field of study in the late eighteenth century, defining it as "what the ancients thought about divine matters," by which he meant the biblical writers.[25] About a century later, William Wrede challenged the discipline in both the object of investigation and the intended results. He defined the object of inquiry as "early Christian religion" rather than the NT. He regarded the canon as nonbinding on modern Christians because it was historically a late development.[26] Thus, "anyone who accepts without question the idea of the canon places himself under the authority of the bishops and theologians of those centuries."[27] With religion as the object of investigation, they grouped the NT with noncanonical literature as the source material. The intended result was a historical description of the religion of the earliest periods.

He was revived, in a sense, in the late twentieth century by Heikki Räisänen, who largely followed and adapted Wrede. This branch of the academy is only interested in history and not bound by a "human decision."[28] When this view of canon is adopted, the term "NT Theology" not only no longer describes the discipline but threatens to pull the plug on the whole enterprise.

The result of such an approach is largely frustration at the banality of the product. As Childs put it, "historical critical exegesis flounders at the crucial junction which must be crossed if one seeks to reflect theologically on what the Bible characterizes as the divine word."[29] The (sometimes wildly idiosyncratic) reconstructions of early Christian religion by these authors are virtually meaningless to modern Christians.

The definition of "canon" among the advocates of the historical-critical model is at the heart of this development. The available records cannot substantiate the canon defined as a purely human achievement. As we have seen, nowhere, in any extant writing, do we see a hint of human decisions determining the NT canon. Instead, we see something more expected from recognizing the intrinsic authority of these works. Immediately, the core of the canon was received, virtually without question. Questions persisted in some circles

---

25. John Sandys-Wunsch and Laurence Eldredge, "J. P. Gabler and the Distinction between Biblical and Dogmatic Theology: Translation, Commentary, and Discussion of His Originality," *SJT* 33 (1980): 137.

26. William Wrede, "The Task and Methods of 'New Testament Theology,'" in Robert Morgan, William Wrede, and Adolf Schlatter, *The Nature of New Testament Theology: The Contribution of William Wrede and Adolf Schlatter*, Studies in Biblical Theology, 2/25 (London: SCM Press, 1973), 70–71.

27. Wrede, *Task and Methods*, 71.

28. Heikki Räisänen, *Beyond New Testament Theology*, 2nd ed. (London: SCM Press, 2000), 160.

29. Brevard S. Childs, *Biblical Theology of OT and NT: Theological Reflection on the Christian Bible* (Philadelphia: Fortress Press, 1979), 525.

around the minor GE. These were "settled" without any known debate or argument. Something more like an overwhelming recognition fits the record better. Localized attempts to remove Revelation and Hebrews from the canon failed. This kind of track history is more in line with a recognized intrinsic authority. Thus, the canon was not the external imposition of old men but the results of the authority identified in these books. The authority then lay outside the churchmen accused of imposing something on modern Christians.

Furthermore, the roots of the dismissal of inspiration as the grounds for a NT canon were flawed. Semler dismissed a uniform inspiration of the NT on the grounds of the so-called centuries-long debate over the canon.[30] This dismissal is faulty on two grounds. First, inspiration was not a criterion for selecting the canon but the assumption about the books received. Second, questions and debates do not necessarily demonstrate a flaw in the NT books. A more plausible venue to assign fault is in the human beings who stubbornly refused to receive these few, mainly small, books. We know by history and personal experience that human beings can miss the divine movement. Thus, the foundation for rejecting a program of NT theology was never on firm ground. Students and scholars should pursue a theological message from the NT.

Summary

The theological implications of the NT canon covered here were threefold. Inspiration, although not a formal criterion for canon selection, was certainly assumed for the NT writings. The NT affirms inspiration and outlines the process as not merely dictation but the movement of God on human beings that included their participation.

The Scripture's description as God's Word also implies its authority. The close association between God and his Word assumes both the truthfulness of the Word and its demands on human beings to obey. Human beings do not have the permission to select agreeable portions of the word to believe or obey.

Finally, the NT is unique among the Christian literature surviving from the earliest periods. It alone is the body of literature handed down from the apostles. It alone bears the authority to set the norms and expectations for believers in Christ. Thus, the search for a NT theology is not only possible but necessary.

REFLECTION QUESTIONS

1. Does inspiration demand dictation?

2. What is the implication of the Bible's self-reference as "God's Word?"

---

30. Semler, *Abhandlung,* 20–21.

3. Is the Bible in conflict with science or history?

4. What is the basis for the doctrine of inerrancy?

5. Why does the definition of canon impact the discipline of biblical theology?

What Are the Hermeneutical Implications of a New Testament Canon?

The intrinsic model espoused here advocates that the books of the NT are ontologically canonical. As such, they are self-authorizing. Therefore, from God's point of view, the canon was closed when the last book was written. The task of believers was recognizing the canon rather than selecting. This view, of course, is roundly criticized in the academy as a faith position.[1] Yet, we would affirm that the underlying theological convictions of the ancients were precisely this, even if they, at times, disagreed about the contents. This internal authorization leads us to approach the text in a certain way. The following is a reflection on the interpretive implications of such a canon of Scripture.

Read as a Whole

The NT canon is the second part of the church's complete canon. The question is, what do we do with the OT? Historically, three influential "camps" solved the problem of OT relevance by either rejection, historical development, or allegorical interpretation. Marcion famously rejected not only the OT but the God of the OT. The early church was rightly offended and denounced his approach, but how should the text be interpreted? The Antiochene school led by Theodore of Mopsuestia promoted literal interpretation, understanding the OT in terms of history and typology. Origen's method (building on his predecessor Clement of Alexandria) sought interpretational relevance for the Israelite Scriptures for Christians through allegory. Later church fathers like Augustine practiced

---

1. See e.g., Karel van der Toorn, *Scribal Culture and the Making of the Hebrew Bible* (Cambridge, MA: Harvard University Press, 2007), 236.

a blend of Antioch and Alexandria.[2] Modern scholarship has approached the question in various permutations over the years. Baker identified four modern solutions: NT as the essential Bible, OT and NT as equally Christian Scripture, the OT as the essential Bible, and The OT and NT as one salvation history.[3]

Our task is not to summarize and critique all the positions but to point out the hermeneutical implications of the Christian canon. Any approach to the canon that does not affirm the necessity and the relevance of both parts of the canon fails to do justice to the concept.

Virtually no "OT priority" scheme in Christian scholarship disparages or ignores the NT. The opposite position certainly does. The church already fought the battle over the necessity of the OT when she censured Marcion in the second century. Some, however, had not remembered the lesson. Prewar Germany saw several neo-Marcionites; the chief was Adolf von Harnack, who averred that the modern church must no longer preserve the OT as a canonical document.[4] The radical *deutsche Christen* movement in the 1930s attempted to do just that, providing a partnership for the Third Reich to radicalize Protestant theology.[5]

The modern Marcionite has no such evil intentions. They either by intimidation or preference, ignore rather than reject the OT. The result is a milder form of Maricon's heresy—a practical Marcionite, if you will.

While the new covenant replaced the older, it did not erase the validity of the old covenant documents in terms of God, his character, his ways, his purposes, and his plans for humanity. The authentication of the new covenant is found in the pages of the older. Thus, when an interpreter ignores the OT and justifies it because they are "a new covenant" preacher/teacher, they practically injure their hearers in three ways. They disparage the older, undermine the foundations for the faith, and provide no vision of the storyline of the Bible. In contrast, the earliest Christians clung to the OT as God's word as if life depended on it.

The best understanding of the OT in relation to the NT is that it presents a history of redemption, from creation to new creation. As the story progresses, so too does God's dealing with humanity. One can hardly prioritize one over the other, but interpret each in light of the other in the totality of the story.

Read as a Unity

A "biblical canon" assumes a certain unity in the books collected. Therefore, the interpreter of the canon should expect a cohesive book. The substance of this cohesion has been challenging to define. Scholars since the

---

2. David Baker, *Two Testaments, One Bible: The Theological Relationship Between the Old and New Testaments*, 3rd ed. rev. and upd. (Downers Grove, IL: IVP Academic, 2010), 36–37.
3. See Baker, *Two Testaments, One Bible*, 267–81.
4. Adolf von Harnack, *Marcion: The Gospel of the Alien God* (Durham, NC: Labyrinth, 1990), 217. Harnack died in 1930, hardly professing the politics of the Nazi party.
5. See Doris L. Bergen, *Twisted Cross: The German Christian Movement in the Third Reich* (Chapel Hill: The University of North Carolina Press, 1996).

enlightenment have claimed repeatedly that the differences within Scripture (particularly between the Testaments) are so significant that little or no such unity exists.[6] As noted above, the early church's interpreters employed harmonization, typology, and allegory to iron out apparent discrepancies. The academy has abandoned most of these on the grounds of historical abuse or incompatibility with their own interpretive methodologies.

Calvin devoted two chapters to the unity and diversity of the canon.[7] His terms were "similarities" and "differences." The unity of the canon is found in a single ongoing covenant, but a different "mode of dispensation."[8] Of course, not all agree with the particulars of his exegesis, but the emphasis on one salvation history undoubtedly binds the two Testaments together as a single canon. Modern writers approach it as a history of redemption approach to the text. Understanding the story arc of the Bible is the best understanding of the unity of the Bible.[9]

Within this unity, there is a diversity that we should not see as contradictory but apparent and appealing. They are only "apparent" when we approach the text too narrowly, with immoveable preconceived notions and imposed methodologies that render only one outcome. Moreover, diversity should be seen as appealing. Art has little appeal without contrast, color, depth, and texture. Likewise, the storyline of the Bible features an aesthetic diversity. Things like various genres, epochs, location, language, culture, and wildly different personalities make a mosaic that invites close inspection and a global overview. Dempster well commented:

> The larger canonical context is able to show how the various parts of the canon connect, interrelate, reveal the major accents and emphases, and dialogue with one another. Thus the canon is not flat and one-dimensional but has depth, contour, and texture and must be understood in its rich and multifaceted totality, what is called *tota Scriptura*.[10]

Read with Equal Value

Luther is credited with advocating a hierarchy within the canon, a canon within the canon. For him, those weighty books were those that showed

---

6. See James D. G. Dunn, *Unity and Diversity in the New Testament: An Inquiry into the Character of Earliest Christianity*, 3rd ed. (London: SCM Press, 2006).
7. Calvin, *Institutes*, 2.10 and 11.
8. Calvin, *Institutes*, 2.10.2.
9. For an overview of the relationship between the OT and NT in various theological systems, see Benjamin L. Merkle, *Discontinuity to Continuity: A Survey of Dispensational and Covenantal Theologies* (Bellingham, WA: Lexham, 2020).
10. Stephen Dempster, "The Canon and Theological Interpretation," in *A Manifesto for Theological Interpretation*, eds. Craig G. Bartholomew and Matthew Y. Emerson (Grand Rapids: Baker Academic, 2016), 140.

Christ, intimately connected with justification by faith. Few would disagree with the importance of the topic, but it echoes the attempt of theologians to find a center for biblical theology.[11] Those who advocate "Christ" or "gospel" as the center are inevitably critiqued for being too vague. Any NT text is only a few degrees separated from the topic. The same is true for Luther's criteria. It is so general that any NT text is hardly separated from it. It is not just the specific criteria that are the problem, though.

The concept of a canon within the canon should be challenged on three fronts. First, it inevitably leads to the devaluation of the "outer canon." It is implicit permission to ignore the "lesser" works. The result is a crypto-Marcionite position. In truth, the church has already recognized all the books of the NT canon. More importantly, the Scriptures do not indicate a hierarchy of divinity. "All Scripture is inspired by God" (2 Tim. 3:16). Second, it is a critical failure for NT theology. NT theology is the synthesis of the teaching of the canon, not privileged texts within the book. We see this in practice when a "Pauline theology" ignores a disputed or "lesser" book(s) to synthesize Paul's message. It is invariably incomplete at best. Finally, and most devastating to the concept, the inherent selectivity brings us back to the question of authority.[12] If the church did not have the privilege to select the canon, it likewise has no jurisdiction to privilege one text over another.

Metzger stated the implications well for NT teachers and preachers:

> New Testament scholars have the responsibility as servants of the Church to investigate, understand, and elucidate, for the development of the Christian life of believers, the full meaning of every book within the canon and not only of those which may be most popular in certain circles and at certain times. Only in such a way will the Church be able to hear the word of God in all of its breadth and depth.[13]

Read Progressively

Although not strictly chronological, the Bible tells the redemption history of humanity. It does not reveal everything at once but progressively unveils biblical truth. Progression is distinct from some theories of "theological development" due to human reflection. For example, many scholars view high

---

11. See Peter Stuhlmacher, *Biblical Theology of the New Testament*, trans. and ed. Daniel P. Bailey (Grand Rapids: Eerdmans, 2018), 772.

12. See Grant R. Osborne, *The Hermeneutical Spiral: A Comprehensive Introduction to Biblical Interpretation*, rev. and exp. (Downers Grove, IL: InterVarsity Press, 2006), 360–61.

13. Bruce Metzger, *The Canon of the New Testament: Its Origin, Development, and Significance* (Oxford: Oxford University Press, 1987), 282.

Christology as a development of years of theological reflection.[14] This theory has led to an array of impossibly late dates for books that demonstrate a high Christology to give room for such a development. Instead, progressive revelation is, first, revelation, God's unveiling of theology. It is, then, chronological. Finally, the progression does not correct the foundational understanding but adds to it. This understanding makes the OT the necessary foundation to comprehend the fuller picture.

Progressive revelation can be viewed from the aspect of the final product as well. Because the NT is so dependent and saturated with citations of the OT, its comments on those previous texts must be received. In other words, when the NT interprets the OT, believers do not have the option to interpret the OT in another way. For example, for many, Jude interprets the "sons of God" in Genesis 6:1–5 as angelic beings. Evangelical NT scholars often embrace this interpretation for both texts.[15] OT scholars are more hesitant but often deny (or ignore) the interpretation of Jude 6 in favor of Luther and Calvin's interpretation as godly men.[16] The point is not who is correct, but if Jude 6 interprets Genesis 6, we have a canonized interpretation.

The problem can also go in the opposite direction, as seen in the interpretation of the Song of Solomon. Both Jews and Christians have interpreted it in various symbolic solutions (like Christ's love for the church). In the early church, it shows up as early as Hippolytus and is consistently allegorical (in various ways).[17] Since no NT writer canonizes such an interpretation, there is no warrant for the approach, however uncomfortable a straightforward interpretation may be.

Summary

Because the Scripture is an ontological and theological unity, the interpretive implications of the canon are at least fourfold. We should read the Scriptures as a whole, as a unity, with equal value to all the parts, and progressively. These implications are hardly exhaustive, but they reflect the approach of the early church in many ways. In his book *Holy Writings, Sacred Text*, John Barton described four axioms of the early church regarding the interpretation of the Bible. The first three are hardly debatable. (1) "A Scriptural

---

14. The foundational example was Wilhelm Bousset, *Kyrios Christos: A History of the Belief in Christ from the Beginnings of Christianity to Irenaeus*, trans. John E. Steely (Nashville: Abingdon, 1970). The best refutation is Larry W. Hurtado, *Lord Jesus Christ: Devotion to Jesus in Earliest Christianity* (Grand Rapids: Eerdmans, 2003).

15. See Thomas R. Schreiner, *The King in His Beauty: A Biblical Theology of the Old and New Testaments* (Grand Rapids: Baker Academic, 2013), 10–11.

16. See Kenneth A. Mathews, *Genesis 1–11:26*, NAC 1A (Nashville: Broadman & Holman, 1996), 329.

17. See the discussion in Duane A. Garrett, *Proverbs, Ecclesiastes, Song of Songs*, NAC 14 (Nashville: Broadman & Holman, 1993), 353–58.

Text is an important text, a text that matters and contains no trivialities, nothing ephemeral."[18] That is, all the Scripture is meaningful; we agree. (2) "Contemporary relevance is clearly related to non-ephemerality: a non-ephemeral work is one relevant to every generation, to all people at all times."[19] That is, the Bible is not meaningful to the original hearers only; we agree. (3) "All reading operates with an assumption of consistency;" we agree.[20] On the fourth axiom, we only partly agree: (4) "Explanations of apparent difficulties and inconsistencies result in a vision of the text as full of mysteries, with many layers of meaning below the surface sense."[21] Apparent difficulties are best handled from the viewpoint of the third axiom (consistency) with a close inspection of the texts in question.

REFLECTION QUESTIONS

1. Why is it important to see the canon made of two parts in a unity?

2. How are the Testaments both diverse and unified?

3. What are the dangers of a canon within the canon?

4. How is progressive revelation different from theories of theological development?

5. What are the interpretive implications of progressive revelation?

---

18. John Barton, *Holy Writings, Sacred Text: The Canon in Early Christianity* (Louisville, KY: Westminster John Knox, 1998), 135.
19. Barton, *Holy Writings, Sacred Text*, 137.
20. Barton, *Holy Writings, Sacred Text*, 139.
21. Barton, *Holy Writings, Sacred Text*, 142.

Glossary of Terms

Apocrypha	In modern usage, the term describes ancient books not in the biblical canon (orthodox or nonorthodox). In antiquity, it referred to heretical books, rejected by the church as having any spiritual value.
Autographs	The original manuscripts of the books of the Greek New Testament.
Byzantine Priorists	Scholars who hold that the Byzantine text contained in the majority of our extant manuscripts best preserves the original text.
Catena	A verse-by-verse commentary supposedly compiled from ancient commentators. They were published as works in their own rights.
CBGM	(Coherence-Based Genealogical Method) A new method for reconstructing the initial text of the New Testament and understanding the history of its transmission by using computer tools and the principles of reasoned eclecticism to analyze the relationship between the texts of the ancient manuscripts.
CNTTS	(Center for New Testament Textual Studies) A research center established in 1998 at New Orleans Baptist Theological Seminary, dedicated to the study of the Greek manuscripts of the New Testament.
Codex	A book consisting of multiple pages attached on one side and constructed in a fashion somewhat similar to the modern book as an alternative to the ancient scroll.
Coincidental Agreement	An agreement between two or more texts that resulted from different scribes independently creating the same reading.

Colophon	A statement at the end of a book that gives information about the composition of the book such as the name of the author and the place of composition.
Conjectural Emendation	A reading believed to be original even though the reading is not found in any extant manuscript of the Greek New Testament.
Contamination	The mixture of readings that results from a scribe consulting more than one exemplar.
Continuous Text	A text of the New Testament or a portion of it that does not disrupt the order of the text or intersperse commentary.
Deluxe Codex	A codex made for public use on the finest parchment and carefully written.
Diaeresis	A mark noting two vowels are not a diphthong (pl. diaereses).
Diphthong	Two consecutive vowels which are pronounced as a single vowel.
Donatists	A group of orthodox Christians in North Africa who were separate from the Catholic Church. They were well-respected but were noted for their strict approaches.
Eclectic Text	An edition of the Greek New Testament that seeks to reconstruct the original text by selecting the best reading for each variant unit from different manuscripts.
Ecumenical Council	A meeting of bishops held to determine matters significant for the life of the church (often addressing specific problems). "Ecumenical" cannot have the sense of "worldwide" but representative of churches from within large districts (e.g., North Africa).
Edict	An official pronouncement of law from the sitting emperor. Sometimes these edicts overturned edicts of previous emperors. For example, the Edict of Toleration by Constantine ended the great persecution demanded by the Edict of Diocletian.
Editio Critica Maior	A multivolume critical edition of the Greek New Testament produced by the Institute for New Testament Textual Research.

Exclusive Definition	An approach to canon formation within the Extrinsic Model that suggests the canon was the result of some sort of declaration (formal or informal). They affirm the ancients had "Scripture" (authoritative writing) but deny "canon" (an authoritative list) until the fourth century.
Exemplar	The manuscript that serves as the source from which a scribe copies his text into another manuscript.
Extant	Still in existence.
External Evidence	The evidence outside of the content of the different readings for a variant unit that is used to evaluate these readings. Evaluation of external evidence considers the age of manuscripts that preserve the reading, the general quality of texts that contain the reading, the geographical distribution of the reading, etc.
Extrinsic Model	A model for canon formation that affirms the canon was chosen purely by a natural, historical process.
Functional Definition	An approach to canon formation within the Extrinsic model that affirms canon at the earliest stages. Ultimately the community determined the canon. Thus, it is no wonder that different communities had different canons. "Canon" is a list of authoritative books rather than an authoritative list.
Genealogical Coherence	An expression used in the CBGM to describe the nature of the relationship between two closely related texts by identifying which text has a larger number of prior readings and is thus the potential ancestor of the close relative.
Haplography	The accidental omission of a portion of the text that is being copied.
Historical-Critical Definition	An approach to canon formation applies rationalist approaches to history to define the process of canon formation. They generally appeal to the fourth-century councils as innovative binding declarations.
Homily	An ancient sermon. A speech of exhortation based on a biblical text.

Homoeoteleuton	Similar endings of lines or words that sometimes caused confusion for copyists resulting in either haplography or dittography.
Homophones	Two words that have identical pronunciations but are spelled differently.
Inerrancy	The view that the original text of Scripture affirms no factual error.
Initial Text	The early text from which the text in all extant copies was derived.
Inspiration	The divine influence upon the human authors of Scripture that ensured that they wrote exactly what God desired to communicate.
Intermediate Category	The ancients did not have two categories of religious writing but three: Canonical, Apocryphal, and Useful for the soul. The third category are orthodox books respected by the church as valuable for discipleship but not canonical. Moderns often call this the "intermediate category."
Internal Evidence	The evidence within specific variants that is used to evaluate these readings. Internal evidence includes intrinsic evidence and transcriptional evidence.
Intrinsic Evidence	Evaluation of internal evidence considers if the reading is in keeping with the author's usual vocabulary, grammar, style and is suitable in the literary context.
Intrinsic Model	A model of canon formation first clarified by the reformers. The books of the Bible are self-authenticating (needing no external authority to select them). Therefore, without the authority to select the books, the task of the church was to recognize the canon.
Intrinsic Probability	A textual critic's assessment of the likelihood that a variant is original based on factors of intrinsic evidence.
Lacuna	A missing portion of a manuscript.
Lection	The specific reading from the Scripture (or lectionary) for an individual worship service.

Lectionary	A manuscript that arranges portions of Scripture for selected public readings assigned to particular days or occasions based on a religious or civil calendar rather than in the order in which they appear in ordinary biblical manuscripts.
Ligature	A combination of two or more letters written like a single character in minuscule script.
Liste	The German term for "catalogue" referring to the official registry of manuscripts of the Greek New Testament maintained by the Institute for New Testament Textual Research in Münster, Germany. The complete name is *Kurzgefasste Liste der griechischen Handschriften des Neuen Testaments* ("Summary Catalogue of Greek Manuscripts of the New Testament"). The catalogue gives a brief profile of each manuscript including information such as the date it was copied, number of leaves, contents, and size.
Magisterial Model	An expression of the Extrinsic model of canon formation employed by the Roman Catholic and Greek Orthodox. Affirming the role of the Holy Spirit in canon formation, these churches see the church as the canonizer of the Bible.
Majuscule	A Greek script with larger, block-style characters written between two imaginary lines or a parchment manuscript that was written in this script.
Manuscript	A document written by the human hand rather than printed mechanically.
Marcion/Marcionite	A heretical sect founded by Marcion in the second century lasting into the fifth. Marcion, a lover of Gnostic doctrine, attempted to separate Christianity from its Jewish foundations. He was most known for editing the Christian Bible down to redacted forms of Luke and Paul.
Miniature Codex	A codex made for private use. By definition it is no bigger than 10cm in any dimension.
Minuscule	A Greek script with smaller, more rounded characters in which some characters extend above or below the two imaginary lines that demarcated majuscule script. The term also refers to manuscripts that were written in this script.
Miscellaneous Codex	A codex containing a hodgepodge of often unconnected works. Most are random collections. Some may be more

connected (see the Bodmer Miscellaneous Codex that was likely liturgical in origin).

Mixture   The variety of readings in a single manuscript copied by two different exemplars, sometimes copying from one and sometimes from the other (see "contamination").

Montanism   A second-century quasi-orthodox movement that was eventually rejected by the church. Montanus, their founder, emphasized charismatic revelation. They referred to themselves as "the New Prophecy" or "the Prophecy."

Moveable Nu   The letter nu (ν), which is sometimes added to a verbal form which would otherwise end in a vowel when the following word begins with a vowel.

Multiple Emergence   The phenomenon in which two copyists independently create the same reading so that their copies agree coincidentally at that point.

Negative Apparatus   A list of witnesses that contain a variant reading different from the one selected for the main text of a critical edition.

Nomen Sacrum   Abbreviated forms of common nouns (several of which refer to persons of the Trinity) written with a horizontal line over them (pl. *nomina sacra*, "sacred names").

Noncontinuous Text   Commentaries, lectionaries, and other presentations of the New Testament text that intersperse new material or rearrange the original order of the New Testament text.

Nonsense Reading   A variant that fits the context so poorly it should not be ruled out as a viable option for the original reading.

Obelus   A sign resembling the modern percentage sign (%) used by ancient scribes to mark texts suspected of being later additions (pl. *obeli*).

Palimpsest   A manuscript that was erased and overwritten with a different text.

Papyrus   A writing material somewhat resembling modern paper and made from reeds that grew in the Nile River Delta in Egypt.

Parablepsis	The act of a scribe looking back and forth between his exemplar and his copy which sometimes resulted in him losing his place so that he accidentally copied some text twice or accidentally skipped some text.
Parchment	Processed animal skin used as a writing surface in ancient books.
Pericope Adulterae	The account of Jesus's forgiveness of the woman caught in adultery in John 7:53–8:11.
Positive Apparatus	A list of witnesses that support the variant reading selected for the main text of a critical edition.
Praxapostoloi	The name for a codex that combined the *praxapostolos* and the epistles of Paul.
Praxapostolos	The name for a codex consisting of Acts and the General Epistles.
Pre-Genealogical Coherence	The degree of similarity between two texts based on their agreement in all the variant units that they share.
Reader	A person in the early church charged with the public reading of Scripture. They were not ordained but took on a semiofficial role in the early church.
Reasoned Eclecticism	An approach to textual criticism that seeks to consider all of the evidence both external and internal.
Receptor Language	The language into which a document originally in another language is translated.
Roll	An ancient book form that was written on one continuous sheet of parchment or papyrus and rolled up. They are usually a little smaller than a two-liter bottle in diameter.
Scholia	Comments by scholars copied into the margins of MSS; sometimes collected and published.
Scriptio Continua	A style of writing that generally does not put spaces between sentences or words and rarely uses punctuation.
Scriptorium	A place in which a group of scribes carry out their work of hand-copying documents.

Singular Reading	A variant that appears in only one extant manuscript of the Greek New Testament.
Staurogram	A kind of *Nomen Sacrum* in certain MSS that are a combination of the Greek letters sigma and rho (from *stauros* and *Christos*) that looks a crucified man. The staurogram does not appear in all biblical MSS.
Sub-Singular Readings	A variant that appears in only two extant manuscripts of the Greek New Testament or in one Greek manuscript and an ancient version.
Text Type	A group of texts which generally share similar readings and are sufficiently distinct from another group of texts which also share similar readings.
Textual Criticism	The science that attempts to reconstruct the original text of a document for which the autograph no longer exists.
Textus Receptus	A term generally used to refer to the Greek Text behind the King James Version.
Thoroughgoing Eclecticism	An approach to textual criticism that greatly emphasizes the evaluation of Internal evidence.
Transcriptional Evidence	Evidence for or against a particular variant based on what is known of ancient scribal practices and the errors which they were most prone to make.
Transcriptional Probability	The likelihood that a scribe made a certain type of common error.
Transposition	A change in the order of letters in a word or words in a sentence.
Variant	One of two or more different readings.
Variant Unit	A place in the text where some manuscripts differ
Vellum	A very high-quality parchment.
Vorlage	The source document from which a copy or translation is made.

Scripture Index

40 QUESTIONS SERIES

4 0 QUESTIONS SERIES

40 Questions About the Historical Jesus
C. Marvin Pate

40 Questions About Interpreting the Bible, 2nd ed.
Robert L. Plummer

40 Questions About Islam
Matthew Aaron Bennett

40 Questions About Pastoral Ministry
Phil A. Newton

40 Questions About Prayer
Joseph C. Harrod

40 Questions About Roman Catholicism
Gregg R. Allison

40 Questions About Salvation
Matthew Barrett

40 Questions About the Text and Canon of the New Testament
Charles L. Quarles and L. Scott Kellum

40 Questions About Typology and Allegory
Mitchell L. Chase

40 Questions About Women in Ministry
Sue G. Edwards and Kelley M. Mathews